LIVING LANGUAGE®
U L T I M A T E
ITALIAN

ULTIMATE
ITALIAN
BASIC–INTERMEDIATE

SALVATORE BANCHERI, PH.D.,

UNIVERSITY OF TORONTO

MICHAEL LETTIERI, PH.D.,

UNIVERSITY OF TORONTO

LIVING LANGUAGE®
A Random House Company

Published by Living Language, A Random House Company,
201 East 50th Street, New York, New York 10022.

Random House, Inc. New York, Toronto, London, Sydney, Auckland
www.livinglanguage.com

Living Language is a registered trademark of Crown Publishers, Inc.

Printed in the United States of America

Library of Congress Cataloging-in-Publication Data is available upon request.

ISBN 0-609-80257-7

10   9   8   7   6   5   4   3   2   1

First Edition

CONTENTS

INTRODUCTION

Living Language® Ultimate Italian is a practical and enjoyable way to learn Italian. The complete course consists of this text and eight hours of recordings. You can, however, use the text on its own if you already know how to pronounce Italian.

With *Ultimate Italian,* you'll speak Italian from the very beginning. Each lesson starts with a dialogue about common situations that you're likely to experience at home or abroad. You'll learn the most common and useful expressions for everyday conversation.

Key grammatical structures introduced in the dialogue are clearly explained in a separate section. The lessons build on one another. The material you've already studied is "recycled," or used again, in later lessons as you learn new words, phrases, and grammatical forms. This method helps you increase your language skills gradually while reinforcing and perfecting material learned previously.

In addition brief notes on cultural topics will add to your understanding of Italian and Italian-speaking people.

COURSE MATERIALS

THE MANUAL

Living Language® Ultimate Italian consists of forty lessons, eight review sections, and four reading sections. The review sections appear after every five lessons, and the reading sections after every ten.

Read and study each lesson before listening to it on the recordings.

DIALOGO (DIALOGUE): Each lesson begins with a dialogue presenting a realistic situation in an Italian locale. The dialogue is followed by a translation in colloquial English. Note that while there are many regional dialects and accents, we will be using standard Italian grammar and vocabulary throughout the course.

PRONUNCIA (PRONUNCIATION): In lessons 1 through 10, you will learn the correct pronunciation of vowels, diphthongs, consonants, and consonant combinations.

GRAMMATICA E SUOI USI (GRAMMAR AND USAGE): This section explains the major grammatical points covered in the lesson. The heading of each topic corresponds to its listing in the table of contents.

VOCABOLARIO (VOCABULARY): In this section you can review the words and expressions from the dialogue and learn additional vocabulary.

ESERCIZI (EXERCISES): These exercises test your mastery of the lesson's essential vocabulary and grammatical structures. You can check your answers in the *CHIAVE PER GLI ESERCIZI* (ANSWER KEY) section.

NOTA CULTURALE (CULTURAL NOTE): These brief notes put the language in its cultural context. Cultural awareness will enrich your understanding of Italian and your ability to communicate effectively.

RIPASSO (REVIEW): Review sections appear after every five lessons. These sections are similar to the Exercises in format, but they integrate material from all of the lessons you have studied to that point.

DA LEGGERE (READING): The four reading passages are not translated. However, the material covered in the preceding lessons, along with the vocabulary notes that accompany the reading, will enable you to infer the meaning, just as you would when reading a newspaper abroad.

APPENDIXES: There are four appendixes: a glossary of Continents, Countries, Cities, and Languages; a Grammar Summary; Verb Charts; and a section on Letter Writing.

GLOSSARY: Be sure to make use of the two-way glossary in the back of the manual to check the meanings and connotations of new words.

INDEX: The manual ends with an index of all the grammar points discussed in the course.

The appendixes, glossary, and index make this manual an excellent source for future reference and study.

RECORDINGS (SETS A & B)

This course provides you with eight hours of audio practice. There are two sets of complementary recordings. The first set is designed for use with the manual, while the second set may be used without it. By listening to and imitating the native speakers, you'll be able to improve your pronunciation and comprehension while learning to use new phrases and structures.

RECORDINGS FOR USE WITH THE MANUAL (SET A)

This set of recordings gives you four hours of audio practice in Italian only, with translations in the manual.

The dialogue of each lesson, the pronunciation section of lessons 1 through 10, the vocabulary section, and parts of the grammar section are featured on these recordings. All the words and expressions that are recorded appear in **boldfaced type** in your manual.

First, you will hear native Italians read the complete dialogue at a normal conversational pace without interruption; then you'll have a chance to listen to the dialogue a second time and repeat each phrase in the pauses provided.

Next, listen carefully to learn the sounds from the pronunciation sections. By repeating after the native speakers, you will gradually master the sounds.

You will then have the opportunity to practice some of the most important grammatical forms from the *Grammatica e suoi usi* section.

Finally, the most important and commonly used vocabulary words will also be modelled by the native speakers for you to repeat in the pauses provided.

After studying each lesson and practicing with Set A, you can go on to the second set of recordings (Set B), which you can use on the go—while driving, jogging, or doing housework.

RECORDINGS FOR USE ON THE GO (SET B)

The "On the Go" recordings give you four hours of audio practice in Italian and English. Because they are bilingual, Set B recordings may be used without the manual, anywhere it's convenient to learn. The forty lessons on Set B correspond to those in the text. A bilingual narrator leads you through the four sections of each lesson:

The first section presents the most important phrases from the original dialogue. You will first hear the abridged dialogue at normal conversational speed. You'll then hear it again, phrase by phrase, with English translations and pauses for you to repeat after the native Italian speakers.

The second section reviews and expands upon the vocabulary in the dialogue. Additional expressions show how the words may be used in other contexts. Again, you are given time to repeat the Italian phrases.

In the third section you'll explore the lesson's most important grammatical structures. After a quick review of the rules, you can practice with illustrative phrases and sentences.

The exercises in the last section integrate what you've learned and help you generate sentences in Italian on your own. You'll take part in brief conversations, respond to questions, transform sentences, and occasionally translate from English into Italian. After you respond, you'll hear the correct answer from a native speaker.

The interactive approach on this set of recordings will teach you to speak, understand, and *think* in Italian.

Now it's time to begin . . .

PRONUNCIATION CHART

Vowels

Italian Spelling	Approximate Sound in English	Phonetic Symbol	Example (Phonetic Transcription)
a	f<u>a</u>ther	ah	*banana* (bah-N<u>AH</u>-nah)
e	m<u>e</u>t	eh	*breve* (BR<u>EH</u>-veh)
i	ma<u>chi</u>ne	ee	*vino* (V<u>EE</u>-noh)
o	h<u>o</u>pe	oh	*moto* (M<u>OH</u>-toh)
u	r<u>u</u>le	oo	*fumo* (F<u>OO</u>-moh)

VOWEL COMBINATIONS

Diphthongs A diphthong is a double vowel combination that produces a single sound. Here is a list of frequent diphthongs and their pronunciation:

Italian Spelling	Approximate Sound in English	Phonetic Symbol	Example (Phonetic Transcription)
ai	r<u>i</u>pe	ahy	*daino* (D<u>AHY</u>-noh)
au	n<u>ow</u>	ow	*auto* (<u>OW</u>-toh)
ei	m<u>ay</u>	ay	*sei* (S<u>AY</u>-ee) (stressed) *seicento* (say-CHEN-toh) (unstressed)
eu	—	ehoo	*neutro* (N<u>EHOO</u>-troh)
ia	<u>y</u>arn	yah	*italiano* (ee-tahl-<u>YAH</u>-noh)
ie	<u>y</u>et	yeh	*miele* (M<u>YEH</u>-leh)
io	<u>y</u>odel	yoh	*campione* (kahm-P<u>YOH</u>-neh)
iu	<u>you</u>	yoo	*fiume* (F<u>YOO</u>-meh)
oi	<u>soy</u>	oy	*poi* (poy)
ua	<u>wa</u>nd	wah	*quando* (KW<u>AHN</u>-doh)
ue	<u>we</u>t	weh	*questo* (KW<u>EH</u>-stoh)
uo	<u>wa</u>r	woh	*suono* (SW<u>OH</u>-noh)
ui	s<u>wee</u>t	wee	*guido* (G<u>WEE</u>-doh)

Words that begin, incorporate, or end in *cia, cie, cio, ciu, gia, gie, gio, giu, scia, scie, scio,* or *sciu* are pronounced as follows: if the *i* is stressed, the two vowels are pronounced separately as in *farmacia* (fahr-mah-CHEE-ah), *bugia*

5

(boo-GEE-ah), *scia* (SHEE-ah). If the *i* is not stresed, follow this chart for pronunciation:

Italian Spelling	Phonetic Symbol	Example (Phonetic Transcription)
cia	chah	*ciambella* (<u>chah</u>m-BEHL-lah)
cie	cheh	*cielo* (<u>CHEH</u>-loh)
cio	choh	*cioccolata* (<u>choh</u>-koh-LAH-tah)
ciu	choo	*ciuffo* (<u>CHOO</u>F-foh)
gia	jah	*giacca* (<u>JAH</u>K-kah)
gie	jeh	*ciliegie* (chee-LYEH-jeh)
gio	joh	*giovane* (<u>JOH</u>-vah-neh)
giu	joo	*giusto* (<u>JOO</u>-stoh)
scia	shah	*fasciare* (fah-<u>SHAH</u>-reh)
scie	sheh	*scienza* (<u>SHEHN</u>-tsah)
scio	shoh	*sciopero* (<u>SHOH</u>-peh-roh)
sciu	shoo	*sciupare* (<u>shoo</u>-PAH-reh)

Hiatus A hiatus is a double vowel combination whose sounds are pronounced separately, rather than elided:

Italian Spelling	Example (Phonetic Transcription)
ae	*maestro* (m<u>ah</u>-<u>EH</u>-stroh)
au	*paura* (p<u>ah</u>-<u>OO</u>-rah)
ea	*reato* (r<u>eh</u>-<u>AH</u>-toh)
ia	*bugia* (boo-<u>JEE</u>-<u>ah</u>)
oa	*boato* (b<u>oh</u>-<u>AH</u>-toh)
oe	*poeta* (p<u>oh</u>-<u>EH</u>-tah)
ue	*bue* (B<u>OO</u>-eh)

Identical Vowels Any same two vowels must be pronounced separately, with the stress on the first vowel:

Italian Spelling	Example (Phonetic Transcription)
ee	*idee* (ee-D<u>EH</u>-<u>eh</u>)
ii	*addii* (ahd-D<u>EE</u>-<u>ee</u>)
oo	*zoo* (DZ<u>OH</u>-<u>oh</u>)

Triphthongs A triphthong is a combination of three vowels:

Italian Spelling	Example (Phonetic Transcription)
aia	*baia* (B<u>AH</u>-<u>yah</u>)
aio	*saio* (S<u>AH</u>-yoh)
iei	*miei* (m<u>ee</u>-<u>AY</u>)
uio	*buio* (B<u>OO</u>-yoh)
uoi	*buoi* (b<u>oo</u>-<u>OY</u>)

Consonants

Italian Spelling	Approximate Sound in English
b/d/f/k/l/m/n/p/q/t/v	similar to English

Italian Spelling	Approximate Sound in English	Phonetic Symbol	Example (Phonetic Transcription)
c (before *e/i*)	<u>ch</u>in	ch	*cena* (<u>CH</u>EH-nah)
			cibo (<u>CH</u>EE-boh)
c (before *a/o/u*)	<u>c</u>atch	k	*caffè* (<u>k</u>ahf-FEH)
			conto (<u>K</u>OHN-toh)
			cupola (<u>K</u>OO-poh-lah)
ch (with *e/i*)	<u>c</u>an	k	*amiche* (ah-MEE-<u>k</u>eh)
			chilo (<u>K</u>EE-loh)
g (before *e/i*)	<u>j</u>elly	j	*gente* (<u>J</u>EHN-teh)
			gita (<u>J</u>EE-tah)
g (before *a/o/u*)	<u>g</u>old	g	*gala* (<u>G</u>AH-lah)
			gondola (<u>G</u>OHN-doh-lah)
			gusto (<u>G</u>OO-stoh)
gh	<u>g</u>et	g	*spaghetti* (spah-<u>G</u>ET-tee)
			ghiotto (<u>G</u>YOHT-toh)
	<u>gh</u>ost	gh	*funghi* (FOON-<u>gh</u>ee)
gl (plus vowel followed by consonant)	<u>gl</u>obe	gl	*globo* (<u>GL</u>OH-boh)
			negligente (neh-<u>gl</u>ee-JEHN-teh)
gli	sca<u>lli</u>on	lyee	*gli* (lyee)
glia		lyah	*famiglia* (fah-MEE-lyah)
glie		lyeh	*moglie* (MOH-lyeh)
glio		lyoh	*aglio* (AH-lyoh)
gn	ca<u>ny</u>on	ny	*Bologna* (Boh-LOH-nyah)
h	silent	—	*hotel* (oh-TEHL)

r	trilled	r	*rumore* (roo-MOH-<u>r</u>eh)
s (generally)	<u>s</u>et	s	*pa<u>s</u>ta* (PAH-<u>s</u>tah)
s (between two vowels and before *b/d/ g/l/m/n/v/r*)	<u>z</u>ero	z	*rosa* (ROH-<u>z</u>ah) *sbaglio* (<u>Z</u>BAH-lyah)
sc (before *e/i*)	fi<u>sh</u>	sh	*pesce* (PEH-<u>sh</u>eh) *sci* (<u>sh</u>ee)
sc (before *a/o/u*)	<u>sc</u>out	sk	*scala* (<u>SK</u>AH-lah) *disco* (DEE-<u>sk</u>oh)
sch (with *e/i*)	<u>sk</u>y	sk	*pesche* (PEH-<u>sk</u>eh) *fischi* (FEE-<u>sk</u>ee)
z (generally like *ts*)	pit<u>s</u>	ts	*zucchero* (<u>TS</u>OOK-keh-roh) *grazie* (GRAH-<u>ts</u>yeh)
z (sometimes like *dz*)	toa<u>ds</u>	dz	*zingaro* (<u>D</u>ZEEN-gah-roh) *zanzara* (<u>dz</u>ahn-<u>DZ</u>AH-rah)

LEZIONE 1

SALUTI E PRESENTAZIONI.   Greetings and introductions.

A. DIALOGO (DIALOGUE)

1. In albergo.

SIGNORINA SMITH: **Buon giorno, signor Rossi.**

SIGNOR ROSSI: **Buon giorno, signorina Smith. Come sta?**

SIGNORINA SMITH: **Bene, grazie. E Lei?**

SIGNOR ROSSI: **Molto bene. Sono contento di rivederLa.**

SIGNORINA SMITH: **Anch'io.**

SIGNOR ROSSI: **Quanto tempo sta in Italia?**

SIGNORINA SMITH: **Non sto molto: solamente una settimana. Signor Rossi, Le presento la signora Wilson.**

SIGNOR ROSSI: **Piacere.**

In a hotel.

MISS SMITH: Good morning, Mr. Rossi.

MR. ROSSI: Good morning, Miss Smith. How are you?

MISS SMITH: Fine, thank you. And you?

MR. ROSSI: Very well. I'm happy to see you again.

MISS SMITH: Me too.

MR. ROSSI: How long will you be staying in Italy?

MISS SMITH: I'm not staying long: only one week. Mr. Rossi, let me introduce you to Mrs. Wilson.

MR. ROSSI: Pleased to meet you.

2. Per la strada.

JANE: **Ciao, Roberto.**

ROBERTO: **Ciao, Jane. Come stai?**

JANE: **Sto bene, grazie. E tu?**

ROBERTO: **Molto bene. Sono contento di rivederti.**

JANE: **Anch'io.**

ROBERTO: **Quanto tempo stai in Italia?**

JANE: **Non sto molto: solamente una settimana.**

ROBERTO: **Andiamo a prendere un caffè?**

JANE: **No, grazie. Aspetto la mia amica Carol. Ecco Carol. Roberto, ti presento Carol.**

ROBERTO: **Molto lieto, Carol. Mi chiamo Roberto.**

———————————

On the street.

JANE: Hi, Roberto.

ROBERTO: Hi, Jane. How are you?

JANE: I'm fine, thank you. And you?

ROBERTO: Very well. I'm happy to see you again.

JANE: Me too.

ROBERTO: How long will you be staying in Italy?

JANE: I'm not staying long: only one week.

ROBERTO: Shall we go for coffee?

JANE: No, thank you. I'm waiting for my friend Carol. Here's Carol. Roberto, let me introduce you to Carol.

ROBERTO: Nice to meet you, Carol. My name is Roberto.

B. PRONUNCIA (PRONUNCIATION)

1. THE ALPHABET

The Italian alphabet consists of 21 letters.

LETTER	NAME	SOUND
a	**a**	father, large, party
b	**bi**	beans, been, boat
c	**ci**	car, cat, case; cheek, chest, church
d	**di**	dark, dime, duck
e	**e**	get, met, let
f	**effe**	farm, force, full
g	**gi**	gas, girl, go; gem, general, giant
h	**acca**	[not pronounced]
i	**i**	machine, marine, police
l	**elle**	lemon, letter, life
m	**emme**	March, market, mother
n	**enne**	no, not, note
o	**o**	cold, no, note
p	**pi**	piano, pizza, potato
q	**cu**	quality, queen, quest
r	**erre**	room, rope, rose
s	**esse**	house, safe; rose
t	**ti**	tone, Tony, toast
u	**u**	boot, moon, spoon
v	**vu/vi**	very, vine, vote
z	**zeta**	beds; bets, lets

The Italian alphabet also recognizes five additional letters found in foreign words. Their sound is the same as in the original language.

LETTER	NAME
j	**i lungo**
k	**cappa**
w	**doppia vi/vu**
x	**ics**
y	**ipsilon/i greca**

2. STRESS

In the majority of Italian words the stress falls on the next-to-last syllable.

capìsco I understand
arrìvo I arrive
domàni tomorrow

When the stress falls on the last syllable, the final vowel is accented (usually with a grave accent, " ` ").

città city
così so
più more

Note that a few monosyllabic words require a marked accent to distinguish them from other words that have the same spelling but a different meaning.

là there   *la* the
è he/she/it is   *e* and
dà he/she/it gives   *da* by, from

C. GRAMMATICA E SUOI USI (GRAMMAR AND USAGE)

1. SUBJECT PRONOUNS

The subject pronouns in Italian are:

	SINGULAR		PLURAL
I	*io*	we	*noi*
you (familiar)	*tu*	you (familiar or polite)	*voi*
he	*lui*	they	*loro*
she	*lei*		
you (polite)	*Lei*	you (polite)	*Loro*

In Italian, subject pronouns are usually omitted because the verb forms reveal who is speaking or being spoken about. They may be used, however, for emphasis or clarity.

Sono contento di rivederti.
I'm happy to see you again.

Come stai?
How are you?

Sto bene, grazie.
I'm fine, thank you.

But:

Come sta Lei?
How are you? (not "he" or "she")

Keep in mind that, unlike in English, *io* ("I") is never capitalized except at the beginning of a sentence.

Tu (singular) and *voi* (plural) are familiar forms generally used to address friends with whom you are on a first-name basis, family, and children. Nowadays, however, the *voi* form is used more and more often as the plural of both *tu* and *Lei*.

Lei (singular) and *Loro* (plural) are used to address both men and women formally and are usually capitalized to distinguish them from *lei* ("she") and *loro* ("they"). However, note that the polite form *Loro* is generally used when addressing people very formally. It is used particularly by elderly people, or by store clerks and waiters when addressing their customers. So, when addressing Mr. Carlo Rossi and Mrs. Luisa Rossi, you have the following possibilities:

FAMILIAR	POLITE
Come stai, Carlo?	*Come sta, signor Rossi?*
How are you, Carlo?	How are you, Mr. Rossi?
Come stai, Luisa?	*Come sta, signora Rossi?*
How are you, Luisa?	How are you, Mrs. Rossi?
Come state, Carlo e Luisa?	*Come state, signori Rossi?*
How are you, Carlo and Luisa?	*Come stanno, signori Rossi?*
	How are you, Mr. and Mrs. Rossi?

2. THE VERBS *ESSERE* AND *STARE*

In the dialogues you encountered the verbs *essere* ("to be") and *stare*. *Stare* usually means "to stay," but in some cases it also signifies "to be." Both verbs are irregular in the present tense.

	ESSERE	TO BE
I am	*io*	*sono*
you are (familiar)	*tu*	*sei*
he is	*lui*	*è*
she is	*lei*	*è*
you are (polite)	*Lei*	*è*
we are	*noi*	*siamo*
you are (familiar or polite)	*voi*	*siete*
they are	*loro*	*sono*
you are (polite)	*Loro*	*sono*

Roberto è italiano.
    Robert is Italian.
Tu sei italiano.
    You are Italian.

Sono contento di rivederti.
    I'm happy to see you again.

	STARE	TO BE; TO STAY
I am/stay	*io*	*sto*
you are/stay (familiar)	*tu*	*stai*
he is/stays	*lui*	*sta*
she is/stays	*lei*	*sta*
you are/stay (polite)	*Lei*	*sta*
we are/stay	*noi*	*stiamo*
you are/stay (familiar or polite)	*voi*	*state*
they are/stay	*loro*	*stanno*
you are/stay (polite)	*Loro*	*stanno*

Stare means "to be" mainly with expressions concerning health.*

    * See lessons 24 and 26 for other uses of *stare*.

Come stai?
How are you?

Sto bene.
I am fine.

Quanto tempo stai in Italia?
How long will you be staying in Italy?

Note that to simply say "I am in Italy," you'd use *essere*.

Sono in Italia.
I am in Italy.

But, when you mean to say "I am staying in Italy," you'd use *stare*.

Sto in Italia tutta l'estate.
I am staying in Italy all summer.

3. SIMPLE NEGATION

In Italian the word for "no" is *no*.

Andiamo a prendere un caffè?
Shall we go for coffee?

No, grazie.
No, thank you.

Siete italiani?
Are you Italian?

No, siamo francesi.
No, we're French.

To make a negative statement, place *non* ("not") before the verb. Compare:

Io sono italiano.
I'm Italian.

Sto bene.
I'm fine.

Mi chiamo Roberto.
My name is Roberto.

Io non sono italiano.
I'm not Italian.

Non sto bene.
I'm not feeling well.

Non mi chiamo Roberto.
My name is not Roberto.

15

4. TITLES

signora	Mrs.
signorina	Miss
signore	Mr., sir
signor Rossi	Mr. Rossi (the final *e* of *signore* is dropped when used before a name)
signori	gentlemen; ladies and gentlemen
signore	ladies

There is no equivalent for "Ms."

Notice that in Italian, titles* are not capitalized (except at the beginning of a sentence).

Buon giorno, signora Rossi.
Good morning, Mrs. Rossi.

Buon giorno, signorina Rossi.
Good morning, Miss Rossi.

Buon giorno, signore.
Good morning, sir; Good morning, ladies.

Buon giorno, signor Rossi.
Good morning, Mr. Rossi.

Buon giorno, signori.
Good morning, gentlemen.

VOCABOLARIO (VOCABULARY)

Ciao!	Hi! Hello! Bye! (familiar)
Buon giorno.	Good morning. Good afternoon.
Buona sera.	Good evening.
Buona notte.	Good night.

* We will learn more about titles in lessons 18 and 22.

A più tardi.	See you later.
A presto.	See you soon.
A domani.	See you tomorrow.
Arrivederci./ArrivederLa.	Good-bye. (familiar/polite)
Come stai/sta?	How are you? (familiar/polite)
Bene.	Fine.
Molto bene./Benissimo.	Very well.
Abbastanza bene.	Pretty good.
Così così.	So so.
Non c'è male.	Not too bad.
Male.	Bad.
E tu/Lei?	And you? (familiar/polite)
Sono contento*(a)* **di rivederti.**	I am happy to see you again. (m./f., familiar)
Sono contento*(a)* **di rivederLa.**	I am happy to see you again. (m./f., polite)
Come ti chiami/si chiama?	What's your name? (familiar/polite)
Mi chiamo . . .	My name is . . .
Ti/Le presento . . .	Let me introduce you to . . . (familiar/polite)
Molto lieto.	Very pleased to meet you.
Piacere.	Pleased to meet you.
Grazie.	Thank you.
Prego.	You're welcome.
Scusa./Scusi.	Excuse me. (familiar/polite)
Aspetto . . .	I'm waiting for . . .
Ecco . . .	Here is/are . . .; There is/are . . .
il mio amico/la mia amica	my friend (m./f.)
Andiamo a prendere un caffè?	Shall we go for coffee?
no	no
non	not
sì	yes
e	and
è	is

ESERCIZI (EXERCISES)

A. *Cambiare le frasi alla forma negativa.* (Change the sentences to the negative form.)

ESEMPIO: Sto bene.
           Non sto bene.

1. *Jane sta bene.*
2. *Mi chiamo Roberto.*
3. *Sono italiano.*
4. *La signorina Smith sta molto in Italia.*
5. *Sono contento.*

B. *Dare l'equivalente italiano.* (Give the Italian equivalent.)

1. I am
2. she is
3. they are
4. we're
5. you are (familiar singular)

C. *Completare le frasi con la forma corretta di "essere" o "stare."* (Complete the sentences with the correct form of *essere* or *stare.*)

ESEMPIO: Paolo _____ italiano.
           Paolo è italiano.

1. *Ciao, Paolo. Come _____?*
2. *Io _____ contento di rivederti.*
3. *Buon giorno, signorina. Come _____?*
4. *Roberto _____ italiano.*
5. *Noi non _____ bene.*

D. *Tradurre.* (Translate.)

1. My name is Anna Bartoli.
2. How are you, Mr. Rossi?—Fine, thank you!
3. Hello. Pleased to meet you.
4. Roberto, let me introduce you to Diana.
5. I'm fine, thank you. And you?

18

NOTA CULTURALE (CULTURAL NOTE)

Greetings in Italy are a little more involved than in the United States. The degree of familiarity or formality of a relationship is reflected by the use of *tu* and *Lei*. When addressing someone for the first time, meeting with a business associate, or purchasing something in a store, you should use the *Lei* form in order to show respect. The *tu* form is reserved for friends, family, and children. Young people also use *tu* among themselves.

In Italy, a handshake is generally used upon meeting someone (along with *Piacere*), and when greeting friends and acquaintances on a daily basis. A hug or a kiss on both cheeks is also common among friends and acquaintances.

CHIAVE PER GLI ESERCIZI (ANSWER KEY)

A. 1. *Jane non sta bene.* 2. *Non mi chiamo Roberto.* 3. *Non sono italiano.*
4. *La signorina Smith non sta molto in Italia.* 5. *Non sono contento.*

B. 1. *Sono* 2. *È* 3. *Sono* 4. *Siamo* 5. *Sei*

C. 1. *stai* 2. *Sono* 3. *sta* 4. *è* 5. *stiamo*

D. 1. *Mi chiamo Anna Bartoli.* 2. *Come sta, signor Rossi?—Bene, grazie!*
3. *Buon giorno. Piacere.* 4. *Roberto, ti presento Diana.* 5. *Sto bene, grazie. E tu/Lei?*

LEZIONE 2

UNO SPUNTINO.   Snack time.

A. DIALOGO

In un bar.

BARISTA: **Buon giorno, signori. Desiderano?**

CLIENTE: **Sì, qualcosa da mangiare . . . Un panino al formaggio per me, una pizzetta per la signora e due tramezzini per i bambini.**

BARISTA: **Benissimo! Qualcosa da bere? Un'aranciata, un bicchiere d'acqua minèrale?**

CLIENTE: **Sì, due aranciate e due bicchieri d'acqua minerale, per piacere.**

BARISTA: **Bene.**

CLIENTE: **Scusi, c'è un telefono?**

BARISTA: **Sì, è lì.**

CLIENTE: **Grazie.**

BARISTA: **Ecco a voi . . . Allora . . . un panino al formaggio, una pizzetta, due tramezzini, due aranciate e due bicchieri d'acqua minerale. Altro?**

CLIENTE: **No, grazie. Quant'è?**

BARISTA: **Dodici mila lire.**

CLIENTE: **Ecco a Lei quattordici mila lire. Tenga pure il resto.**

BARISTA: **Grazie.**

In a café.

BARTENDER: Hello. May I help you?

CLIENT: Yes, something to eat . . . A cheese sandwich for me, a small pizza for the lady, and two club sandwiches for the children.

BARTENDER: Great! Something to drink? An orange drink, a glass of mineral water?

CLIENT: Yes, two orange drinks and two glasses of mineral water, please.

BARTENDER: Okay.

CLIENT: Excuse me, is there a telephone here?

BARTENDER: Yes, it's over there.

CLIENT: Thank you.

BARTENDER: Here you are . . . So . . . a cheese sandwich, a small pizza, two club sandwiches, two orange drinks, and two glasses of mineral water. Anything else?

CLIENT: No, thank you. How much do I owe you? (How much is it?)

BARTENDER: Twelve thousand lire.

CLIENT: Here are fourteen thousand lire. Keep the change.

BARTENDER: Thank you.

B. PRONUNCIA

1. THE VOWELS

Unlike English vowels, Italian vowels are always pronounced the same way, whatever their position in a word. They must always be articulated clearly and accurately.

VOWEL	PRONUNCIATION	EXAMPLE
a	father, large, party	acqua, aranciata, birra
e	get, met, let	bere, desiderano, resto
i	machine, marine, police	panino, pizzetta, tramezzino
o	cold, gold, note	coca cola, formaggio, qualcosa
u	boot, moon, spoon	due, pure, tu

21

2. THE LETTERS *C* AND *G*

The letter *c* has two different sounds.

$$c + \begin{matrix} a \\ o \\ u \end{matrix} = c \text{ as in "cat"}$$

$$c + \begin{matrix} e \\ i \end{matrix} = ch \text{ as in "church"}$$

LETTER	SOUND	EXAMPLE
c	car, cat, case	**caffè, coca cola, qualcosa**
	cheek, chest, church	**aranciata, dodici, piacere**

The letter *g* also has two different sounds.

$$g + \begin{matrix} a \\ o \\ u \end{matrix} = g \text{ as in "go"}$$

$$g + \begin{matrix} e \\ i \end{matrix} = g \text{ as in "general"}$$

LETTER	SOUND	EXAMPLE
g	gas, girl, go	**tenga, gola, gusto**
	gem, general, giant	**formaggio, mangiare, gelato**

C. GRAMMATICA E SUOI USI

1. CARDINAL NUMBERS 0–20

zero	0	**sei**	6
uno	1	**sette**	7
due	2	**otto**	8
tre	3	**nove**	9
quattro	4	**dieci**	10
cinque	5	**undici**	11

dodici	12	**diciassette**	17
tredici	13	**diciotto**	18
quattordici	14	**diciannove**	19
quindici	15	**venti**	20
sedici	16		

2. GENDER OF NOUNS

Italian nouns are either masculine or feminine. Nouns ending in *-o* are generally masculine.

panino	sandwich
tramezzino	club sandwich
formaggio	cheese

Nouns ending in *-a* are generally feminine.

birra	beer
aranciata	orange drink
acqua	water

Nouns ending in *-e* can be either masculine or feminine.

bicchiere (m.)	glass
cameriere (m.)	waiter
consonante (f.)	consonant

In the vocabulary sections we will indicate the gender of words ending in *-e*, as well as that of words that do not follow these basic rules.

3. THE PLURAL OF NOUNS

In the plural, the final vowels of nouns are changed in the following way:

GENDER	SINGULAR		PLURAL
MASCULINE	*-o*		
MASCULINE/FEMININE	*-e*	>	*-i*
FEMININE	*-a*		*-e*

23

un panino	*due panini*
un bicchiere	*due bicchieri*
una consonante	*due consonanti*
una birra	*due birre*

4. THE INDEFINITE ARTICLE

The English indefinite articles are: "a" and "an." In Italian, the indefinite article (*l'articolo indeterminativo*) must agree with the gender and number of the noun it accompanies.

MASCULINE	FEMININE
Before most nouns:	Before nouns beginning with a consonant:
un	*una*
Before nouns beginning with *s* plus consonant or with *z*:	Before nouns beginning with a vowel:
uno	*un'*

un panino	a sandwich
uno zero	a zero
una coca cola	a coke
un'aranciata	an orange drink

5. *C'È, CI SONO* VERSUS *ECCO*

The English equivalents of *c'è* (singular) and *ci sono* (plural) are "there is" and "there are."

C'è un telefono.
There is a telephone.

C'è un bar?
Is there a café?

Ci sono due caffè.
There are two cafés.

However, when the expressions "here is/are" or "there is/are" are used to point at or draw attention to someone or something, they all translate into Italian as: *ecco*.

Ecco il caffè.
　　Here is your coffee.

Ecco il panino.
　　Here is your sandwich.

VOCABOLARIO

bar (m.)	café
caffè (m.)	café; coffee
gelateria	ice cream parlor/café
pasticceria	pastry shop/café
barista (m./f.)	bartender
cameriere (m.)	waiter
acqua tonica	tonic water
aperitivo	aperitif
aranciata	orange drink
bicchiere (m.) **d'acqua minerale**	glass of mineral water
birra	beer
caffè (m.) **ristretto**	extra strong coffee
caffè (m.) **lungo**	weak coffee
caffè (m.) **macchiato**	coffee with a dash of milk
caffè (m.) **corretto**	laced coffee
caffellatte (m.)	coffee with milk
cappuccino	cappuccino
espresso	espresso coffee
latte (m.)	milk
limonata	lemonade
spremuta d'arancia	freshly squeezed orange juice
succo di frutta	fruit juice
tè (m.)	tea
gelato	ice cream
panino	sandwich

pasta	pastry
pizzetta	small pizza
spuntino	snack
Desidera?/Desiderano?	May I help you? What would you like? (polite, singular/plural)
per favore/per piacere	please
Qualcosa da bere?	Something to drink?
Qualcosa da mangiare?	Something to eat?
Quant'è?	How much do I owe you? How much is it?
Tenga pure.	Keep the change.
lì/là	there
per	for

ESERCIZI

A. *Dare l'articolo indeterminativo appropriato.* (Give the appropriate indefinite article.)

ESEMPIO: birra
        una birra

1. *aperitivo*
2. *limonata*
3. *bicchiere*
4. *cappuccino*
5. *aranciata*

B. *Ricostruire il seguente dialogo.* (Unscramble the following dialogue.)

BARISTA: *Ecco! Una pasta e un cappuccino.*
JANE: *Bene, grazie. E Lei?*
BARISTA: *Altro?*
JANE: *Grazie. Quant'è?*
BARISTA: *Buon giorno, signorina. Come sta oggi?*
JANE: *Sì, una pasta.*
BARISTA: *Così così. Desidera?*
JANE: *Un cappuccino, per favore.*

C. *Dare il numero in italiano e cambiare il nome al plurale.* (Give the number in Italian, and change the noun to plural.)

ESEMPIO: un cappuccino; 7
      sette cappuccini

1. *un gelato;* 5
2. *una birra;* 3
3. *un panino;* 15
4. *un'aranciata;* 12
5. *uno zero;* 6
6. *un bicchiere;* 20

NOTA CULTURALE

Sitting at a sidewalk café on a lovely piazza with a *cappuccino,* watching the world go by, is one of the great pleasures of visiting Italy.

Italian cafés are different from American bars. At an Italian café you would get something to drink (coffee, soda, beer, an aperitif) and a quick bite to eat (a brioche, sandwich, pastry, or some ice cream). Food and drinks can be ordered at a counter or sitting down at a table, but the latter is more expensive. In a *bar,* you usually pay for your order first at the cashier, and then take the receipt to the counter, where you place your order.

In Italy, coffee is prepared in many different ways. If you order just a *caffè,* the waiter will assume you want an *espresso.* A café may also be called a *gelateria, pasticceria,* or a *caffè: Bar Dante, Caffè Dante, Gelateria Dante,* or *Pasticceria Dante.*

CHIAVE PER GLI ESERCIZI

A. 1. *un* 2. *una* 3. *un* 4. *un* 5. *un'*
B. BARISTA: *Buon giorno, signorina. Come sta oggi?*
    JANE: *Bene, grazie. E Lei?*
    BARISTA: *Così così. Desidera?*
    JANE: *Un cappuccino, per favore.*
    BARISTA: *Altro?*
    JANE: *Sì, una pasta.*
    BARISTA: *Ecco! Una pasta e un cappuccino.*
    JANE: *Grazie. Quant'è?*
C. 1. *cinque gelati* 2. *tre birre* 3. *quindici panini* 4. *dodici aranciate*
    5. *sei zeri* 6. *venti bicchieri*

LEZIONE 3

VIAGGIARE IN AEREO.   Traveling by plane.

A. DIALOGO

All'aeroporto.

PASSEGGERO: Buon giorno. Il volo per New York è in orario?

IMPIEGATA: No, è in ritardo di quaranta minuti. Il biglietto e il passaporto, per piacere.

PASSEGGERO: Ecco.

IMPIEGATA: Ha bagagli?

PASSEGGERO: Sì, ho due valigie e una borsa a mano.

IMPIEGATA: Fumatori o non fumatori?

PASSEGGERO: Non fumatori e un posto vicino al finestrino o al corridoio, per piacere.

IMPIEGATA: Va bene. Il posto 24A è vicino al finestrino.

PASSEGGERO: Grazie.

IMPIEGATA: Ecco il biglietto, il passaporto e la carta d'imbarco. Uscita venticinque. L'imbarco è previsto per le ventidue e cinquanta; la partenza per le ventitrè e trentacinque.

PASSEGGERO: E l'arrivo a New York?

IMPIEGATA: L'arrivo è previsto per le sei e cinquantacinque di mattina.

PASSEGGERO: Grazie.

IMPIEGATA: ArrivederLa e buon viaggio.

At the airport.

PASSENGER: Good morning. Is the flight to New York on time?

AIRLINE AGENT: No, it's forty minutes late. Your ticket and passport, please.

PASSENGER: Here you are.

AIRLINE AGENT: Do you have any luggage?

PASSENGER: Yes, I have two suitcases and one piece of hand luggage.

AIRLINE AGENT: Smoking or nonsmoking?

PASSENGER: Nonsmoking and a window or aisle seat, please.

AIRLINE AGENT: Okay. Seat 24A is a window seat.

PASSENGER: Thank you.

AIRLINE AGENT: Here are your ticket, passport and boarding pass. Gate twenty-five. Boarding is scheduled for 10:50 P.M.; departure for 11:35 P.M.

PASSENGER: And the arrival in New York?

AIRLINE AGENT: The arrival is scheduled for 6:55 A.M.

PASSENGER: Thank you.

AIRLINE AGENT: Good-bye, and have a nice trip.

B. PRONUNCIA

1. THE COMBINATION *GLI*

The *gli* sound is not used in English; the closest English approximation would be the combination "lli," as in "million."

biglietto	ticket
bagaglio	luggage
figlio	son

2. THE LETTER *H*

In Italian the letter *h* is always silent.

ho	I have	**hai**	you have
ha	he/she has	**hanno**	they have

At the beginning of words, *h* is used mainly to distinguish words with the same pronunciation.

ho	I have	*o*	or
ha	he/she has	*a*	to
hanno	they have	*anno*	year

In the combinations *ch/gh* plus *e/i,* the *h* gives a hard sound to the *c* and the *g:*

LETTER	SOUND	EXAMPLE
ch	<u>c</u>ar, <u>c</u>ase, <u>c</u>afè	an<u>ch</u>e, <u>ch</u>e, per<u>ch</u>é bi<u>cch</u>iere, <u>ch</u>iamo, fa<u>cch</u>ino
gh	<u>g</u>as, <u>gh</u>etto, <u>g</u>irl	<u>gh</u>etto, lar<u>gh</u>e, lun<u>gh</u>e la<u>gh</u>i, lun<u>gh</u>i, ma<u>gh</u>i

C. GRAMMATICA E SUOI USI

1. THE DEFINITE ARTICLE

The definite article (*l'articolo determinativo*) is the equivalent of "the." In Italian, "the" can have one of several forms, depending on whether a noun is masculine or feminine, singular or plural, and what its first letter is:

	SINGULAR	PLURAL
Before masculine nouns beginning with a:		
consonant	*il*	*i*
s plus consonant, or with z	*lo*	*gli*
vowel	*l'*	*gli*
Before feminine nouns beginnning with a:		
consonant	*la*	*le*
vowel	*l'*	*le*

il passaporto	*i passaporti*	passport(s)
lo studente	*gli studenti*	student(s)
lo zero	*gli zeri*	zero(s)

l'arrivo	*gli arrivi*	arrival(s)
la borsa	*le borse*	bag(s)
l'uscita	*le uscite*	exit(s)

2. THE VERB *AVERE*

The verb *avere* ("to have") is a common irregular verb. Here it is in the present tense.

	AVERE	TO HAVE
I have	*io*	*ho*
you have (familiar)	*tu*	*hai*
he has	*lui*	*ha*
she has	*lei*	*ha*
you have (polite)	*Lei*	*ha*
we have	*noi*	*abbiamo*
you have (familiar or polite)	*voi*	*avete*
they have	*loro*	*hanno*
you have (polite)	*Loro*	*hanno*

Note that the Italian present tense has several equivalents in English.

io ho
I have
I am having
I do have

Ha bagagli?
Do you have any luggage?

Ho due valigie.
I have two suitcases.

Lei ha una borsa a mano.
She has a piece of hand luggage.

3. CARDINAL NUMBERS 21–60

ventuno	21	**ventitrè**	23
ventidue	22	*ventiquattro*	24

venticinque	25	quarantatrè	43
ventisei	26	quarantaquattro	44
ventisette	27	quarantacinque	45
ventotto	28	quarantasei	46
ventinove	29	**quarantasette**	47
trenta	30	**quarantotto**	48
trentuno	31	**quarantanove**	49
trentadue	32	**cinquanta**	50
trentatrè	33	cinquantuno	*51*
trentaquattro	34	cinquantadue	52
trentacinque	35	cinquantatrè	53
trentasei	36	cinquantaquattro	54
trentasette	37	cinquantacinque	55
trentotto	38	cinquantasei	56
trentanove	39	cinquantasette	57
quaranta	40	cinquantotto	58
quarantuno	41	cinquantanove	59
quarantadue	42	**sessanta**	60

Note that the number *uno* follows the same rules as the indefinite article.

un caffè, uno studente, un aereo, un'aranciata

Numbers ending with *-uno* and *-otto* (21, 31, 41, 51, etc.; 28, 38, 48, 58, etc.) drop the final vowel of the ten-unit (*venti—vent, trenta—trent,* etc.) before adding *-uno* or *-otto.*

ventuno, trentuno, quarantuno, cinquantuno, etc.
ventotto, trentotto, quarantotto, cinquantotto, etc.

Numbers ending in *-uno* (21, 31, etc.) drop the final *-o* when they precede a plural noun.

ventun birre, trentun aranciate, etc.

4. TELLING TIME

To ask for the time in Italian, say:

Che ora è?
What time is it?

Che ore sono?

What time is it?

The feminine definite articles *l'* and *le* are used when expressing the time. They agree with *ora* and *ore* ("hour" and "hours"), which are not expressed. The only exceptions to this rule are "noon" and "midnight" which do not require the use of an article. Time is usually expressed in the plural, except with one o'clock, noon, and midnight, which are singular.

È l'una.

It's one o'clock.

Sono le due.

It's two o'clock.

Sono le tre.

It's three o'clock.

Sono le dodici.

It's twelve o'clock.

È mezzanotte.

It's midnight.

È mezzogiorno.

It's noon.

To indicate minutes past the hour, from the hour to half past, use the current hour and *e*, "and," plus the number of minutes elapsed.

È l'una e cinque.

It's five after one; 1:05.

Sono le quattro e quindici.

It's four fifteen; 4:15.

È l'una e trenta.

It's one-thirty; 1:30.

To express the time from the half hour to the hour, use the coming hour and *meno*, "minus," plus the number of minutes to go; or use the same construction as above (the current hour plus *e* plus the minutes elapsed).

Sono le due meno venti.
> It's twenty to two; 1:40.

È l'una e quaranta.
> It's one forty; 1:40.

Sono le sei meno dieci.
> It's ten to six; 5:50.

Sono le cinque e cinquanta.
> It's five fifty; 5:50.

Sono le otto meno quindici.
> It's fifteen minutes to eight; 7:45.

Sono le sette e quarantacinque.
> It's seven forty-five; 7:45.

Instead of numbers, you may also use the following terms, as in English: *un quarto* ("a quarter"), *tre quarti* ("three quarters"), and *mezzo/a* ("half").

È l'una e un quarto.
> It's a quarter past one; 1:15.

Sono le sei meno un quarto.
> It's a quarter to six; 5:45.

Sono le cinque e tre quarti.
> It's five forty-five; 5:45.

È l'una e mezzo*(a).*
> It's half past one; 1:30.

In everyday language, "A.M." and "P.M." are expressed with *di mattina, di (del) pomeriggio, di (della) sera,* and *di (della) notte.*

Sono le otto di mattina.
> It's eight A.M.

Sono le tre del pomeriggio.
> It's three P.M.

Sono le otto di sera.
> It's eight P.M.

34

Sono le tre di notte.
> It's three A.M.

In official language (train and airplane schedules, television and radio announcements, etc.), Italians use the twenty-four-hour system. After twelve noon, continue counting up to twenty-four o'clock (midnight).

le quattordici	14:00 (2:00 P.M.)
le diciotto e mezzo	18:30 (6:30 P.M.)
le ventidue e cinquanta	22:50 (10:50 P.M.)
le ventitrè e trentacinque	23:35 (11:35 P.M.)

Another popular time-related expression is *in punto* ("sharp").

Sono le tre in punto.
> It's three o'clock sharp.

VOCABOLARIO

viaggiare	to travel, traveling
aeroporto	airport
biglietto	ticket
passaporto	passport
prenotazione (f.)	reservation
carta d'imbarco	boarding pass
bagaglio (pl., *bagagli*)	luggage
borsa a mano	hand luggage
valigia (pl., *valigie*)	suitcase
facchino	porter
banco d'accettazione	check-in counter
dogana	customs
sala d'aspetto	waiting room
uscita	gate
aereo	airplane
assistente (m., f.) **di volo**	flight attendant
passeggero	passenger
volo	flight
Buon viaggio!	Have a nice trip!

arrivo	arrival
partenza	departure
essere in ritardo	to be late
essere in orario	to be on time
compagnia aerea	airline
posto	seat
prima classe (f.)	first class
classe (f.) turistica	economy class
corridoio	aisle
finestrino	window
zona fumatori	smoking area
zona non fumatori	nonsmoking area
cintura di sicurezza	seat belt
Che ora è?/Che ore sono?	What time is it?
di mattina	in the morning
di *(del)* pomeriggio	in the afternoon
di *(della)* sera	in the evening
di *(della)* notte	at night
previsto	foreseen, anticipated
vicino	near
al	to the/at the
in punto	sharp

ESERCIZI

A. *Dare l'articolo determinativo e poi cambiare al plurale.* (Give the appropriate definite article, then change to the plural.)

ESEMPIO: passaporto
       il passaporto, i passaporti

1. *prenotazione*
2. *biglietto*
3. *aereo*
4. *uscita*
5. *partenza*

B. *Dare la forma corretta di "avere."* (Give the correct form of *avere.*)

ESEMPIO: Loro _____ *il passaporto.*
         Loro hanno il passaporto.

1. *Io* _____ *due valigie.*
2. *La signora Rossi non* _____ *una prenotazione.*
3. *Noi* _____ *una borsa a mano.*
4. *Tu* _____ *la carta d'imbarco?*
5. *Voi* _____ *i biglietti?*

C. *Tradurre.* (Translate.)

1. What time is it?
2. It's 1:15.
3. It's noon.
4. It's 6:45.
5. It's 9:00 sharp.

D. *Ricostruire il seguente dialogo.* (Unscramble the following dialogue.)

PASSEGGERO: *No, non ho bagagli.*
IMPIEGATO: *Ecco la carta d'imbarco: uscita sette. Buon viaggio.*
PASSEGGERO: *Buona sera. Ecco il passaporto e il biglietto. Un posto vicino
     al finestrino, per piacere.*
IMPIEGATO: *Ha bagagli?*
PASSEGGERO: *Grazie e arrivederLa.*
IMPIEGATO: *Buona sera.*

NOTA CULTURALE

Alitalia is the national airline of Italy. Rome's Leonardo da Vinci International Airport at Fiumicino is ranked fourth in Europe in terms of number of passengers served. There are also international airports in Milan, Venice, Pisa, and Naples, as well as smaller airports in Bologna, Genoa, Palermo, Turin, and Verona. All visitors from the United States and Canada must have a valid passport. A visa is not required unless you expect to stay in Italy more than 90 days, or you expect to work there. Once you arrive at the airport, you go through immigration and customs control, *Dogana,* which, for American visitors, should present no problem.

Tourist information about Italy can be obtained at the counters of the Rome Provincial Tourism Board (*EPT*) or the Italian National Tourism Board (*ENIT*) located at the airport. In the arrival hall there are also taxi, bus, and car rental counters. English, French, German, and Spanish are spoken in most hotels and shops, and aboard most ships, planes, trains, and tour buses.

CHIAVE PER GLI ESERCIZI

A. 1. *la prenotazione, le prenotazioni*   2. *il biglietto, i biglietti*   3. *l'aereo, gli aerei*   4. *l'uscita, le uscite*   5. *la partenza, le partenze*

B. 1. *ho*   2. *ha*   3. *abbiamo*   4. *hai*   5. *avete*

C. 1. *Che ora è?/Che ore sono?* 2. *È l'una e un quarto./È l'una e quindici.*
3. *È mezzogiorno.* 4. *Sono le sei e tre quarti./Sono le sette meno un quarto./ Sono le sei e quarantacinque.* 5. *Sono le nove in punto.*

D. IMPIEGATO: *Buona sera.*
PASSEGGERO: *Buona sera. Ecco il passaporto e il biglietto. Un posto vicino al finestrino, per piacere.*
IMPIEGATO: *Ha bagagli?*
PASSEGGERO: *No, non ho bagagli.*
IMPIEGATO: *Ecco la carta d'imbarco: uscita sette. Buon viaggio.*
PASSEGGERO: *Grazie e arrivederLa.*

LEZIONE 4

LE NAZIONALITÀ.   Nationalities.

A. DIALOGO

All'Università per Stranieri di Perugia.

ROBERTO: **Mi chiamo Roberto. E tu?**

SUSAN: **Mi chiamo Susan.**

ROBERTO: **Sei americana?**

SUSAN: **Sì, sono di New York. E tu di dove sei? Sei italiano?**

ROBERTO: **No, sono spagnolo. Sono di Madrid.**

SUSAN: **Parli bene l'italiano. Abiti e lavori in Italia?**

ROBERTO: **No, non lavoro.**

SUSAN: **E che cosa fai?**

ROBERTO: **Sono studente. Anche tu parli bene l'italiano. Da quanto tempo sei in Italia?**

SUSAN: **Sono in Italia da quattro anni.**

ROBERTO: **Che cosa fai?**

SUSAN: **Frequento l'università da tre anni. Studio Belle Arti e insegno l'inglese.**

ROBERTO: **Andiamo a prendere un caffè?**

SUSAN: **Sì, grazie. Molto gentile.**

––––––––––––––

At the University for Foreign Students at Perugia.

ROBERTO: My name is Roberto. And yours?

SUSAN: My name is Susan.

ROBERTO: Are you American?

SUSAN: Yes, I'm from New York. And where are you from? Are you Italian?

ROBERTO: No, I'm Spanish. I'm from Madrid.

SUSAN: You speak Italian very well. Do you work and live in Italy?

ROBERTO: No, I don't work.

SUSAN: What do you do then?

ROBERTO: I'm a student. You speak Italian very well, too. How long have you been in Italy?

SUSAN: I've been in Italy for four years.

ROBERTO: What do you do?

SUSAN: I have been attending the university for three years. I study fine arts, and I teach English.

ROBERTO: Shall we go for coffee?

SUSAN: Yes, thank you. That's very kind of you.

B. PRONUNCIA

1. THE COMBINATION *GN*

Gn is a sound not found in English; the closest English approximation would be the combination "ni," as in "onion."

spagnolo	Spanish
signorina	Miss
insegno	I teach

2. THE LETTER *D*

The sound of the letter *d* is similar to the corresponding English letter, but it is more dentalized (pronounced with the tip of the tongue closer to the upper front teeth) and more explosive.

dove	where
studio	I study

C. GRAMMATICA E SUOI USI

1. SIMPLE PREPOSITIONS

There are nine simple prepositions in Italian.

MEANING	PREPOSITION
of	*di*
at, to	*a*
from	*da*
in	*in*
with	*con*
on	*su*
through, by means of, for, on	*per*
between, among	*tra/fra*

Note, however, that the translation of these prepositions may vary according to the context.

Noi abitiamo in Italia.
   We live in Italy.

Andiamo in Italia.
   We are going to Italy.

Sono di New York.
   I'm from New York.

There is no difference between *tra* and *fra*.

2. NATIONS AND NATIONALITIES

In the following list, under "Nationalities," the forms in parentheses represent the plural of the adjective. We will study the plural of adjectives later on in this lesson. Notice that, in Italian, adjectives of nationality and names of languages are not capitalized.

NATIONS		NATIONALITIES	
Canada	Canada	*canadese (-i)*	Canadian
Cina	China	*cinese (-i)*	Chinese
Francia	France	*francese (-i)*	French
Germania	Germany	*tedesco, -a (-hi, -he)*	German
Giappone	Japan	*giapponese (-i)*	Japanese
Inghilterra	England	*inglese (-i)*	English
Italia	Italy	*italiano, -a (-i, -e)*	Italian
Russia	Russia	*russo, -a (-i, -e)*	Russian
Spagna	Spain	*spagnolo, -a (-i, -e)*	Spanish
Stati Uniti	United States	*americano -a (-i, -e)*	American

3. *SONO DI . . .*

When asked: *Di dov'è Lei?* or *Di dove sei?* ("Where are you from?" polite or familiar), you may respond with *sono di* plus the name of a city, or *sono* plus an adjective of nationality.

Di dove sei?
Where are you from? (familiar)

Sono di Firenze.
I'm from Florence.

Siete italiani?
Are you Italian? (plural)

Sì, siamo italiani.
Yes, we're Italian.

Sei di New York?
Are you from New York? (familiar)

Sì, sono di New York.
Yes, I'm from New York.

Sono americana.
I'm American. (f.)

4. AGREEMENT OF ADJECTIVES

As with nationalities, Italian adjectives agree in gender and number with the nouns they modify. Many adjectives end in *-o* in the masculine and *-a* in the feminine singular forms.

Paul è americano.
    Paul is American.

Jane è americana.
    Jane is American.

The plural forms are as follows:

Paul e John sono americani.
    Paul and John are American.

Jane e Lisa sono americane.
    Jane and Lisa are American.

	SINGULAR	PLURAL
MASCULINE	*americano*	*americani*
FEMININE	*americana*	*americane*

You have also seen the adjective *contento,* which functions the same way.

Susan è contenta.
    Susan is happy.

Roberto e Susan sono contenti.
    Robert and Susan are happy.

Remember that when an adjective refers to a mixed group of males and females, it takes the masculine plural form.
    Some adjectives end in *-e* in both the masculine and feminine singular forms.

Brian è canadese.
    Brian is Canadian.

Mary è canadese.
    Mary is Canadian.

The plural form of these adjectives is also both masculine and feminine and ends in -*i.*

Brian e Louis sono canadesi.
   Brian and Louis are Canadian.

Mary e Lisa sono canadesi.
   Mary and Lisa are Canadian.

	SINGULAR	PLURAL
MASCULINE	*canadese*	*canadesi*
FEMININE	*canadese*	*canadesi*

In Italian, adjectives (such as those of nationality) generally follow the noun to which they refer.

un ragazzo americano   an American boy

5. INTRODUCTION TO THE CONJUGATION OF VERBS

Italian verbs are divided into three groups, according to their infinitive endings: *-are, -ere, -ire.*

1st group *-are:*	*parlare* (to speak)	*abitare* (to live)
2nd group *-ere:*	*scrivere* (to write)	*vedere* (to see)
3rd group *-ire:*	*partire* (to leave)	*sentire* (to hear)

To conjugate a verb, drop the infinitive ending (*-are, -ere, -ire*), and add the appropriate personal verb ending in the desired tense to the verb root (*parl-, abit-,* etc.).

6. THE PRESENT TENSE OF REGULAR *-ARE* VERBS

Verbs ending in *-are* are the most numerous. All regular verbs in this group are conjugated in the same way. Their singular personal endings are: *-o, -i, -a,* and the plural are: *-iamo, -ate, -ano.*

PARLARE		TO SPEAK
I speak	*io*	*parlo*
you speak (familiar)	*tu*	*parli*
he speaks	*lui*	*parla*
she speaks	*lei*	*parla*
you speak (polite)	*Lei*	*parla*
we speak	*noi*	*parliamo*
you speak (familiar or polite)	*voi*	*parlate*
they speak	*loro*	*parlano*
you speak (polite)	*Loro*	*parlano*

As mentioned in lesson 1, the verb endings indicate the subject of the verb, and the subject pronouns are, therefore, usually omitted (except when necessary for emphasis or to avoid ambiguity).

Notice that, as mentioned before, Italian verbs can be translated into English in three different ways.

Studio Belle Arti.
I'm studying Fine Arts.

Parli bene l'italiano.
You speak Italian well.

Lavoriamo in Italia.
We do work in Italy.

7. IDIOMATIC USES OF THE PRESENT TENSE PLUS *DA* PLUS A TIME EXPRESSION

In addition to its basic meaning "from," the preposition *da* has several other meanings and uses. For instance, *da* can mean both "since" or "for" in sentences expressing an action that began in the past and continues into the present.

Abito in Italia da cinque anni.
I have been living in Italy for five years.

Frequento l'università dal 1992.
I have been attending university since 1992.

VOCABOLARIO

Canada	Canada
canadese *(-i)*	Canadian
Cina	China
cinese *(-i)*	Chinese
Francia	France
francese *(-i)*	French
Germania	Germany
tedesco *(-a, -hi, -he)*	German
Giappone	Japan
giapponese *(-i)*	Japanese
Inghilterra	England
inglese *(-i)*	English
Italia	Italy
italiano *(-a, -i, -e)*	Italian
Messico	Mexico
messicano, *(-a, -i, -e)*	Mexican
Russia	Russia
russo *(-a, -i, -e)*	Russian
Spagna	Spain
spagnolo *(-a, -i, -e)*	Spanish
Stati Uniti	United States
americano *(-a, -i, -e)*	American
abitare in Italia	to live in Italy
insegnare l'inglese	to teach English
lavorare in Canada	to work in Canada
parlare *(il)* **francese**	to speak French
studiare l'italiano	to study Italian
aspettare	to wait for
frequentare	to attend
ambasciata	embassy
da	from, since, for
Da quanto tempo è in Italia?	How long have you been in Italy?
dove	where
Di dov'è Lei?	Where are you from? (polite)
Di dove sei tu?	Where are you from? (familiar)
qui	here

anno	year
Sono in Italia da quattro anni.	I've been in Italy for four years.
Sono di . . .	I am from . . .
Belle Arti	Fine Arts
università	university
anche *(anch')*	too, also
ma	but

ESERCIZI

A. *Completare con la forma appropriata del verbo "parlare."* (Complete with the appropriate form of the verb *parlare*.)

1. *Marco* _____ *l'italiano?*
2. *Io* _____ *italiano.*
3. *E anche tu* _____ *spagnolo?*
4. *Elisa e Maria* _____ *spagnolo.*
5. *Elisa, Maria, voi* _____ *spagnolo?*
6. *Anche noi* _____ *inglese.*

B. *Completare in modo opportuno.* (Fill in the appropriate ending.)

1. *Franz è tedesc_____.*
2. *La signorina Rossi è italian_____.*
3. *Roberto e Carlos sono spagnol_____.*
4. *Frank e Jane sono canades_____.*
5. *Susan e Liz sono american_____.*
6. *Emily Sung e Richard Fong sono cines_____.*

C. *Completare con la forma appropriata del verbo fra parentesi.* (Complete with the appropriate form of the verb in parentheses.)

1. *Roberto e Susan* _____ *bene l'italiano. (parlare)*
2. *Noi* _____ *a New York da due anni. (abitare)*
3. *Tu* _____ *l'Università per Stranieri. (frequentare)*
4. *Io* _____ *l'aereo. È in ritardo! (aspettare)*
5. *Susan* _____ *l'inglese. (insegnare)*

47

NOTA CULTURALE

Many Italian universities and language centers offer Italian language courses for foreigners. Among the most important are: *Università Italiana per Stranieri* (Perugia), *Centro di Cultura per Stranieri* (Florence), *Centro Linguistico Italiano* of the "Dante Alighieri Society" (Florence, Rome), *Scuola di Lingua e Cultura Italiana per Stranieri* (*Università degli Studi,* Siena), and *Fondazione "Giorgio Cini"* (Venice). Courses are generally available at the elementary, intermediate, and advanced levels. Courses offered deal not only with the Italian language but also with subjects such as Italian literature, history, geography, and fine arts.

CHIAVE PER GLI ESERCIZI

A. 1. *parla*   2. *parlo*   3. *parli*   4. *parlano*   5. *parlate*   6. *parliamo*
B. 1. *tedesco*   2. *italiana*   3. *spagnoli*   4. *canadesi*   5. *americane*   6. *cinesi*
C. 1. *parlano*   2. *abitiamo*   3. *frequenti*   4. *aspetto*   5. *insegna*

LEZIONE 5

PROGETTI PER IL WEEK-END.   Plans for the weekend.

A. DIALOGO

Un week-end intenso.

BARBARA: **Che cosa fai questo week-end?**

RENZO: **Vado a Roma . . . Vado da Sandra. Sabato sera andiamo al ristorante e domenica restiamo a casa. E tu come passi il week-end?**

BARBARA: **Ho molto da fare. Sabato pomeriggio prima vado a fare delle spese e poi faccio una passeggiata in centro. La sera vado al cinema con le amiche.**

RENZO: **Che film danno?**

BARBARA: **Danno un film di Tornatore.**

RENZO: **E domenica?**

BARBARA: **Di mattina vado a messa e poi vado all'aeroporto con Gianni. Alle undici e mezzo arriva un amico di Gianni dagli Stati Uniti. Poi la sera Gianni dà una festa.**

RENZO: **Un week-end intenso!**

A busy weekend.

BARBARA: What are you doing this weekend?

RENZO: I'm going to Rome . . . to Sandra's. Saturday night we're going to the restaurant, and Sunday we'll stay at home. And how are you going to spend your weekend?

BARBARA: I have a lot to do. Saturday afternoon first I'm going shopping, and then I'm going for a walk downtown. In the evening I'm going to the movies with my friends.

RENZO: What movie is playing?

BARBARA: They're showing a movie by Tornatore.

RENZO: And on Sunday?

BARBARA: In the morning I'm going to mass, and then I'm going to the airport with Gianni. A friend of Gianni's is arriving from the United States at eleven thirty. Then in the evening Gianni's throwing a party.

RENZO: A busy weekend!

B. PRONUNCIA

1. THE LETTERS *B, F, M, N,* AND *V*

The letters *b, f, m, n,* and *v* have the same sound as the corresponding English letters.

LETTER	PRONUNCIATION	EXAMPLE
b	beans, been, boat	sabato, Barbara, abitare
f	feet, force, full	fare, Firenze, festa
m	machine, marine, mother	domenica, pomeriggio, mattina
n	near, no, note	cinema, non, undici
v	veal, Vince, victory	vado, arrivare, venerdì

2. THE APOSTROPHE

The apostrophe (') indicates the elision (omission) of the final unaccented vowel of a word in front of another word beginning with a vowel. Articles and the combined forms of prepositions and articles often take the apostrophe.

all'aeroporto
un'aranciata
l'aereo
anch'io
dov'è

C. GRAMMATICA E SUOI USI

1. PREPOSITIONS AND DEFINITE ARTICLES: COMBINED FORMS

When used in connection with the definite article, the prepositions *di, a, da, in, con,* and *su* are contracted. *Per* and *tra/fra* are never contracted. *Con* has both noncontracted and contracted forms.

Here is a complete scheme of the prepositions and definite articles.

PREPOSITION				ARTICLE			
	LO	L'	GLI	IL	I	LA	LE
DI	*dello*	*dell'*	*degli*	*del*	*dei*	*della*	*delle*
A	*allo*	*all'*	*agli*	*al*	*ai*	*alla*	*alle*
DA	*dallo*	*dall'*	*dagli*	*dal*	*dai*	*dalla*	*dalle*
IN	*nello*	*nell'*	*negli*	*nel*	*nei*	*nella*	*nelle*
SU	*sullo*	*sull'*	*sugli*	*sul*	*sui*	*sulla*	*sulle*
CON	*con lo*	*con l'*	*con gli*	*con il* / *col*	*con i* / *coi*	*con la*	*con le*
PER	*per lo*	*per l'*	*per gli*	*per il*	*per i*	*per la*	*per le*
TRA/FRA	*tra/fra lo*	*tra/fra l'*	*tra/fra gli*	*tra/fra il*	*tra/fra i*	*tra/fra la*	*tra/fra le*

2. USES OF *DI, A,* AND *DA*

The preposition *di* (*d'* in front of a vowel) is used to express: place of origin (see lesson 4, section C3).

Sono di Firenze.
I'm from Florence.

possession, expressed in English with -'s and -s'.

L'amico di Gianni
Gianni's friend

Note that the English equivalent of "to" or "in" a city is translated in Italian with *a:*

Vado a Roma.
I'm going to Rome.

Abito a Roma.

I live in Rome.

As you learned in lesson 4, *da* is used idiomatically in sentences expressing an action that began in the past and continues into the present.

Da quanto tempo sei in Italia?

How long have you been in Italy?

Abito in Italia da due anni.

I have been living in Italy for two years.

When used before a name, surname, or profession, *da* (plus definite article, if required) expresses "to" or "at" somebody's house, office, or workplace.

Vado da Gianni.

I am going to Gianni's.

Sono dal dottore.

I am at the doctor's office.

Take note also of the construction *molto* plus *da* plus an infinitive.

Ho molto da fare.

I have a lot to do.

3. IRREGULAR VERBS: *ANDARE, DARE,* AND *FARE*

	ANDARE	TO GO
I go	*io*	*vado*
you go (familiar)	*tu*	*vai*
he goes	*lui*	*va*
she goes	*lei*	*va*
you go (polite)	*Lei*	*va*
we go	*noi*	*andiamo*
you go (familiar or polite)	*voi*	*andate*
they go	*loro*	*vanno*
you go (polite)	*Loro*	*vanno*

Dove vai?
   Where are you going?

Vado a Roma.
   I'm going to Rome.

Andiamo al ristorante.
   We're going to the restaurant.

	DARE	TO GIVE
I give	*io*	*do*
you give (familiar)	*tu*	*dai*
he gives	*lui*	*dà*
she gives	*lei*	*dà*
you give (polite)	*Lei*	*dà*
we give	*noi*	*diamo*
you give (familiar or polite)	*voi*	*date*
they give	*loro*	*danno*
you give (polite)	*Loro*	*danno*

Danno un film di Tornatore.
   They're showing a movie by Tornatore.

Gianni dà una festa.
   Gianni is giving a party.

	FARE	TO DO; TO MAKE
I do/make	*io*	*faccio*
you do/make (familiar)	*tu*	*fai*
he does/makes	*lui*	*fa*
she does/makes	*lei*	*fa*
you do/make (polite)	*Lei*	*fa*
we do/make	*noi*	*facciamo*
you do/make (familiar or polite)	*voi*	*fate*
they do/make	*loro*	*fanno*
you do/make (polite)	*Loro*	*fanno*

Che fai questo week-end?
   What are you doing this weekend?

Vado a fare delle spese.
I'm going shopping.

Facciamo una passeggiata.
We're going for a walk.

4. DAYS OF THE WEEK

lunedì	Monday
martedì	Tuesday
mercoledì	Wednesday
giovedì	Thursday
venerdì	Friday
sabato	Saturday
domenica	Sunday

The days of the week, with the exception of *domenica,* are masculine; they are never capitalized, unless they begin a sentence. Note also the accent on the first five days. The definite article is used to express "on Mondays," "on Tuesdays," etc. Compare the following sentences.

Carla lavora venerdì.
Carla is working on Friday.

Carla lavora il venerdì.
Carla works on Fridays.

VOCABOLARIO

giorno	day
settimana	week
lunedì (m.)	Monday
martedì (m.)	Tuesday
mercoledì (m.)	Wednesday
giovedì (m.)	Thursday
venerdì (m.)	Friday
sabato	Saturday
domenica	Sunday

Che giorno è oggi?	What day is today?
Oggi è lunedì.	Today is Monday.
sabato mattina	Saturday morning
sabato pomeriggio	Saturday afternoon
sabato sera	Saturday evening
progetti per il week-end	plans for the weekend
Cosa fai/fa questo week-end?	What are you doing this weekend? (familiar/polite)
Come passi/passa il week-end?	How will you spend your weekend? (familiar/polite)
andare al cinema (m.)	to go to the movies
andare a messa	to go to mass
andare dal dottore (m.)	to go to the doctor
andare in centro	to go downtown
andare al ristorante (m.)	to go to a restaurant
dare un film	to show a movie
dare una festa	to have a party
andare a fare delle spese	to go shopping
fare una passeggiata	to go for a walk
restare a casa	to stay at home
dare	to give
solo	only
prima	first
poi	then
questo	this

ESERCIZI

A. *Rispondere affermativamente alle seguenti domande.* (Answer the following questions affirmatively.)

1. *Vai da Sandra questo week-end?*
2. *Andate in centro oggi?*
3. *Vai a messa la domenica?*
4. *Date una festa sabato?*
5. *Fai una passeggiata oggi?*

B. *Tradurre le seguenti frasi.* (Translate the following sentences.)

1. I'm from Florence.
2. Sandra lives in Rome.
3. We go to the restaurant on Saturdays.
4. Sunday I'm going to the airport.
5. He's arriving from the United States Monday.
6. Friday they're going to the movies.

C. *Completare con la forma corretta di "andare," "dare," o "fare."* (Complete with the correct form of *andare, dare,* or *fare.*)

1. *La domenica voi* _____ *una passeggiata.*
2. *Carla e Marisa* _____ *al ristorante.*
3. *Oggi* _____ *un film di Fellini.*
4. *Barbara* _____ *dal dottore.*
5. *Io* _____ *in centro.*

NOTA CULTURALE

For the majority of Italians, Saturday is a work day, and for children it's a school day. As in many other countries, Saturday nights are reserved for the movies, going to a restaurant, a gathering at a friend's home, or a party. In general, on Sundays, after mass, the family gathers for lunch. Then in the afternoon, from September to May, many soccer fans go to the stadium to watch their favorite team, or gather around a radio or a television set to watch or listen to the games. In the evening, everyone traditionally goes for a walk in the piazza or on the main street. Quite often during summer weekends, the towns and cities are deserted, as everyone leaves for the beach or on a picnic in the country.

CHIAVE PER GLI ESERCIZI

A. 1. *Sì, vado da Sandra questo weekend.* 2. *Sì, andiamo in centro oggi.* 3. *Sì, vado a messa la domenica.* 4. *Sì, diamo una festa sabato.* 5. *Sì, faccio una passeggiata oggi.*

B. 1. *Sono di Firenze.* 2. *Sandra abita a Roma.* 3. *Andiamo al ristorante il sabato.* 4. *Domenica io vado all'aeroporto.* 5. *Arriva dagli Stati Uniti lunedì.* 6. *Venerdì vanno al cinema.*

C. 1. *fate* 2. *vanno* 3. *danno* 4. *va* 5. *vado*

PRIMO RIPASSO (FIRST REVIEW)

A. *Dare l'articolo indeterminativo appropriato.* (Give the appropriate indefinite article.)

1. *zero*
2. *aranciata*
3. *telefono*
4. *gelateria*
5. *studente*
6. *americano*

B. *Dare l'articolo determinativo appropriato e poi cambiare al plurale.* (Give the appropriate definite article, and then change to the plural.)

1. *signora*
2. *bicchiere*
3. *panino*
4. *consonante*
5. *studente*
6. *arrivo*
7. *uscita*
8. *pizzetta*

C. *Completare con la forma appropriata del verbo fra parentesi.* (Complete with the appropriate form of the verb in parentheses.)

1. *Io _____ italiano. (essere)*
2. *Roberto, come _____? (stare)*
3. *Il passeggero _____ due valigie e una borsa a mano. (avere)*
4. *Susan _____ Belle Arti. (studiare)*
5. *Loro _____ bene l'italiano. (parlare)*
6. *Questo week-end noi _____ all'aeroporto. (andare)*
7. *Voi che cosa _____ domenica? (fare)*
8. *Sabato Gianni _____ una festa. (dare)*

D. *Completare in modo opportuno quando è necessario.* (Fill in the appropriate ending where necessary.)

1. *Buon giorno, signor_____ Smith.*
2. *Lei, signorina, è american_____?*

3. *Brian è canades_____.*
4. *Maria e Anna sono italian_____.*
5. *Paul e Susan sono american_____.*

E. *Tradurre.* (Translate.)

1. Mr. Smith, here is the ticket and the boarding pass.
2. Excuse me, is there a telephone here?
3. What time is it?—It's four twenty-five.
4. I'm from New York.
5. Friday night we're going to the restaurant.
6. On Saturdays Barbara goes to the doctor.

CHIAVE PER GLI ESERCIZI

A. 1. *uno* 2. *un'* 3. *un* 4. *una* 5. *uno* 6. *un*

B. 1. *la signora, le signore* 2. *il bicchiere, i bicchieri* 3. *il panino, i panini* 4. *la consonante, le consonanti* 5. *lo studente, gli studenti* 6. *l'arrivo, gli arrivi* 7. *l'uscita, le uscite* 8. *la pizzetta, le pizzette*

C. 1. *sono* 2. *stai* 3. *ha* 4. *studia* 5. *parlano* 6. *andiamo* 7. *fate* 8. *dà*

D. 1. *signor* 2. *americana* 3. *canadese* 4. *italiane* 5. *americani*

E. 1. *Signor Smith, ecco il biglietto e la carta d'imbarco.* 2. *Scusi, c'è un telefono qui?* 3. *Che ora è?/Che ore sono?—Sono le quattro e venticinque.* 4. *Sono di New York.* 5. *Venerdì sera andiamo al ristorante.* 6. *Il sabato Barbara va dal dottore.*

LEZIONE 6

ABBIGLIAMENTO.   Clothing.

A. DIALOGO

1. Davanti alla vetrina di un negozio di abbigliamento.

SANDRA: **Come è bello quel maglione in vetrina!**

DANIELE: **Quale?**

SANDRA: **Quello blu.**

DANIELE: **Sì, è molto bello.**

SANDRA: **Però costa molto!**

DANIELE: **Certo! È di Armani.**

SANDRA: **Anche quella camicia bianca è molto bella.**

DANIELE: **Sì, è una bella camicia.**

SANDRA: **Entriamo!**

In front of a clothing store window.

SANDRA: How pretty that pullover in the window is!

DANIELE: Which one?

SANDRA: The blue one.

DANIELE: Yes, it's very beautiful.

SANDRA: But it costs a lot!

DANIELE: Of course. It's an Armani.

SANDRA: That white shirt is also very beautiful.

DANIELE: Yes, it is.

SANDRA: Let's go in.

2. In un negozio di abbigliamento.

SANDRA: **Vorrei vedere la camicetta che è in vetrina.**

COMMESSO: **Che taglia porta?**

SANDRA: **La quarantasei.**

COMMESSO: **Vuole provare questa rosa o questa gialla?**

SANDRA: **Provo la bianca . . . Mmh . . . È un po' stretta. Non c'è una taglia più grande?**

COMMESSO: **Ma va bene . . . Le sta anche bene.**

SANDRA: **Quanto costa?**

COMMESSO: **Centomila lire.**

SANDRA: **È l'ultimo prezzo? Non fate lo sconto?**

COMMESSO: **Mi dispiace, abbiamo prezzi fissi.**

SANDRA: **Posso pagare in dollari?**

COMMESSO: **Sì . . .**

SANDRA: **Allora, se ha la mia taglia, compro anche quell'abito.**

In a clothing store.

SANDRA: I'd like to see the blouse in the window.

SALESMAN: What size are you?

SANDRA: Forty-six.

SALESMAN: Would you like to try on this pink or this yellow one?

SANDRA: I'll try on the white one . . . Mmh . . . It's a bit tight. Do you have a bigger size?

SALESMAN: But it's fine . . . It also suits you well.

SANDRA: How much is it?

SALESMAN: A hundred thousand lire.

SANDRA: Is this your final price? Don't you give discounts?

SALESMAN: I'm sorry, but we have fixed prices.

SANDRA: May I pay in dollars?

SALESMAN: Yes . . .

SANDRA: In that case, if you have my size, I'll also buy that outfit.

B. PRONUNCIA

1. THE LETTER Q

In Italian the letter *q* is followed by the vowel *u* and is always pronounced like the *qu* of the English words "quick," "queen," and "quest."

quello
questo
quale

2. DOUBLE CONSONANTS

Double consonants indicate that the consonant sound is to be prolonged and emphasized while the preceding vowel sound is shortened. The only consonant that cannot be doubled is *q,* but the combination *cq* is the equivalent of a double *q,* i.e., **acqua** (water).

quello
rosso
camicetta

The proper pronunciation of single and double consonants is important, as it prevents confusion between similar words.

casa	house	**cassa**	trunk
sete	thirst	**sette**	seven
sono	I am, they are	**sonno**	sleep

C. GRAMMATICA E SUOI USI

1. QUESTION WORDS

The following are some of the question words used to introduce interrogative sentences. We have already encountered some of them in previous lessons.

che	what	*Che fai?*	What are you doing?
che cosa	what	*Che cosa fai?*	What are you doing?
chi	who	*Chi parla?*	Who is speaking?
come	how	*Come stai?*	How are you?
dove	where	*Dove vai?*	Where are you going?
perché	why	*Perché non entriamo?*	Why don't we go in?
quale	which	*Quale maglione compri?*	Which pullover are you buying?
quando	when	*Quando vai?*	When are you going?
quanto(a)	how much	*Quanto caffè compri?*	How much coffee are you buying?
quanti(e)	how many	*Quanti dollari hai?*	How many dollars do you have?

All of these question words are invariable except for *quanto* and *quale*, which always agree with the noun to which they refer. *Quale* has two forms.

	SINGULAR	PLURAL
MASCULINE	*quale*	*quali*
FEMININE	*quale*	*quali*

Quale camicetta compri?
   Which blouse are you buying?

Quale maglione compri?
   Which pullover are you buying?

Quali maglioni compri?
   Which pullovers are you buying?

Quali camicette compri?
   Which blouses are you buying?

Quale compri?
   Which one are you buying?

Quali compri?
   Which ones are you buying?

Quanto has four forms.

	SINGULAR	PLURAL
MASCULINE	*quanto*	*quanti*
FEMININE	*quanta*	*quante*

Quanto denaro hai?
   How much money do you have?

Quanti maglioni compri?
   How many pullovers are you buying?

Quante camicette compri?
   How many blouses are you buying?

Quanto costa?
   How much does it cost?

2. DEMONSTRATIVE ADJECTIVES AND PRONOUNS: *QUESTO* AND *QUELLO*

Questo ("this") indicates something close to the speaker; *quello* ("that") indicates something at a distance from the speaker. Both words can function as adjectives or pronouns.

As an adjective *questo* agrees with the noun that it qualifies and has four different forms.

	SINGULAR	PLURAL
MASCULINE	*questo*	*questi*
FEMININE	*questa*	*queste*

Before masculine and feminine singular nouns beginning with a vowel, *questo*/*questa* may take an apostrophe.

questo maglione	this pullover
questi maglioni	these pullovers
questa camicetta	this blouse
queste camicette	these blouses
quest'abito	this outfit

As a pronoun, *questo* agrees with the noun to which it refers, and its forms are the same as those of the adjective.

Compro questo (= *maglione,* m.).
  I'm buying this one.

Compro questa (= *camicetta,* f.).
  I'm buying this one.

Compro queste (= *camicette,* f. pl.).
  I'm buying these.

Compro questi (= *maglioni,* f. pl.).
  I'm buying these.

As an adjective, *quello* agrees with the noun it modifies. Here are the possible forms (They resemble the forms and follow the rules of the definite article.):

	SINGULAR	PLURAL
Before masculine nouns beginning with a:		
consonant	*quel*	*quei*
s plus consonant, or with z	*quello*	*quegli*
vowel	*quell'*	*quegli*
Before feminine nouns beginning with a:		
consonant	*quella*	*quelle*
vowel	*quell'*	*quelle*

quel maglione	that pullover
quei maglioni	those pullovers
quella camicetta	that blouse
quelle camicette	those blouses
quell'abito	that outfit

As a pronoun, *quello* agrees with the noun to which it refers and has only four forms.

	SINGULAR	PLURAL
MASCULINE	*quello*	*quelli*
FEMININE	*quella*	*quelle*

Quale maglione compri?
  Which pullover are you buying?

Compro quello.
  I'm buying that one.

Quali maglioni compri?
  Which pullovers are you buying?

Compro quelli.
  I'm buying those.

Quale camicetta compri?
  Which blouse are you buying?

Compro quella.
  I'm buying that one.

Quali camicette compri?
  Which blouses are you buying?

Compro quelle.
  I'm buying those.

3. THE ADJECTIVE *BELLO*

The adjective *bello* ("beautiful") generally precedes the noun and has the following forms (which resemble the forms of *quello* above).

	SINGULAR	PLURAL
Before masculine nouns beginning with a:		
consonant	*bel*	*bei*
s plus consonant, or with z	*bello*	*begli*
vowel	*bell'*	*begli*
Before feminine nouns beginning with a:		
consonant	*bella*	*belle*
vowel	*bell'*	*belle*

65

bel maglione	beautiful pullover
bei maglioni	beautiful pullovers
bella camicetta	beautiful blouse
belle camicette	beautiful blouses
bell'abito	beautiful outfit

However, *bello* may follow the noun when used for emphasis or contrast, or when it is modified by an adverb. It then follows the same pattern as all the other adjectives and has four forms.

	SINGULAR	PLURAL
MASCULINE	*bello*	*belli*
FEMININE	*bella*	*belle*

un maglione bello
   a beautiful pullover

una camicetta bella
   a beautiful blouse

due maglioni belli
   two beautiful pullovers

due camicette belle
   two beautiful blouses

una cravatta molto bella
   a very beautiful tie

4. THE PLURAL OF ADJECTIVES OF COLOR

Adjectives of color always follow the noun, and they are generally regular.

il maglione verde	the green pullover
la camicetta rossa	the red blouse
i maglioni neri	the black pullovers

However, the adjective *blu* ("blue"), and adjectives derived from nouns, like *rosa* ("pink," "rose") and *viola* ("purple," "violet"), are invariable.

il maglione viola	the purple pullover
la camicetta rosa	the pink blouse
i pantaloni blu	the blue pants

5. VERBS ENDING IN *-GARE*

In the present tense, verbs that end in *-gare* add an *h* before the second person singular and first person plural endings.

	PAGARE	TO PAY
I pay	*io*	*pago*
you pay (familiar)	*tu*	*paghi*
he pays	*lui*	*paga*
she pays	*lei*	*paga*
you pay (polite)	*Lei*	*paga*
we pay	*noi*	*paghiamo*
you pay (familiar or polite)	*voi*	*pagate*
they pay	*loro*	*pagano*
you pay (polite)	*Loro*	*pagano*

VOCABOLARIO

abbigliamento	clothing
abito	outfit, suit, dress
camicetta	blouse
camicia	shirt
cappello	hat
cappotto	coat
cravatta	tie
giacca	jacket
gonna	skirt
guanti (m., pl.)	gloves
maglione (m.)	pullover/sweater
pantaloni (m., pl.)	pants
vestito	suit, dress
negozio di abbigliamento	clothing store

negozio di scarpe	shoe store
grande magazzino	department store
commesso(a)	salesman/saleswoman
Che numero/taglia porta?	What size do you wear?
Quanto costa/costano?	How much does it cost/do they cost?
È troppo caro.	It's too expensive.
La mia taglia è . . .	My size is . . .
Vorrei provare . . .	I would like to try on . . .
È un po' stretto(a).	It's a bit tight.
pagare	to pay
comprare	to buy
colore (m.)	color
bianco	white
blu	blue
giallo	yellow
marrone	brown
nero	black
rosa	pink
rosso	red
verde	green
viola	purple

ESERCIZI

A. *Usare le seguenti parole interrogative per completare le frasi.* (Use the following question words to complete the sentences.)

quando che cosa quanto chi come

1. *Pronto!* _____ *parla?*
2. *Antonio,* _____ *vai in Italia?*
3. *John,* _____ *stai?*
4. *Marco,* _____ *fai?*
5. *Signorina,* _____ *costa questo vestito?*

B. *Cambiare al plurale.*

1. *Quel signore è italiano.*
2. *Quale camicetta compra?*
3. *È un bel vestito.*
4. *Questa cravatta è molto bella.*
5. *Quella camicetta rosa è bella ma costa molto.*

C. *Tradurre seguendo le istruzioni.* (Translate using the clues.)

1. This (= hat) is very expensive.
2. Miss, I'll try on that sweater.
3. Sir, which coat are you going to buy?
4. Those (= skirts) are very beautiful.
5. Roberta has a beautiful outfit.

NOTA CULTURALE

Italy is considered one of the best countries for shopping. In fact, Italian fashion designers (Versace, Ferré, Laura Biagiotti, Valentino, Fendi, Armani, Missoni, etc.) are famous all over the world. The main fashion centers are Milan, Florence, Rome, and Turin.

In Italy, most people shop in small boutiques. Morning store hours are generally from 8:30 A.M. or 9:00 A.M. until 1:00 P.M.; afternoon hours are from 3:30 P.M. or 4:00 P.M. until 8:00 P.M. or 9:00 P.M. Italians like to take a long lunch!

Large department stores, such as *La Rinascente, Coin, UPIM,* and *Standa,* can also be found in virtually every city and are open all day. In addition, many tourist resorts offer outdoor flea markets where bargaining is routine. You can try bargaining in just about any shop in Italy, though some stores, especially the large department stores, have a *prezzi fissi* (fixed-price) policy.

CHIAVE PER GLI ESERCIZI

A. 1. *chi* 2. *quando* 3. *come* 4. *che cosa* 5. *quanto*
B. 1. *Quei signori sono italiani.* 2. *Quali camicette comprano?* 3. *Sono dei bei vestiti.* 4. *Queste cravatte sono molto belle.* 5. *Quelle camicette rosa sono belle ma costano molto.*
C. 1. *Questo costa molto.* 2. *Signorina, provo quel maglione.* 3. *Signore, quale cappotto compra?* 4. *Quelle sono molto belle.* 5. *Roberta ha un bel vestito.*

LEZIONE 7

GLI STUDI. Studies.

A. DIALOGO

Un incontro fortuito.

ANTONIO: **Ester, come stai? Come stanno Sandro e Silvana?**

ESTER: **Bene. E tu e Lina come state? E i ragazzi?**

ANTONIO: **Benissimo. Io e Lina lavoriamo. I ragazzi vanno a scuola.**

ESTER: **Giovanni va già all'università, vero?**

ANTONIO: **Sì, fa il primo anno. Studia a Roma. Oggi ha l'esame d'italiano, domani quello di francese. Deve sempre studiare. Non lo vediamo mai.**

ESTER: **Anche Silvana studia sempre, legge sempre, scrive sempre. L'ultimo anno di liceo è sempre difficile.**

ANTONIO: **Sai, anch'io seguo un corso serale, un corso d'inglese. Voglio imparare bene l'inglese.**

ESTER: **Bravo!**

ANTONIO: **Sì, ma non posso più fare niente.**

ESTER: **Giochi ancora a tennis con gli amici?**

ANTONIO: **No, non ho più tempo.**

A chance meeting.

ANTONIO: Ester, how are you? How are Sandro and Silvana?

ESTER: Fine. And how are you and Lina? And the children?

ANTONIO: Very well. Lina and I work. The children go to school.

ESTER: Giovanni is already in college, isn't he?

ANTONIO: Yes, he's in his first year. He's studying in Rome. Today he has an Italian exam, tomorrow French. He always has to study. We never see him.

ESTER: Silvana, too, is always studying, always reading, always writing. The last year of the *liceo* is always hard.

ANTONIO: You know, I, too, am taking a night course, an English course. I want to learn English well.

ESTER: Bravo!

ANTONIO: Yes, but I can't do anything else anymore.

ESTER: Do you still play tennis with your friends?

ANTONIO: No, I don't have the time anymore.

B. PRONUNCIA

1. THE LETTER *S*

The letter *s* can have two different sounds. In the following cases it is voiceless, as in the English words "soft" and "sell":

a. at the beginning of a word if followed by a vowel: **sempre**
b. in front of the consonants *c, f, p, q, t:* **scuola**
c. if it is doubled: **posso**

In all other cases, it is voiced (as in "rose").

inglese
esame
sbaglio

2. THE LETTER *L*

In Italian, the *l* is pronounced more toward the front of the mouth than in English, and its sound is sharper.

leggere
scuola
l'esame

C. GRAMMATICA E SUOI USI

1. THE PRESENT TENSE OF REGULAR *-ERE* VERBS

As with *-are* verbs, the present tense of regular *-ere* verbs is formed by adding the appropriate endings to the root of the verb. The singular personal endings are: *-o, -i, -e*; the plural are: *-iamo, -ete, -ono*.

	VEDERE	TO SEE
I see	io	vedo
you see (familiar)	tu	vedi
he sees	lui	vede
she sees	lei	vede
you see (polite)	Lei	vede
we see	noi	vediamo
you see (familiar or polite)	voi	vedete
they see	loro	vedono
you see (polite)	Loro	vedono

We have already encountered a few regular *-ere* verbs; for example, *leggere* ("to read") and *scrivere* ("to write").

Io vedo Luigi.
   I see Luigi.

Tu leggi sempre.
   You are always reading.

Scrive un saggio.
   He is writing an essay.

2. THE PRESENT TENSE OF *DOVERE, POTERE,* AND *VOLERE*

Dovere ("to have to, must"), *potere* ("to be able to, can, may"), and *volere* ("to want") are called modal verbs and are irregular in the present tense. They are often followed by a dependent infinitive.

72

Deve leggere.
>He has to read.

Lei non può studiare.
>She can't study.

Non voglio studiare.
>I don't want to study.

	DOVERE	TO HAVE TO
I have to	*io*	*devo*
you have to (familiar)	*tu*	*devi*
he has to	*lui*	*deve*
she has to	*lei*	*deve*
you have to (polite)	*Lei*	*deve*
we have to	*noi*	*dobbiamo*
you have to (familiar or polite)	*voi*	*dovete*
they have to	*loro*	*devono*
you have to (polite)	*Loro*	*devono*

Devo studiare.
>I have to study.

Loro devono andare a scuola.
>They must go to school.

Noi dobbiamo scrivere un saggio.
>We have to write an essay.

	POTERE	TO BE ABLE TO
I am able to	*io*	*posso*
you are able to (familiar)	*tu*	*puoi*
he is able to	*lui*	*può*
she is able to	*lei*	*può*
you are able to (polite)	*Lei*	*può*
we are able to	*noi*	*possiamo*
you are able to (familiar or polite)	*voi*	*potete*
they are able to	*loro*	*possono*
you are able to (polite)	*Loro*	*possono*

Non posso.
I can't.

Non posso studiare.
I can't study.

Non possiamo bere.
We can't drink.

	VOLERE	TO WANT
I want	*io*	*voglio*
you want (familiar)	*tu*	*vuoi*
he wants	*lui*	*vuole*
she wants	*lei*	*vuole*
you want (polite)	*Lei*	*vuole*
we want	*noi*	*vogliamo*
you want (familiar or polite)	*voi*	*volete*
they want	*loro*	*vogliono*
you want (polite)	*Loro*	*vogliono*

Vuoi studiare con Eva?
Do you want to study with Eva?

Non vogliamo studiare.
We don't want to study.

Voglio leggere.
I want to read.

3. VERBS ENDING IN *-CARE*

In the present tense, verbs ending in *-care* (e.g., *giocare,* "to play") add an *h* before the second person singular and the first person plural endings, in order to retain their hard *k* sound.

GIOCARE		TO PLAY
I play	*io*	*gioco*
you play (familiar)	*tu*	*giochi*
he plays	*lui*	*gioca*
she plays	*lei*	*gioca*
you play (polite)	*Lei*	*gioca*
we play	*noi*	*giochiamo*
you play (familiar or polite)	*voi*	*giocate*
they play	*loro*	*giocano*
you play (polite)	*Loro*	*giocano*

Giochi a tennis?
   Do you play tennis?

Noi giochiamo a tennis.
   We play tennis.

Loro giocano a tennis.
   They play tennis.

4. THE POSITION OF *SEMPRE*

The adverb of time *sempre* ("always") usually follows the verb.

Noi studiamo sempre.
   We always study.

Tu leggi sempre.
   You always read.

Silvana studia sempre.
   Silvana is always studying.

5. THE POSITION OF *ANCHE*

Anche ("too, also") always precedes the noun, pronoun, or infinitive to which it refers. Notice that when *anche* precedes *io* it becomes *anch'*.

Vuole anche questo libro.
   He wants that book, too.

Anch'io devo studiare.
    I, too, have to study.

Devi anche studiare.
    You also have to study.

VOCABOLARIO

studi	studies
classe (f.)	class, classroom
corso	course
libro	book
penna	pen
quaderno	notebook
saggio	essay
laurea	degree
diploma (m.)	diploma
insegnante (m./f.)	teacher
professore (m.)	professor
professoressa (f.)	professor
studente (m.)	student
studentessa (f.)	student
scuola materna	kindergarten
scuola elementare	elementary school
scuola media	junior high school, middle school
scuola superiore	high school
liceo	*liceo* (type of high school)
corso serale	night course
andare a lezione (f.)	to go to class
andare a scuola	to go to school
andare all'università	to attend university
fare i compiti	to do the homework
fare il primo anno	to be in the first year (of school)
prendere appunti	to take notes
avere un esame	to have an examination
imparare	to learn
spiegare	to explain
studiare	to study

correggere	to correct
leggere	to read
scrivere	to write
insegnare	to teach
anche	too, also
sempre	always
incontro fortuito	chance meeting

ESERCIZI

A. *Rispondere affermativamente alle seguenti domande.*

1. *Gli studenti devono fare i compiti?*
2. *Devi andare a lezione?*
3. *Dobbiamo prendere appunti?*
4. *Voi dovete studiare?*
5. *Anna vuole andare all'università?*

B. *Completare con la forma appropriata del verbo fra parentesi.*

1. *Noi _____ (scrivere) un saggio.*
2. *Roberto _____ (leggere) molto.*
3. *Loro _____ (leggere) sempre e _____ (scrivere) sempre saggi.*
4. *Il professore _____ (correggere) gli esami.*
5. *Carla _____ (dovere) andare a scuola.*

C. *Rimettere le parole in ordine.* (Put the words in order.)

ESEMPIO: professore / l' / insegna / quel / italiano
   Quel professore insegna l'italiano.

1. *lezione / la / deve / professoressa / spiegare / la*
2. *i / io / fare / devo / compiti*
3. *studente / prende / lo / appunti*
4. *lezione / vado / io / sempre / a*
5. *gli / scrivono / l' / esame / studenti*

NOTA CULTURALE

In Italy education is compulsory until fourteen years of age. Children may, but don't have to, go to the *scuola materna* (kindergarten), but must attend five years of elementary school (*la scuola elementare*) and three years of junior high school (*la scuola media inferiore*). They may choose to continue their education in high school (*la scuola media superiore*), in a *liceo* (a secondary school that focuses on the Humanities or Science), or in an *istituto* (a vocational high school, usually providing technical or business education). Students who graduate from a *liceo* or an *istituto* may continue their studies at a university. Every major city has a university, some of which are very old. The *Università di Bologna,* for example, was founded in the twelfth century and is the oldest university in Europe.

CHIAVE PER GLI ESERCIZI

A. 1. *Sì, (gli studenti) devono fare i compiti.* 2. *Sì, devo andare a lezione.* 3. *Sì, dobbiamo/dovete prendere appunti.* 4. *Sì, dobbiamo studiare.* 5. *Sì, Anna vuole andare all'università.*

B. 1. *scriviamo* 2. *legge* 3. *leggono, scrivono* 4. *corregge* 5. *deve*

C. 1. *La professoressa deve spiegare la lezione.* 2. *Io devo fare i compiti.* 3. *Lo studente prende appunti.* 4. *Io vado sempre a lezione.* 5. *Gli studenti scrivono l'esame.*

LEZIONE 8

AL TELEFONO.   On the telephone.

A. DIALOGO

1. Il centralino.

MICHELE: **Vorrei telefonare a New York, per favore.**

CENTRALINISTA: **Qual è il prefisso?**

MICHELE: **Il prefisso è due–uno–due.**

CENTRALINISTA: **E il numero telefonico?**

MICHELE: **Il numero è sei–due–otto–quindici–ventotto.**

CENTRALINISTA: **Resti in linea . . . Mi dispiace, la linea è occupata.**

MICHELE: **Va bene, richiamo più tardi . . .**

The operator.

MICHELE: I would like to make a telephone call to New York, please.

OPERATOR: What's the area code?

MICHELE: The area code is two–one–two.

OPERATOR: And the telephone number?

MICHELE: The number is six–two–eight–fifteen–twenty-eight.

OPERATOR: Hold on . . . I'm sorry, the line is busy.

MICHELE: Okay, I'll call again later . . .

---

2. Una telefonata interurbana.

MARIA: **Pronto, chi parla?**

MICHELE: **Pronto. Sono Michele . . . Come stai?**

MARIA: **Sei Michele? Non ti sento bene . . . La linea non è buona.**

MICHELE: **Chiamo da Roma. Sono in una cabina telefonica. Parto fra un'ora.**

MARIA: **Che cosa dici?**

MICHELE: **Dico che vengo a casa. Arrivo a New York questo pomeriggio. Capisci?**

MARIA: **Vieni oggi? Quando parti, e quando arrivi? Non ti sento bene e non capisco quello che dici.**

MICHELE: **Chiudiamo . . . Chiamo il centralino e poi ti richiamo subito.**

A long-distance call.

MARIA: Hello! Who's speaking?

MICHELE: Hello! It's Michele . . . How are you?

MARIA: It's Michele? I can't hear you well . . . It's a bad connection.

MICHELE: I'm calling from Rome. I'm at a public phone. I'm leaving in one hour.

MARIA: What?

MICHELE: I'm saying that I'm coming home. I will arrive in New York this afternoon. Do you understand?

MARIA: You're coming today? When are you leaving, and when will you arrive? I can't hear you well, and I don't understand what you're saying.

MICHELE: Let's hang up . . . I'll call the operator, and I'll call you right back.

B. PRONUNCIA

1. THE COMBINATION *SC*

Like the letter *c*, the combination *sc* can have two different sounds. Before *a, o, u* it is equivalent to the English *sc* in "scar." Before *e* or *i* it is equivalent to the English *sh* in "shoe."

LETTER	SOUND	EXAMPLE
sc	scar, scope, scarf	conosco, scuola, scala
	shoe, shine, she	conosci, conoscere, scena

2. THE COMBINATION *SCH*

The combination *sch* occurs only before *i* or *e* and is always equivalent to the English *sch* in "school" or *sk* in "disk."

LETTER	SOUND	EXAMPLE
sch	school, disk, skeleton	scheletro, pesche, dischi

C. GRAMMATICA E SUOI USI

1. THE PRESENT TENSE OF REGULAR *-IRE* VERBS

The present tense of regular *-ire* verbs is formed by adding the appropriate endings to the verb root. The singular personal endings are: *-o, -i, -e,* and the plural are: *-iamo, -ite, -ono.*

	SENTIRE	TO HEAR
I hear	io	sento
you hear (familiar)	tu	senti
he hears	lui	sente
she hears	lei	sente
you hear (polite)	Lei	sente
we hear	noi	sentiamo
you hear (familiar or polite)	voi	sentite
they hear	loro	sentono
you hear (polite)	Loro	sentono

Non ti sento.
I can't hear you.

Sentite quel rumore?
Do you hear that noise?

Other verbs conjugated like *sentire* are: *offrire* ("to offer") and *partire* ("to leave, to depart").

Quando parti?
When are you leaving?

Offriamo noi stasera.
We're treating tonight.

2. THE PRESENT TENSE OF VERBS IN *-ISC*

Some verbs of the third group are not conjugated like *sentire*. They are referred to as verbs in *-isc* because an *-isc* is inserted between their root and the regular endings in all but the first and second persons plural.

	CAPIRE	TO UNDERSTAND
I understand	*io*	*capisco*
you understand (familiar)	*tu*	*capisci*
he understands	*lui*	*capisce*
she understands	*lei*	*capisce*
you understand (polite)	*Lei*	*capisce*
we understand	*noi*	*capiamo*
you understand (familiar or polite)	*voi*	*capite*
they understand	*loro*	*capiscono*
you understand (polite)	*Loro*	*capiscono*

Other verbs conjugated like *capire* are: *finire* ("to finish") and *preferire* ("to prefer"). Verbs that follow the model of *capire* will be indicated in the vocabulary sections by *-isc* in parentheses.

Non capisco.
I don't understand.

Loro capiscono l'italiano.
They understand Italian.

Noi capiamo questa lezione.
We understand this lesson.

3. IRREGULAR *-IRE* VERBS: *DIRE* AND *VENIRE*

Dire and *venire* are irregular in the present tense.

	DIRE	TO SAY
I say	*io*	*dico*
you say (familiar)	*tu*	*dici*
he says	*lui*	*dice*
she says	*lei*	*dice*
you say (polite)	*Lei*	*dice*
we say	*noi*	*diciamo*
you say (familiar or polite)	*voi*	*dite*
they say	*loro*	*dicono*
you say (polite)	*Loro*	*dicono*

Che cosa dici?
   What are you saying?

Dico che parto.
   I'm saying that I'm leaving.

	VENIRE	TO COME
I come	*io*	*vengo*
you come (familiar)	*tu*	*vieni*
he comes	*lui*	*viene*
she comes	*lei*	*viene*
you come (polite)	*Lei*	*viene*
we come	*noi*	*veniamo*
you come (familiar or polite)	*voi*	*venite*
they come	*loro*	*vengono*
you come (polite)	*Loro*	*vengono*

Vengo in Italia.
   I'm coming to Italy.

Venite a Roma?
   Are you coming to Rome?

4. IDIOMATIC USES OF *FRA*

The preposition *fra* means "among" and "between" (see chapter 5), but when referring to time it also means "in."

Parto fra un'ora.
  I'm leaving in one hour.

Arrivo fra due giorni.
  I'm arriving in two days.

Vengo fra dieci minuti.
  I'm coming in ten minutes.

VOCABOLARIO

telefono	telephone
cabina telefonica	telephone booth
carta telefonica	telephone card
centralino (place)	operator
centralinista (m./f.)	operator
elenco telefonico	telephone book
gettone (m.)	telephone token
interurbana	long-distance call
fare una telefonata "erre"	to call collect
pagine gialle	yellow pages
prefisso	area code
la segreteria telefonica	answering machine
La linea è occupata.	The line is busy.
La linea è libera.	The line is free.
Posso parlare con . . .?	May I speak to . . .?
Pronto! Chi parla?	Hello! Who's speaking?
Qual'è il prefisso di . . .?	What is the area code for . . .?
Resta/i in linea.	Hold on./Stay on the line. (familiar/ polite)
rispondere al telefono	to answer the phone
telefonare	to telephone
fare una telefonata	to make a telephone call
ricevere una telefonata	to receive a telephone call

Scusi, ho sbagliato numero.   I'm sorry, I dialed the wrong number.
capire (isc)   to understand
dire   to say
sentire   to hear
richiamare   to call back, to call again
telefonare   to phone
finire (isc)   to finish
offrire   to offer
partire   to leave, to depart
venire   to come
preferire (isc)   to prefer

ESERCIZI

A. *Dare la forma corretta del verbo.*

1. *io (partire)*
2. *noi (offrire)*
3. *loro (finire)*
4. *lei (sentire)*
5. *voi (capire)*

B. *Dare la forma appropriata del verbo.*

1. *Io _____ stasera. (partire)*
2. *Il signor Carli _____ un caffè corretto a Carlo. (offrire)*
3. *Signor Meli, quando _____ a New York? (venire)*
4. *Noi non _____ molto. (dire)*
5. *Io non _____ il centralinista. (capire)*

C. *Tradurre.*

1. Hello! Who is speaking?
2. I dialed the wrong number.
3. May I speak to Luigi?
4. What's the area code for New York?
5. Stay on the line, please.

NOTA CULTURALE

Italian public telephones take coins, a token called a *gettone,* or a *carta telefonica* (a telephone card). *Gettoni* and *carte telefoniche* can be bought where public telephones are found (at cafés, tobacco shops, and telephone offices) and from vending machines at most airports and railway stations. To use the *carta telefonica,* tear off the perforated corner of the card, and insert the card as indicated by the arrow. The value of the card will appear in a display window on the telephone. After you hang up, the card will be returned. You may continue to use it until the full value of the card has been used up. If you use coins or *gettoni,* make sure that you insert enough of them (even for a local call). In the telephone display window you will see the amount that you have inserted or that is still unused. Unused coins or *gettoni* will be returned.

You can make collect calls from any phone by dialing 170, or by dialing the number of the international operator of the country that you want to reach. The latter method may be cheaper (especially for the United States and Canada) because you will be charged according to the rates and times of the country you call. In both cases, however, if you use a public telephone, you still need to insert the minimum value for a phone call, which will be returned after your call has been completed.

Phone calls can also be made from offices of *S.I.P.* (a state-owned company) found in every city and at most airports and train stations. Operators will assign you a booth, help you place the call, and collect payment when you finish.

CHIAVE PER GLI ESERCIZI

A. 1. *parto*   2. *offriamo*   3. *finiscono* 4. *sente*   5. *capite*
B. 1. *parto*   2. *offre*   3. *viene*   4. *diciamo*   5. *capisco*
C. 1. *Pronto, chi parla?* 2. *Ho sbagliato numero.* 3. *Posso parlare con Luigi?* 4. *Qual'è il prefisso di New York?* 5. *Resta/i* (familiar/polite) *in linea, per favore.*

LEZIONE 9

MESI, STAGIONI, DATE E TEMPO.
Months, Seasons, Dates, and Weather.

A. DIALOGO

Alla spiaggia.

SIGNORA ROSSI: **Che bella giornata! C'è molta gente . . .**

SIGNOR ROSSI: **Eh sì, con l'estate e il caldo arrivano molti turisti
. . . Ma quanti ne abbiamo oggi?**

SIGNORA ROSSI: **È già il primo luglio . . . Finalmente un po' di
gente . . .**

SIGNOR ROSSI: **Un po' di gente!?! Vuoi dire tanta gente! Vengono
tutti qui al mare! Vengono tutti qui in vacanza! In luglio e in
agosto è impossibile fare il bagno . . . E fa molto caldo!**

SIGNORA ROSSI: **Quanto sei esagerato! Qui in estate non fa troppo
caldo! Questa città non è molto bella d'inverno. È vuota. Quando
fa freddo e piove sempre, qui ci sono poche persone, non c'è
quasi nessuno.**

SIGNOR ROSSI: **Eh sì, tu preferisci il caldo e l'estate perché ami la
confusione.**

———————

At the beach.

MRS. ROSSI: What a beautiful day! There are a lot of people . . .

MR. ROSSI: Oh yes, with the summer and the heat a lot of tourists arrive
. . . But what's today's date?

MRS. ROSSI: It's already the first of July. Finally some people.

MR. ROSSI: Some people!?! You mean a lot of people . . . They all come to
the beach here! They all come here on vacation! In July and August it's
impossible to go for a swim . . . And it's very hot!

MRS. ROSSI: How you exaggerate! It's not too hot here in the summer! This city isn't very beautiful in winter. It's empty. When it's too cold and it's always raining, there are few people here, there's hardly anyone.

MR. ROSSI: Oh yes, you prefer the heat and the summer because you love confusion.

B. PRONUNCIA

1. THE LETTER *T*

In Italian, the *t* is more dentalized and is pronounced without aspiration.

giornata	day
tutti	everybody
gente	people

2. THE LETTER *P*

In Italian, the *p* sound is less explosive than in English.

per piacere	please
pesce	fish
dopo	after

3. THE LETTER *J*

In Italian, the letter *j* is pronounced the same as *i* and is seldom used.

il Mar Jonio	the Jonic Sea
la Juventus	Juventus (an Italian soccer team)

Remember, however, that in words borrowed from English, the *j* is pronounced as in English.

jogging	jogging
juke-box	jukebox

C. GRAMMATICA E SUOI USI

1. ORDINAL NUMBERS

Ordinal numbers indicate position in a sequence: first, second, third . . .

primo, -a	first
secondo, -a	second
terzo, -a	third
quarto, -a	fourth
quinto, -a	fifth
sesto, -a	sixth
settimo, -a	seventh
ottavo, -a	eighth
nono, -a	ninth
decimo, -a	tenth
undicesimo, -a	eleventh
dodicesimo, -a	twelfth
tredicesimo, -a	thirteenth
quattordicesimo, -a	fourteenth
quindicesimo, -a	fifteenth
sedicesimo, -a	sixteenth
diciassettesimo, -a	seventeenth
diciottesimo, -a	eighteenth
diciannovesimo, -a	nineteenth
ventesimo, -a	twentieth
trentesimo, -a	thirtieth
quarantesimo, -a	fortieth
centesimo, -a	hundredth
millesimo, -a	thousandth
milionesimo, -a	millionth

From "eleventh" (*undicesimo, -a*) on, drop the final vowel of the cardinal number, and add *-esimo, -a*. For numbers like *ventitrè, trentatrè*, etc., add *-esimo, -a*, but do not drop the final *e* from the cardinal number (*ventitreesimo, -a:* no accent on the *e*). Ordinal numbers are adjectives and must agree in gender and number with the nouns they modify.

Il primo mese dell'anno è gennaio.
The first month of the year is January.

Il primo giorno della settimana è lunedì.
The first day of the week is Monday.

Passo la terza settimana delle vacanze in Francia.
I'm spending the third week of vacation in France.

2. THE MONTHS

The months in Italian are all masculine and are never capitalized.

gennaio	January
febbraio	February
marzo	March
aprile	April
maggio	May
giugno	June
luglio	July
agosto	August
settembre	September
ottobre	October
novembre	November
dicembre	December

The prepositions *a* or *in* plus the name of a month express "in January," "in February," etc.

A luglio fa caldo.
In July it's hot.

In dicembre fa freddo.
In December it's cold.

The first day of the month is expressed with the ordinal number *primo*.

È il primo *(di)* **luglio.**
It's the first of July.

90

Cardinal numbers are used for the other days.

Oggi è il due *(di)* **marzo.**
Today is the second of March.

Oggi è il sette *(di)* **agosto.**
Today is the seventh of August.

Notice that the preposition *di* before the name of a month is optional.

3. THE SEASONS

l'inverno	winter
la primavera	spring
l'estate (f.)	summer
l'autunno	fall

The names of the seasons are not capitalized and should be preceded by the definite article.

Io preferisco l'estate.
I prefer summer.

Amo la primavera.
I love spring.

Italian expresses "in" a certain season in the following manner:

in primavera	in spring
in estate/d'estate	in summer
in autunno	in autumn
in inverno/d'inverno	in winter

4. THE USE OF *MOLTO, TROPPO, TANTO,* AND *POCO* AS ADVERBS AND ADJECTIVES

When *molto* ("a lot, many"), *tanto* ("so much, so many"), *troppo* ("too much, too many"), and *poco* ("a little, a few") modify a noun, they act as adjectives and must agree with the noun.

	SINGULAR	PLURAL
MASCULINE	*molto, tanto, troppo, poco*	*molti, tanti, troppi, pochi*
FEMININE	*molta, tanta, troppa, poca*	*molte, tante, troppe, poche*

Arrivano molti turisti.
> Many tourists are arriving.

C'è tanta gente.
> There are a lot of people.

Ci sono poche persone.
> There are few people.

When *molto, poco, tanto,* and *troppo* are used before an adjective or after a verb, they act as adverbs and are invariable. Their equivalents in English are "very" (*molto*), "so, so much" (*tanto*), "too, too much" (*troppo*), and "a bit, little" (*poco*).

Fa molto caldo.
> It's very hot.

Qui in estate non fa troppo caldo.
> It's not too hot here in the summer.

A luglio piove poco.
> It rains little in July.

VOCABOLARIO

mese (m.)	month
gennaio	January
febbraio	February
marzo	March
aprile (m.)	April
maggio	May
giugno	June
luglio	July
agosto	August
settembre (m.)	September
ottobre (m.)	October

novembre (m.)	November
dicembre (m.)	December
stagione (f.)	season
inverno	winter
primavera	spring
estate (f.)	summer
autunno	fall
data	date
Quanti ne abbiamo oggi?	What's today's date?
Oggi è il primo . . .	Today is the first . . .
Oggi è il due . . .	Today is the second . . .
Che tempo fa?	What's the weather like?
È una bella giornata.	It's a beautiful day.
È una brutta giornata.	It's a miserable day.
Fa caldo.	It's hot.
Fa freddo.	It's cold.
Fa bel tempo.	It's nice out.
Piove.	It's raining.
Nevica.	It's snowing.
Tira vento.	It's windy.
andare in vacanza	to go on vacation
andare al mare	to go to the shore
andare alla spiaggia	to go to the beach
fare il bagno	to go swimming
troppo	too much, too many, too
molto	a lot of, many, very
tanto	so much, so many, so
poco	a few, a bit, little

ESERCIZI

A. *Completare la sequenza con i due numeri successivi.* (Give the next two numbers of each sequence.)

1. *primo, secondo, terzo*
2. *nono, undicesimo, tredicesimo*

3. *diciannovesimo, ventesimo, ventunesimo*
4. *trentesimo, quarantesimo, cinquantesimo*
5. *quinto, decimo, quindicesimo*

B. *Completare con la forma corretta della parola fra parentesi.*

1. *C'è _____ gente alla spiaggia. (tanto)*
2. *La primavera è _____ bella. (molto)*
3. *In estate fa _____ caldo. (troppo)*
4. *Ci sono _____ turisti. (tanto)*
5. *D'inverno fa _____ freddo. (troppo)*
6. *In estate piove _____. (poco)*

C. *Tradurre le seguenti frasi.*

1. What's the weather like in March?
2. It's cold and rainy in winter.
3. In the summer it's too hot.
4. It's a beautiful day today.
5. Tomorrow is the second of July.
6. Today is October first.

NOTA CULTURALE

Italy's climate is mild and balmy, making it possible to travel and sightsee in comfort all year round. The main tourist season runs from mid-April to the end of September. The best months for sightseeing are April, May, June, September, and October, when the weather is generally pleasant and not too hot. July and August, the hottest months of the year, are most popular for Italian vacationers. During these months the heat can be oppressive, and people cram roads, trains, and planes on their way to shore and mountain resorts. This is especially true around the national holiday on August 15 *(Ferragosto),* when cities are deserted, and many restaurants are closed. Winters in Italy are relatively mild in most places on the main tourist circuit, but always include some rainy spells.

CHIAVE PER GLI ESERCIZI

A. 1. *quarto, quinto* 2. *quindicesimo, diciassettesimo* 3. *ventiduesimo, ventitreesimo* 4. *sessantesimo, settantesimo* 5. *ventesimo, venticinquesimo*

B. 1. *tanta* 2. *molto* 3. *troppo* 4. *tanti* 5. *troppo* 6. *poco*

C. 1. *Che tempo fa a marzo?* 2. *Fa freddo e piove d'/in inverno.* 3. *D'/In estate fa troppo caldo.* 4. *È una bella giornata oggi.* 5. *Domani è il due (di) luglio.* 6. *Oggi è il primo (di) ottobre.*

LEZIONE 10
LA FAMIGLIA.   The family.

A. DIALOGO

Una festa in famiglia.

MONICA: **Ma dove vai, Matteo?**

MATTEO: **Ho fretta. Devo comprare un regalo per mio nonno. Oggi
è il suo compleanno. Facciamo una bella festa.**

MONICA: **Quanti anni ha tuo nonno?**

MATTEO: **Ha ottant'anni, ma è ancora molto vivace.**

MONICA: **Anche il mio è molto vivace ed ha settantasei anni. Alla
festa vengono tutti i tuoi parenti?**

MATTEO: **Sì, viene tutta la mia famiglia: mia sorella, mio fratello e
tutti i nostri zii e cugini. Viene anche la mia fidanzata e suo
fratello.**

MONICA: **Beh, ciao e buon compleanno a tuo nonno!**

MATTEO: **Grazie. Ciao!**

A family party.

MONICA: But where are you going, Matteo?

MATTEO: I'm in a hurry. I have to buy a gift for my grandfather. Today is
his birthday. We're going to have a big party.

MONICA: How old is your grandfather?

MATTEO: He's 80 years old, but he's still very active.

MONICA: Mine is very active, too, and he's 76. Are all your relatives coming
to the party?

MATTEO: Yes, my whole family is coming: my sister, my brother, and all
our aunts, uncles and cousins. My fiancée and her brother are also coming.

96

MONICA: Well, good-bye, and happy birthday to your grandfather!

MATTEO: Thank you. Good-bye!

B. PRONUNCIA

1. DIPHTHONGS AND TRIPHTHONGS

A diphthong consists of two vowels pronounced with a single sound and single syllable: *ia, ie, io; ai, ei, oi; ua, ue, uo; au, eu, ou; iu; ui*. Likewise, a triphthong consists of three vowels pronounced together: *iei, iuo, uoi, uai*. Many of the possessive forms contain diphthongs or triphthongs: *mio, sue, miei, suoi*.

piano slowly	**noi** we	**buono** good
vai you go	**uguale** equal	**pausa** pause
guidare to drive	**quello** that	**più** more

2. THE LETTER *Z*

The letter *z* can be voiced, like the *ds* in "beds," or voiceless, like the *ts* in "bets." Unfortunately, there are no set rules to distinguish between the two pronunciations.

VOICELESS	**zio**	uncle
	negozio	store
	fidanzata	fiancée
VOICED	**grande magazzino**	department store
	zero	zero

3. THE LETTER *R*

In Italian, the letter *r* is trilled.

sera	evening
bere	to drink
ristorante	restaurant

4. *E* VERSUS *ED*

When the word *e* ("and") precedes a word beginning with a vowel (especially another *e* or an *a*) or an *h*, a *d* may be added in order to facilitate pronunciation.

Dico "Ciao" ed esco.
I say "Bye" and go out.

C. GRAMMATICA E SUOI USI

1. POSSESSIVE ADJECTIVES

	MASCULINE		FEMININE	
	SINGULAR	PLURAL	SINGULAR	PLURAL
my	*il mio*	*i miei*	*la mia*	*le mie*
your (familiar singular)	*il tuo*	*i tuoi*	*la tua*	*le tue*
his, her, its	*il suo*	*i suoi*	*la sua*	*le sue*
your (polite singular)	*il Suo*	*i Suoi*	*la Sua*	*le Sue*
our	*il nostro*	*i nostri*	*la nostra*	*le nostre*
your (familiar/ polite, plural)	*il vostro*	*i vostri*	*la vostra*	*le vostre*
their	*il loro*	*i loro*	*la loro*	*le loro*
your (polite plural)	*il Loro*	*i Loro*	*la Loro*	*le Loro*

In Italian, the definite article is used before the possessive adjective.

Oggi è il suo compleanno.
Today is his/her birthday.

The possessive adjective agrees in gender and number with the noun it modifies.

il mio compleanno	my birthday
la sua torta	his/her cake
i tuoi regali	your presents

Notice that *loro,* however, has only one form.

il loro fratello	their brother
i loro fratelli	their brothers
le loro sorelle	their sisters

The definite article, commonly used before the possessive adjective, is omitted before a singular, unmodified noun denoting family relationship.

mio fratello	my brother
mia sorella	my sister

However, the following cases are exceptions to this rule and require an article before the possessive adjective:

a. when the noun is plural:

i nostri cugini	our cousins

b. when *loro* is the possessive adjective:

il loro fratello	their brother

c. when the noun is modified by another adjective:

il mio cugino americano	my American cousin

With *mamma* (mommy) and *papà* (daddy), the use of the article is optional:

(Il) mio papà è giovane.
My father is young.

The article is used with nouns like *amico, bambino, fidanzato/a, famiglia* ("friend, child, fiancé/e, family") because these nouns do not actually refer to a family relationship.

99

La mia fidanzata è americana.
   My fiancée is American.

Don't forget to distinguish between familiar and polite forms.

Mario, questo è il tuo vestito?
   Mario, is this your suit?

Signor Rossi, questo è il Suo vestito?
   Mr. Rossi, is this your suit?

Unlike English, Italian does not differentiate between "his," "her," and "its."

È il suo compleanno.
   It's his/her birthday.

Sono i suoi cugini.
   They are his/her cousins.

2. POSSESSIVE PRONOUNS

Possessive pronouns ("mine, yours, hers," etc.) replace a noun. They have the same forms as the possessive adjectives. They always require an article, even when refering to singular, unmodified nouns that indicate family relationships.

Non parlo a tuo padre.—Parlo al mio.
   I'm not talking to your father.—I'm talking to mine.

The only exception to this rule is when the possessive pronoun follows the verb *essere,* in which case the article is omitted.

Questo vestito è mio.
   This suit is mine.

3. CARDINAL NUMBERS 61–100

sessantuno	61		*ottantuno*	81
sessantadue	62		*ottantadue*	82
sessantatrè	63		*ottantatrè*	83
sessantaquattro	64		*ottantaquattro*	84
sessantacinque	65		*ottantacinque*	85
sessantasei	66		*ottantasei*	86
sessantasette	67		**ottantasette**	87
sessantotto	68		**ottantotto**	88
sessantanove	69		**ottantanove**	89
settanta	70		**novanta**	90
settantuno	71		*novantuno*	91
settantadue	72		*novantadue*	92
settantatrè	73		*novantatrè*	93
settantaquattro	74		*novantaquattro*	94
settantacinque	75		*novantacinque*	95
settantasei	76		*novantasei*	99
settantasette	77		*novantasette*	97
settantotto	78		*novantotto*	98
settantanove	79		*novantanove*	99
ottanta	80		**cento**	100

4. THE PLURAL OF NOUNS ENDING IN *-IO*

Singular nouns ending in *-io* end in a single *-i* in the plural if the *-io* is not stressed.

il figlio	*i figli*	son(s)
il premio	*i premi*	prize(s)

If the *-io* is stressed, however, the plural form ends in *-ii*.

lo zio	*gli zii*	uncle(s)
l'addio	*gli addii*	good-bye(s)

5. IDIOMS WITH *AVERE*

In the dialogue, Monica and Matteo use the verb *avere* to express age.

Quanti anni ha tuo nonno?
   How old is your grandfather?

Ha ottant'anni.
   He's eighty years old.

Here are some more useful idiomatic expressions with *avere*.

avere ragione	to be right
avere torto	to be wrong
avere fretta	to be in a hurry
avere bisogno di	to need
avere voglia di	to feel like
avere paura	to be afraid

VOCABOLARIO

famiglia	family
padre (m.)	father
madre (f.)	mother
papà (m.)	daddy
mamma	mommy
figlio/a	son/daughter
sorella	sister
fratello	brother
nonno/a	grandfather/grandmother
zio/a	uncle/aunt
nipote (m./f.)	grandson, granddaughter, nephew, niece
cugino/a	cousin
parenti (m.), (f., pl.)	relatives
fidanzato/a	fiancé/fiancée
marito	husband
moglie (f.)	wife

genitori (m., pl.)	parents
nuora	daughter-in-law
genero	son-in-law
suocero/a	father/mother-in-law
cognato/a	brother/sister-in-law
bambino/a	child, son/daughter
compleanno	birthday
onomastico	name day
Quando è il tuo compleanno?	When is your birthday?
Quando è il tuo onomastico?	When is your name day?
Quanti anni hai/ha?	How old are you? (familiar/polite)
avere . . . anni	to be . . . years old
Buon compleanno!	Happy birthday!
Buon onomastico!	Happy name day!
Tanti auguri!	Best Wishes!
regalo	gift
festa	party, feast
torta	cake
andare al negozio	to go to the store
essere vivace	to be active, vivacious
avere ragione	to be right
avere torto	to be wrong
avere fretta	to be in a hurry
avere bisogno di	to need
avere voglia di	to feel like
avere paura	to be afraid

ESERCIZI

A. *Rispondere affermativamente alle seguenti domande usando l'aggettivo possessivo appropriato.*

1. *Questo è vostro zio?*
2. *Oggi è il tuo compleanno?*
3. *Questo è il fratello di Paolo?*
4. *Questi sono i figli dei signori Rossi?*

5. *Questa è la sorella di Paolo?*
6. *Questi sono i parenti di Maria?*

B. *Tradurre.*

1. My uncle is 25 years old.
2. Happy birthday!
3. They are in a hurry.
4. My brother and my cousins are coming to the party.
5. How old is your father?

C. *Completare con la forma appropriata dell' aggettivo possessivo e l'articolo determinativo, quando è necessario.*

1. _____ *padre ha cinquantadue anni. (tuo)*
2. _____ *cugina americana si chiama Lisa. (nostro)*
3. _____ *famiglia è molto numerosa. (vostro)*
4. *Oggi è* _____ *compleanno. (suo)*
5. _____ *sorella è bella. (loro)*

NOTA CULTURALE

Italy has one of the lowest birth rates in the world. A typical Italian family consists of the father, the mother, and two children. As in many modern industrialized countries, in Italy the family unit is not as close-knit as it used to be. In fact, due to the difficulties in finding work or even a place to live, the younger generations have had to relocate outside their hometowns. However, the family often gathers on Sundays, holidays, family birthdays, or name days. In Italy, name days are given the same importance as birthdays.

CHIAVE PER GLI ESERCIZI

A. 1. *Sì, è nostro zio.* 2. *Sì, è il mio compleanno.* 3. *Sì, è suo fratello.* 4. *Sì, sono i loro figli.* 5. *Sì, è sua sorella.* 6. *Sì, sono i suoi parenti.*
B. 1. *Mio zio ha venticinque anni.* 2. *Buon compleanno!* 3. *Loro hanno fretta.* 4. *Mio fratello e i miei cugini vengono alla festa.* 5. *Quanti hanni ha tuo padre?*
C. 1. *Tuo* 2. *La nostra* 3. *La vostra* 4. *il suo* 5. *La loro*

SECONDO RIPASSO

A. *Tradurre.*

1. Is that pink sweater yours?
2. We are leaving in two hours.
3. Today is September first.
4. What's the date today?
5. This is my coat.
6. She is my sister.
7. Where are your parents?
8. These are her gloves.

B. *Accoppiare la domanda nella colonna a sinistra con la risposta appropriata nella colonna a destra.* (Match each question with the appropriate answer in the right-hand column.)

1. *Come stai?*
2. *Dove vai?*
3. *Quando parte Cristina?*
4. *Quale camicia compri?*
5. *Quanto costa questo maglione?*

a. *Parte domenica.*
b. *Quella bianca.*
c. *Centomila lire.*
d. *Bene, grazie.*
e. *Vado da Carlo.*

C. *Completare con la forma appropriata di "bello" o "quello."*

1. *Quale camicetta compri?*
   Compro _____.
2. *Quali pantaloni compri?*
   Compro _____.
3. *_____ cappotto è molto bello.*
4. *Compro anche _____ due vestiti.*
5. *Questo è un _____ abito.*
6. *È un _____ vestito, ma è un po' stretto.*

D. *Completare in modo opportuno.*

1. *Chi paga? Pag_____ tu o pag_____ io?*
2. *Marianna legg_____ sempre.*
3. *Oggi Simona e Monica scriv_____ un saggio.*
4. *Io e John non cap_____ l'italiano.*
5. *Oggi c'è molt_____ gente alla spiaggia.*

6. *Qui in inverno ci sono poc*_____ *turisti.*
7. *Tu prefer*_____ *l'estate o l'inverno?*
8. *Questa città non è molt*_____ *bella d'inverno.*
9. *In estate fa tropp*_____ *caldo.*
10. *Quel maglione viol*_____ *è molt*_____ *bello.*

E. *Completare con la forma appropriata del verbo fra parentesi.*

1. *Antonio* _____ *sempre studiare. (dovere)*
2. *Io* _____ *imparare bene l'inglese. (volere)*
3. *Oggi loro non* _____ *studiare. (potere)*
4. *Tu capisci quello che noi* _____*? (dire)*
5. *Domenica io e Michele* _____ *a casa. (venire)*

CHIAVE PER GLI ESERCIZI

A. 1. *Quel maglione rosa è tuo?* 2. *Partiamo fra due ore.* 3. *Oggi è il primo (di) settembre.* 4. *Quanti ne abbiamo oggi?* 5. *Questo è il mio cappotto.* 6. *Lei è mia sorella.* 7. *Dove sono i tuoi genitori?* 8. *Questi sono i suoi guanti.*

B. 1-d; 2-e; 3-a; 4-b; 5-c

C. 1. *quella* 2. *quelli* 3. *Quel* 4. *quei* 5. *bell'* 6. *bel*

D. 1. *paghi, pago* 2. *legge* 3. *scrivono* 4. *capiamo* 5. *molta* 6. *pochi* 7. *preferisci* 8. *molto* 9. *troppo* 10. *viola, molto*

E. 1. *deve* 2. *voglio* 3. *possono* 4. *diciamo* 5. *veniamo*

DA LEGGERE (READING)

Now you're ready to practice your reading skills! While indeed you've been "reading" the dialogues, the four reading sections (*Da Leggere*) offer you the chance to practice reading as you would read a newspaper article or essay abroad. First, read through each passage without referring to the accompanying vocabulary notes. Try to understand the main idea of the text, inferring the meaning of the new words from context. Don't worry if a passage seems long or if you don't know each word; you can go back and reread it, checking the vocabulary notes to learn the exact meaning of new words and phrases. Now, let's begin!

L'Italia è una penisola,[1] ha la forma di uno stivale[2] e copre una superficie[3] di 301,264 Km.[2] È circondata[4] dal Mar Mediterraneo, che comprende il Mar Adriatico, il Mar Ligure, il Mar Tirreno e il Mar Ionio. Le Alpi, una catena[5] montuosa,[6] dividono[7] l'Italia dal resto dell'Europa. Gli Appennini, un'altra catena di monti, attraversano[8] tutta l'Italia. Il monte più alto[9] delle Alpi è il Monte Bianco.

Il territorio italiano è occupato per il 40% dalla collina,[10] per il 30% dalla montagna[11] e per il 30% dalla pianura.[12] I principali fiumi[13] italiani sono: il Po (652 Km), l'Adige (410 Km), il Tevere (405 Km), l'Adda (313 Km) e il Ticino (248 Km). I laghi[14] più importanti sono: il lago di Garda (il più grande d'Italia), il lago di Como, il lago Maggiore e il lago Trasimeno (il più vasto dell'Italia centrale).

L'Italia ha un clima che varia da regione a regione. Le regioni alpine, per esempio, hanno inverni lunghi e freddi, estati brevi e fresche. Le regioni marittime[15] hanno, per esempio, estati calde e inverni abbastanza miti.[16]

VOCABULARIO

1. *penisola*	peninsula
2. *stivale* (m.)	boot
3. *superficie* (f.)	area, surface
4. *circondato, -a*	surrounded
5. *catena*	chain
6. *montuoso, -a*	mountainous
7. *dividere*	to divide
8. *attraversare*	to cross, to pass through
9. *alto, -a*	high
10. *collina*	hill
11. *montagna*	mountain
12. *pianura*	plain, lowland
13. *fiume* (m.)	river
14. *lago*	lake
15. *marittimo, -a*	of the sea, coastal
16. *mite*	mild

LEZIONE 11

MANGIARE E BERE.   Food and drink.

A. DIALOGO

Al ristorante.

CAMERIERE: Ecco il menu.

SIGNOR SMITH: Ma oggi il ristorante è vuoto . . . Non c'è nessuno . . .

CAMERIERE: È ancora presto . . . In Italia non ceniamo mai prima delle otto.

SIGNORA SMITH: Noi invece mangiamo verso le sei.

CAMERIERE: Desiderate ordinare adesso?

SIGNORA SMITH: Sì, abbiamo fame. Io vorrei del pesce ai ferri. È buono il pesce oggi?

CAMERIERE: Sì, è molto buono. E per Lei Signore?

SIGNOR SMITH: Io vorrei una bistecca, per favore. E ben cotta.

CAMERIERE: E per contorno?

SIGNOR SMITH: Per me un po' di verdura e delle patate fritte.

SIGNORA SMITH: E io vorrei dell'insalata.

CAMERIERE: E da bere? Del vino? Abbiamo un buon vino.

SIGNOR SMITH: Niente vino. Non beviamo vino. Ma abbiamo sete. Una bottiglia d'acqua minerale.

SIGNORA SMITH: E dopo un dolce . . .

CAMERIERE: Un gelato, una pasta?

SIGNOR SMITH: Io ho caldo—un gelato al cioccolato per me.

SIGNORA SMITH: E una pasta per me. Grazie.

At the restaurant.

WAITER: Here's the menu.

MR. SMITH: But the restaurant is empty today . . . Nobody is here . . .

WAITER: It's still early . . . In Italy we never have dinner before eight o'clock.

MRS. SMITH: We eat around six o'clock, instead.

WAITER: Would you like to order now?

MRS. SMITH: Yes, we're hungry. I would like some grilled fish. Is the fish good today?

WAITER: Yes, it's very good. And for you, sir?

MR. SMITH: I would like a steak, please. Well done.

WAITER: And as a side dish?

MR. SMITH: For me some vegetables and some french fries.

MRS. SMITH: And I would like some salad.

WAITER: And to drink? Some wine? We have a good wine.

MR. SMITH: No wine. We don't drink wine. But we're thirsty. A bottle of mineral water.

MRS. SMITH: And later some dessert . . .

WAITER: Some ice cream, a pastry?

MR. SMITH: I'm hot—chocolate ice cream for me.

MRS. SMITH: And a pastry for me. Thank you.

B. GRAMMATICA E SUOI USI

1. VERBS ENDING IN -GIARE

In the present tense, verbs ending in -giare have only one i in the second person singular and the first person plural forms.

MANGIARE	TO EAT	
I eat	*io*	*mangio*
you eat (familiar)	*tu*	*mangi*
he eats	*lui*	*mangia*
she eats	*lei*	*mangia*
you eat (polite)	*Lei*	*mangia*
we eat	*noi*	*mangiamo*
you eat (familiar or polite)	*voi*	*mangiate*
they eat	*loro*	*mangiano*
you eat (polite)	*Loro*	*mangiano*

Io mangio il pesce.
   I eat fish.

Noi mangiamo verso le sei.
   We eat around six o'clock.

Loro non mangiano verdura.
   They don't eat vegetables.

2. PARTITIVE PREPOSITIONS

The partitive expresses a part or portion of something. In English, it is expressed by "some," "any," or with a noun alone.

I want some fish.
Do you want any fish?
Do you want fish?

In Italian, the partitive can be expressed with the preposition *di* plus a form of the definite article (*il, lo, la,* etc.).

Vorrei del pesce.
   I would like some fish.

Vorrei dell'insalata.
   I would like some salad.

Vorrei delle patate fritte.
   I would like some french fries.

110

3. DOUBLE NEGATIVES

We have already seen that the word *non* before the verb expresses negation.

Io non mangio pesce.
> I don't eat fish.

There are other words which form negative sentences. They are often used with *non* in a double negative construction.

a. *nessuno* (no one)

As a pronoun it is invariable. It can follow *non* and the verb.

Non viene nessuno.
> No one is coming.

It can also begin the sentence, in which case *non* is omitted.

Nessuno viene.
> No one is coming.

b. *niente* and *nulla* (nothing, not . . . anything)

Niente and *nulla* are pronouns. They are invariable and are used in the singular. Like *nessuno,* they can begin a sentence.

Niente vino, per favore.
> No wine, please.

or they can follow *non* and the verb.

Non voglio niente/nulla.
> I don't want anything.

c. *mai* (never)

The negative word *mai* can also either begin the sentence or follow *non* and the verb.

Non ceniamo mai prima delle otto.
We never have dinner before eight o'clock.

Mai ceniamo prima delle otto.
We never have dinner before eight o'clock.

Other negative expressions commonly used in Italian include:

non . . . più (anymore/no longer)

Sandra non mangia più pesce.
Sandra doesn't eat fish anymore.

non . . . né . . . né (neither . . . nor)

Non beve né vino né acqua.
He drinks neither wine nor water.

non . . . ancora (not yet, still)

Non so ancora.
I don't know yet. I still don't know.

4. THE ADJECTIVE *BUONO*

The adjective *buono* may precede or follow the noun. When it follows the noun, it has the same four forms as regular adjectives ending in *-o*.

	SINGULAR	PLURAL
MASCULINE	*buono*	*buoni*
FEMININE	*buona*	*buone*

una pizza buona	a good pizza
un gelato buono	good ice cream
una bistecca buona	a good steak

When preceding the noun, the singular forms of *buono* resemble those of the indefinite article and follow the same rules.

	MASCULINE	FEMININE
Before most nouns:		Before nouns beginning with a consonant:
	buon	*buona*
Before nouns beginning with s + consonant, or with z:		Before nouns beginning with a vowel:
	buono	*buon'*

Buon appetito!	Enjoy your meal!
una buona pizza	a good pizza
un buon pesce	a good fish

5. THE PRESENT TENSE OF *BERE*

	BERE	TO DRINK
I drink	*io*	*bevo*
you drink (familiar)	*tu*	*bevi*
he drinks	*lui*	*beve*
she drinks	*lei*	*beve*
you drink (polite)	*Lei*	*beve*
we drink	*noi*	*beviamo*
you drink (familiar or polite)	*voi*	*bevete*
they drink	*loro*	*bevono*
you drink (polite)	*Loro*	*bevono*

Non bevo vino.
 I don't drink wine.

Lisa beve acqua minerale.
 Lisa drinks mineral water.

6. MORE IDIOMS WITH *AVERE*

In Italian, *avere* is often used to express states of being.

avere fame	to be hungry
avere sete	to be thirsty
avere caldo	to be warm/hot
avere freddo	to be cold
avere sonno	to be sleepy

VOCABOLARIO

ristorante (m.)	restaurant
menu (m.)	menu
coperto	cover charge
conto	bill
mancia	tip
coltello	knife
cucchiaio	spoon
forchetta	fork
piatto	dish
tavolo	table
tovagliolo	napkin
contorno *(di verdura, patate fritte)*	side dish (of vegetables, french fries)
dolce (m.)	dessert
frutta	fruit
insalata	salad
spaghetti (m., pl.) **(al dente, al sugo)**	spaghetti (al dente, with sauce)
bistecca (ben cotta, al sangue)	steak (well done, rare)
pesce (m.) **(ai ferri, lesso, fritto)**	fish (grilled, boiled, fried)
gelato (al cioccolato, alla vaniglia)	ice cream (chocolate, vanilla)
vino	wine
Cameriere*(a)*, **il menu, per favore!**	Waiter *(waitress)*, the menu, please!

Desidera ordinare adesso?	Would you like to order now?
Il conto, per favore.	The bill, please.
Il servizio è compreso?	Is service included?
Buon appetito!	Enjoy your meal!
avere fame	to be hungry
avere sete	to be thirsty
avere caldo	to be warm/hot
avere freddo	to be cold
avere sonno	to be sleepy
mangiare	to eat
cenare	to have dinner
bere	to drink
nessuno	no one, nobody
niente/nulla	nothing
mai	never
non . . . più	anymore/no longer
né . . . né	neither . . . nor
non . . . ancora	not . . . yet

ESERCIZI

A. *Rispondere negativamente alle seguenti domande usando "nessuno, niente, mai, né . . . né" oppure "non . . . più."*

1. *Carla vuole qualcosa? (niente)*
2. *Preferisci vino o acqua minerale? (né . . . né)*
3. *Paola telefona sempre a Marco? (mai)*
4. *Cosa fai? (niente)*
5. *Chi c'è oggi al ristorante? (nessuno)*
6. *Sandra abita ancora a Roma? (non . . . più)*

B. *Completare con la forma appropriata di "buono."*

1. *Voglio un _____ caffé.*
2. *Lucia è una _____ amica.*
3. *Gianni e Marco sono _____ amici.*
4. *Questa pizza è _____.*

5. _____ *appetito!*

6. _____ *sera, signorina.*

C. *Tradurre.*

1. Some fish, some french fries, and some salad, please.
2. No wine, please.
3. John isn't coming anymore.
4. At what time are we eating tonight?
5. This is a good restaurant.
6. This fish is good.
7. I don't understand anything.

NOTA CULTURALE

Dining in Italy is a pleasant experience, a chance to enjoy authentic Italian specialties and ingredients. There are a variety of eating places in Italy, ranging from a *ristorante* (restaurant) to a *trattoria, tavola calda* (hot buffet), or *rosticceria* (rotisserie). A *trattoria* is usually family run—simpler in decor, menu, and service than a *ristorante,* and also slightly less expensive. In addition, countless fast-food places are opening up everywhere. They are variations of the older Italian institutions, such as the *tavola calda* and the *rosticceria,* and offer a selection of hot and cold dishes to take out or eat on the premises.

In all but the simplest places there's a *coperto* (cover charge), as well as a *servizio* (service charge) of 10 to 15 percent.

Lunch is generally served from 1:00 to 3:00, and dinner from 8:00 to 10:00, or even later in some restaurants.

CHIAVE PER GLI ESERCIZI

A. 1. *No, Carla non vuole niente.* 2. *Non preferisco né vino né acqua minerale.* 3. *No, Paola non telefona mai a Marco.* 4. *Non faccio niente.* 5. *Non c'è nessuno oggi al ristorante.* 6. *No, Sandra non abita più a Roma.*

B. 1. *buon* 2. *buon'* 3. *buoni* 4. *buona* 5. *Buon* 6. *Buona*

C. 1. *Del pesce, delle patate fritte e dell'insalata, per favore.* 2. *Niente vino, per favore.* 3. *John non viene più.* 4. *A che ora mangiamo questa sera?* 5. *Questo è un buon ristorante.* 6. *Questo pesce è buono.* 7. *Non capisco niente/nulla.*

LEZIONE 12

UNA GIORNATA TIPICA.   A typical day.

A. DIALOGO

Parliamo di lavoro!

CARLA: **Ciao. Come stai?**

LUIGI: **Non ci vediamo da un anno.**

CARLA: **Sì, finalmente ci incontriamo! Ma sei sempre occupato?**

LUIGI: **Sempre occupato, sempre al lavoro. Sono molto stressato.**

CARLA: **Anch'io, sai. La mia giornata comincia prestissimo. La mattina mi sveglio alle sei, mi alzo, mi lavo, mi vesto, mi siedo un attimo per prendere un caffè ed esco subito per andare al lavoro.**

LUIGI: **Ma tu almeno fai colazione.**

CARLA: **E tu no?**

LUIGI: **È proprio così . . . E in ufficio sto seduto alla scrivania tutto il giorno. Mi sento stanco. Non ho mai un minuto per divertirmi.**

CARLA: **Ma hai un bel posto!**

LUIGI: **Neanche tu puoi lamentarti!**

CARLA: **È vero, neanch'io mi posso lamentare.**

Let's talk about work!

CARLA: Hi. How are you?

LUIGI: We haven't seen each other for a year.

CARLA: Yes, we finally meet! But are you always busy?

LUIGI: Always busy, always working. I'm under a lot of stress.

CARLA: Me too, you know. My day starts very early. I wake up at six in the morning, I get up, I wash, I get dressed, I sit down for a second to have coffee, and right away I go out to go to work.

LUIGI: But at least you have breakfast.

CARLA: You don't?

LUIGI: That's the way it is . . . And in my office, I sit at my desk all day. I feel tired. I never have a moment to enjoy myself.

CARLA: But you have a good job!

LUIGI: You can't complain either!

CARLA: That's true. I can't complain either.

B. GRAMMATICA E SUOI USI

1. REFLEXIVE PRONOUNS

Reflexive pronouns "reflect" the action of the verb back to the subject. In Italian the reflexive pronouns (*pronomi riflessivi*) are:

myself	*mi*
yourself (familiar)	*ti*
himself, herself, itself, oneself, yourself (polite)	*si*
ourselves	*ci*
yourselves (familiar or polite)	*vi*
themselves, yourselves (polite)	*si*

2. REFLEXIVE VERBS

Reflexive verbs (*verbi riflessivi*) express actions performed by the subject on the subject.

Io mi lavo.
I wash myself.

A reflexive verb is conjugated like all other verbs in its group, but a reflexive pronoun precedes the verb form. The reflexive pronoun always corresponds to the subject.

118

Mi vesto.

I get dressed.

Ti alzi.

You get up.

In their infinitive form, reflexive verbs have *-si* ("oneself") attached to the regular infinitive with the final *e* dropped: *lavarè* + *si* = *lavarsi*.

	LAVARSI (-ARE) TO WASH ONESELF	METTERSI (-ERE) TO PUT ON	VESTIRSI (-IRE) TO GET DRESSED
io	mi lavo	mi metto	mi vesto
tu	ti lavi	ti metti	ti vesti
lui	si lava	si mette	si veste
lei	si lava	si mette	si veste
Lei	si lava	si mette	si veste
noi	ci laviamo	ci mettiamo	ci vestiamo
voi	vi lavate	vi mettete	vi vestite
loro	si lavano	si mettono	si vestono
Loro	si lavano	si mettono	si vestono

Some verbs are reflexive in Italian, but not in English.

Io mi sveglio alle otto.

I wake up at eight o'clock.

Noi ci alziamo presto.

We get up early.

3. RECIPROCAL VERBS

The plural reflexive pronouns (*ci, vi,* and *si*) may also be used with nonreflexive verbs to indicate a reciprocal action (the plural subjects act on each other, rather than on themselves). These verbs are thus called reciprocal verbs.

reflexive: We see ourselves in the mirror.
reciprocal: We see each other often.

Ci scriviamo ogni settimana.
    We write to each other every week.

Vi vedete spesso?
    Do you see each other often?

Loro si telefonano tutte le sere.
    They phone each other every night.

4. THE USE OF MODAL VERBS WITH REFLEXIVE VERBS

When used with a modal verb (*potere, dovere, volere*), the reflexive pronoun can either precede the verb or be attached to the infinitive as a suffix (in which case the final *-e* of the infinitive is dropped).

Io non mi posso lamentare.
    I can't complain.

Io non posso lamentarmi.
    I can't complain.

5. THE PRESENT TENSE OF *SEDERSI*

	SEDERSI	TO SIT DOWN
I sit down	*io*	*mi siedo*
you sit down (familiar)	*tu*	*ti siedi*
he sits down	*lui*	*si siede*
she sits down	*lei*	*si siede*
you sit down (polite)	*Lei*	*si siede*
we sit down	*noi*	*ci sediamo*
you sit down (familiar or polite)	*voi*	*vi sedete*
they sit down	*loro*	*si siedono*
you sit down (polite)	*Loro*	*si siedono*

Mi siedo alla scrivania.
    I sit down at my desk.

6. THE PRESENT TENSE OF *USCIRE*

	USCIRE	TO GO OUT
I go out	*io*	*esco*
you go out (familiar)	*tu*	*esci*
he goes out	*lui*	*esce*
she goes out	*lei*	*esce*
you go out (polite)	*Lei*	*esce*
we go out	*noi*	*usciamo*
you go out (familiar or polite)	*voi*	*uscite*
they go out	*loro*	*escono*
you go out (polite)	*Loro*	*escono*

Stasera esco con Maria.
Tonight I am going out with Maria.

Usciamo alle otto.
We're going out at eight o'clock.

7. VERBS ENDING IN *-CIARE* AND *-GLIARE*

In the present tense, verbs ending in *-ciare* and *-gliare* drop the final *i* from the stem of the second person singular and first person plural forms.

	COMINCIARE	TO START
I start	*io*	*comincio*
you start (familiar)	*tu*	*cominci*
he starts	*lui*	*comincia*
she starts	*lei*	*comincia*
you start (polite)	*Lei*	*comincia*
we start	*noi*	*cominciamo*
you start (familiar or polite)	*voi*	*cominciate*
they start	*loro*	*cominciano*
you start (polite)	*Loro*	*cominciano*

Tu cominci a lavorare alle otto.
> You start working at eight o'clock.

La mia giornata comincia presto.
> My day starts early.

Noi cominciamo la giornata presto.
> We start our day early.

	SVEGLIARSI	TO WAKE UP
I wake up	io	mi sveglio
you wake up (familiar)	tu	ti svegli
he wakes up	lui	si sveglia
she wakes up	lei	si sveglia
you wake up (polite)	Lei	si sveglia
we wake up	noi	ci svegliamo
you wake up (familiar or polite)	voi	vi svegliate
they wake up	loro	si svegliano
you wake up (polite)	Loro	si svegliano

Noi ci svegliamo prestissimo.
> We wake up very early.

Tu ti svegli alle sei?
> Do you wake up at six?

VOCABOLARIO

addormentarsi	to fall asleep
svegliarsi	to wake up
alzarsi	to get up
lavarsi	to get washed
vestirsi	to get dressed
mettersi	to put on (clothing)
fare colazione	to have breakfast
andare al lavoro	to go to work
essere in ufficio	to be in the office
avere un bel posto	to have a good job

non avere un minuto/ momento per . . .	not to have a moment for . . .
essere occupato	to be busy
essere stressato	to be under stress
uscire	to go out
divertirsi	to enjoy oneself
lamentarsi	to complain
sentirsi	to feel
chiamarsi	to be called (used when saying "My name is . . ." etc.)
sedersi	to sit down
cominciare	to start
È proprio così!	That's the way it is!
presto	early
prestissimo	very early
finalmente	finally
almeno	at least
neanche	not even
attimo	moment, instant

ESERCIZI

A. *Rispondere negativamente alle seguenti domande.* (Answer the following questions negatively.)

1. *La mattina ti alzi presto?*
2. *Vi svegliate presto?*
3. *Si divertono al lavoro?*
4. *Ti chiami Paolo?*
5. *Si sente bene oggi, signor Rossi?*

B. *Tradurre le seguenti frasi.*

1. We wake up at eight o'clock.
2. They never see each other.
3. Giovanni gets up early.
4. Miss, how do you feel today?
5. We wash ourselves.

C. *Completare con la forma appropriata del verbo fra parentesi.*

1. *La mattina Paolo _____ presto. (alzarsi)*
2. *La sera noi _____ sempre i denti. (lavarsi)*
3. *Come _____ Lei, signorina? (chiamarsi)*
4. *Giovanni e Roberto _____ spesso. (vedersi)*
5. *Io e Laura non _____. (salutarsi)*
6. *Noi _____ stasera. (incontrarsi)*
7. *Carlo, come _____? (sentirsi)*
8. *Io non _____ stasera. (uscire)*

NOTA CULTURALE

In general, life in Italy has a slower pace than in the United States. In fact, in Italy, life practically comes to a halt in the early afternoon. Streets are almost deserted. Stores, offices, banks, and post offices are all closed, as Italians enjoy a lengthy lunch break and rest period. Life resumes at about 5:00 P.M.

CHIAVE PER GLI ESERCIZI

A. 1. *No, non mi alzo presto.* 2. *No, non ci svegliamo presto.* 3. *No, non si divertono al lavoro.* 4. *No, non mi chiamo Paolo.* 5. *No, oggi non mi sento bene.*

B. 1. *Noi ci svegliamo alle otto.* 2. *Loro non si vedono mai.* 3. *Giovanni si alza presto.* 4. *Signorina, come si sente oggi?* 5. *Noi ci laviamo.*

C. 1. *si alza*   2. *ci laviamo*   3. *si chiama*   4. *si vedono*   5. *ci salutiamo*   6. *ci incontriamo*   7. *ti senti*   8. *esco*

LEZIONE 13

CHIEDERE E DARE INDICAZIONI. Asking for and giving directions.

A. DIALOGO

Alla Stazione Termini.

SIGNORINA VALLI: **Scusi, devo andare alla Biblioteca Nazionale. È lontana?**

VIGILE: **No, è a cinquecento metri. Può andare a piedi. È qui dietro, in Viale Castro Pretorio. Alla piazza giri a destra e poi vada sempre dritto.**

SIGNORINA VALLI: **Può dirmi anche dov'è il Museo Nazionale Romano?**

VIGILE: **Anche il museo è vicino. È a due passi. Ritorni indietro e prosegua fino a Piazza della Repubblica. È proprio lì, sulla sinistra, dietro la Basilica di Santa Maria e di fronte al Ministero del Tesoro.**

SIGNORINA VALLI: **E per Villa Borghese?**

VIGILE: **È distante circa tre chilometri.**

SIGNORINA VALLI: **Devo prendere il tram, l'autobus . . . ?**

VIGILE: **No, prenda la metropolitana a Piazza della Repubblica e scenda a Piazza di Spagna. È la seconda fermata.**

SIGNORINA VALLI: **Grazie. Lei è molto gentile.**

At the *Stazione Termini.*

MISS VALLI: Pardon me, I have to go to the National Library. Is it far?

TRAFFIC POLICEMAN: No, it's five hundred meters away. You can walk there. It's behind here, on Viale Castro Pretorio. At the piazza turn right, and then go straight.

MISS VALLI: Can you also tell me where the *Museo Nazionale Romano* is?

TRAFFIC POLICEMAN: The museum is also close by. It's very close. Go back the way you came, and then continue as far as the *Piazza della Repubblica*. It's right there, on the left, behind the *Basilica of Santa Maria* and in front of the *Ministero del Tesoro*.

MISS VALLI: And to go to the *Villa Borghese?*

TRAFFIC POLICEMAN: It's about three kilometers from here.

MISS VALLI: Do I have to take the streetcar, the bus . . . ?

TRAFFIC POLICEMAN: No, take the subway at the *Piazza della Repubblica* and get off at the *Piazza di Spagna*. It's the second stop.

MISS VALLI: Thank you. You're very kind.

B. GRAMMATICA E SUOI USI

1. THE IMPERATIVE

Just as in English, the imperative (*l'imperativo*) can express a command, an invitation, an exhortation, or a suggestion. Subject pronouns are not used. In Italian, the imperative is used in all but the first person singular. It is formed by dropping the infinitive ending, and adding the appropriate imperative ending to the root of the verb. Study the following tables.

	GIRARE	TO TURN
turn (familiar)	*tu*	*gira*
turn (polite)	*Lei*	*giri*
let's turn	*noi*	*giriamo*
turn (familiar or polite)	*voi*	*girate*
turn (polite)	*Loro*	*girino*

Gira a destra.
   Turn right. (singular, familiar)

Ritorni indietro.
   Go back the way you came. (singular, formal)

126

PRENDERE		TO TAKE
take (familiar)	tu	prendi
take (polite)	Lei	prenda
let's take	noi	prendiamo
take (familiar or polite)	voi	prendete
take (polite)	Loro	prendano

Prendete la metropolitana.
  Take the subway. (plural)

Prendiamo l'autobus.
  Let's take the bus.

PROSEGUIRE		TO CONTINUE
continue (familiar)	tu	prosegui
continue (polite)	Lei	prosegua
let's continue	noi	proseguiamo
continue (familiar or polite)	voi	proseguite
continue (polite)	Loro	proseguano

Prosegua fino alla stazione.
  Continue as far as the station. (singular, polite)

Proseguite dritto.
  Keep going straight. (plural)

FINIRE (-ISC)		TO FINISH
finish (familiar)	tu	finisci
finish (polite)	Lei	finisca
let's finish	noi	finiamo
finish (familiar or polite)	voi	finite
let's finish (polite)	Loro	finiscano

Finite i compiti.
  Finish your homework. (plural)

Finisca i compiti.
  Finish your homework. (singular, polite)

Here are a few points to help you learn the forms of the imperative.

a. The verbs in *-isc* follow the same pattern as the present indicative: add *-isc* before the endings of the *tu, Lei,* and *Loro* forms.
b: The *noi* and *voi* forms of all three conjugations are identical to their respective present indicative forms.
c. The *tu* form of verbs in *-ere* and *-ire* (including verbs in *-isc*) are identical to that of the indicative.

Finisci di mangiare.
Finish eating.

Prendi il tram.
Take the streetcar.

2. ADVERBIAL PREPOSITIONS

The following adverbs may also be used as prepositions.

accanto (a)	beside, next to
davanti (a)	in front of, before, facing
dietro	behind, after
lontano (da)	far (from)
vicino (a)	near, next to, beside, close by

Il museo è lontano.
The museum is far.

La biblioteca è vicino.
The library is close by.

Il museo è dietro la stazione.
The museum is behind the station.

Remember that *vicino* and *lontano* could also be considered adjectives, in which case they must agree with the noun to which they refer.

La biblioteca è vicina.
The library is close by.

La biblioteca è lontana.
The library is far.

3. ADVERBS OF PLACE: *QUI/QUA, LÌ/LÀ*

The adverbs of place *qui/qua* and *lì/là* mean "here" and "there," respectively.

Il museo è qui.
   The museum is here.

La biblioteca è là.
   The library is there.

4. THE PLURAL OF FOREIGN NOUNS

Foreign nouns (usually ending in a consonant) are generally masculine and do not change form in the plural.

l'autobus	*gli autobus*	*il tram*	*i tram*
il film	*i film*	*lo sport*	*gli sport*
il bar	*i bar*	*il club*	*i club*
il gas	*i gas*	*il garage*	*i garage*

5. PREPOSITIONS AND MEANS OF TRANSPORTATION

The preposition "by" in expressions like "to go by" a certain means of transportation are translated into Italian with *in*.

Noi andiamo in macchina.
   We're going by car.

Loro vanno in autobus.
   They go by bus.

Tu vai in treno.
   You go by train.

However, when the means of transportation are modified, you must use *con* plus the appropriate definite article.

Vado con il treno delle otto.
   I'm going on the eight o'clock train.

Andiamo con l'autobus numero nove.
   We're going with bus number nine.

Tu vai con la macchina di Marco.
   You're going with Mark's car.

Remember that "to go by foot, to walk (to a place)" is expressed by *andare a piedi.*

Puoi andare a piedi al museo.
   You can walk to the museum.

VOCABOLARIO

chiedere indicazioni	to ask for directions
dare indicazioni	to give directions
Può dirmi dov'è . . . ?	Can you tell me where is . . . ?
È vicino.	It's close by.
È lontano.	It's far.
È a due passi.	It's very close. (literally, "It's at two steps.")
È in via . . .	It is on . . . Street.
È distante circa un chilometro.	It's a kilometer away.
È a cento metri.	It's one hundred meters from here.
A che fermata devo scendere?	At which stop do I have to get off?
Lei è molto gentile.	You're very kind.
prendere la metropolitana	to take the subway
prendere il tram	to take the tram/streetcar
prendere l'autobus (m.)	to take the bus
andare a piedi	to walk
girare a destra/sinistra	to turn right/left
sempre dritto	straight ahead

sulla destra	on the right
sulla sinistra	on the left
proseguire	to continue
ritornare indietro	to go back (to retrace one's steps)
stazione (f.)	(train) station
museo	museum
chiesa	church
duomo	cathedral
biblioteca	library
piazza	square
pinacoteca	art gallery
palazzo	palace, building
cinema (m.)	movie theater
lì/là	there
qui/qua	here
accanto (a)	beside
davanti (a)	in front of, before
dietro	behind, after
lontano (da)	far (from)
vicino (a)	beside, near, next to, close by
vigile	traffic policeman
proprio	just, really

ESERCIZI

A. *Cambiare i seguenti comandi dalla forma familiare alla forma di cortesia.*
   (Transform the following commands from the familiar to the polite form.)

   1. *Aspetta un momento!*
   2. *Scendi alla Stazione Termini!*
   3. *Gira a destra!*
   4. *Continua dritto!*
   5. *Prendi la metropolitana.*

B. *Completare le frasi con l'imperativo del verbo fra parentesi.*

   1. *Signorina, _____ il panino! (mangiare)*
   2. *Ragazzi, _____ fino al museo! (proseguire)*

131

3. *Signor Valli, _____ italiano! (parlare)*
4. *Michele, _____ il biglietto dell'autobus! (comprare)*
5. *Signorina, _____ indietro! (ritornare)*

C. *Tradurre.*

1. Is the museum far?
2. No, it's very close.
3. You (polite, singular) can take the subway or the bus.
4. The library is behind the cathedral.
5. Get off (polite, singular) at the second stop.

NOTA CULTURALE

In Italy most of the major cities have urban bus services that usually operate with prepurchased tickets (from a machine, a tobacco store, or even a newsstand). Passengers generally board at the back of the bus and exit at the middle. Upon boarding they must stamp their tickets in a machine located at the back of the bus. These bus services are inexpensive, but the buses may become unbearably jammed during rush hours. During hot periods, particularly in the south, there are also lunchtime rush hours when people go home for siesta. Buses operated by members of *ANAC* and *SITA* travel the length of the country, and most are air-conditioned and comfortable.

You can also get around by taxi. Taxis wait at designated stands or may be requested by phone, in which case there is a small additional charge. There's usually an extra charge for service after 10:00 P.M. and on Sundays or holidays, as well as for each piece of luggage.

Rome and Milan have subway systems. Tickets should be purchased at newspaper stands or tobacco shops and must be validated by machines located at the station entrances before you board.

CHIAVE PER GLI ESERCIZI

A. 1. *Aspetti un momento!* 2. *Scenda alla Stazione Termini!* 3. *Giri a destra!* 4. *Continui dritto!* 5. *Prenda la metropolitana.*

B. 1. *mangi* 2. *proseguite* 3. *parli* 4. *compra* 5. *ritorni*

C. 1. *Il museo è lontano?* 2. *No, è molto vicino.* 3. *Può prendere la metropolitana o l'autobus.* 4. *La biblioteca è dietro il duomo.* 5. *Scenda alla seconda fermata.*

LEZIONE 14

RADIO E TELEVISIONE.   Radio and television.

A. DIALOGO

1. Alla televisione.

LUCIA: **Marco, dov'è il telecomando?**

MARCO: **È qui!**

LUCIA: **Accendi il televisore.**

MARCO: **Cosa c'è alla televisione?**

LUCIA: **Sii gentile! Accendi.**

MARCO: **C'è un programma speciale?**

LUCIA: **Metti sul Canale 5.**

MARCO: **Ecco! C'è solo della pubblicità.**

LUCIA: **Aspetta un momento. Abbi pazienza.**

MARCO: **Ma cosa c'è? La tua telenovela preferita? Stasera c'è l'ultima puntata, vero?**

LUCIA: **No. Ascolta! Non parlare!**

MARCO: **C'è forse un film? Il telegiornale? Ma cosa c'è?**

LUCIA: **Sei seccante! C'è il concerto di Pavarotti. Senti! È bravissimo.**

On television.

LUCIA: Marco, where's the remote control?

MARCO: It's here!

LUCIA: Turn on the television.

MARCO: What's on?

LUCIA: Be nice! Turn it on.

133

MARCO: Is there a special program on?

LUCIA: Put it on Channel 5.

MARCO: Here you are! It's only a commercial.

LUCIA: Wait a second. Be patient.

MARCO: But what's on? Your favorite soap opera? Tonight's the last episode, right?

LUCIA: No. Listen! Don't talk!

MARCO: Maybe there's a movie on? The news? But what's on?

LUCIA: You're a pain! Pavarotti's concert is on. Listen! He's great.

---

2. Alla radio.

CARLO: **Mentre aspetta, vuole ascoltare un po' di musica alla radio?**

SIGNORA PETRINI: **Sì, grazie. Accenda la radio. Ascoltiamo un po' di musica.**

CARLO: **Senta questa canzone. È molto bella!**

SIGNORA PETRINI: **Sì, è carina, ma abbassi il volume!**

On the radio.

CARLO: While you're waiting, would you like to listen to some music on the radio?

MRS. PETRINI: Yes, thank you. Turn on the radio. Let's listen to some music.

CARLO: Listen to this song. It's very beautiful!

MRS. PETRINI: Well, it's nice, but turn down the volume!

B. GRAMMATICA E SUOI USI

1. THE IMPERATIVE OF *AVERE* AND *ESSERE*

	AVERE	TO HAVE
have (familiar)	*tu*	*abbi*
have (polite)	*Lei*	*abbia*
let's have	*noi*	*abbiamo*
have (familiar or polite)	*voi*	*abbiate*
have (polite)	*Loro*	*abbiano*

Abbi pazienza!
   Be patient! (familiar, singular)

Abbiamo pazienza!
   Let's be patient!

	ESSERE	TO BE
be (familiar)	*tu*	*sii*
be (polite)	*Lei*	*sia*
let's be	*noi*	*siamo*
be (familiar or polite)	*voi*	*siate*
be (polite)	*Loro*	*siano*

Sii gentile!
   Be nice! (familiar, singular)

Siate buoni!
   Be good! (plural)

2. THE NEGATIVE IMPERATIVE

The negative imperative follows this scheme:

tu form: *non* plus infinitive
Lei/noi/voi/Loro forms: *non* plus imperative

Paolo, non parlare!
   Paolo, don't talk! (familiar, singular)

Signorina, non esageri!
   Miss, don't exaggerate! (polite, singular)

Non accendete il televisore!
   Don't turn on the television! (plural)

3. THE GENDER OF NOUNS: SOME EXCEPTIONS

Generally, nouns ending in -*o* are masculine, and those ending in -*a* are feminine.* However, there are exceptions. Some words are feminine, even though they end in -*o;* others are masculine, even though they end in -*a. Radio* ("radio"), for example, is feminine, while *programma* ("program") is masculine. The plural of *radio* is invariable. The plural of *programma* is *programmi.*

Accendi la radio.
   Turn on the radio. (familiar, singular)

Ho due radio.
   I have two radios. (plural)

C'è un programma speciale?
   Is there a special program on?

Ci sono dei programmi speciali?
   Are there special programs on?

* Please refer back to lesson 2 for more information on general gender rules.

4. IDIOMATIC USES OF THE PREPOSITION *A*

The expressions "on the radio" and "on television" translate into Italian as *alla radio* and *alla televisione*.

Ascoltate un po' di musica alla radio.
Listen to some music on the radio.

Cosa c'è alla televisione?
What's on television?

VOCABOLARIO

radio (f.)	radio
televisione (f.)	television
televisore (m.)	television set
stazione (f.) **radio**	radio station
stazione (f.) **televisiva**	TV station
telecomando	remote control
ascoltare la radio	to listen to the radio
guardare la televisione	to watch television
accendere il televisore	to turn on the television
accendere la radio	to turn on the radio
spegnere il televisore	to turn off the television
spegnere la radio	to turn off the radio
Cosa c'è alla radio?	What's on the radio?
Cosa c'è alla televisione?	What's on television?
C'è qualche programma speciale?	Is there a special program on?
Il mio programma preferito è . . .	My favorite program is . . .
Metti sul canale 5.	Put on channel five.
cambiare canale	to change channels
telegiornale (m.)	news
gioco a premi/a quiz	game show
film (m.)	film
commedia	comedy
telenovela/teleromanzo	soap opera

puntata	episode
spettacolo di varietà	variety show
trasmissione (f.) in diretta	live broadcast
documentario	documentary
cartoni animati (m., pl.)	cartoons
concerto	concert
pubblicità	commercial
presentatore (m.)	host
ascoltare/sentire una canzone	to listen to/to hear a song
ascoltare un po' di musica	to listen to some music
abbassare il volume	to turn down the volume
carina	nice, pretty
avere pazienza	to be patient
Sei seccante!	You're a pain!

ESERCIZI

A. *Cambiare i seguenti comandi al negativo.*

1. *Accendete la radio!*
2. *Sii gentile!*
3. *Marco, mangia!*
4. *Parlate!*
5. *Ascoltino la canzone!*

B. *Tradurre.*

1. Don't change (familiar, singular) the channel.
2. Listen (familiar, plural) to the song on the radio.
3. There are two special programs on television.
4. I have two radios.
5. Watch (polite, singular) television!

C. *Rimettere le parole in ordine.*

1. *un / ascolto / radio / io / programma / alla*
2. *spettacolo / di / televisione / c'è / alla / varietà / uno*
3. *preferito / mio / è / programma / telegiornale / il / il*
4. *pubblicità / canale / c'è / sul / nove / sempre / la*
5. *la / la / o / guardiamo / commedia / telenovela?*

NOTA CULTURALE

Much like in North America, in Italy television and radio are the most popular means of communication. Together with newspapers, cinema, and education, they have greatly contributed to the unification of the Italian language.

The Italian Broadcasting Corporation, RAI-TV (*Radiotelevisione italiana*), is run by the state and broadcasts programs on three different channels (*Raiuno, Raidue, Raitre*). In the last few years, numerous private (*Canale 5, Italia Uno, Rete 4*, etc.) and foreign (*Tele-Montecarlo, Antenne-deux, Capodistria*, etc.) television stations have begun to compete with RAI-TV.

CHIAVE PER GLI ESERCIZI

A. 1. *Non accendete la radio!* 2. *Non essere gentile!* 3. *Marco, non mangiare!* 4. *Non parlate!* 5. *Non ascoltino la canzone!*
B. 1. *Non cambiare canale.* 2. *Ascoltate la canzone alla radio.* 3. *Ci sono due programmi speciali alla televisione.* 4. *Io ho due radio.* 5. *Guardi la televisione!*
C. 1. *Io ascolto un programma alla radio.* 2. *Alla televisione c'è uno spettacolo di varietà.* 3. *Il mio programma preferito è il telegiornale.* 4. *Sul canale nove c'è sempre la pubblicità.* 5. *Guardiamo la commedia o la telenovela?*

LEZIONE 15

VIAGGIARE IN TRENO.   Traveling by train.

A. DIALOGO

Alla stazione ferroviaria.

SIGNOR BRIZI: **Quand'è il prossimo treno per Milano?**

IMPIEGATA: **Alle 22,30.**

SIGNOR BRIZI: **È in orario?**

IMPIEGATA: **No, sfortunatamente ha un ritardo di trenta minuti.**

SIGNOR BRIZI: **Recentemente il treno per Milano è sempre in ritardo. È in ritardo ogni giorno. Un biglietto di prima classe, per piacere.**

IMPIEGATA: **Solo andata?**

SIGNOR BRIZI: **No, andata e ritorno.**

IMPIEGATA: **Con cuccetta?**

SIGNOR BRIZI: **Sì, preferisco viaggiare comodamente.**

IMPIEGATA: **Va spesso a Milano?**

SIGNOR BRIZI: **Sì, ci vado regolarmente. Faccio il pendolare tra Napoli e Milano per motivi di lavoro, ma a giugno finalmente rimango fisso a Napoli. Da che binario parte il treno?**

IMPIEGATA: **Dal binario 23.**

SIGNOR BRIZI: **Questo treno ferma a Roma?**

IMPIEGATA: **Sì, ferma a Roma. Ecco a Lei il biglietto. Buon viaggio.**

SIGNOR BRIZI: **Grazie. ArrivederLa.**

At the train station.

MR. BRIZI: When is the next train for Milan?

CLERK: At 10:30 P.M.

MR. BRIZI: Is it on time?

CLERK: No, unfortunately it's thirty minutes late.

MR. BRIZI: Lately the train for Milan is always late. It's late every day. A first-class ticket, please.

CLERK: One way only?

MR. BRIZI: No, round trip.

CLERK: With couchette?

MR. BRIZI: Yes, I prefer to travel comfortably.

CLERK: Do you often go to Milan?

MR. BRIZI: Yes, I go there regularly. I commute between Naples and Milan for business. But in June I'll stay in Naples permanently. Which track is the train leaving from?

CLERK: Track 23.

MR. BRIZI: Does this train stop in Rome?

CLERK: Yes, it stops in Rome. Here's your ticket. Have a nice trip!

MR. BRIZI: Thank you. Good-bye.

B. GRAMMATICA E SUOI USI

1. PUNCTUATION MARKS

.	*punto*	:	*due punti*
,	*virgola*	!	*punto esclamativo*
;	*punto e virgola*	?	*punto interrogativo*
. . .	*puntini sospensivi*	( )	*parentesi*

2. THE ADVERB OF PLACE *CI*

We have already seen *ci* meaning "there," in the expressions *c'è, ci sono.* *Ci* is also used to replace any phrase indicating location or place. *Ci* usually precedes the verb.

Lei va spesso a Milano?
Do you often go to Milan?

Si, ci vado spesso.
Yes, I go there often.

Quando vai da Paolo?
When are you going to Paolo's?

Ci vado stasera.
I'm going (there) tonight.

3. ADVERBS ENDING IN *-MENTE*

Many adverbs end in *-mente.*

sfortunatamente	unfortunately
recentemente	recently

These adverbs are formed by adding *-mente* to the feminine singular form of the adjective.

FEMININE ADJECTIVE	ADVERB	
comoda	*comodamente*	comfortably
sfortunata	*sfortunatamente*	unfortunately
recente	*recentemente*	recently

Adjectives ending in *-le* or *-re* drop the final *e* before adding *-mente,* if the *l* or the *r* is preceded by a vowel.

finale → finalmente	final → finally
gentile → gentilmente	kind → kindly
regolare → regolarmente	regular → regularly

142

The adverbs that correspond to *buono* ("good") and *cattivo* ("bad") are *bene* and *male*.

Oggi non sto bene. Sto male.
   Today I'm not feeling well. I'm sick.

4. THE PRESENT TENSE OF *RIMANERE*

	RIMANERE	TO REMAIN, TO STAY
I remain	*io*	*rimango*
you remain (familiar)	*tu*	*rimani*
he remains	*lui*	*rimane*
she remains	*lei*	*rimane*
you remain (polite)	*Lei*	*rimane*
we remain	*noi*	*rimaniamo*
you remain (familiar or polite)	*voi*	*rimanete*
they remain	*loro*	*rimangono*
you remain (polite)	*Loro*	*rimangono*

Io rimango a Napoli.
   I'm staying in Naples.

Noi rimaniamo a casa.
   We're staying at home.

5. THE ADJECTIVE *OGNI*

The adjective *ogni* ("every") always precedes a singular noun.

Il treno è in ritardo ogni giorno.
   The train is late every day.

Io vado a Milano ogni giorno.
   I go to Milan every day.

Andiamo alla stazione ogni sabato.
   We go to the station every Saturday.

VOCABOLARIO

stazione (f.) ferroviaria	train station
biglietto di andata	one-way ticket
biglietto di andata e ritorno	round-trip ticket
biglietto di prima classe	first-class ticket
biglietto di seconda classe	second-class ticket
biglietteria	ticket booth
bigliettaio	ticket collector
Ferrovie dello Stato	Italy's state-owned railroad system
ufficio informazioni	information office
binario	train track
treno	train
scompartimento	compartment
cuccetta	couchette
vagone (m.)	railroad car
vagone letto	sleeping car
vagone ristorante	dining car
viaggiare in treno	to travel by train
fare il pendolare	to commute
Questo treno va a . . . ?	Does this train go to . . . ?
Questo treno ferma a . . . ?	Does this train stop at . . . ?
Dove devo cambiare per . . . ?	Where do I have to transfer for . . . ?
Quando è il prossimo treno per . . . ?	When is the next train for . . . ?
Da quale binario parte il treno?	Which track is the train leaving from?
A che binario arriva il treno?	Which track is the train arriving on?
A che ora arriva il treno?	At what time does the train arrive?
A che ora parte il treno?	At what time does the train leave?
È libero questo posto?	Is this seat vacant?
È occupato questo posto?	Is this seat taken?
comodamente	comfortably
recentemente	recently
regolarmente	regularly
sfortunatamente	unfortunately
gentilmente	politely, kindly
rimanere a casa	to stay at home
ogni	every

ESERCIZI

A. *Dare l'avverbio corrispondente per ognuno dei seguenti aggettivi.* (Give the corresponding adverb for each of the following adjectives.)

1. *regolare*
2. *sfortunato*
3. *recente*
4. *comodo*
5. *gentile*

B. *Tradurre.*

1. He goes to Milan regularly.
2. He goes there by train.
3. He prefers to travel comfortably.
4. He goes there every month.
5. He remains there for three days.
6. The train for Rome is late every day.

C. *Usare le seguenti parole per completare le frasi.*

classe	ritorno	treno
posto	binario	biglietto

1. *Un biglietto di andata e _____, per favore.*
2. *Da quale _____ parte il treno per Roma?*
3. *Io viaggio sempre in prima _____.*
4. *Quando arriva il _____ per Napoli?*
5. *Voglio un _____ di seconda classe.*
6. *Questo _____ è occupato?*

NOTA CULTURALE

The fastest trains on the *FS* (*Ferrovie dello Stato*), the state-owned railroad, are *Intercity* and *Rapido* trains. *Espresso* trains usually make more stops and are a little slower. *Diretto* and *Locale* are the slowest. Rail travel is very popular in Italy, particularly on weekends and during the main vacation periods.

To avoid long lines at station windows, you may buy tickets and make reservations at least a day in advance at travel agencies displaying the *FS* emblem.

Refreshments are offered on all long-distance trains with mobile carts, cafeterias, or dining cars.

Most trains have first- and second-class cars, though some top trains have only first-class, and some local trains only second-class.

CHIAVE PER GLI ESERCIZI

A. 1. *regolarmente* 2. *sfortunatamente* 3. *recentemente*
   4. *comodamente* 5. *gentilmente*
B. 1. *Lui va a Milano regolarmente.* 2. *Ci va in treno.* 3. *Preferisce viaggiare comodamente.* 4. *Ci va ogni mese.* 5. *Ci rimane tre giorni.* 6. *Il treno per Roma è in ritardo ogni giorno.*
C. 1. *ritorno* 2. *binario* 3. *classe* 4. *treno* 5. *biglietto* 6. *posto*

TERZO RIPASSO

A. *Tradurre.*

1. I would like some grilled fish.
2. Today there is no one here.
3. I don't want anything.
4. We're thirsty.
5. Please, Antonio, don't turn off the radio.
6. Do you (singular, familiar) go to Rome every day?—Yes, I go there regularly.

B. *Completare con la forma corretta dell'imperativo.*

1. *Signorina, _____ pazienza! (avere)*
2. *Marco, _____ il televisore! (accendere)*

3. *John, _____ gentile! (essere)*
4. *Carlo, non _____! (parlare)*
5. *Signorina, _____ la metropolitana a Piazza della Repubblica e _____ a Piazza di Spagna. (prendere) (scendere)*
6. *Signor Rossi, non _____! (esagerare)*
7. *Signorina, alla piazza _____ a destra e poi vada sempre dritto. (girare)*
8. *Michele, _____! (mangiare)*

C. *Fare delle frasi complete con gli elementi dati e dare la forma corretta del verbo.* (Form complete sentences using the elements provided and give the correct form of the verb.)

1. *Noi / non / bere / mai / vino*
2. *Io / Antonio / non / vedersi / da / anno*
3. *La / mattina / io / alzarsi / sei / mezzo*
4. *Il / week-end / noi / uscire / mai*
5. *Tu / oggi / cominciare / a lavorare / dieci?*
6. *Carlo / andare / ristorante / autobus*
7. *Oggi / loro / rimanere / casa*

D. *Indicare la parola che non appartiene al gruppo.* (Cross out the word that does not belong in each category.)

1. *coltello, cucchiaio, frutta*
2. *uscire, lavarsi, vestirsi*
3. *lontano, biblioteca, vicino*
4. *recentemente, gentilmente, comodo*
5. *il tram, l'autobus, lo sport*

E. *Completare con la forma corretta di "buono."*

1. *Voglio bere un _____ caffè.*
2. *Maria è una _____ amica.*
3. *John è un _____ amico.*
4. *Marco è un ragazzo _____.*
5. *Questa è una _____ macchina.*
6. *Mario e Roberto sono _____ amici.*

A. 1. *Vorrei del pesce ai ferri.* 2. *Oggi non c'è nessuno qui.* 3. *Non voglio niente/ nulla.* 4. *Noi abbiamo sete.* 5. *Per favore, Antonio, non spegnere la radio.* 6. *Vai a Roma ogni giorno?—Sì, ci vado regolarmente.*

B. 1. *abbia* 2. *accendi* 3. *sii* 4. *parlare* 5. *prenda, scenda* 6. *esageri* 7. *giri* 8. *mangia*

C. 1. *Noi non beviamo mai vino.* 2. *Io e Antonio non ci vediamo da un anno.* 3. *La mattina io mi alzo alle sei e mezzo.* 4. *Il week-end noi non usciamo mai.* 5. *Tu oggi cominci a lavorare alle dieci?* 6. *Carlo va al ristorante in autobus.* 7. *Oggi loro rimangono a casa.*

D. 1. *frutta* 2. *uscire* 3. *biblioteca* 4. *comodo* 5. *lo sport*

E. 1. *buon* 2. *buon'* 3. *buon* 4. *buono* 5. *buona* 6. *buoni*

LEZIONE 16
IN ALBERGO.   In a hotel.

A. DIALOGO

Vorrei una camera singola.

SIGNORA DONATI: **Ci sono delle camere libere?**

PORTIERE: **Sì, signora.**

SIGNORA DONATI: **Vorrei una camera singola, per due notti.**

PORTIERE: **Con bagno? Con doccia? Oppure senza bagno?**

SIGNORA DONATI: **Con bagno, per piacere. Qual'è il prezzo per una notte?**

PORTIERE: **Centomila lire.**

SIGNORA DONATI: **La prima colazione è inclusa?**

PORTIERE: **No. Vuole vedere la camera?**

SIGNORA DONATI: **Non è necessario. La prendo. Mi può svegliare alle sette?**

PORTIERE: **Senz'altro. La sveglio alle sette in punto.**

SIGNORA DONATI: **Dove posso lasciare le valigie?**

PORTIERE: **Le può lasciare qui. Il facchino le porterà in camera. Il passaporto, per piacere.**

SIGNORA DONATI: **Ecco. Dove posso parcheggiare la macchina?**

PORTIERE: **La può parcheggiare nel posteggio dietro l'albergo. Ecco a Lei le chiavi. Camera numero trentadue.**

SIGNORA DONATI: **Grazie. ArrivederLa.**

I'd like a single room.

MRS. DONATI: Are there any rooms available?

CONCIERGE: Yes, madam.

MRS. DONATI: I would like a single room for two nights.

CONCIERGE: With a bathroom? With a shower? Or without a bathroom?

MRS. DONATI: With a bathroom, please. What is the price for one night?

CONCIERGE: One hundred thousand lire.

MRS. DONATI: Is breakfast included?

CONCIERGE: No. Would you like to see the room?

MRS. DONATI: It's not necessary. I'll take it. Can you wake me up at seven?

CONCIERGE: Of course. I'll wake you up at seven sharp.

MRS. DONATI: Where can I leave my suitcases?

CONCIERGE: You can leave them here. The porter will take them to your room. Your passport, please.

MRS. DONATI: Here it is. Where can I park my car?

CONCIERGE: You can park it in the parking lot behind the hotel. Here are your keys. Room number thirty-two.

MRS. DONATI: Thank you. Good-bye.

B. GRAMMATICA E SUOI USI

1. DIRECT OBJECT PRONOUNS

Direct objects receive the action of the verb directly.

| I'll take the room. | Direct object: room |
| Leave your suitcases here. | Direct object: suitcases |

Direct object pronouns (*pronomi oggetto diretto*) replace direct object nouns or noun phrases.

Parli italiano?
Do you speak Italian?

Sì, lo parlo.
> Yes, I speak it.

In the first sentence, *italiano* is the direct object; in the second sentence *lo* is the direct object pronoun.

The direct object pronouns are:

me	*mi*
you (familiar)	*ti*
him, it (m.)	*lo*
her, it (f.)	*la*
you (polite)	*La*
us	*ci*
you (familiar or polite)	*vi*
them (m.)	*li*
them (f.)	*le*
you (polite m.)	*Li*
you (polite f.)	*Le*

The pronouns *lo* and *la* drop the final vowel before a verb that starts with a vowel sound.

Lo amo = L'amo.
> I love him.

La amo = L'amo.
> I love her.

Direct object pronouns precede the verb.

La (= la camera) prendo.
> I'll take it.

Le (= le valigie) può lasciare qui.
> You can leave them here.

In negations *non* comes before the object pronoun.

Non la (= la camera) prendo.
> I will not take it.

Non le (= le valigie) può lasciare qui.
You can't leave them here.

The direct object pronoun that corresponds to the subject pronoun *Lei* (polite) is *La* (also usually capitalized). *La,* just like *Lei,* is used to address either a man or a woman.

Signor Rossi, La sveglio alle sette in punto.
Mr. Rossi, I'll wake you up at seven sharp.

Signorina, La sveglio alle sette in punto.
Miss, I'll wake you up at seven sharp.

2. THE POSITION OF DIRECT OBJECT PRONOUNS WITH MODAL VERBS

With the modal auxiliaries (*dovere, potere, volere*), the direct object pronoun either precedes the verb or is attached to the end of the infinitive (in which case the final *-e* of the infinitive is dropped).

Vuole vedere la camera?
Do you want to see the room?

Sì, la voglio vedere.
Yes, I want to see it.

Sì, voglio vederla.
Yes, I want to see it.

3. THE PLURAL OF NOUNS AND ADJECTIVES ENDING IN -CIA, -GIA

Nouns and adjectives ending in *-cia/-gia* form the plural in *-ce/-ge,* if the *i* in *-cia/-gia* is not stressed.

la pioggia, le piogge	rain, rains
la doccia, le docce	shower, showers

If the *i* in *-cia/-gia* is stressed, the plural will end in *-cie/gie*.

la farmacia, le farmacie	pharmacy, pharmacies
la bugia, le bugie	lie, lies

4. OMISSION OF THE POSSESSIVE ADJECTIVE

Contrary to English, in Italian it is not necessary to use the possessive adjective if the possessor is obvious.

Dove posso lasciare le valigie?
Where can I leave my suitcases?

Dove posso parcheggiare la macchina?
Where can I park my car?

VOCABOLARIO

albergo	hotel
pensione (f.)	pensione
hotel (m.)	hotel
hotel di prima categoria	first-class hotel
albergo di seconda classe	second-class hotel
hotel a due stelle	two-star hotel
albergo a tre stelle	three-star hotel
portiere (m.)	concierge
Vorrei una camera.	I would like a room.
Desidero una camera per una notte.	I would like a room for one night.
Desidero una camera per due notti.	I would like a room for two nights.
prenotare una camera	to reserve a room
Ho la prenotazione.	I have a reservation.
camera singola	single room
camera doppia/matrimoniale	double room
camera con bagno	room with a bathroom
camera senza bagno	room without a bathroom
camera con doccia	room with a shower

Qual è il prezzo per una notte?	What's the price for one night?
La camera ha il telefono?	Does the room have a telephone?
La camera ha il televisore?	Does the room have a television set?
La prima colazione è inclusa?	Is breakfast included?
Dove posso lasciare la macchina?	Where can I leave my (the) car?
C'è un garage?	Is there a garage?
C'è un parcheggio custodito?	Is there a supervised parking lot?
Può far portare su i bagagli?	Can you have my luggage brought up?
Può far portare giù i bagagli?	Can you have my luggage brought down?
chiavi (f., pl.) della camera	room keys
Mi chiami alle sette, per favore.	Please, call me at seven.
Mi svegli alle sette, per favore.	Please wake me up at seven.
Per favore, mi prepari il conto.	Please prepare my bill.
soltanto	only
oppure	or
senza	without
prendere	to take
è necessario	it is necessary
senz'altro	certainly

ESERCIZI

A. *Sostituire l'oggetto diretto con un pronome.* (Replace the direct object with a direct object pronoun.)

ESEMPIO: Lascio le valigie in camera?
Le lascio in camera?

1. *Vuole il passaporto?*
2. *Porto le valigie in camera?*
3. *Parcheggio la macchina nel garage?*
4. *Do le chiavi all'impiegato?*
5. *Il facchino porta i bagagli in macchina?*

B. *Rispondere affermativamente, usando un pronome oggetto diretto. Mettere il pronome PRIMA del verbo.* (Answer affirmatively using a direct object pronoun. Place the pronoun BEFORE the verb.)

1. *Possono parcheggiare la macchina nel garage?*
2. *Signore, vuole vedere la stanza?*
3. *Possiamo portare le valigie in camera?*
4. *Dobbiamo dare le chiavi all'impiegato?*
5. *Devono dare il passaporto all'impiegato?*

C. *Rispondere affermativamente alle domande dell' esercizio B, usando un pronome oggetto diretto. Mettere il pronome DOPO il verbo.* (Answer the questions from excercise B affirmatively using a direct object pronoun. Place the pronoun AFTER the verb.)

D. *Tradurre. Fare attenzione ai possessivi.* (Translate. Pay attention to the possessives.)

1. I'm taking my suitcases to my room.
2. Here are your keys.
3. Where can I park my car?
4. Your passport, please.
5. Where can I leave my suitcases?

NOTA CULTURALE

Italy offers a good choice of accommodations. Throughout the country, you'll find everything: deluxe five-star hotels, charming country inns, villas for rent, campgrounds, hostels, well-equipped vacation villages in remote areas, etc.

Major cities have hotel reservation service booths in train stations or airports. CIGA, Jolly, Space, Atahotels, and Italhotels are among the hotel chains or groups operating in Italy.

Camping is becoming a popular choice for vacationers who take to the hills and lakes, where there are many campgrounds and bungalows.

There are more than 150 youth hostels in Italy, some in such beautiful settings as the fourteenth-century *Castello di Rocca degli Alberi* at Montagnana, near Padua; the *Castello di Murat,* at Pizzo, in Calabria; and the *Castello di Scilla,* near the Straits of Messina.

A. 1. *Lo vuole?* 2. *Le porto in camera?* 3. *La parcheggio nel garage?* 4. *Le do all'impiegato?* 5. *Il facchino li porta in macchina?*

B. 1. *Sì, la possono parcheggiare nel garage.* 2. *Sì, la voglio vedere.* 3. *Sì, le potete/possiamo portare in camera.* 4. *Sì, le dovete/dobbiamo dare all'impiegato.* 5. *Sì, lo devono dare all'impiegato.*

C. 1. *Sì, possono parcheggiarla nel garage.* 2. *Sì, voglio vederla.* 3. *Sì, potete/ possiamo portarle in camera.* 4. *Sì, dovete/dobbiamo darle all'impiegato.* 5. *Sì, devono darlo all'impiegato.*

D. 1. *Porto le valigie in camera.* 2. *Ecco le chiavi.* 3. *Dove posso parcheggiare la macchina?* 4. *Il passaporto, per favore.* 5. *Dove posso lasciare le valigie?*

LEZIONE 17

L'AGENZIA DI VIAGGI.   The travel agency.

A. DIALOGO

Un giro organizzato.

SIGNOR CARLI: **Ci sono giri organizzati dell'Italia meridionale?**

AGENTE DI VIAGGI: **Sì. Ma Lei non ha già viaggiato con noi l'anno scorso?**

SIGNOR CARLI: **Sì. Sono andato in America con mia sorella e due sue amiche.**

AGENTE DI VIAGGI: **Quali città ha visitato?**

SIGNOR CARLI: **Siamo andati a New York, Boston, Chicago, Toronto e Montreal.**

AGENTE DI VIAGGI: **Un bel giro!**

SIGNOR CARLI: **Lì ho conosciuto due ragazze americane molto simpatiche. Ho avuto occasione di parlare un po' d'inglese. Ho passato una vacanza favolosa! E quest'anno vorrei fare un giro del mio paese con due miei amici. Non siamo mai stati a sud di Roma.**

AGENTE DI VIAGGI: **Bene . . . Abbiamo prezzi da sogno: alberghi di prima categoria, guide preparate . . . Il giro parte da Roma e va a Napoli, in Calabria e in Sicilia.**

An organized tour.

MR. CARLI: Are there organized tours of southern Italy?

TRAVEL AGENT: Yes. But didn't you already travel with us last year?

MR. CARLI: Yes. I went to America with my sister and two of her friends.

TRAVEL AGENT: Which cities did you visit?

MR. CARLI: We went to New York, Boston, Chicago, Toronto, and Montreal.

TRAVEL AGENT: A nice tour!

MR. CARLI: There I met two very nice American girls. I had the opportunity to speak a bit of English. I had a fabulous vacation! And this year I would like to tour my country with two of my friends. We've never been south of Rome.

TRAVEL AGENT: Well . . . We have fabulous prices: first-class hotels, well-prepared guides . . . The tour starts in Rome and goes to Naples, Calabria, and Sicily.

B. GRAMMATICA E SUOI USI

1. REGULAR PAST PARTICIPLES

In Italian the past participle of regular verbs is formed by adding the appropriate ending to the root of the verb. Remember that the root of the verb is the infinitive minus *-are/-ere/-ire*.

	INFINITIVE	ENDING	PAST PARTICIPLE
First Conjugation	*parlare*	*-ato*	*parl-ato*
Second Conjugation	*vedere*	*-uto*	*ved-uto*
Third Conjugation	*capire*	*-ito*	*cap-ito*

As in English, in Italian the past participle can be used as an adjective; it then agrees in gender and number with the noun it modifies.

un giro organizzato
   an organized tour

2. THE PRESENT PERFECT

The *passato prossimo* is used to indicate a completed past action and corresponds to the English present perfect tense. It is formed with the present tense of *avere* or *essere* and the past participle of the verb.

Io sono andato in Italia.
   I went to Italy.

158

Io ho visitato Roma.
  I visited Rome.

There are three possible English translations of the Italian *passato prossimo*.

Io ho visitato Roma.	I have visited Rome. I visited Rome. I did visit Rome.

In negative sentences, *non* is placed before the auxiliary or helping verb, *essere* or *avere*.

Io non sono andato a Roma.
  I didn't go to Rome.

Tu non hai visitato gli Stati Uniti.
  You didn't visit the United States.

Verbs that take a direct object (referred to as transitive verbs) are generally conjugated with *avere*.

	PARLARE	TO SPEAK
I spoke	*io*	*ho parlato*
you spoke (familiar)	*tu*	*hai parlato*
he spoke	*lui*	*ha parlato*
she spoke	*lei*	*ha parlato*
you spoke (polite)	*Lei*	*ha parlato*
we spoke	*noi*	*abbiamo parlato*
you spoke (familiar or polite)	*voi*	*avete parlato*
they spoke	*loro*	*hanno parlato*
you spoke (polite)	*Loro*	*hanno parlato*

In Italia ho comprato molti regali.
  In Italy I bought a lot of gifts.

Abbiamo conosciuto due ragazze.
  We met two girls.

You should already know the meaning of these common verbs that, like *parlare,* are conjugated with *avere.*

amare	to love	*aspettare*	to wait for
avere	to have	*capire*	to understand
cominciare	to start	*comprare*	to buy
dare	to give	*finire*	to finish
vedere	to see	*visitare*	to visit
fare	to do	*bere*	to drink

Verbs that do not take a direct object (intransitive verbs) are generally conjugated with *essere,* and their participle must always agree in gender and number with the subject. These are generally verbs of movement.

	ANDARE	TO GO
I went	*io*	*sono andato/a*
you went (familiar)	*tu*	*sei andato/a*
he went	*lui*	*è andato*
she went	*lei*	*è andata*
you went (polite)	*Lei*	*è andato/a*
we went	*noi*	*siamo andati/e*
you went (familiar or polite)	*voi*	*siete andati/e*
they went	*loro*	*sono andati/e*
you went (polite)	*Loro*	*sono andati/e*

Mario è andato in Italia.
  Mario went to Italy.

Maria è andata in Italia.
  Maria went to Italy.

Mario e Ivo sono andati in Italia.
  Mario and Ivo went to Italy.

Maria e Lisa sono andate in Italia.
  Maria and Lisa went to Italy.

When the subject is a mixed group of masculine and feminine nouns, the past participle takes the masculine plural ending *i*.

Maria e Mario sono andati in Italia.
Maria and Mario went to Italy.

Here are some very common verbs that, like *andare,* are conjugated with *essere.*

arrivare	to arrive	*partire*	to leave
ritornare	to return	*stare*	to stay, to be
uscire	to go out	*venire*	to come

3. THE PRESENT PERFECT OF *AVERE* AND *ESSERE*

	AVERE	TO HAVE
I had	*io*	*ho avuto*
you had (familiar)	*tu*	*hai avuto*
he had	*lui*	*ha avuto*
she had	*lei*	*ha avuto*
you had (polite)	*Lei*	*ha avuto*
we had	*noi*	*abbiamo avuto*
you had (familiar or polite)	*voi*	*avete avuto*
they had	*loro*	*hanno avuto*
you had (polite)	*Loro*	*hanno avuto*

Non abbiamo avuto tempo.
We didn't have time.

Ho avuto occasione di parlare inglese.
I had the opportunity to speak English.

Non ha mai avuto mal di stomaco.
He never had a stomachache.

161

	ESSERE	TO BE
I was	io	sono stato/a
you were (familiar)	tu	sei stato/a
he was	lui	è stato
she was	lei	è stata
you were (polite)	Lei	è stato/a
we were	noi	siamo stati/e
you were (familiar or polite)	voi	siete stati/e
they were	loro	sono stati/e
you were (polite)	Loro	sono stati/e

Siamo stati a Roma.
  We were in Rome.

L'anno scorso, Giovanni è stato molto malato.
  Last year, Giovanni was very sick.

4. THE PLURAL OF NOUNS AND ADJECTIVES ENDING IN -CA/-GA AND -CO/-GO

Nouns and adjectives ending in *-ca* or *-ga* in the singular form, end in *-che* or *-ghe* in the plural form.

amica	*amiche*	friend, friends
simpatica	*simpatiche*	nice
lunga	*lunghe*	long

Nouns and adjectives ending in *-co* or *-go* in the singular, end in *-chi* or *-ghi* in the plural, if the accent falls on the next to last syllable.

lungo	*lunghi*	long
ricco	*ricchi*	rich
albergo	*alberghi*	hotel, hotels
bianco	*bianchi*	white

Exception:

amico	*amici*	friend, friends

162

If, however, the accent falls on the second to last syllable, the plural ends in -*ci* or -*gi*.

meccanico	*meccanici*	mechanic, mechanics
simpatico	*simpatici*	nice
teologo	*teologi*	theologian, theologians
psicologo	*psicologi*	psychologist, psychologists

VOCABOLARIO

agenzia di viaggi	travel agency
agente (m./f.) **di viaggi**	travel agent
operatore (m.) **turistico**	tour operator
viaggiare	to travel
viaggio d'affari	business trip
luna di miele	honeymoon
fare una crociera	to go on a cruise
visitare un paese	to visit a country
visitare una città	to visit a city
giro organizzato	organized tour
fare un giro	to take a tour
Il giro parte da . . .	The tour leaves from . . .
passare una vacanza favolosa	to spend a fabulous vacation
un viaggio lungo	a long trip
Ci sono dei giri organizzati per . . . ?	Are there any organized tours for . . . ?
L'hotel è incluso?	Is the hotel included?
I pasti sono inclusi?	Are meals included?
L'autobus ha l'aria condizionata?	Does the bus have air conditioning?
La guida è molto preparata.	The guide is well-prepared.
Abbiamo prezzi da sogno.	We have fabulous prices.
Quant'è la tariffa?	How much is the fare?
tariffa ridotta	reduced fare
pagare metà prezzo	to pay half price
Vorrei partire di mattina.	I would like to leave in the morning.
Vorrei partire di pomeriggio.	I'd like to leave in the afternoon.

Vorrei partire di sera.	I'd like to leave in the evening.
Vorrei fare la prenotazione.	I would like to make a reservation.
prenotare	to book/reserve
itinerario	itinerary
destinazione (f.)	destination
escursione (f.)	excursion
l'anno scorso	last year
avere occasione di . . .	to have the opportunity to . . .
Italia meridionale	Southern Italy
sud	south
amico	friend
ragazza	girl
simpatico	nice, likeable, pleasant

ESERCIZI

A. *Cambiare le seguenti frasi al passato prossimo.*

1. *Anna va in Italia con sua sorella.*
2. *Roberto e Paolo vanno a New York.*
3. *Io parlo con Luisa.*
4. *Voi passate le vacanze a Firenze.*
5. *A che ora parte il giro organizzato?*
6. *Io sono a Roma.*
7. *Visitiamo delle città italiane.*

B. *Completare le frasi con il passato prossimo del verbo fra parentesi.*

1. *L'anno scorso noi _____ in America. (andare)*
2. *In Italia io _____ due ragazze molto simpatiche. (incontrare)*
3. *In Italia John _____ occasione di parlare un po' d'italiano. (avere)*
4. *L'anno scorso noi _____ una vacanza favolosa. (passare)*
5. *I signori Jones non _____ mai _____ a sud di Roma. (essere)*

C. *Cambiare al plurale.*

1. *amico simpatico*
2. *giacca lunga*

3. *ragazza simpatica*
4. *nonno ricco*
5. *gonna bianca*

NOTA CULTURALE

Although today's Southern Italy is quite modernized and as avid about progress and industrial development as any other part of the western world, it remains less industrialized than its richer and more contemporary Northern counterpart. Southern Italy, however, boasts natural and artistic beauties that are second to none.

Campania is the region of Naples, Mt. Vesuvius, Capri, Ischia, Amalfi, Sorrento, Pompei, and Paestum—places which have become familiar to people of all nationalities and have inspired filmmakers from all over the world, in particular, filmmakers from Hollywood.

In pre-Roman times, modern Apulia, Basilicata, and Calabria comprised one of the most opulent Greek colonies. The Greeks had a Latin name for it: Magna Graecia. Although these regions are less popular with tourists than other areas of Italy, they, nevertheless, offer visitors many rewards. The sandy beaches of Calabria's Tyrrhenian coast and the rocky promontories of the Ionic coast have become Italy's newest playgrounds.

Just off the toe of the Italian boot lies Sicily, home to Palermo, Taormina, Siracusa, and the Valley of Temples. This largest of the Mediterranean islands is known for its perfect climate, the mountain-to-sea beauty of its landscape, and for its ancient Greek temples and theaters that make the monuments of Rome seem almost new.

CHIAVE PER GLI ESERCIZI

A. 1. *Anna è andata in Italia con sua sorella.* 2. *Roberto e Paolo sono andati a New York.* 3. *Io ho parlato con Luisa.* 4. *Voi avete passato le vacanze a Firenze.* 5. *A che ora è partito il giro organizzato?* 6. *Io sono stato/a a Roma.* 7. *Abbiamo visitato delle città italiane.*
B. 1. *siamo andati/e* 2. *ho incontrato* 3. *ha avuto* 4. *abbiamo passato* 5. *sono . . . stati*
C. 1. *amici simpatici* 2. *giacche lunghe* 3. *ragazze simpatiche* 4. *nonni ricchi* 5. *gonne bianche*

LEZIONE 18

IL LAVORO. Employment.

A. DIALOGO

Un colloquio di lavoro.

DOTT. JONES: **Sono nato a New York e mi sono laureato in economia e commercio alla New York University.**

INTERVISTATRICE: **Dove ha lavorato, dottore?**

DOTT. JONES: **A Londra, Madrid, Parigi, sempre nell'industria turistica. Ho sempre voluto lavorare nel settore privato e sempre nel settore dirigenziale.**

INTERVISTATRICE: **Ha viaggiato molto!**

DOTT. JONES: **Sì, possiamo dire che ho fatto il giro del mondo. Ho visto tante città. Ho anche scritto un libro sulle mie esperienze di viaggio.**

INTERVISTATRICE: **Come mai ha deciso di fare domanda?**

DOTT. JONES: **Mi sono innamorato dell'Italia. Vorrei vivere qui. Nell'avviso economico ho letto che cercate qualcuno con capacità manageriali.**

INTERVISTATRICE: **Sì, infatti. E offriamo possibilità di fare carriera, uno stipendio fisso, un orario lavorativo regolare e un mese di ferie all'anno.**

A job interview.

DR. JONES: I was born in New York, and I received my degree in economics and business from New York University.

INTERVIEWER: Where have you worked, Doctor?

DR. JONES: In London, Madrid, Paris, always in tourism. I always wanted to work in the private sector in a managerial position.

INTERVIEWER: You've traveled a lot!

DR. JONES: Yes, you could say that I've traveled around the world. I visited so many cities. I've also written a book about my traveling experiences.

INTERVIEWER: Why did you decide to apply for the job?

DR. JONES: I fell in love with Italy. I'd like to live here. In the ad I read that you're looking for someone with managerial abilities.

INTERVIEWER: Yes, of course. And we offer the opportunity for a successful career, a steady income, regular working hours, and a month of vacation every year.

B. GRAMMATICA E SUOI USI

1. IRREGULAR PAST PARTICIPLES

Some verbs have irregular past participles. The following are some of the most common.

	INFINITIVE	PAST PARTICIPLE
to be	*essere*	*stato*
to drink	*bere*	*bevuto*
to know	*conoscere*	*conosciuto*
to read	*leggere*	*letto*
to do, to make	*fare*	*fatto*
to say	*dire*	*detto*
to put	*mettere*	*messo*
to write	*scrivere*	*scritto*
to see	*vedere*	*visto/veduto*
to come	*venire*	*venuto*
to take	*prendere*	*preso*
to close	*chiudere*	*chiuso*
to open	*aprire*	*aperto*
to be born	*nascere*	*nato*
to die	*morire*	*morto*

Other than *essere, nascere, morire,* and *venire,* all of the above verbs are conjugated with *avere.*

2. THE PRESENT PERFECT OF REFLEXIVE VERBS

Reflexive verbs always take *essere* as their auxiliary verb in the present perfect and in all compound tenses. The past participle of the main verb must agree in gender and number with the subject.

	LAVARSI	TO WASH ONESELF
I washed myself	*io*	*mi sono lavato/a*
you washed yourself (familiar)	*tu*	*ti sei lavato/a*
he washed himself	*lui*	*si è lavato*
she washed herself	*lei*	*si è lavata*
you washed yourself (polite)	*Lei*	*si è lavato/a*
we washed ourselves	*noi*	*ci siamo lavati/e*
you washed yourselves (familiar or polite)	*voi*	*vi siete lavati/e*
they washed themselves	*loro*	*si sono lavati/e*
you washed yourselves (polite)	*Loro*	*si sono lavati/e*

Marco si è lavato.
Marco washed himself.

Anna si è lavata.
Anna washed herself.

As you can see, the only difference in conjugation between reflexive verbs and all the other verbs conjugated with *essere* is that the reflexive verbs are preceded by the reflexive pronouns. This is true for all compound tenses.

3. THE PRESENT PERFECT OF MODAL VERBS

When *dovere, potere,* and *volere* are in the present perfect and are accompanied by an infinitive, the infinitive determines which auxiliary verb should be used. Compare:

Io ho voluto visitare l'Italia.
I wanted to visit Italy.

Io sono voluto andare in Italia.
I wanted to go to Italy.

In the former example we use *ho voluto* because we say *Io ho visitato l'Italia.* In the latter example we use *sono voluto* because we say *Io sono andato in Italia.* Remember that when the auxiliary verb is *essere,* the past participle must agree with the subject in gender and number.

Le signore sono volute andare in Italia.
   The ladies wanted to go to Italy.

In current spoken Italian, however, the auxiliary *avere* may be used in all cases.

Io ho voluto andare in Italia.
   I wanted to go to Italy.

4. THE PLURAL OF NOUNS WITH AN ACCENTED FINAL VOWEL

Singular nouns with a written accent on the last vowel do not change form in the plural.

possibility	*la possibilità*	*le possibilità*	possibilities
capacity	*la capacità*	*le capacità*	capacities
city	*la città*	*le città*	cities
coffee	*il caffè*	*i caffè*	coffees
tea	*il tè*	*i tè*	teas

Ho visto tante città.
   I saw so many cities.

Cercate qualcuno con capacità manageriali?
   Are you looking for someone with managerial abilities?

Offriamo possibilità di fare carriera.
   We offer the chance for a successful career.

5. ABBREVIATIONS OF TITLES

The following abbreviations are used when writing titles.

TITLE	ABBREVIATION	TRANSLATION
signore	*sig.*	Mr.
signora	*sig.a*	Mrs.

TITLE	ABBREVIATION	TRANSLATION
signorina	*sig.na*	Miss
professore	*prof.*	Prof. (m.)
professoressa	*prof.essa*	Prof. (f.)
dottore	*dott.*	Dr. (m.)
dottoressa	*dott.essa*	Dr. (f.)
ingegnere	*ing.*	engineer
avvocato	*avv.*	lawyer

Signore, professore, dottore, and *ingegnere* drop the final *e* if followed by a last name.

il signor Carli
  Mr. Carli

dottor Jones
  Dr. Jones

VOCABOLARIO

lavoro	work, employment, job
colloquio	interview
ditta	company
lavorare nel settore privato	to work in the private sector
lavorare nel settore dirigenziale	to work in the managerial sector
lavorare in fabbrica	to work in a factory
lavorare in ufficio	to work in an office
lavorare in proprio	to have one's own business
fare domanda per lavoro	to apply for a job
essere al lavoro	to be at work
paga	pay
stipendio fisso	steady income
orario lavorativo regolare	regular working hours
vacanze (f., pl.)	vacation
ferie (f., pl.)	vacation

prendere le ferie	to take vacation
cercare qualcuno con capacità manageriali	to look for someone with managerial abilities
fare carriera	to have a successful career
avere/ottenere una promozione	to get a promotion
assumere	to hire
licenziare	to fire
cercare lavoro	to look for a job
trovare lavoro	to find a job
essere disoccupato	to be unemployed
avere esperienza	to have experience
laurearsi in economia e commercio	to get a degree in economics and business
avviso economico	newspaper ad
posto (di lavoro)	position, job
avere un bel lavoro/posto	to have a good job
fare il giro del mondo	to travel around the world
scrivere un libro su . . .	to write a book on . . .
decidere (pp. *deciso*)	to decide
nascere (pp. *nato*)	to be born
morire (pp. *morto*)	to die

ESERCIZI

A. *Cambiare le frasi al passato prossimo.*

1. *Anna legge un avviso economico.*
2. *Noi lavoriamo a New York.*
3. *Noi facciamo il giro del mondo.*
4. *Tu scrivi un libro.*
5. *Lui si laurea in economia e commercio.*

B. *Scrivere la forma corretta del verbo nello schema.* (Write the correct form of the verb in the table below.)

	PRESENTE	PASSATO
ESEMPIO:	io parlo	io ho parlato
1.	io rispondo	
2.		noi abbiamo finito
3.	voi prendete	
4.		lei si è lavata
5.	loro dicono	

C. *Tradurre.*

1. Yesterday we got up at 7:30.
2. John wrote a book.
3. I was born in September.
4. I have seen many cities.
5. Dr. Jones had to go to Italy.

NOTA CULTURALE

Italy today is not just the classic land of history, beauty, and art. With its industrial centers of Milan, Genoa, and Turin, Italy is one of the most industrialized countries in the world. Today in Washington, D.C., subway passengers ride in subway cars made in Italy. Italian fashion designers such as Giorgio Armani, Nino Cerruti, Versace, Ferragamo, Valentino, and others have become forerunners in the fashion world. Fiat is one of the major automobile companies in Europe. Olivetti has become one of the world leaders in sales of office machines and data-processing equipment. And, of course, Italian wines are world famous.

CHIAVE PER GLI ESERCIZI

A. 1. *Anna ha letto un avviso economico.* 2. *Noi abbiamo lavorato a New York.* 3. *Noi abbiamo fatto il giro del mondo.* 4. *Tu hai scritto un libro.* 5. *Lui si è laureato in economia e commercio.*

B. 1. *io ho risposto*   2. *noi finiamo*   3. *voi avete preso*   4. *lei si lava*   5. *loro hanno detto*

C. 1. *Ieri ci siamo alzati/e alle 7,30.* 2. *John ha scritto un libro.* 3. *Io sono nato/a a settembre.* 4. *Io ho visto molte città.* 5. *Il dottor Jones è/ha dovuto andare in Italia.*

LEZIONE 19

GLI SPORT. Sports.

A. DIALOGO

Il calcio o il pugilato?

ANNA: **Mi dai il telecomando, per favore? C'è la partita di calcio. Gioca la mia squadra preferita.**

MARCO: **Chi ti ha detto che oggi c'è la partita?**

ANNA: **Mi ha telefonato Claudio. Gli ho parlato proprio un minuto fa.**

MARCO: **Ma io voglio vedere l'incontro di pugilato.**

ANNA: **Ma quante volte ti devo dire che il pugilato non mi piace. È uno sport troppo violento e gli sport violenti non mi piacciono!**

MARCO: **Se il pugilato non ti interessa, cosa dobbiamo guardare allora? La partita di calcio? Mi dispiace, il calcio non mi piace affatto!**

ANNA: **Va bene! Se non ti piace guardare la partita di calcio, guardiamo l'incontro di pugilato. Ma la prossima volta guardiamo quello che voglio io! Okay?!**

Soccer or boxing?

ANNA: Can you give me the remote control, please? There's a soccer game on. My favorite team is playing.

MARCO: Who told you that there's a game on today?

ANNA: Claudio phoned me. I just talked to him a minute ago.

MARCO: But I want to see the boxing match.

ANNA: But how many times do I have to tell you that I don't like boxing. It's too violent a sport, and I don't like violent sports!

MARCO: Since you don't like boxing, what should we watch then? The soccer game? I'm sorry, I don't like soccer at all!

ANNA: Okay! Since you don't want to watch the soccer game, let's watch the boxing match. But next time we'll watch what I want! Okay?!

B. GRAMMATICA E SUOI USI

1. INDIRECT OBJECT PRONOUNS

The object of a verb can be either direct or indirect.

direct:	I'm writing a letter.
indirect:	I'm writing to Marco.

The indirect object expresses to whom or for whom an action is being performed. A verb can have both a direct and an indirect object.

I'm writing a letter to Marco.
She is buying a gift for her father.

In English an indirect object is often introduced by the preposition "to" or "for." In Italian, it is usually introduced by the preposition *a*.

Scrivo a Marco.
I'm writing to Marco.

Parliamo a Marco.
We're talking to Marco.

Indirect object pronouns (*pronomi oggetto indiretto*) replace indirect objects and the preposition *(a)* that introduces them.

Scrivi a Marco?
Are you writing to Marco?

Sì, gli scrivo.
Yes, I'm writing to him.

Italian has the following indirect object pronouns:

to me	*mi*
to you (familiar)	*ti*
to him, to it (m.)	*gli*
to her, to it (f.)	*le*
to you (polite)	*Le*
to us	*ci*
to you (familiar or polite)	*vi*
to them	*loro (gli)*
to you (polite)	*Loro (gli)*

Note that, except in the third person singular and plural, indirect object pronouns have the same form as direct object pronouns.

Except for *loro* and *Loro,* indirect object pronouns generally precede the verb.

Parli a Monica?
Are you talking to Monica?

Sì, le parlo.
Yes, I'm talking to her.

In negative sentences they follow *non.*

Non vi telefono.
I'm not phoning you.

In colloquial Italian, *loro* and *Loro* are replaced by *gli,* which precedes the verb.

Gli scrivo oggi. / Scrivo loro oggi.
I'm writing to them today.

Gli scrivo oggi. / Scrivo Loro oggi.
I'm writing to you (polite) today.

With the modal auxiliaries, indirect object pronouns may either precede the verb or be attached to the infinitive as suffixes (in which case the final *-e* of the infinitive is dropped).

Le devo parlare.
I have to talk to her.

Devo parlarle.
I have to talk to her.

Verbs that commonly take an indirect object include *parlare* ("to speak"), *telefonare* ("to phone"), *dare* ("to give"), *scrivere* ("to write"), *dire* ("to say"), *rispondere* ("to answer"), etc.

Note that in Italian *telefonare* takes an indirect object, whereas the English verb "to telephone" takes a direct object. In this respect, Italian verbs and their English counterparts may or may not differ.

Remember, too, that certain verbs can take both a direct and an indirect object (e.g., *dare*, *scrivere*).

Io scrivo una lettera.
I'm writing a letter.

Io scrivo a Paola.
I'm writing to Paola.

Io scrivo una lettera a Paola.
I'm writing a letter to Paola.

2. THE PRESENT TENSE OF *PIACERE*

In Italian the verb *piacere* ("to like") always takes an indirect object pronoun. Its construction is quite different from the corresponding English verb "to like." To illustrate this difference, it may be useful to translate *piacere* as "to be pleasing (to someone)."

SUBJECT	VERB	OBJECT
Mark	likes	soccer.
Il calcio	*piace*	*a Marco.*
Soccer	is pleasing	to Marco.

SUBJECT	VERB	OBJECT
Mark	likes	Simona and Monica.
Simona e Monica	*piacciono*	*a Marco.*
Simona and Monica	are pleasing	to Marco.

177

In English, people like things or persons. In Italian, things or persons are pleasing to people.

Although *piacere* can be conjugated in all persons, just like any other verb, it is mostly used in the third person singular and plural forms, *piace* and *piacciono*.

I like	*mi piace/piacciono*
you like (familiar)	*ti piace/piacciono*
he likes	*gli piace/piacciono*
she likes	*le piace/piacciono*
you like (polite)	*Le piace/piacciono*
we like	*ci piace/piacciono*
you like (familiar or polite)	*vi piace/piacciono*
they like	*a loro (gli) piace/piacciono*
you like (polite)	*a Loro (gli) piace/piacciono*

If the thing or person liked is in the singular, use *piace;* if it is in the plural, use *piacciono.*

Mi piace il calcio.
I like soccer.

Ti piacciono questi sport?
Do you like these sports?

When the verb *piacere* is followed by an infinitive, use the singular form *piace*.

Ti piace guardare la partita?
Do you like watching the game?

Mi piace giocare al calcio.
I like playing soccer.

Notice also that word order is relatively free.

Ti piace il calcio?
Do you like soccer?

Il calcio ti piace?
Do you like soccer?

Here is the complete conjugation of *piacere* in the present.

I am pleasing to	*io*	*piaccio*
you are pleasing to (familiar)	*tu*	*piaci*
he is pleasing to	*lui*	*piace*
she is pleasing to	*lei*	*piace*
you are pleasing to (polite)	*Lei*	*piace*
we are pleasing to	*noi*	*piacciamo*
you are pleasing to (familiar or polite)	*voi*	*piacete*
they are pleasing to	*loro*	*piacciono*
you are pleasing to (polite)	*Loro*	*piacciono*

3. THE POSITION OF SUBJECT PRONOUNS

In Italian the subject may follow the verb for emphasis.

Lo faccio io.
 I'll do it.

Lo fa Maria.
 Maria will do it.

4. *NON . . . AFFATTO*

The word *affatto* ("at all") is always used with *non* in a double negative construction.*

Il calcio non ci piace affatto.
 We don't like soccer at all.

Non capisco affatto.
 I don't understand at all.

* Please see lesson 11.

sport (m.)	sport
calcio	soccer
pugilato	boxing
pallacanestro (f.)	basketball
ciclismo	cycling
nuoto	swimming
sci (m.)	skiing
tennis (m.)	tennis
automobilismo	car racing
motociclismo	motorcycling
atletica	athletics
partita	game
incontro	match
incontro di calcio	soccer game
partita di pallacanestro	basketball game
guardare la partita	to watch the game
squadra	team
giocatore (m.)	player
professionista (m.)	professional
dilettante (m.)	amateur
allenatore (m.)	coach
arbitro	referee
campionato	championship
allenamento	training
praticare uno sport	to play a sport
giocare	to play
perdere	to lose
vincere	to win
Mi dispiace.	I'm sorry.
Va bene!	Okay!
stasera	tonight
allora	then
la prossima volta	next time
non . . . affatto	not at all

ESERCIZI

A. *Dire che le seguenti attività piacciono. Usare "mi piace" o "mi piacciono."*
(Say that you like the following activities. Use *mi piace* or *mi piacciono*.)

ESEMPIO: Lo sport?
Mi piace lo sport.

1. *Il ciclismo?*
2. *Gli sport violenti?*
3. *Questi giocatori?*
4. *Giocare a tennis?*
5. *La pallacanestro?*

B. *Sostituire le parole sottolineate con un pronome indiretto.* (Substitute the underlined words with an indirect object pronoun.)

1. *Ho scritto all'allenatore.*
2. *Avete parlato agli arbitri.*
3. *Abbiamo telefonato alla nonna.*
4. *Abbiamo dato il vestito alla commessa.*
5. *Avete parlato alle vostre cugine.*

C. *Tradurre.*

1. I like watching soccer.
2. Luisa phoned Claudio.
3. I don't like sports at all.
4. I spoke to him yesterday.
5. Who told you that there is a game today?

NOTA CULTURALE

Italians are enthusiastic sports fans, and there are several daily newspapers devoted solely to sports. *Calcio* (soccer) is the most popular spectator sport in Italy. All major cities and most smaller ones have teams playing in one league or another. Big-league games are played on Sunday afternoons from September to May. Other popular sports are basketball, tennis, skiing, car racing, and cycling. Basketball is gaining a big following around the country, and many Americans play on Italian professional teams.

CHIAVE PER GLI ESERCIZI

A. 1. *Mi piace il ciclismo.* 2. *Mi piacciono gli sport violenti.* 3. *Mi piacciono questi giocatori.* 4. *Mi piace giocare a tennis.* 5. *Mi piace la pallacanestro.*

B. 1. *Gli ho scritto.* 2. *Gli avete parlato. / Avete parlato loro.* 3. *Le abbiamo telefonato.* 4. *Le abbiamo dato il vestito.* 5. *Gli avete parlato. / Avete parlato loro.*

C. 1. *Mi piace guardare il calcio.* 2. *Luisa ha telefonato a Claudio.* 3. *Non mi piacciono affatto gli sport.* 4. *Gli ho parlato ieri.* 5. *Chi ti ha detto che oggi c'è la partita?*

LEZIONE 20
LA CASA.   The home.

A. DIALOGO

Una casa ideale.

GINA: **Hai visto la casa nuova di Rosanna?**

RITA: **Sì, l'ho vista. È bella, vero?**

GINA: **Sì, ed è anche molto grande.**

RITA: **Hai visto le camere da letto?**

GINA: **Sì. Ma quante camere da letto ha? Non ricordo.**

RITA: **Ne ha cinque. Ed ha tre bagni e una cucina immensa . . .**

GINA: **Ma è costata molto!**

RITA: **Ma che cosa credi? Ha una piscina, un bell'ingresso, tanti armadi a muro, una cantina, un giardino . . . Ha anche l'aria condizionata!**

GINA: **Allora per arredarla ha dovuto comprare molti mobili nuovi?**

RITA: **Sì, ne ha comprati molti: un divano, un televisore, diversi quadri . . . Ha anche usato molti mobili della vecchia casa . . .**

GINA: **E ha un garage?**

RITA: **Sì, ne ha due!! Non li hai visti!?**

An ideal house.

GINA: Did you see Rosanna's new house?

RITA: Yes, I saw it. It's beautiful, isn't it?

GINA: Yes, and it's also very big.

RITA: Did you see the bedrooms?

GINA: Yes. But how many bedrooms does it have? I don't remember.

RITA: It has five. And it has three bathrooms and a huge kitchen . . .

GINA: But it cost a lot!

RITA: Well, what do you expect? It has a swimming pool, a beautiful entrance, so many closets, a wine cellar, a garden. . . . It also has air conditioning!

GINA: Then, to furnish it, she had to buy a lot of new furniture?

RITA: Yes, she bought a lot: a sofa, a televison set, several paintings . . . She also used a lot of furniture from the old house . . .

GINA: And does it have a garage?

RITA: Yes, it has two!! Didn't you see them!?

B. GRAMMATICA E SUOI USI

1. THE CONJUNCTIVE PRONOUN *NE*

The pronoun *ne* precedes the verb and is used as a partitive meaning "some/any (of it, of them)."

Quante camere da letto ha?—Ne ha cinque.
How many bedrooms does it have? It has five (of them).

Ho comprato molti mobili.—Ne ho comprati molti.
I bought a lot of furniture. I bought a lot (of it).

Vuole del vino?—Sì, ne voglio. No, non ne voglio.
Do you want some wine? Yes, I want some. No, I don't want any.

Ne can also be used as a pronoun meaning "of/about him/her/them/it."

Avete parlato della casa?—Sì, ne abbiamo parlato.
Did you speak about the house? Yes, we spoke about it.

Avete parlato di Antonio?—Sì, ne abbiamo parlato.
Did you speak about Antonio? Yes, we spoke about him.

2. AGREEMENT OF PAST PARTICIPLES WITH DIRECT OBJECT PRONOUNS

When one of the following direct object pronouns—*lo, la, li, le,* and *ne* in its partitive meaning—precedes a verb in the past tense, the past participle must agree with the pronoun in gender and number. With *mi, ti, ci,* and *vi* agreement is not mandatory.

Hai visto il giardino?—Sì, l'ho visto.
Did you see the garden? Yes, I saw it.

Hai visto la casa?—Sì, l'ho vista.
Did you see the house? Yes, I saw it.

Hai visto le stanze?—Sì, le ho viste.
Did you see the rooms? Yes, I saw them.

Hai comprato i mobili?—Sì, li ho comprati.
Did you buy the furniture? Yes, I bought it.

Hai comprato i mobili?—Sì, ne ho comprati molti.
Did you buy the furniture? Yes, I bought a lot of it.

3. THE ADJECTIVE *GRANDE*

The adjective *grande* may precede or follow the noun. When it follows the noun, it has two forms (like regular adjectives ending in -*e*): *grande* (singular) and *grandi* (plural).

un armadio grande
a big closet

una casa grande
a big house

due case grandi
two big houses

When it precedes the noun, there are several different possibilities.

SINGULAR	PLURAL
Before masculine and feminine	Before all masculine and
nouns beginning with a consonant:	feminine nouns:
gran or *grande*	*grandi*

Before masculine and feminine nouns
  beginning with any vowel:
    grand' or *grande*

È un grande/gran bagaglio.
  It's a big piece of luggage.

È una grande/grand'amica.
  She's a great friend.

Siamo grandi amiche.
  We're great friends.

4. THE POSITION OF ADJECTIVES: SPECIAL CASES

Qualifying adjectives, such as adjectives of nationality or color, usually follow the noun.

un vestito nero
  a black suit

un signore americano
  an American gentleman

Some common adjectives (*bello, buono, grande, brutto*), however, generally precede the noun.

una bella casa
  a beautiful house

un buon libro
  a good book

una brutta giornata
  a miserable day

186

These common adjectives can follow the noun when they are modified by
an adverb or are used for emphasis or contrast.

una casa molto bella
    a very beautiful house

È una casa grande, non è piccola.
    It's a big house, not a small house.

Certain adjectives (*grande, vecchio, nuovo, diverso*) have a literal meaning
when they come after the noun, and a figurative meaning when they come
before the noun. Study the following examples.

un libro grande
    a big book

un grande libro
    a great book

La casa è vecchia.
    The house is old.

Questa è la mia vecchia casa.
    This is my former house.

Ho comprato una casa nuova.
    I bought a new house.

Ho comprato una nuova casa.
    I bought another house.

Ho comprato due quadri diversi.
    I bought two different paintings.

Ho comprato diversi quadri.
    I bought several paintings.

VOCABOLARIO

casa	house, home
appartamento	apartment
stanza/camera	room
camera da letto	bedroom
salotto/soggiorno	living room
sala da pranzo	dining room
bagno	bathroom
cantina	wine cellar
cucina	kitchen, stove
ingresso	entrance, foyer
giardino	garden
piscina	swimming pool
mobili (m., pl.)	furniture
aria condizionata	air conditioning
armadio a muro	closet
televisore (m.)	television set
divano	sofa
quadro	painting
frigorifero	refrigerator
letto	bed
abitare al primo piano	to live on the second floor
abitare al secondo piano	to live on the third floor
arredare	to furnish
cambiare casa	to move
nuovo	new
vecchio	old, former
usato	used
piccolo	small
grande	big, large, great
immenso	immense
diversi/e	different, several
caro	expensive
certamente	certainly
infatti	in fact
Non ricordo.	I don't remember.

ESERCIZI

A. *Rispondere affermativamente alle domande usando il pronome oggetto diretto.*

1. *Hai visto la casa?*
2. *Hai visto il bagno?*
3. *Hai visto il nuovo televisore?*
4. *Avete visto le stanze da letto?*
5. *Avete comprato i quadri?*

B. *Rispondere alle seguenti domande usando il pronome "ne" e servendosi delle indicazioni fra parentesi.* (Answer the following questions using *ne* and the clues in parentheses.)

ESEMPIO: Quante case avete? (2)
　　　　　Ne abbiamo due.

1. *Quante camere da letto ha la casa? (4)*
2. *Quanti garage ha? (1)*
3. *Quanti quadri avete comprato? (8)*
4. *Quanti televisori avete visto? (2)*
5. *Quanti armadi a muro ha la casa? (6)*

C. *Tradurre.*

1. I bought several paintings.
2. Mary lives in a brand new apartment.
3. This television set is old.
4. The house has a swimming pool and a garden.
5. The rooms are very big.

NOTA CULTURALE

In Italy in the last few decades, as industrialization has grown and claimed more and more of the land, agricultural lands have shrunk. People have moved en masse from the country into the cities. This exodus has caused congestion problems. Urban centers were forced to expand, and many Italian cities have experienced major changes. New districts consisting of modern apartment buildings (*palazzi*), government low-rent houses (*case popolari*), and luxurious detached houses (*ville*) have risen around the old city centers. The post-war economic boom has also enabled many Italians to buy a second home in a resort area (*zona di villeggiatura*)—a house or apartment by the beach, near a lake, or in the mountains.

CHIAVE PER GLI ESERCIZI

A. 1. *Sì, l'ho vista.* 2. *Sì, l'ho visto.* 3. *Sì, l'ho visto.* 4. *Sì, le abbiamo viste.* 5. *Sì, li abbiamo comprati.*

B. 1. *Ne ha quattro.* 2. *Ne ha uno.* 3. *Ne abbiamo comprati otto.* 4. *Ne abbiamo visti due.* 5. *Ne ha sei.*

C. 1. *Io ho comprato diversi quadri.* 2. *Mary abita in un appartamento nuovo.* 3. *Questo televisore è vecchio.* 4. *La casa ha una piscina e un giardino.* 5. *Le stanze sono molto grandi.*

QUARTO RIPASSO

A. *Rispondere affermativamente, usando un pronome oggetto diretto.*

 1. *Compri questo vestito?*
 2. *Volete questi pantaloni?*
 3. *Signore, parcheggio la macchina qui?*
 4. *Carla, mi svegli alle sette?*
 5. *Ti sveglia alle sette Carla?*

B. *Rispondere negativamente, usando un pronome oggetto diretto.*

 1. *Hai visto quel film?*
 2. *Hai visto la casa di Gianna?*
 3. *Hai comprato i mobili?*
 4. *Hai fatto i compiti?*
 5. *Hai visto quelle camere?*

C. *Completare con un pronome oggetto indiretto.*

 1. *Ti piace il calcio?*
   Sì, _____ piace molto.

2. *Franco, a che ora mi telefoni?*
   _____ *telefono alle otto, Mario.*
3. *Signor Rossi, a che ora mi telefona?*
   _____ *telefono alle dieci, signorina.*
4. *Hai già parlato ai tuoi genitori?*
   Sì, _____ *ho già parlato.*
5. *Che cosa hai detto a Luigi?*
   Non _____ *ho detto niente.*
6. *Hai scritto a Marianna?*
   Sì, _____ *ho scritto ieri.*

D. *Completare con la forma appropriata del verbo.*

	PRESENTE	PASSATO
ESEMPIO:	io parlo	io ho parlato
1.		tu sei stato
2.	voi andate	
3.		loro hanno avuto
4.	lei esce	
5.		lei ha letto
6.	noi facciamo	
7.		loro si sono divertiti
8.	noi scriviamo	
9.		lui ha detto

E. *Completare in modo opportuno.*

1. *Vuoi vedere le valig_____?*
   Sì, voglio veder_____.
2. *Monica e Simona sono grand_____ amic_____.*
3. *In Italia abbiamo conosciut_____ due ragazze italiane molt_____*
   simpatic_____.
4. *Quegli alberg_____ sono di prima categoria.*
5. *Quella ditta cerca qualcuno con capacit_____ manageriali.*
6. *Il tennis mi piac_____ molto.*
7. *Questi sport ti piac_____?*

191

8. *Ti piac_____ guardare le partite di calcio alla televisione?*
9. *Vuoi del vino?*
    Sì, _____ voglio.
10. *Avete parlato di Antonio?*
    Sì, _____ abbiamo parlato.

CHIAVE PER GLI ESERCIZI

A. 1. *Sì, lo compro.* 2. *Sì, li vogliamo.* 3. *Sì, la parcheggi qui.* 4. *Sì, ti sveglio alle sette.* 5. *Sì, mi sveglia alle sette.*

B. 1. *No, non l'ho visto.* 2. *No, non l'ho vista.* 3. *No, non li ho comprati.* 4. *No, non li ho fatti.* 5. *No, non le ho viste.*

C. 1. *mi* 2. *ti* 3. *Le* 4. *gli* 5. *gli* 6. *le*

D. 1. *tu sei* 2. *voi siete andati/e* 3. *loro hanno* 4. *lei è uscita* 5. *lei legge* 6. *noi abbiamo fatto* 7. *loro si divertono* 8. *noi abbiamo scritto* 9. *lui dice*

E. 1. *valigie, vederle* 2. *grandi amiche* 3. *conosciuto, molto, simpatiche* 4. *alberghi* 5. *capacità* 6. *piace* 7. *piacciono* 8. *piace* 9. *ne* 10. *ne*

DA LEGGERE

L'ITALIA POLITICA

L'Italia ha venti regioni: il Piemonte, la Valle D'Aosta, la Liguria, la Lombardia, il Veneto, il Trentino-Alto Adige, il Friuli-Venezia Giulia, l'Emilia Romagna, la Toscana, le Marche, l'Umbria, il Lazio, gli Abruzzi, il Molise, la Campania, la Puglia, la Basilicata, la Calabria, la Sicilia e la Sardegna. Ogni regione ha il suo capoluogo.[1] Per esempio, Milano è il capoluogo della Lombardia, Torino è il capoluogo del Piemonte e Palermo quello della Sicilia. La capitale[2] d'Italia è Roma.

L'Italia ha una popolazione di circa[3] cinquantasette milioni di abitanti.[4] È una repubblica. Il Presidente della Repubblica, che è il Capo dello Stato,[5] è eletto[6] ogni sette anni dai membri[7] del Parlamento. Il Parlamento, composto[8] di senatori[9] e deputati[10] che sono eletti ogni cinque anni, formula[11] le leggi.[12] Il Governo, invece,[13] ha il potere esecutivo.[14] L'incarico[15] di formare il Governo è conferito[16] dal Presidente della Repubblica al Presidente del Consiglio dei Ministri. I Ministri sono scelti, normalmente, dal Presidente del Consiglio.

VOCABOLARIO

1. *capoluogo* — capital of a province
2. *capitale* (f.) — capital of a country
3. *circa* — around, about
4. *abitante* (m.) — inhabitant
5. *Capo dello Stato* — Head of State
6. *eletto, -a* — elected, chosen
7. *membro* — member
8. *composto, -a* — composed
9. *senatore* (m.) — Senator
10. *deputato* — member of parliament
11. *formulare* — to formulate, to set forth
12. *legge* (f.) — law
13. *invece* — on the other hand, instead
14. *esecutivo, -a* — executive
15. *incarico* — task, appointment
16. *conferire* — to bestow, to grant

LEZIONE 21

I GIORNALI.   Newspapers.

A. DIALOGO

Sfogliando il quotidiano.

SERGIO: **Hai comprato *La Stampa*?**

GIANNA: **No, ho comprato *Il Corriere della Sera*. È lì. Ma non l'ho ancora letto. C'è qualche notizia interessante?**

SERGIO: **L'editoriale parla del presidente americano. La settimana prossima verrà in Italia, si incontrerà con le autorità politiche e . . .**

GIANNA: **E andrà dal papa. Cosa c'è in terza pagina?**

SERGIO: **Presto uscirà un altro libro di Eco.**

GIANNA: **Cosa dice il mio oroscopo?**

SERGIO: **Vediamo . . . Leone. Farai conoscenze interessanti . . . Incontrerai un ragazzo alto, bruno, gentile . . . Vincerai un premio . . . Partirai per un viaggio . . .**

GIANNA: **Ma sarà vero?**

SERGIO: **Non so . . . Ora ti leggo il mio.**

GIANNA: **Non ora. Non ho tempo ora. Devo uscire per trovare il mio ragazzo alto, bruno, gentile . . .**

SERGIO: **Va bene! Se partirai, potrò leggere in pace la pagina sportiva.**

Leafing through the daily paper.

SERGIO: Did you buy *La Stampa?*

GIANNA: No, I bought the *Corriere della Sera*. It's there. But I haven't read it yet. Is there any interesting news?

SERGIO: The editorial is about the American president. Next week he'll come to Italy; he will meet with the political leaders, and . . .

GIANNA: And he will meet the pope. What's on the cultural page?

SERGIO: Another book by Eco will come out soon.

GIANNA: What does my horoscope say?

SERGIO: Let's see . . . Leo. You'll meet interesting people . . . You're going to meet a tall, dark-haired, kind man . . . You'll win a prize . . . You'll go on a trip . . .

GIANNA: But will it come true?

SERGIO: I don't know . . . Now I'll read you mine.

GIANNA: Not now. I don't have time now. I have to go out and look for my tall, dark-haired, kind boyfriend . . .

SERGIO: Great! If you leave, I'll be able to read the sports page in peace.

B. GRAMMATICA E SUOI USI

1. THE FUTURE TENSE OF REGULAR VERBS

Just as in English, the future tense generally expresses a future action. The future of regular verbs is formed by dropping the final *e* of the infinitive and adding the appropriate personal endings *-ò, -ai, -à, -emo, -ete, -anno*. For the first verb group, the *a* in the infinitive ending changes to *e*.

	PARLARE	TO SPEAK
I will speak	*io*	*parlerò*
you will speak (familiar)	*tu*	*parlerai*
he will speak	*lui*	*parlerà*
she will speak	*lei*	*parlerà*
you will speak (polite)	*Lei*	*parlerà*
we will speak	*noi*	*parleremo*
you will speak (familiar or polite)	*voi*	*parlerete*
they will speak	*loro*	*parleranno*
you will speak (polite)	*Loro*	*parleranno*

Stasera comprerete il giornale.
Tonight you'll buy the newspaper.

Il presidente americano incontrerà il papa.

The American president will meet the pope.

Domani parlerò a Luigi.

Tomorrow I'll speak to Luigi.

	PRENDERE	TO TAKE
I will take	io	prenderò
you will take (familiar)	tu	prenderai
he will take	lui	prenderà
she will take	lei	prenderà
you will take (polite)	Lei	prenderà
we will take	noi	prenderemo
you will take (familiar or polite)	voi	prenderete
they will take	loro	prenderanno
you will take (polite)	Loro	prenderanno

Tu vincerai un premio.

You'll win a prize.

Leggeranno il giornale domani.

They'll read the newspaper tomorrow.

	PARTIRE	TO LEAVE
I will leave	io	partirò
you will leave (familiar)	tu	partirai
he will leave	lui	partirà
she will leave	lei	partirà
you will leave (polite)	Lei	partirà
we will leave	noi	partiremo
you will leave (familiar or polite)	voi	partirete
they will leave	loro	partiranno
you will leave (polite)	Loro	partiranno

Presto uscirà un altro libro di Eco.

Another book by Eco will come out soon.

Partiremo per un lungo viaggio.

We'll leave on a long trip.

2. THE FUTURE TENSE OF *AVERE* AND *ESSERE*

Avere and *essere* are irregular in the future tense.

	AVERE	TO HAVE
I will have	*io*	*avrò*
you will have (familiar)	*tu*	*avrai*
he will have	*lui*	*avrà*
she will have	*lei*	*avrà*
you will have (polite)	*Lei*	*avrà*
we will have	*noi*	*avremo*
you will have (familiar or polite)	*voi*	*avrete*
they will have	*loro*	*avranno*
you will have (polite)	*Loro*	*avranno*

Non avrò tempo.
I won't have time.

Avremo sete.
We'll be thirsty.

	ESSERE	TO BE
I will be	*io*	*sarò*
you will be (familiar)	*tu*	*sarai*
he will be	*lui*	*sarà*
she will be	*lei*	*sarà*
you will be (polite)	*Lei*	*sarà*
we will be	*noi*	*saremo*
you will be (familiar or polite)	*voi*	*sarete*
they will be	*loro*	*saranno*
you will be (polite)	*Loro*	*saranno*

Sarai in ufficio domani?
Will you be in the office tomorrow?

Sarete a casa stasera?
Will you be at home tonight?

3. THE FUTURE TENSE OF VERBS ENDING IN *-CARE, -GARE, -CIARE,* AND *-GIARE*

Verbs ending in *-care* and *-gare* add an *h* after the *c* and *g* in the future tense in order to retain the hard *k* and *g* sounds.

	GIOCARE	TO PLAY
I will play	io	giocherò
you will play (familiar)	tu	giocherai
he will play	lui	giocherà
she will play	lei	giocherà
you will play (polite)	Lei	giocherà
we will play	noi	giocheremo
you will play (familiar or polite)	voi	giocherete
they will play	loro	giocheranno
you will play (polite)	Loro	giocheranno

Domani giocheremo a pallacanestro.
Tomorrow we'll play basketball.

Domani giocheranno a tennis.
Tomorrow they'll play tennis.

	PAGARE	TO PAY
I will pay	io	pagherò
you will pay (familiar)	tu	pagherai
he will pay	lui	pagherà
she will pay	lei	pagherà
you will pay (polite)	Lei	pagherà
we will pay	noi	pagheremo
you will pay (familiar or polite)	voi	pagherete
they will pay	loro	pagheranno
you will pay (polite)	Loro	pagheranno

Ti pagherò domani.
I'll pay you tomorrow.

Il professore spiegherà la lezione.
The professor will explain the lesson.

198

Verbs ending in *-ciare* and *-giare* drop the *i* from their stems in the future tense.

COMINCIARE		TO START
I will start	io	comincerò
you will start (familiar)	tu	comincerai
he will start	lui	comincerà
she will start	lei	comincerà
you will start (polite)	Lei	comincerà
we will start	noi	cominceremo
you will start (familiar or polite)	voi	comincerete
they will start	loro	cominceranno
you will start (polite)	Loro	cominceranno

Le partite cominceranno alle due.
The games will start at two.

La lezione comincerà alle dieci.
The lesson will start at ten.

MANGIARE		TO EAT
I will eat	io	mangerò
you will eat (familiar)	tu	mangerai
he will eat	lui	mangerà
she will eat	lei	mangerà
you will eat (polite)	Lei	mangerà
we will eat	noi	mangeremo
you will eat (familiar or polite)	voi	mangerete
they will eat	loro	mangeranno
you will eat (polite)	Loro	mangeranno

Stasera mangerò pesce.
I'll eat fish tonight.

Domani mangerai carne.
Tomorrow you'll eat meat.

4. THE FUTURE TENSE OF IRREGULAR VERBS

Some verbs have irregular stems in the future tense, but they all use regular endings.

to give	*dare*	*darò, darai, darà, daremo, darete, daranno*
to do	*fare*	*farò, farai, farà, faremo, farete, faranno*
to stay	*stare*	*starò, starai, starà, staremo, starete, staranno*
to go	*andare*	*andrò, andrai, andrà, andremo, andrete, andranno*
to have to	*dovere*	*dovrò, dovrai, dovrà, dovremo, dovrete, dovranno*
to see	*vedere*	*vedrò, vedrai, vedrà, vedremo, vedrete, vedranno*
to know	*sapere*	*saprò, saprai, saprà, sapremo, saprete, sapranno*
to be able to	*potere*	*potrò, potrai, potrà, potremo, potrete, potranno*
to drink	*bere*	*berrò, berrai, berrà, berremo, berrete, berranno*
to come	*venire*	*verrò, verrai, verrà, verremo, verrete, verranno*
to want	*volere*	*vorrò, vorrai, vorrà, vorremo, vorrete, vorranno*

Il presidente americano verrà in Italia.
   The American president will come to Italy.

Noi andremo a Roma.
   We'll go to Rome.

Domani farà caldo.
   Tomorrow it will be hot.

5. USES OF THE FUTURE TENSE

In Italian the present tense, along with an expression indicating future time, may be used to express the future.

Stasera leggiamo il giornale.
   Tonight we'll read the newspaper.

Domani vado a New York.
Tomorrow I'll go to New York.

The future tense in Italian may be used to express probability, uncertainty, or conjecture.

Che ora sarà?
What time can it be?

Sarà l'una.
It must be one o'clock.
It's probably one o'clock.

The future tense is also commonly used after *se* ("if") and *quando* ("when") to express a future action.

Quando il presidente americano arriverà in Italia, si incontrerà con le autorità politiche.
When the American president arrives in Italy, he will meet with the political leaders.

Se te ne vai, potrò leggere in pace la pagina sportiva.
If you leave, I'll be able to read the sports page in peace.

VOCABOLARIO

giornale (m.)	newspaper
quotidiano	daily newspaper
settimanale (m.)	weekly newspaper
rivista	magazine
leggere il giornale	to read the newspaper
sfogliare il giornale	to leaf through the newspaper
comprare il giornale	to buy the newspaper
C'è qualche notizia interessante?	Is there any interesting news?
Cosa dice il giornale?	What does the newspaper say?
Cosa c'è sul giornale?	What's in the newspaper?
direttore (m.)	editor
giornalista (m./f.)	journalist

giornalaio	newspaper vendor
edicola	newsstand
reporter (m./f.)	reporter
editoriale (m.)	editorial
titolo	title
testata	headline
articolo	article
servizio	report
rubrica	column, section, page
servizio speciale	special report, feature
terza pagina	cultural page
rubrica/pagina sportiva	sports page
rubrica finanziaria	business page
rubrica teatrale	theater section
cronaca mondana	gossip column
cronaca nera	crime news
annunci economici (m., pl.)	classified ads
oroscopo	horoscope
la settimana prossima	next week
l'anno prossimo	next year
alto	tall
bruno	dark-haired

ESERCIZI

A. *Cambiare le frasi al futuro.*

1. *Io scrivo un articolo.*
2. *Tu compri il giornale.*
3. *Lui legge la pagina sportiva.*
4. *Noi sfogliamo la rubrica finanziaria.*
5. *Voi leggete gli annunci economici.*
6. *Loro ascoltano le notizie.*

B. *Scrivere la forma corretta del verbo nello schema.*

	PRESENTE	FUTURO
ESEMPIO:	io parlo	io parlerò
1.		tu comincerai
2.	voi mangiate	
3.		noi faremo
4.	io ho	
5.		loro potranno
6.	lei è	

C. *Tradurre.*

1. It must be one o'clock.
2. I'll read the newspaper.
3. They'll go to Italy.
4. We'll come to New York next week.
5. You (singular, familiar) will see a tall, young man.

NOTA CULTURALE

Italy publishes more than 70 daily newspapers and approximately 6,000 weekly and monthly periodicals. Some of the most important newspapers are *Il Corriere della Sera* (published in Milan), *La Stampa* (Turin), *La Repubblica* (Rome), *La Nazione* (Florence), and *Il Mattino* (Naples). The major political parties have their own newspapers. The Italian political system is one of the most dynamic in the world and is continually undergoing major changes. Political newspapers, naturally, follow these changes, resulting in a constant flux of new publications appearing and old ones disappearing. Foreign language newspapers, such as *The Daily American* (Rome), are also published. The most popular financial newspapers are *Sole 24 Ore* (Milan) and *Il Corriere Mercantile* (Genoa). *Il Corriere dello Sport* (Rome) and *La Gazzetta dello Sport* (Milan) are among the most popular daily papers dedicated entirely to sports.

Some of the most widely circulated weekly and monthly magazines are *Famiglia Cristiana, L'Espresso, Panorama, Epoca, Gente, Oggi, Amica. Sorrisi e Canzoni* is the most popular TV guide. Comic books and children's papers like *Topolino* and *Il Corriere dei Piccoli* are also very popular.

CHIAVE PER GLI ESERCIZI

A. 1. *Io scriverò un articolo.* 2. *Tu comprerai il giornale.* 3. *Lui leggerà la pagina sportiva.* 4. *Noi sfoglieremo la rubrica finanziaria.* 5. *Voi leggerete gli annunci economici.* 6. *Loro ascolteranno le notizie.*

B. 1. *tu cominci* 2. *voi mangerete* 3. *noi facciamo* 4. *io avrò* 5. *loro possono* 6. *lei sarà*

C. 1. *Sarà l'una.* 2. *Io leggerò il giornale.* 3. *Loro andranno in Italia.* 4. *Verremo a New York la settimana prossima.* 5. *Vedrai un ragazzo alto e giovane.*

LEZIONE 22

IN BANCA.   At the bank.

A. DIALOGO

Aprire un conto.

SIGNOR BROWN: **C'è il dottor Ranieri? Sono John Brown.**

IMPIEGATA: **Non so. Un momento, per piacere . . . No, il direttore oggi non è di servizio. C'è il vice direttore, il dottor Miceli. Vuole parlare con lui?**

SIGNOR BROWN: **Non importa. Non conosco Miceli.**

IMPIEGATA: **Posso aiutarLa io?**

SIGNOR BROWN: **Sì, vorrei aprire un conto in banca e depositare dei soldi. Non mi piace portare con me troppo denaro liquido.**

IMPIEGATA: **Bene. Ci penso io. Desidera un conto corrente o un libretto di risparmi?**

SIGNOR BROWN: **Conto corrente.**

IMPIEGATA: **Lei ha la residenza in Italia?**

SIGNOR BROWN: **Sì.**

IMPIEGATA: **Ha un documento d'identità?**

SIGNOR BROWN: **Ecco.**

IMPIEGATA: **Si accomodi allo sportello numero tre. Deve compilare alcuni moduli. Le daranno anche dei libretti degli assegni e il numero di conto corrente.**

Opening an account.

MR. BROWN: Is Dr. Ranieri in? I'm John Brown.

TELLER: I don't know. One moment, please . . . No, he's not on duty today, but the assistant manager, Dr. Miceli, is in. Do you want to speak with him?

MR. BROWN: It's not important. I don't know Dr. Miceli.

TELLER: Can I help you?

MR. BROWN: Yes, I'd like to open a bank account and deposit some money. I don't like to have a lot of cash on me.

TELLER: Okay. I'll take care of it. Would you like a checking or a savings account?

MR. BROWN: Checking account.

TELLER: Do you have your residence in Italy?

MR. BROWN: Yes.

TELLER: Do you have some identification?

MR. BROWN: Here you are.

TELLER: Go to window three. You have to fill out some forms. They'll also give you some checkbooks and the account number.

B. GRAMMATICA E SUOI USI

1. USE OF THE DEFINITE ARTICLE

As we have already seen, there are many instances in which Italian requires a definite article, while English doesn't. Here are a few more.

The definite article precedes nouns used in a general or abstract way.

La pazienza è una virtù.
Patience is a virtue.

Il denaro è necessario.
Money is necessary.

The definite article is used with possessive adjectives or pronouns.

Questo è il mio assegno. Il tuo è là.
This is my check. Yours is there.

206

The definite article is also used with names of countries, continents, provinces, etc.

L'Italia è bellissima.
Italy is very beautiful.

However, it is not used with the names of cities or after *in* plus names of countries, continents, etc.

Io sono andato in Italia.
I went to Italy.

Io sono andato a Roma.
I went to Rome.

Roma è una bella città.
Rome is a beautiful city.

The definite article is required with titles, when speaking about people in the third person.

C'è il dottor Ranieri?
Is Dr. Ranieri in?

Il dottor Ranieri non è di servizio.
Dr. Ranieri is not on duty.

When addressing someone directly, however, the article is omitted.

Signor Brown, si accomodi allo sportello numero tre.
Mr. Brown, go to window number three.

Signora Clinton, ha un documento d'identità?
Mrs. Clinton, do you have some identification?

The definite article is also used before names of languages.

L'italiano mi piace.
I like Italian.

Il francese è una bella lingua.
French is a beautiful language.

But, when the name of the language is preceded by *in* or *di*, the article is omitted.

Vado a lezione di francese.
I'm going to French class.

Come si dice questa parola in italiano?
How do you say this word in Italian?

Note that with the verbs *parlare* and *studiare,* both possibilities are acceptable.

Io parlo l'italiano.
I speak Italian.

Io parlo italiano.
I speak Italian.

The definite article should be used with colors.

Il rosso è il mio colore preferito.
Red is my favorite color.

The definite article is always used with expressions of time including the hour, days of the week, years, and seasons.

Sono le due.
It is two o'clock.

Il lunedì lavoro in banca.   but: *Lunedì comincio a lavorare in banca.*
On Mondays I work at the bank.   Monday I start working at the bank.

Abito qui dal 1980.
I've been living here since 1980.

L'estate è la mia stagione preferita.
Summer is my favorite season.

With *in* plus seasons, no article is used.

In estate vado in Italia.
During the summer I go to Italy.

2. CARDINAL NUMBERS FROM 100

cento	100	mille	1.000
centouno	101	milleuno	1.001
centodue	102	milledue	1.002
centotrè	103	milletrè	1.003
centodieci	110	millecento	1.100
centoventi	120	milleduecento	1.200
centoventitrè	123	milletrecento	1.300
centotrenta	130	duemila	2.000
duecento	200	tremila	3.000
trecento	300	diecimila	10.000
quattrocento	400	ventimila	20.000
cinquecento	500	centomila	100.000
seicento	600	duecentomila	200.000
settecento	700	un milione	1.000.000
ottocento	800	due milioni	2.000.000
novecento	900	un miliardo	1.000.000.000

Remember the following points:

a. *Cento* and *mille* do not require an indefinite article, while *milione* and *miliardo* do.

Ho mille lire.
I have one thousand lire.

Ho cento dollari.
I have one hundred dollars.

Ho un milione di dollari.
I have one million dollars.

b. The plural of *mille* is *mila.*

Ho guadagnato duemila dollari.
I earned 2,000 dollars.

c. *Milione* and *miliardo* take the preposition *di* when followed by a noun.

Roma ha circa 5.000.000 di abitanti.

Rome has about 5,000,000 inhabitants.

d. When capitalized and preceded by the article, numbers like *duecento, trecento, quattrocento,* etc., refer to a century. Therefore, *il Duecento* is the thirteenth century; *il Trecento* is the fourteenth century, etc. The word *mille* (e.g., *milleduecento:* 1,200) is understood.

Michelangelo è vissuto nel Cinquecento.

Michelangelo lived in the sixteenth century.

3. THE VERBS *CONOSCERE* AND *SAPERE*

Both *conoscere* and *sapere* mean "to know," but they are not interchangeable.

Conoscere implies a familiarity or acquaintance with people, places, and things. It is always followed by a direct object.

	CONOSCERE	TO KNOW, TO BE ACQUAINTED WITH
I know	*io*	*conosco*
you know (familiar)	*tu*	*conosci*
he knows	*lui*	*conosce*
she knows	*lei*	*conosce*
you know (polite)	*Lei*	*conosce*
we know	*noi*	*conosciamo*
you know (familiar or polite)	*voi*	*conoscete*
they know	*loro*	*conoscono*
you know (polite)	*Loro*	*conoscono*

Conosci Paola?

Do you know Paola?

Conoscono bene Roma.

They know Rome well.

Sapere, on the other hand, indicates knowledge of a fact. If followed by an infinitive, *sapere* means "to know how."

	SAPERE	TO KNOW, TO KNOW HOW
I know	*io*	*so*
you know (familiar)	*tu*	*sai*
he knows	*lui*	*sa*
she knows	*lei*	*sa*
you know (polite)	*Lei*	*sa*
we know	*noi*	*sappiamo*
you know (familiar or polite)	*voi*	*sapete*
they know	*loro*	*sanno*
you know (polite)	*Loro*	*sanno*

Sai, viene anche Paola.
> You know, Paola is coming, too.

Lo so.
> I know.

Non so giocare a tennis.
> I don't know how to play tennis.

4. IDIOMATIC USES OF *CI*

In lesson 15 you learned that *ci* can be used as an adverb of place meaning "here" or "there."

Vado in banca. Ci vado.
> I'm going to the bank. I'm going there.

Ci may also replace *a/in* plus a noun or phrase in expressions like *credere* plus *a/in* ("to believe in") or *pensare* plus *a* ("to think about"). Study these examples:

Credi in Dio?
> Do you believe in God?

Sì, ci credo.
> Yes, I believe in him.

211

Pensi all'Italia?
   Are you thinking about Italy?

Sì, ci penso.
   Yes, I'm thinking about it.

VOCABOLARIO

banca	bank
bancomat (m.)	instant teller
cassiere (m.)	cashier
direttore (m.)	manager
denaro	money
soldi (m., pl.)	money
denaro liquido	cash
spiccioli (m., pl.)	small change
conto corrente	checking account
conto sociale	joint account
libretto di risparmi	savings account
assegno	check
libretto degli assegni	checkbook
firma	signature
cassaforte (f.)	safe
debito	debt
credito	credit
cassetta di sicurezza	safety deposit box
Vorrei riscuotere questo assegno.	I'd like to cash this check.
Vorrei aprire un conto.	I'd like to open an account.
Vorrei depositare dei soldi.	I'd like to deposit some money.
Vorrei prelevare dei soldi.	I'd like to withdraw some money.
Il mio numero di conto è . . .	My account number is . . .
Vorrei un prestito.	I would like a loan.
Il tasso di interesse è al dieci per cento.	The interest rate is ten percent.
Si accomodi allo sportello numero cinque.	Please go to window number five.
Si accomodi alla cassa.	Please go to the cashier's window.

Desidera biglietti di grosso taglio?	Would you like big bills?
Desidera biglietti di piccolo taglio?	Would you like small bills?
Deve compilare alcuni moduli.	You have to fill out some forms.
Mi dà un documento?	Can I see some identification? (Can you give me some identification?)
Lei ha la residenza in Italia?	Do you have your residence in Italy?
Non importa.	It's not important.
Un momento, per piacere . . .	One moment, please . . .
essere di servizio	to be on duty
Ci penso io.	I'll take care of it.
conoscere	to know, to be acquainted with
sapere	to know, to know how

ESERCIZI

A. *Rispondere affermativamente alle seguenti domande.*

1. *Luigi, sai usare il bancomat?*
2. *Voi conoscete Firenze?*
3. *Carla conosce bene il direttore della banca?*
4. *Sai che devo depositare questi soldi?*
5. *Signorina, sa a che ora apre la banca?*
6. *Sapete dov'è la banca?*

B. *Ricostruire le seguenti frasi.*

1. *trecentomila / io / prelevare / vorrei / lire*
2. *moduli / noi / compilare / questi / dobbiamo*
3. *e / aprire / depositare / conto / dei / soldi / corrente / vorrei / un*
4. *documento / per / un / identità / d' / ha / favore?*
5. *assegno / vorrei / riscuotere / quest'*
6. *direttore / di / non / servizio / è / il*

C. *Tradurre.*

1. Your checking account number is 27836.
2. I would like to open a savings account.

3. I've had my residence in Italy since 1986.
4. Mr. Brown is going to the bank.
5. Mr. Brown, go to the next window, please.

NOTA CULTURALE

The Italian monetary unit is the *lira*. Coins are currently issued in 50, 100, 200, and 500 lire denominations (5, 10, and 20 lire coins are disappearing); bills are in denominations of 1,000; 2,000; 5,000; 10,000; 50,000; and 100,000. Copper *gettoni* (telephone tokens) worth 200 lire are sometimes given as change. Banks are open weekdays from approximately 8:30 A.M. to 1:30 P.M. and from 3:00 P.M. to 4:30 P.M.

CHIAVE PER GLI ESERCIZI

A. 1. *Sì, so usare il bancomat.* 2. *Sì, conosciamo Firenze.* 3. *Sì, Carla conosce bene il direttore della banca.* 4. *Sì, lo so. / Sì, so che devi depositare questi soldi.* 5. *Sì, lo so. / Sì, so a che ora apre la banca.* 6. *Sì, lo sappiamo. / Sì, sappiamo dov'è la banca.*

B. 1. *Io vorrei prelevare trecentomila lire.* 2. *Noi dobbiamo compilare questi moduli.* 3. *Vorrei aprire un conto corrente e depositare dei soldi.* 4. *Ha un documento d'identità, per favore?* 5. *Vorrei riscuotere quest'assegno.* 6. *Il direttore non è di servizio.*

C. 1. *Il numero del Suo conto corrente è 27836.* 2. *Vorrei aprire un libretto di risparmi.* 3. *Ho la residenza in Italia dal 1986.* 4. *Il signor Brown va alla banca.* 5. *Signor Brown, vada/si accomodi allo sportello accanto, per piacere.*

LEZIONE 23

LA POSTA. The mail.

A. DIALOGO

1. Verso l'ufficio postale.

FRANCO: **Paola, vuoi venire con me?**

PAOLA: **Certo, vengo con te, ma prima devo telefonare a Lucia . . .
Dove devi andare?**

FRANCO: **Alla posta. Devo prendere la pensione della mamma e
pagare la bolletta del telefono.**

PAOLA: **Anch'io ci devo andare. Devo comprare dei francobolli e
spedire qualche cartolina. Anche Lucia deve andare alla posta.
Deve spedire alcune lettere. Possiamo chiamarla?**

FRANCO: **Ma le lettere non possiamo spedirle noi per lei?**

PAOLA: **Perché? Lucia non può venire con noi?**

FRANCO: **Sì, può venire.**

Going to the post office.

FRANCO: Paola, would you like to come with me?

PAOLA: Of course, I'll come with you, but first I have to phone Lucia . . .
Where do you have to go?

FRANCO: To the post office. I have to pick up Mom's pension check and pay
the telephone bill.

PAOLA: I have to go there, too. I have to buy some stamps and mail some
postcards. Lucia has to go to the post office, too. She has to mail some
letters. Can we call her?

FRANCO: Can't we mail the letters for her?

PAOLA: Why? Can't Lucia come with us?

FRANCO: Yes, she can come.

---

2. All'ufficio postale.

FRANCO: **Quattro francobolli per cartolina, per favore.**

IMPIEGATA: **Ecco.**

FRANCO: **Vorrei fare un telegramma e spedire questo pacchetto . . .**

IMPIEGATA: **Per il telegramma riempia questo modulo. Scriva chiaramente il messaggio e gli indirizzi del mittente e del destinatario.**

FRANCO: **Ecco fatto.**

At the post office.

FRANCO: Four postcard stamps, please.

CLERK: Here you are.

FRANCO: I'd like to send a telegram and mail this small parcel . . .

CLERK: For the telegram fill out this form. Write the message and the addresses of the sender and recipient clearly.

FRANCO: All done.

B. GRAMMATICA E SUOI USI

1. DISJUNCTIVE PRONOUNS

Disjunctive pronouns (*pronomi tonici*) are so called because they are used independently of the verb. The disjunctive pronouns are:

SINGULAR		PLURAL	
me	*me*	us	*noi*
you (familiar)	*te*	you (familiar or polite)	*voi*
him	*lui*	them	*loro*
her	*lei*		
you (polite)	*Lei*	you (polite)	*Loro*

216

These pronouns are used as follows:

a. after a preposition (*di, a, da, in, con, su,* etc.)

Paola, vuoi venire con me?
Paola, do you want to come with me?

Certo, vengo con te.
Of course, I'll come with you.

b. immediately after a verb, for emphasis or contrast

Amo te.
I love <u>you</u>.

Amo te, non lui.
I love <u>you</u>, not <u>him</u>.

c. in exclamations

Povero te!
Poor you!

Fortunati voi!
Lucky you!

2. THE PARTITIVE

As we have already seen in lesson 11, the partitive can be expressed with
the preposition *di* plus a form of the definite article.

Devo comprare dei francobolli.
I have to buy some stamps.

Devo spedire delle lettere.
I have to mail some letters.

The partitive can also be expressed by using *qualche* with a singular noun.

Devo spedire qualche cartolina.
    I have to mail some postcards.

Devo comprare qualche francobollo.
    I have to buy some stamps.

Another possibility is to use *alcuni/e* with a plural noun.

Devo scrivere alcune lettere.
    I have to write some letters.

Ho spedito alcuni pacchi.
    I sent some parcels.

And finally, the partitive can be expressed by *un po' di* ("a bit of, some") with a singular noun.

Vuoi un po' di pane?
    Would you like some bread?

Mangio solo un po' di insalata.
    I'll only eat some salad.

Abbiamo bisogno di un po' di tempo.
    We need some time.

In some cases, especially in negative sentences, Italian does not require a partitive at all.

Non scrivo mai lettere.
    I never write (any) letters.

Non abbiamo francobolli.
    We don't have (any) stamps.

3. SUFFIXES AND THEIR USES

Suffixes are special endings that may be attached to nouns, adjectives, or adverbs in order to alter the meaning of the word. The final vowel of a word should be dropped before adding a suffix.

The endings *-ino, -ina, -ello, -ella, -etto, -etta, -uccio,* and *-uccia* are diminutive suffixes that express smallness.

parcel	*pacco*	*pacchetto*	small parcel
letter	*lettera*	*letterina*	a short letter
Carlo	*Carlo*	*Carletto*	little Carlo

The endings *-one* and *-ona* are augmentative suffixes that indicate largeness.

| parcel | *pacco* | *paccone* | large parcel |
| letter | *lettera* | *letterona* | long letter |

The endings *-ino* and *-uccio* also express endearment.

Tesorino mio!
  My sweetheart!

Amoruccio mio!
  My sweet love!

The endings *-accio, -accia, -astro, -astra, -azzo,* and *-azza* are depreciative suffixes that imply ugliness or poor quality.

letter	*lettera*	*letteraccia*	nasty letter
boy	*ragazzo*	*ragazzaccio*	bad boy
gray	*grigio*	*grigiastro*	grayish, dirty gray

VOCABOLARIO

posta	mail
ufficio postale	post office
lettera	letter
espresso	express letter
raccomandata	registered letter
corriere (m.)	courier
per via aerea	by air mail
cartolina	postcard
telegramma (m.)	telegram
francobollo	stamp
francobollo per l'estero	stamp for a foreign country
timbro	postmark
carta da lettere	writing paper
busta	envelope
indirizzo	address
mittente (m.)	sender
destinatario	addressee, recipient
casella postale	post office box
codice (m.) postale	postal code
postino	mailman
fermo posta	"poste restante"
Dov'è la posta?	Where is the post office?
Dov'è la buca delle lettere?	Where is the mailbox?
andare alla posta	to go to the post office
riscuotere la pensione	to cash the pension check
pagare la bolletta del telefono	to pay the telephone bill
pagare la bolletta della luce	to pay the lighting bill
fare una raccomandata	to send a registered letter
spedire/imbucare una lettera	to mail a letter
fare un telegramma	to send a telegram
affrancare una lettera	to put a stamp on a letter
spedire un pacco	to send a parcel
assicurare un pacco	to insure a parcel
fare un vaglia	to draft a money order
Ecco fatto!	All done!

ESERCIZI

A. *Rispondere affermativamente alle seguenti domande, usando un pronome tonico.*

 1. *Hai parlato al telefono con mio fratello?*
 2. *Hai telefonato ai tuoi genitori?*
 3. *Hai spedito la lettera alla tua amica?*
 4. *Giovanni viene con te alla posta?*
 5. *Scriverai una cartolina anche a me e a Luisa?*

B. *Completare le frasi usando "qualche" o "alcuni/alcune."*

 1. *Dall'Italia ho spedito _____ cartolina.*
 2. *Devo spedire _____ pacchi.*
 3. *Vado alla posta perché devo comprare _____ francobollo.*
 4. *Sono stato alla posta per pagare _____ bollette.*
 5. *Per il compleanno ho ricevuto anche _____ telegrammi.*

C. *Dire all'impiegato dell'ufficio postale che Lei vuole fare le seguenti operazioni. Usare "Vorrei . . ."* (Tell the post office clerk that you want to perform the following transactions. Use *"Vorrei . . ."*)

ESEMPIO: to buy a stamp
 Vorrei comprare un francobollo.

 1. mail a letter
 2. pay the telephone bill
 3. send a registered letter
 4. mail and insure a small parcel
 5. mail a postcard

NOTA CULTURALE

Postage rates in Italy change frequently, following the upward trend in prices. Current rates can generally be obtained at a tobacco shop, where stamps can also be purchased. A postcard requires less postage than a letter. However, you must pay the full letter rate on postcards if they contain more than a simple greeting and a signature.

At the post office you can also send telegrams or cables; pay the house bills; collect, cash, or deposit your pension check; and buy money orders.

CHIAVE PER GLI ESERCIZI

A. 1. *Sì, ho parlato al telefono con lui.* 2. *Sì, ho telefonato a loro.* 3. *Sì, ho spedito la lettera a lei.* 4. *Sì, Giovanni viene con me alla posta.* 5. *Sì, scriverò una cartolina anche a voi (a te e a lei).*
B. 1. *qualche* 2. *alcuni* 3. *qualche* 4. *alcune* 5. *alcuni*
C. 1. *Vorrei spedire/imbucare una lettera.* 2. *Vorrei pagare la bolletta del telefono.* 3. *Vorrei fare una raccomandata.* 4. *Vorrei spedire e assicurare un pacchetto.* 5. *Vorrei spedire una cartolina.*

LEZIONE 24

UN APPUNTAMENTO MEDICO.   A doctor's appointment.

A. DIALOGO

Dal dottore.

SIGNORA MANCINI: **Oggi non sto molto bene: ho la febbre e anche mal di gola e mal di stomaco. Mi gira la testa e mi sento le braccia pesanti. Prima o poi mi verrà l'esaurimento nervoso.**

DOTTORE: **Sta prendendo delle medicine?**

SIGNORA MANCINI: **Sì, sto prendendo queste. Me le ha prescritte Lei. Sto anche seguendo una cura dimagrante. Non sto mangiando molto . . .**

DOTTORE: **Vorrei farLe una serie di accertamenti: una radiografia, l'analisi del sangue . . .**

SIGNORA MANCINI: **Me li farà oggi?**

DOTTORE: **Certo.**

SIGNORA MANCINI: **Mi misura la pressione?**

DOTTORE: **Sì, ora gliela misuro . . . È un po' bassa . . . Prenda queste pillole.**

SIGNORA MANCINI: **Occorre la ricetta?**

DOTTORE: **No, gliene do alcune io . . . Deve prenderne una tre volte al giorno dopo i pasti.**

SIGNORA MANCINI: **E il prossimo appuntamento?**

DOTTORE: **Glielo fisserà la segretaria.**

At the doctor's office.

MRS. MANCINI: I don't feel very well today: I have a fever and a sore throat and stomachache, too. I'm dizzy, and my arms feel heavy. Sooner or later I'm going to have a nervous breakdown.

DOCTOR: Are you taking any medication at the moment?

MRS. MANCINI: Yes, I'm taking these. You prescribed them. I'm also on a diet. I'm not eating much . . .

DOCTOR: I'd like to conduct a series of tests: X rays, blood tests . . .

MRS. MANCINI: Will you conduct them today?

DOCTOR: Of course.

MRS. MANCINI: Are you going to measure my blood pressure?

DOCTOR: Yes, I'll measure it now . . . It's a bit low . . . Take these pills.

MRS. MANCINI: Do I need a prescription?

DOCTOR: No, I'll give you some . . . You must take one three times a day, after meals.

MRS. MANCINI: And the next appointment?

DOCTOR: The secretary will arrange it.

B. GRAMMATICA E SUOI USI

1. DOUBLE OBJECT PRONOUNS

When two object pronouns are used with the same verb, the indirect object pronoun precedes the direct object pronoun. In English, on the other hand, one pronoun is often omitted. Here are the double object pronoun constructions.

IND. OBJ.	+ LO	+ LA	+ LI	+ LE	+ NE
mi	me lo	me la	me li	me le	me ne
ti	te lo	te la	te li	te le	te ne
gli/le/Le	glielo	gliela	glieli	gliele	gliene
ci	ce lo	ce la	ce li	ce le	ce ne
vi	ve lo	ve la	ve li	ve le	ve ne
gli	glielo	gliela	glieli	gliele	gliene
loro	lo . . . loro	la . . . loro	li . . . loro	le . . . loro	ne . . . loro

Glielo dirò fra poco.
I'll tell (it to) you in a while.

224

Gliene do alcune io.
    I'll give you some (of them).

Me l'ha prescritta Lei.
    You prescribed it (to me).

Ora gliela misuro.
    I'll measure it now (for you).

Glielo fisserà la segretaria.
    The secretary will arrange it (for you).

Note that *loro* and *Loro* ("to you, to them") always follow the verb and are never attached to the direct object pronoun.

Il dottore dà loro la medicina.
    The doctor gives them the medicine.

Il dottore la dà loro.
    The doctor gives it to them.

Double object pronouns (*pronomi doppi*) formed with *lo/la* may drop the final vowel before verbs that begin with a vowel sound.

Gliel'ho misurata.
    I measured it.

Gliel'ho prescritta.
    I prescribed it.

Remember that with modal verbs plus infinitives the double object pronouns may either be placed before the modal verb or attached to the end of the infinitive as a suffix (in which case the final -*e* of the infinitive is dropped).

Me lo devi dire./Devi dirmelo.
    You must tell me.

Gliene vuoi parlare tu?/Vuoi parlargliene tu?
    Do you want to speak to her about it?

2. THE PRESENT PROGRESSIVE

Sentences like "I am speaking" and "I am eating" are normally expressed in the present tense: *parlo, mangio*. However, to stress the fact that an action is in progress, Italian uses the verb *stare* plus the gerund.

Sta prendendo delle medicine?
Are you taking any medication?

Non sto mangiando molto.
I'm not eating much.

The gerund of regular verbs is formed by adding the appropriate ending to the root of the verb (infinitive minus *-are/-ere/-ire*).

	INFINITIVE	ENDING	GERUND
first conjugation	*mangiare*	*-ando*	*mangiando*
second conjugation	*prendere*	*-endo*	*prendendo*
third conjugation	*seguire*	*-endo*	*seguendo*

3. THE PLURAL OF NOUNS ENDING IN *-I* AND *-IE*

Singular nouns ending in *-i* and *-ie* are generally feminine and do not change in the plural.

la serie	*le serie*	series
la specie	*le specie*	species, type(s)
la crisi	*le crisi*	crisis, crises
l'analisi	*le analisi*	analysis, analyses

One exception to this rule is the word *la moglie* ("wife"), whose plural is *le mogli*.

4. NOUNS WITH IRREGULAR PLURAL FORMS

A group of singular masculine nouns ending in *-o*, when changed to plural, end in *-a* and become feminine. The majority of them refer to parts of the body.

il braccio	le braccia	arm, arms
il dito	le dita	finger, fingers
il labbro	le labbra	lip, lips
l'osso	le ossa	bone, bones
l'uovo	le uova	egg, eggs
il miglio	le miglia	mile, miles
il paio	le paia	pair, pairs

Mi sento le braccia pesanti.
> My arms feel heavy.

Mi fanno male le dita.
> My fingers hurt.

VOCABOLARIO

appuntamento	appointment
dottore/medico	doctor
Chiamate un medico, per piacere.	Call a doctor, please.
Dov'è l'ospedale?	Where is the hospital?
Ho bisogno di un'ambulanza.	I need an ambulance.
Portatemi al Pronto Soccorso.	Take me to the Emergency Room.
Sono malata(o).	I'm sick.
Non sto bene.	I'm not well.
Mi gira la testa.	My head is spinning.
Mi sento le braccia pesanti.	My arms feel heavy.
Mi sono rotta(o) un dito.	I broke my finger.
Mi sono rotta(o) un braccio.	I broke my arm.
Mi sono rotta(o) il piede.	I broke my foot.
Mi fanno male le orecchie.	My ears hurt.
Ho il diabete.	I have diabetes.
Sono allergica(o) a . . .	I'm allergic to . . .
avere la febbre	to have a fever
avere mal di testa	to have a headache
avere mal di gola	to have a sore throat
avere mal di stomaco	to have a stomachache
esaurimento nervoso	nervous breakdown

Mi misura la pressione?	Are you going to take my blood pressure?
La pressione è bassa.	Your blood pressure is low.
La pressione è alta.	Your blood pressure is high.
seguire una cura dimagrante	to be on a diet
fare degli accertamenti	to conduct tests
analisi del sangue	blood test
analisi dell'urina	urine test
radiografia	X ray
prendere una medicina	to take a medication
tre volte al giorno	three times a day
prima dei pasti	before meals
dopo i pasti	after meals
durante i pasti	during meals
prescrivere una medicina	to prescribe a medication
Occorre la ricetta?	Do I need a prescription?
aspirina	aspirin
pillola	pill
Vorrei fissare un appuntamento.	I would like to make an appointment.
segretaria	secretary
moglie	wife

ESERCIZI

A. *Rispondere alle seguenti domande usando un pronome doppio.*

1. *Il dottore ha prescritto la medicina a Luigi?*
2. *Il dottore ha misurato la pressione alla paziente?*
3. *Voi ci avete dato le pillole?*
4. *Il dottore ha fatto degli accertamenti alla signora?*
5. *La segretaria fisserà l'appuntamento alla signora Carli oggi?*

B. *Trasformare le seguenti frasi usando "stare" e il gerundio.*

ESEMPIO: *Mangio.*
    Sto mangiando.

1. *Seguiamo una cura dimagrante.*
2. *Prendono delle medicine.*
3. *Andate dal dottore.*
4. *Fisso un appuntamento.*
5. *Misuri la pressione.*

C. *Seguire le istruzioni.* (Follow the instructions.)

1. Tell the doctor that you have a fever and a headache.
2. Tell the doctor that you are taking medication.
3. Tell the doctor that you are not eating too much.
4. Tell your patient that you would like to conduct a series of tests.
5. Tell your patient to take these pills.

NOTA CULTURALE

In Italy, medicine is socialized. Doctors' visits are free for all residents, and the price of medicine is relative to one's income. Foreign tourists, however, are not covered and must pay their own medical fees. Many doctors, especially in the larger cities, speak English. Otherwise, American embassies and consulates are often helpful in locating English-speaking doctors. The emergency number for first aid is "113." First aid is available in all hospitals, and in most airports and train stations.

CHIAVE PER GLI ESERCIZI

A. 1. *Sì, gliela (gliel') ha prescritta.* 2. *Sì, gliela (gliel') ha misurata.* 3. *Sì, ve le abbiamo date.* 4. *Sì, glieli ha fatti.* 5. *Sì, glielo fisserà oggi.*
B. 1. *Stiamo seguendo una cura dimagrante.* 2. *Stanno prendendo delle medicine.* 3. *State andando dal dottore.* 4. *Sto fissando un appuntamento.* 5. *Stai misurando la pressione.*
C. 1. *Ho la febbre e mal di testa.* 2. *Sto prendendo delle medicine.* 3. *Non sto mangiando molto.* 4. *Vorrei farLe una serie di accertamenti.* 5. *Prenda queste pillole.*

LEZIONE 25

LE MACCHINE.   Cars.

A. DIALOGO

1. Un meccanico in casa.

ROBERTA: **Papà, sii gentile! Dammi una mano!**

SIGNOR RANIERI: **Dimmi!**

ROBERTA: **La mia Fiat Uno perde olio e il motore scalda.**

SIGNOR RANIERI: **Fammela vedere. Mettiti in macchina. Metti in moto. Accelera! Basta così!**

ROBERTA: **Allora?**

SIGNOR RANIERI: **Aspetta un attimo. Abbi pazienza! Fammi vedere. Dammi quella chiave!**

ROBERTA: **L'hai aggiustata?**

SIGNOR RANIERI: **Penso di sì.**

ROBERTA: **Andiamo a fare un giro!**

SIGNOR RANIERI: **Okay, però va' piano. Non guidare velocemente! Sta' attenta!**

A mechanic at home.

ROBERTA: Daddy, be nice! Give me a hand!

MR. RANIERI: What is it? (Tell me.)

ROBERTA: My Fiat Uno is leaking oil, and the engine is overheating.

MR. RANIERI: Let me take a look. Get in the car. Turn on the engine. Accelerate! That's enough!

ROBERTA: So?

MR. RANIERI: Wait a second. Be patient! Let me see. Give me that wrench!

ROBERTA: Did you fix it?

MR. RANIERI: I think so.

ROBERTA: Let's go for a ride!

MR. RANIERI: Okay, but go slowly. Don't drive fast! Be careful!

---

2. *Alla stazione di servizio.*

BENZINAIO: **Dica?**

SIGNORA: **Faccia il pieno, per favore.**

BENZINAIO: **Super? Normale?**

SIGNORA: **Super.**

BENZINAIO: **Controllo l'olio?**

SIGNORA: **Sì, lo controlli.**

BENZINAIO: **Spenga il motore, per piacere.**

SIGNORA: **Ecco fatto.**

BENZINAIO: **Bisogna cambiare l'olio.**

SIGNORA: **Okay, lo cambi. Senta, c'è un meccanico qui vicino?**

BENZINAIO: **Sì. Vada sempre dritto, poi al semaforo giri a destra
. . . È proprio lì all'angolo. Non dimentichi di girare a destra . . .**

At the gas station.

ATTENDANT: Yes?

WOMAN: Fill it up, please.

ATTENDANT: Super? Regular?

WOMAN: Super.

ATTENDANT: Should I check the oil?

WOMAN: Yes, check it.

ATTENDANT: Turn off the engine, please.

WOMAN: Done.

ATTENDANT: The oil needs changing.

WOMAN: Okay, change it. Excuse me, is there a mechanic close by?

ATTENDANT: Yes. Go straight, then turn right at the light . . . It's right there on the corner . . . Don't forget to turn right . . .

B. GRAMMATICA E SUOI USI

1. THE IMPERATIVE OF IRREGULAR VERBS

to go	*andare*	*va', vada, andiamo, andate, vadano*
to give	*dare*	*da', dia, diamo, date, diano*
to say	*dire*	*di', dica, diciamo, dite, dicano*
to do, to make	*fare*	*fa', faccia, facciamo, fate, facciano*
to know	*sapere*	*sappi, sappia, sappiamo, sappiate, sappiano*
to turn off	*spegnere*	*spegni, spenga, spegniamo, spegnete, spengano*
to stay	*stare*	*sta', stia, stiamo, state, stiano*
to go out	*uscire*	*esci, esca, usciamo, uscite, escano*
to come	*venire*	*vieni, venga, veniamo, venite, vengano*

Va' piano!
   Go slowly.

Faccia il pieno.
   Fill it up.

Spenga il motore.
   Turn off the engine.

Note that the *noi* and *voi* forms of these verbs (except *sapere)* are identical to their respective present tense forms.

Andiamo a casa.
   Let's go home./We're going home.

2. THE IMPERATIVE WITH PRONOUNS

For the position of pronouns (direct, indirect, double, reflexive, *ci, ne*) with the imperative, follow this scheme:

for the *tu/noi/voi* forms: pronoun is attached to the end of the verb

for *Lei/Loro* forms: pronoun precedes the verb

Scrivile.
> Write to her.

Lo faccia.
> Do it.

Diglielo.
> Tell it to him/her/them.

When any pronoun (except *gli)* is attached to one of these five verb forms—*da', di', fa', sta',* and *va'*—the first letter of the pronoun is doubled.

Falla vedere a me.
> Let me see it.

Dimmelo.
> Tell me.

Vacci subito.
> Go there right away.

3. THE NEGATIVE IMPERATIVE WITH PRONOUNS

To place pronouns correctly in a negative imperative sentence, follow this scheme:

tu form: pronoun precedes or is attached to the end of the infinitive (drop -*e*)

noi/voi forms: pronoun precedes or is attached to the end of the imperative verb

Lei/Loro forms: pronoun precedes the verb

Non andarci./Non ci andare.
   Don't go there.

Non lo fate./Non fatelo.
   Don't do it.

Non glielo dica.
   Don't tell her.

4. THE WORD *MANO*

Even though it ends in *-o, mano* ("hand") is feminine and has an irregular plural form: *le mani.*

Dammi una mano, per piacere.
   Give me a hand, please.

Le mie mani sono sporche.
   My hands are dirty.

VOCABOLARIO

meccanico	mechanic
stazione (f.) **di servizio**	gas station
Può darmi un passaggio fino alla stazione di servizio?	Can you give me a ride to the gas station?
Sono rimasto senza benzina.	I'm out of gas.
benzinaio	gas station attendant
fare benzina	to get gas
Faccia il pieno, per favore.	Fill it up, please.
Benzina super *(normale, senza piombo/verde)*	super (regular, unleaded) gas
Può controllare l'olio, per favore?	Can you check the oil, please?
Può pulirmi il parabrezza, per favore?	Can you clean the windshield, please?
C'è un meccanico qui vicino?	Is there a mechanic nearby?
La macchina perde olio.	The car is leaking oil.
Il motore scalda.	The engine is overheating.

Può cambiare l'olio?	Can you change the oil?
Può cambiare il filtro?	Can you change the filter?
Controlli i freni, per favore.	Can you check the brakes, please?
La freccia non funziona.	The turn signal doesn't work.
La macchina non si mette in moto.	The car won't start.
mettere la prima	to put in first gear
mettere la seconda	to put in second gear
La terza non ingrana.	The car won't go into third gear.
Ho le gomme a terra.	My tires are low.
Mi può riparare la gomma?	Can you repair my tire?
Spenga il motore, per piacere.	Turn off the engine, please.
aggiustare la macchina	to fix the car
mettere in moto	to start the car
accelerare	to accelerate
frenare	to put on the brakes
frizione (f.)	clutch
cambio	gear
chiave (f.)	wrench
Andiamo a fare un giro.	Let's go for a ride.
Va' piano.	Go slowly.
Non guidare velocemente!	Don't drive fast!
Sta' attento!	Be careful!
Dammi una mano!	Give me a hand!

ESERCIZI

A. *Cambiare i seguenti comandi dalla forma familiare alla forma di cortesia.*

1. *Fammi vedere la macchina.*
2. *Dammi quella chiave.*
3. *Sta' attento.*
4. *Va' piano!*
5. *Spegni la macchina.*

B. *Sostituire le parole sottolineate con un pronome.*

1. *Metti la macchina in moto.*
2. *Cambia l'olio.*
3. *Mi dia la chiave.*
4. *Controlli la frizione.*
5. *Fa' vedere la macchina al meccanico.*

C. *Cambiare i seguenti comandi alla forma affermativa.*

1. *Non accelerare.*
2. *Non aggiustarla.*
3. *Non la metta in moto.*
4. *Non lo cambi.*
5. *Non andare dritto.*

NOTA CULTURALE

Driving in Italy is made easy by the extensive *autostrada* (toll highway) network connecting all major towns. These roads are complemented by equally well-maintained *superstrade* (highways), which are free of tolls. When you enter an *autostrada,* you are issued a ticket that must be presented when exiting the highway to determine the amount of your toll. It's quite expensive.

In most Italian towns the use of the car horn is prohibited in certain areas designated by a large notice reading *zona di silenzio.* Parking in a *zona disco* is permitted for limited periods of time, and parking discs *(dischi rossi)* can be purchased at gas stations. You should observe the following speed restrictions: 50 km/h in metropolitan areas, 130 km/h on highways, and 100 km/h on all other roads.

The Italian Automobile Club *(ACI)* has branches in all major towns as well as information offices at most border crossings and will be able to help you with any motoring problems you may have.

Gas stations are usually closed for a couple of hours at lunchtime and after 7:00 P.M. Only a few gas stations are open on Sundays. However, many gas stations have a computerized self-service system. Gas stations on the highways usually provide 24-hour service.

Italy uses the metric system. A U.S. gallon is approximately equal to 3.7 liters; an Imperial gallon is about 4.2 liters. One mile is equivalent to 1.6 kilometers.

A. 1. *Mi faccia vedere la macchina.* 2. *Mi dia quella chiave.* 3. *Stia attento.* 4. *Vada piano!* 5. *Spenga la macchina.*

B. 1. *Mettila in moto.* 2. *Cambialo.* 3. *Me la dia.* 4. *La controlli.* 5. *Fagliela vedere.*

C. 1. *Accelera.* 2. *Aggiustala.* 3. *La metta in moto.* 4. *Lo cambi.* 5. *Va' dritto.*

QUINTO RIPASSO

A. *Rispondere affermativamente usando "stare" e il gerundio.*

ESEMPIO: *Cosa fate, studiate?*
   Sì, stiamo studiando.

1. *Cosa fa Maria, legge?*
2. *Cosa fai, bevi il caffè?*
3. *Cosa fanno Roberto e Riccardo, escono?*
4. *Cosa fai, scrivi a Paolo?*
5. *Cosa fai, ascolti la radio?*

B. *Cambiare le frasi al futuro, incominciando le nuove frasi con "domani."* (Rewrite the following sentences in the future tense, starting the new sentences with *domani.*)

1. *Oggi vado a scuola. La mia amica Paola viene con me.*
2. *Ora mangiamo una pizza e beviamo un caffè.*
3. *Oggi non posso venire con te perché devo lavorare.*
4. *Stasera loro finiscono il lavoro.*
5. *Oggi Sergio parte per un viaggio.*
6. *Oggi noi non usciamo: stiamo a casa.*

C. *Usare le seguenti parole per completare le frasi.*

qualche   ci   conosci   delle   so   braccia

1. *Tu* _____ *bene Paola?*
2. *C'è il signor Smith?—Non lo* _____.
3. *Dove vai?—Alla posta. Devo spedire* _____ *cartolina e* _____ *lettere.*

4. *Non sto bene. Ho la febbre e mi sento le* _____ *pesanti.*

5. *Pensi all'Italia?—Sì,* _____ *penso sempre.*

D. *Rispondere affermativamente alle domande usando un pronome doppio.*

1. *Ti ho dato i biglietti?*
2. *Hai dato il cappotto a Paolo?*
3. *Avete spedito la lettera ai vostri genitori?*
4. *Per favore, mi compri il giornale?*
5. *Vi hanno misurato la pressione?*
6. *Mi dai la medicina stasera?*

E. *Tradurre.*

1. Roberto, go to school.
2. Miss, tell me.
3. Paolo, don't phone him.
4. Daddy, give me that book.
5. John, do your homework.
6. Miss Smith, come here, please.
7. Red is my favorite color.
8. French is a beautiful language.

CHIAVE PER GLI ESERCIZI

A. 1. *Sì, sta leggendo.* 2. *Sì, sto bevendo il caffè.* 3. *Sì, stanno uscendo.* 4. *Sì, sto scrivendo a Paolo.* 5. *Sì, sto ascoltando la radio.*

B. 1. *Domani andrò a scuola. La mia amica Paola verrà con me.* 2. *Domani mangeremo una pizza e berremo un caffè.* 3. *Domani non potrò venire con te perché dovrò lavorare.* 4. *Domani loro finiranno il lavoro.* 5. *Domani Sergio partirà per un viaggio.* 6. *Domani noi non usciremo: staremo a casa.*

C. 1. *conosci* 2. *so* 3. *qualche, delle* 4. *braccia* 5. *ci*

D. 1. *Sì, me li hai dati.* 2. *Sì, gliel'ho dato.* 3. *Sì, gliel'abbiamo spedita./Sì, l'abbiamo spedita loro.* 4. *Sì, te lo compro.* 5. *Sì, ce l'hanno misurata.* 6. *Sì, te la do.*

E. 1. *Roberto, va' a scuola.* 2. *Signorina, mi dica.* 3. *Paolo, non gli telefonare./ Non telefonargli.* 4. *Papà, dammi quel libro.* 5. *John, fa' i compiti.* 6. *Signorina Smith, venga qui, per favore.* 7. *Il rosso è il mio colore preferito/ favorito.* 8. *Il francese è una bella lingua.*

LEZIONE 26

LE ARTI.   The arts.

A. DIALOGO

Al cinema o all'opera?

MARIO: **Che film davano ieri?**

GIULIA: **Un film di Fellini, il tuo regista preferito.**

MARIO: **È vero, quando ero giovane andavo sempre a vedere i suoi film.**

GIULIA: **E allora perché non sei venuto?**

MARIO: **Volevo venire, ma non ho potuto. Stavo per uscire quando mi ha telefonato Carla. Voleva andare all'opera.**

GIULIA: **E ci sei andato?**

MARIO: **Sì, ma che giornataccia!**

GIULIA: **Perché?**

MARIO: **Mentre aspettavamo in fila per i biglietti, è cominciato a piovere. Pioveva a dirotto e non avevamo nemmeno un ombrello.**

GIULIA: **Tutto qui?**

MARIO: **Quando siamo arrivati al botteghino non riuscivo a trovare i soldi. Poi finalmente li ho trovati . . .**

GIULIA: **E lo spettacolo?**

MARIO: **Bellissimo! Fantastica la messinscena. Bravissimi i cantanti. Pavarotti è un tenore stupendo.**

GIULIA: **E il direttore d'orchestra?**

MARIO: **È stato impeccabile.**

To the movies or to the opera?

MARIO: What movie were they showing yesterday?

GIULIA: A film by Fellini, your favorite director.

MARIO: That's true. When I was young I always used to go to see his films.

GIULIA: Then why didn't you come?

MARIO: I wanted to come, but I couldn't. I was about to go out when Carla phoned me. She wanted to go to the opera.

GIULIA: And did you go?

MARIO: Yes, but what a terrible day!

GIULIA: Why?

MARIO: While we were waiting in line for the tickets, it started to rain. It was raining cats and dogs, and we didn't even have an umbrella.

GIULIA: Is that all?

MARIO: When we got to the ticket booth, I couldn't find my money. Then I finally found it . . .

GIULIA: And the show?

MARIO: Wonderful! The staging was fantastic. The singers were great. Pavarotti is a great tenor.

GIULIA: And the conductor?

MARIO: He was impeccable.

B. GRAMMATICA E SUOI USI

1. THE IMPERFECT OF REGULAR VERBS

The imperfect (*l'imperfetto*) is also known as the past descriptive tense. In English it is expressed in the following way:

We were speaking Italian.
We used to speak Italian.

The imperfect has the same endings for all three verb groups. It is formed by dropping the *-re* of the infinitive and adding the following endings to the stem: *-vo, -vi, -va, -vamo, -vate, -vano.*

	PARLARE	TO SPEAK
I used to speak	*io*	*parlavo*
you used to speak (familiar)	*tu*	*parlavi*
he used to speak	*lui*	*parlava*
she used to speak	*lei*	*parlava*
you used to speak (polite)	*Lei*	*parlava*
we used to speak	*noi*	*parlavamo*
you used to speak (familiar or polite)	*voi*	*parlavate*
they used to speak	*loro*	*parlavano*
you used to speak (polite)	*Loro*	*parlavano*

Parlava molto.
> He used to talk a lot.

Aspettavamo in fila.
> We were waiting in line.

	PRENDERE	TO TAKE
I used to take	*io*	*prendevo*
you used to take (familiar)	*tu*	*prendevi*
he used to take	*lui*	*prendeva*
she used to take	*lei*	*prendeva*
you used to take (polite)	*Lei*	*prendeva*
we used to take	*noi*	*prendevamo*
you used to take (familiar or polite)	*voi*	*prendevate*
they used to take	*loro*	*prendevano*
you used to take (polite)	*Loro*	*prendevano*

Pioveva molto.
> It was raining a lot.

Prendevo sempre l'autobus.
> I always used to take the bus.

DORMIRE	TO SLEEP	
I used to sleep	*io*	*dormivo*
you used to sleep (familiar)	*tu*	*dormivi*
he used to sleep	*lui*	*dormiva*
she used to sleep	*lei*	*dormiva*
you used to sleep (polite)	*Lei*	*dormiva*
we used to sleep	*noi*	*dormivamo*
you used to sleep (familiar or polite)	*voi*	*dormivate*
they used to sleep	*loro*	*dormivano*
you used to sleep (polite)	*Loro*	*dormivano*

Non riuscivo a trovare i biglietti.
I couldn't find the tickets.

Alle otto dormivo.
At eight o'clock, I was sleeping.

2. THE IMPERFECT OF *AVERE* AND *ESSERE*

The auxiliary verb *avere* is regular in the imperfect.

AVERE	TO HAVE	
I used to have	*io*	*avevo*
you used to have (familiar)	*tu*	*avevi*
he used to have	*lui*	*aveva*
she used to have	*lei*	*aveva*
you used to have (polite)	*Lei*	*aveva*
we used to have	*noi*	*avevamo*
you used to have (familiar or polite)	*voi*	*avevate*
they used to have	*loro*	*avevano*
you used to have (polite)	*Loro*	*avevano*

Avevo fame.
I was hungry.

Avevate sete.
You were thirsty.

Essere is irregular in the imperfect.

	ESSERE	TO BE
I used to be	io	ero
you used to be (familiar)	tu	eri
he used to be	lui	era
she used to be	lei	era
you used to be (polite)	Lei	era
we used to be	noi	eravamo
you used to be (familiar or polite)	voi	eravate
they used to be	loro	erano
you used to be (polite)	Loro	erano

Era tardi.
   It was late.

Fellini era il mio regista preferito.
   Fellini was my favorite director.

3. THE IMPERFECT OF *BERE, DIRE,* AND *FARE*

Bere, dire, and *fare* have irregular stems (*beve-, dice-, face-*) in the imperfect, but their endings are regular.

to drink	bere	bevevo, bevevi, beveva,
		bevevamo, bevevate, bevevano
to say, to tell	dire	dicevo, dicevi, diceva,
		dicevamo, dicevate, dicevano
to do, to make	fare	facevo, facevi, faceva,
		facevamo, facevate, facevano

Faceva freddo.
   It was cold.

Non diceva niente.
   He wasn't saying anything.

Bevevo molto.
   I used to drink a lot.

4. USES OF THE IMPERFECT

The imperfect is used to describe a continued or habitual action in the past.

Quando ero giovane, andavo al cinema tutte le settimane.
When I was young, I used to go to the movies every week.

The imperfect also describes an action that was occurring in the past, while something else was happening or happened.

Mentre aspettavamo, si è messo a piovere.
While we were waiting, it started raining.

Mentre mangiava, guardava la televisione.
While she was eating, she was watching television.

And finally, the imperfect expresses mental and physical states in the past, as well as time, age, and weather conditions.

Avevo sete.
I was thirsty.

Era l'una.
It was one o'clock.

Quando avevo 18 anni, ero molto ottimista.
When I was 18 years old I was very optimistic.

Pioveva a dirotto.
It was raining cats and dogs.

5. *STARE PER* PLUS INFINITIVE

Stare per plus an infinitive translates into English as "to be about to" do something.

Stavo per uscire.
I was about to go out.

Stiamo per mangiare.
We're about to eat.

6. THE PLURAL OF NOUNS AND ADJECTIVES ENDING IN *-ISTA*

Nouns ending in *-ista* generally refer to a profession and can be either masculine or feminine. In the singular they have only one form (*-ista*) for both genders. In the plural, if masculine, they end in *-isti;* if feminine, in *-iste.*

il regista (m.)	*i registi*	director(s)
la regista (f.)	*le registe*	director(s)
il protagonista (m.)	*i protagonisti*	protagonist(s)
la protagonista (f.)	*le protagoniste*	protagonist(s)
il pianista (m.)	*i pianisti*	pianist(s)
la pianista (f.)	*le pianiste*	pianist(s)

Il pianista è bravo.
> The pianist is good.

I pianisti sono bravi.
> The pianists are good.

La pianista è brava.
> The pianist is good.

Le pianiste sono brave.
> The pianists are good.

The word *atleta* (athlete) follows the same pattern.

l'atleta (m.)	*gli atleti*	athlete(s)
l'atleta (f.)	*le atlete*	athlete(s)

Adjectives in *-ista* follow the same pattern as the nouns.

un ragazzo ottimista	an optimistic boy
dei ragazzi ottimisti	optimistic boys
una ragazza ottimista	an optimistic girl
delle ragazze ottimiste	optimistic girls

VOCABOLARIO

arte (f.), *le arti*	art, the arts
andare al cinema *(a teatro, all'opera)*	to go to the movies (to the theater, to the opera)
Che film danno?	What movie are they showing?
A che ora inizia lo spettacolo?	At what time does the show begin?
A che ora termina lo spettacolo?	At what time does the show end?
assistere ad uno spettacolo	to attend a show
aspettare in fila	to wait in line
botteghino	ticket booth
biglietto	ticket
messinscena	staging
fare la parte di	to play the part of
protagonista (m./f.)	protagonist
attore (m.)	actor
attrice (f.)	actress
regista (m./f.)	director
tenore (m.)	tenor
direttore (m.) **d'orchestra**	conductor
ballerina	ballerina
balletto	ballet
commedia	comedy
tragedia	tragedy
dramma (m.)	dramatic play
palcoscenico	stage
sipario	curtain
trama	plot
recitare	to recite, to perform
applaudire	to applaud
Lo spettacolo era *(è stato)* **stupendo.**	The show/performance was wonderful.
Il tenore era *(è stato)* **bravissimo.**	The tenor was great.
La messinscena era *(è stata)* **fantastica.**	The staging was fantastic.

246

Il direttore d'orchestra è stato impeccabile.	The conductor was impeccable.
Il mio attore preferito è . . .	My favorite actor is . . .
La mia attrice preferita è . . .	My favorite actress is . . .
È un film ottimista.	It's an optimistic movie.
È un film pessimista.	It's a pessimistic film.
Il pianista era *(è stato)* eccezionale.	The pianist was exceptional.
stare per	to be about to
Tutto qui?	Is that all?

ESERCIZI

A. *Cambiare le frasi al plurale.*

1. *Quel regista era molto bravo.*
2. *La pianista è stata impeccabile.*
3. *Questo film è troppo pessimista.*
4. *Quel ragazzo è ottimista.*
5. *La protagonista è stata stupenda.*

B. *Completare con il verbo fra parentesi all'imperfetto.*

1. *Che film _____ ieri sera? (dare)*
2. *Loro _____ sempre al cinema. (andare)*
3. *Bertolucci _____ il mio regista preferito. (essere)*
4. *Noi _____ andare al cinema. (volere)*
5. *Quel giorno _____. (piovere)*

C. *Completare, scegliendo tra il passato prossimo e l'imperfetto.* (Complete the sentences choosing between the present perfect and the imperfect.)

1. *Quando Carla _____ (essere) giovane, _____ (andare) spesso a teatro.*
2. *C'_____ (essere) la fila per entrare, pioveva e noi non _____ (avere) l'ombrello.*
3. *Noi volevamo venire, ma non _____ (potere).*
4. *Tu _____ (stare) per uscire, quando ha telefonato Carla.*
5. *Ieri voi _____ (assistere) ad un bello spettacolo?*

NOTA CULTURALE

The performing arts, particularly the opera, are an essential part of Italian culture. The celebrated *Teatro alla Scala* in Milan is perhaps the most famous opera house in the world. In the summer, spectacular operas are performed outdoors at the *Arena Sferisterio* in Macerata (July) and the *Terme di Caracalla* in Rome (July/August). In the *Arena di Verona,* before the performance begins, it is customary for the audience to light up small candles that flicker like stars.

Two of the most important festivals of the performing arts—featuring art exhibits, opera, ballet, and theater performances—are the *Maggio Musicale Fiorentino* in Florence and the Festival of Two Worlds in Spoleto.

Italy is also a leader in cinematic art and hosts several important film festivals. The most famous is the Venice International Film Festival, the oldest in the world. Also notable are the Florence Film Festival and the International Film Festival in Taormina, Sicily.

CHIAVE PER GLI ESERCIZI

A. 1. *Quei registi erano molto bravi.* 2. *Le pianiste sono state impeccabili.* 3. *Questi film sono troppo pessimisti.* 4. *Quei ragazzi sono ottimisti.* 5. *Le protagoniste sono state stupende.*

B. 1. *davano* 2. *andavano* 3. *era* 4. *volevamo* 5. *pioveva*

C. 1. *era, andava* 2. *era, avevamo* 3. *abbiamo potuto* 4. *stavi* 5. *avete assistito.*

LEZIONE 27

LA MUSICA. Music.

A. DIALOGO

Un concerto di Baglioni.

ANTONIO: **Sono stato a vedere lo spettacolo di Claudio Baglioni. Lo conosci?**

MARY: **Certo. È un cantautore molto bravo. L'ho visto in un programma televisivo in America e subito sono diventata una sua fan.**

ANTONIO: **Va bene, me l'avevi già detto!**

MARY: **Ho tutti i suoi dischi. Amo ascoltare la sua musica. Ma dove è stato il concerto?**

ANTONIO: **Al teatro Ariston di Sanremo.**

MARY: **Eri mai stato ad un suo concerto prima?**

ANTONIO: **Sì, c'ero già andato due anni fa. Ora però c'era anche un gruppo che non avevo avuto ancora occasione di vedere.**

MARY: **Ha cantato canzoni del suo ultimo album?**

ANTONIO: **Il suo ultimo hit. La sua musica però è un po' cambiata.**

MARY: **L'avevo già notato nel suo ultimo video.**

A Baglioni concert.

ANTONIO: I went to see Claudio Baglioni's concert. Do you know him?

MARY: Of course. He's a very good singer-songwriter. I saw him on a television program in America, and I instantly became his fan.

ANTONIO: That's right, you had already told me!

MARY: I have all his records. I love listening to his music. Where was the concert?

ANTONIO: At the *Ariston* theater in Sanremo.

MARY: Had you ever been to one of his concerts before?

ANTONIO: Yes, I had gone to one two years ago. But this time there was also a group that I hadn't had an opportunity to see yet.

MARY: Did he sing any songs from his latest album?

ANTONIO: His latest hit. But his music has changed a bit.

MARY: I had already noticed it in his latest video.

B. GRAMMATICA E SUOI USI

1. THE PLUPERFECT INDICATIVE

The pluperfect indicative (*il trapassato prossimo*) is used to indicate an event that happened prior to another event in the past. It consists of the imperfect of *avere* or *essere* plus the past participle of the main verb. The use of the auxiliaries *avere* and *essere* is determined as with the present perfect tense: transitive verbs take *avere,* and intransitive verbs (usually verbs of motion) take *essere.*

	PARLARE	TO SPEAK
I had spoken	*io*	*avevo parlato*
you had spoken (familiar)	*tu*	*avevi parlato*
he had spoken	*lui*	*aveva parlato*
she had spoken	*lei*	*aveva parlato*
you had spoken (polite)	*Lei*	*aveva parlato*
we had spoken	*noi*	*avevamo parlato*
you had spoken (familiar or polite)	*voi*	*avevate parlato*
they had spoken	*loro*	*avevano parlato*
you had spoken (polite)	*Loro*	*avevano parlato*

Me l'avevi già detto.
  You had already told me.

L'avevo già notato.
  I had already noticed it.

ANDARE		TO GO
I had gone	io	ero andato/a
you had gone (familiar)	tu	eri andato/a
he had gone	lui	era andato
she had gone	lei	era andata
you had gone (polite)	Lei	era andato/a
we had gone	noi	eravamo andati/e
you had gone (familiar or polite)	voi	eravate andati/e
they had gone	loro	erano andati/e
you had gone (polite)	Loro	erano andati/e

Ero già andato ad un suo concerto.
I had already been to one of his concerts.

Il disco era già uscito.
The record had already come out.

2. THE PLUPERFECT OF *AVERE* AND *ESSERE*

AVERE		TO HAVE
I had had	io	avevo avuto
you had had (familiar)	tu	avevi avuto
he had had	lui	aveva avuto
she had had	lei	aveva avuto
you had had (polite)	Lei	aveva avuto
we had had	noi	avevamo avuto
you had had (familiar or polite)	voi	avevate avuto
they had had	loro	avevano avuto
you had had (polite)	Loro	avevano avuto

Non avevo avuto ancora occasione di vedere quel gruppo.
I hadn't had the opportunity to see that group yet.

	ESSERE	TO BE
I had been	*io*	*ero stato/a*
you had been (familiar)	*tu*	*eri stato/a*
he had been	*lui*	*era stato*
she had been	*lei*	*era stata*
you had been (polite)	*Lei*	*era stato/a*
we had been	*noi*	*eravamo stati/e*
you had been (familiar or polite)	*voi*	*eravate stati/e*
they had been	*loro*	*erano stati/e*
you had been (polite)	*Loro*	*erano stati/e*

Non ero mai stato ad un concerto.
I had never been to a concert.

Erano già stati a Sanremo.
They had already been in Sanremo.

3. USE OF THE INFINITIVE AS A NOUN

In Italian the infinitive can be used as a noun, in which case it is considered masculine and singular. In English, this construction is often expressed with the "-ing" form of the verb.

Amo ascoltare le sue canzoni.
I love listening to his songs.

Andare all'opera è la mia passione.
Going to the opera is my passion.

Non mi piace ballare.
I don't like dancing.

4. MASCULINE NOUNS ENDING IN -A

Usually, singular nouns ending in *-a* are feminine.* Some, however, are masculine. They are often words of Greek origin, and most of them end in *-ma,* and form their plural in *-i.*

* Please see lesson 2 for more information.

il problema	*i problemi*	problem(s)
il telegramma	*i telegrammi*	telegram(s)
il programma	*i programmi*	program(s)

The word *cinema* (movie theater) is an abbreviated form of *cinematografo* and is also masculine. It does not change in the plural.

il cinema	*i cinema*	movie theater(s)

VOCABOLARIO

concerto	concert
andare ad un concerto di . . .	to go to a concert by . . .
Dov'è il concerto?	Where is the concert held?
concerto all'aperto	open-air concert
festival della canzone (m.)	Song Festival
cantante (m./f.)	singer
cantautore (m./f.)	singer-songwriter
gruppo/complesso	musical group
musicista (m./f.)	musician
musica	music
cantare una canzone	to sing a song
disco	record
l'ultimo album *(hit, CD, video)*	the latest album (hit, CD, video)
incidere un disco	to cut a record
registrare	to record
registratore (m.)	tape recorder
cassetta	cassette
strumento musicale	musical instrument
musica classica	classical music
musica leggera	pop music
musica rock	rock music
musica di . . .	music by . . .
parole di . . .	lyrics by . . .
fare una tournée	to go on tour
suonare il violino	to play the violin
suonare la chitarra	to play the guitar

pubblico	public, audience
successo	success
chiedere il bis	to ask for an encore
concedere un bis	to give an encore
essere un *(una)* **fan di** . . .	to be a fan of . . .
la discoteca	discotheque
juke-box	jukebox
ascoltare una canzone	to listen to a song
ballare il rock	to dance to rock and roll
ballare il liscio	to dance to a slow song

ESERCIZI

A. *Rispondere negativamente alle domande usando il trapassato prossimo.*

ESEMPIO: Quando sono arrivato, tu dovevi ancora vedere lo spettacolo?
No, avevo già visto lo spettacolo.

1. *Quando sono arrivato, tu dovevi ancora andare al concerto?*
2. *Quando sono arrivato, voi dovevate ancora andare al cinema?*
3. *Quando sono arrivato, lui doveva ancora cantare?*
4. *Quando sono arrivato, tu dovevi ancora ascoltare il disco?*
5. *Quando sono arrivato, quel gruppo doveva ancora fare una tournée in America?*

B. *Eliminare la parola che non appartiene al gruppo.* (Cross out the word which does not belong to the group.)

1. *cantante / professore / cantautore*
2. *concerto / spettacolo / lezione*
3. *mangiare / ballare / cantare*
4. *disco / aranciata / compact disc*
5. *il violino / la chitarra / il libro*

C. *Tradurre.*

1. He had already told me.
2. You (familiar, singular) had already heard that record.
3. We hadn't had the opportunity to see that group.

4. Going to the opera is my passion.
5. I heard his song on a television program in Italy.

NOTA CULTURALE

The Festival of Sanremo (near Genoa) is the most famous festival of Italian popular music. It takes place every year, usually during the month of February. The three-day festival is a competition for the best song of the year. The most famous Italian popular musicians appear at the festival, and some songs achieve international acclaim. Favorite performers at Sanremo include Peppino di Capri, *Ricchi e Poveri*, Anna Oxa, Al Bano and Romina Power, Toto Cutugno, and Marcella Bella.

CHIAVE PER GLI ESERCIZI

A. 1. *No, ero già andato/a al concerto.* 2. *No, eravamo già andati/e al cinema.* 3. *No, aveva già cantato.* 4. *No, avevo già ascoltato il disco.* 5. *No, aveva già fatto una tournée in America.*
B. 1. *professore* 2. *lezione* 3. *mangiare* 4. *aranciata* 5. *il libro*
C. 1. *Me l'aveva già detto.* 2. *Tu avevi già sentito quel disco.* 3. *Non avevamo avuto l'occasione di vedere quel gruppo.* 4. *Andare all'opera è la mia passione.* 5. *Ho sentito la sua canzone in un programma televisivo in Italia.*

LEZIONE 28

FRUTTA E VERDURA.   Fruits and vegetables.

A. DIALOGO

Al mercato.

FRUTTIVENDOLO: Frutta! Verdura! Ciliege! Fragole! Pomodori! Spinaci! Fagiolini! La roba più fresca del mondo! Signora, guardi queste fragole: sono buonissime.

SIGNORA MARINI: Le ciliege mi sembrano più buone delle fragole. Quanto costano?

FRUTTIVENDOLO: Cinquemila lire al chilo . . .

SIGNORA MARINI: Troppo!

FRUTTIVENDOLO: Alla bancarella di fronte sono più care.

SIGNORA MARINI: E le fragole?

FRUTTIVENDOLO: Più o meno quanto le ciliege. Le mele e le arance, però, sono meno costose e sono molto buone.

SIGNORA MARINI: Perché costano meno?

FRUTTIVENDOLO: In questo periodo ci sono più mele e arance che ciliege e fragole.

SIGNORA MARINI: Compro due chili di mele. Ai miei bambini piacciono più le mele che le arance. E poi le mele fanno bene, vero?

FRUTTIVENDOLO: Certo: "Una mela al giorno toglie il medico di torno!" Vuole anche della verdura?

SIGNORA MARINI: No, grazie.

At the open market.

FRUIT VENDOR: Fruits! Vegetables! Cherries! Strawberries! Tomatoes! Spinach! String beans! The freshest stuff in the world! Madame, look at these strawberries: they're very good.

MRS. MARINI: The cherries seem to be better than the strawberries. How much do they cost?

FRUIT VENDOR: Five thousand lire a kilo . . .

MRS. MARINI: Too much!

FRUIT VENDOR: At the stand in front they're more expensive.

MRS. MARINI: And the strawberries?

FRUIT VENDOR: They cost more or less the same as the cherries. However, the apples and oranges are less expensive, and they're very good.

MRS. MARINI: Why do they cost less?

FRUIT VENDOR: Because at this time of year there are more apples and oranges than strawberries and cherries.

MRS. MARINI: I'll take two kilos of apples. My children like apples more than oranges. And apples are good for you, right?

FRUIT VENDOR: Of course: "An apple a day keeps the doctor away!" Would you also like some vegetables?

MRS. MARINI: No, thank you.

B. GRAMMATICA E SUOI USI

1. COMPARISONS

In Italian comparisons are expressed as follows:

più . . . di/che	more . . . than
meno . . . di/che	less . . . than
così . . . come	as . . . as
tanto . . . quanto	as . . . as

Più and *meno* can be used in conjunction with either *di* or *che*. *Di* (or *di* plus article, when necessary) is used when comparing two different things. *Che* must be used if the comparison is between two qualities of the same thing, two adjectives, two verbs, or two adverbs.

Le ciliege sono più buone delle fragole.
Cherries are better than strawberries.

Ci sono più mele che arance.
There are more apples than oranges.

La mela è più verde che rossa.
The apple is more green than red.

If the second term of the comparison is a pronoun, the direct object form of the pronoun should be used.

Franco è più alto di me.
Frank is taller than I (me).

Io sono più intelligente di lui.
I'm more intelligent than he (him).

2. THE RELATIVE SUPERLATIVE

The relative superlative compares two or more things; it expresses the greatest or least degree of something.

the richest woman (of the group)
the most intelligent student (in the class)
the least successful person (of those I know)

In Italian, the relative superlative is formed by placing the article before the comparative form of the adjective. In place of the English prepositions "in" and "of," Italian uses *di*.

Le mele sono la frutta meno costosa del mondo.
Apples are the least expensive fruit in the world.

Queste sono le fragole più buone del mondo.
These are the best strawberries in the world.

3. THE ABSOLUTE SUPERLATIVE

The absolute superlative expresses an extreme degree or absolute state of something without comparison.

Strawberries are very sweet.
The orange is quite good.
She speaks very softly.

In Italian, the absolute superlative can be expressed in several ways:

a. by dropping the last vowel of the adjective and adding *-issimo, -issima, -issimi,* or *-issime:*

Le fragole sono dolcissime.
Strawberries are very sweet.

La mela è buonissima.
The apple is very good.

b. by placing the words *molto, troppo,* or *assai* before the adjective:

Questa arancia è molto buona.
This orange is very good.

Queste ciliege sono troppo care.
These cherries are too expensive.

L'arancia è assai dolce.
The orange is quite sweet.

c. by using the prefixes *stra-* or *arci-:*

Quel signore è straricco/arciricco.
That man is very rich.

Quella donna è straricca/arciricca.
That woman is very rich.

d. by repeating the adjective or adverb:

La frutta è dolce dolce.
The fruit is very sweet.

Carlo parla piano piano.
Carlo speaks very softly.

4. NOUNS USED MAINLY IN THEIR PLURAL FORM

The following nouns are mainly used in the plural form.

zucchini	zucchini
spinaci	spinach
piselli	peas
fagiolini	string beans

VOCABOLARIO

mercato	outdoor market
bancarella	stand
fruttivendolo	fruit seller
Quanto costa al chilo?	How much is it a kilo?
Cinquemila lire al chilo.	Five thousand lire a kilo.
La frutta è fresca.	The fruit is fresh.
frutta	fruit(s)
anguria	watermelon
arancia	orange
banana	banana
ciliegia	cherry
fragola	strawberry
limone (m.)	lemon
mela	apple
melone (m.)	melon
pera	pear
pesca	peach
prugna	plum
uva	grapes
legumi (m., pl.)	vegetables
verdura	vegetables
aglio	garlic
carota	carrot
cetriolo	cucumber
cipolla	onion

fagiolini (m., pl.)	string beans
lattuga	lettuce
melanzana	eggplant
patata	potato
peperone (m.)	pepper
piselli (m., pl.)	peas
pomodoro	tomato
sedano	celery
spinaci (m., pl.)	spinach
zucchini (m., pl.)	zucchini

ESERCIZI

A. *Rispondere affermativamente alle seguenti domande, usando il suffisso "-issimo."*

1. *Sono buone queste fragole?*
2. *È dolce questa mela?*
3. *Costano molto queste ciliege?*
4. *Sono cari questi spinaci?*
5. *È fresca questa lattuga?*

B. *Rispondere negativamente alle domande, esprimendo l'opinione contraria.* (Answer the questions negatively, and state the reverse to be true.)

ESEMPIO: *Giorgio è più bravo di Claudio?*
No, Claudio è più bravo di Giorgio.

1. *I piselli sono più freschi degli spinaci?*
2. *Le mele sono più buone delle banane?*
3. *L'uva è più dolce delle fragole?*
4. *I pomodori sono più costosi delle patate?*
5. *Le pere sono più care delle arance?*

C. *Tradurre.*

1. These peas are as expensive as the spinach.
2. These cherries are less expensive than the melons.
3. Today there are more apples than oranges.

4. These grapes are the sweetest in the world.
5. That man is very rich.

NOTA CULTURALE

Food and flea markets are popular all over Italy, where food and a vast array of items, new and old, are displayed in open-air stalls. The markets normally open early in the morning, and at most of them bargaining is still the rule.

Rome's biggest and most colorful outdoor food markets are at *Campo dei Fiori, Via Andrea Doria,* and *Piazza Vittorio.* In Florence, an open-air market takes place in the *Parco Cascine* every Tuesday morning, while in Milan, on Saturdays, there is a huge market called *Fiera di Senigallia* in *Viale Papiniano* and *Via Calatafimi.*

Remember that Italians use the metric system. To change kilograms into pounds, multiply by 2.2. One U.S. quart equals 0.946 liters.

CHIAVE PER GLI ESERCIZI

A. 1. *Sì, sono buonissime.* 2. *Sì, è dolcissima.* 3. *Sì, costano moltissimo.* 4. *Sì, sono carissimi.* 5. *Sì, è freschissima.*
B. 1. *No, gli spinaci sono più freschi dei piselli.* 2. *No, le banane sono più buone delle mele.* 3. *No, le fragole sono più dolci dell'uva.* 4. *No, le patate sono più costose dei pomodori.* 5. *No, le arance sono più care delle pere.*
C. 1. *Questi piselli sono (tanto/così) cari quanto/come gli spinaci.* 2. *Queste ciliege sono meno care dei meloni.* 3. *Oggi ci sono più mele che arance.* 4. *Quest'uva è la più dolce del mondo.* 5. *Quell'uomo è ricchissimo.*

LEZIONE 29
GLI ALIMENTARI.   Groceries.

A. DIALOGO

Al supermercato.

DANIELE: **Maria, che cosa ci serve?**

MARIA: **Pasta, sale, olio, aceto, zucchero, latte, burro, pane . . . Un po' di carne, della senape, del ketchup, del miele, dei dadi di manzo, una dozzina di uova . . . Dentifricio, tovaglioli, carta igienica, detersivo . . .**

DANIELE: **Servono degli affettati?**

MARIA: **Sì, cinquecento grammi di mortadella, del salame, del formaggio e un po' di prosciutto.**

DANIELE: **Prendiamo anche della carne in scatola, del tonno e della marmellata per i bambini. E quale vino vuoi comprare?**

MARIA: **Del vino italiano: è il migliore del mondo.**

DANIELE: **Anche quello francese è ottimo.**

MARIA: **Sì, ma i vini italiani sono superiori a tutti i vini del mondo.**

DANIELE: **Ci servono dei surgelati?**

MARIA: **No. Andiamo alla cassa.**

At the supermarket.

DANIELE: Maria, what do we need?

MARIA: Pasta, salt, oil, vinegar, sugar, milk, butter, bread . . . Some meat, mustard, ketchup, honey, some beef bouillon cubes, a dozen eggs . . . Toothpaste, napkins, toilet paper, detergent . . .

DANIELE: Do we need cold cuts?

MARIA: Yes, five hundred grams of mortadella, some salami, some cheese, and some prosciutto.

DANIELE: Let's also get some luncheon meat, some tuna, and some jam for the children. And which wine do you want to buy?

MARIA: An Italian wine: it's the best in the world.

DANIELE: The French ones are excellent, as well.

MARIA: Yes, but Italian wines are superior to all the wines in the world.

DANIELE: Do we need any frozen food?

MARIA: No. Let's go to the checkout.

B. GRAMMATICA E SUOI USI

1. IRREGULAR COMPARATIVES AND SUPERLATIVES

Some commonly used adjectives have both regular and irregular comparative and superlative forms.

ADJECTIVE	COMPARATIVE	RELATIVE SUPERLATIVE	ABSOLUTE SUPERLATIVE
good	better	the best	very good
buono	*più buono, migliore*	*il più buono, il migliore*	*ottimo*
bad	worse	the worst	very bad
cattivo	*più cattivo, peggiore*	*il più cattivo, il peggiore*	*pessimo*
big, great, old	bigger, greater, older	the biggest, greatest, oldest	very big, great
grande	*più grande, maggiore*	*il più grande, il maggiore*	*massimo*
little, small	smaller	the smallest	very small
piccolo	*il più piccolo, minore*	*il minore*	*minimo*

Note that *migliore, peggiore, maggiore,* and *minore* may drop the *e* when they precede singular nouns that do not start with *s* plus consonant or with *z*.

Il vino italiano è il miglior*(e)* vino del mondo.
Italian wine is the best in the world.

Maggiore/il maggiore is often used to mean "older/the oldest."

Luigi è il figlio maggiore.
Luigi is the oldest son.

Minore/il minore is often used to mean "younger/the youngest."

Marco è il figlio minore.
Marco is the youngest son.

The adverbs *bene* and *male* also have irregular comparative forms:
bene → meglio; male → peggio.

Come ti senti?
How do you feel?

Sto meglio.
I am better.

Sto peggio.
I am worse.

2. NOUNS USED MAINLY IN THEIR SINGULAR FORM

The following nouns are used mainly in their singular form.

senape	mustard
zucchero	sugar
miele	honey
aceto	vinegar
sale	salt
marmellata	jam

Voglio della marmellata.

I want some jam.

Mi dai lo zucchero, per favore?

Can you give me the sugar, please?

3. THE VERB *SERVIRE*

The verb *servire* ("to need") has the same construction as *piacere* ("to like, to please"): it is used primarily in the third person singular and plural forms and takes an indirect object. Remember that it differs from its English counterpart "to need."

SUBJECT	VERB	DIRECT OBJECT
Mark	needs	bread.
Il pane	*serve*	*a Marco.*
The bread	is needed	by Marco.

SUBJECT	VERB	DIRECT OBJECT
Mark	needs	cold cuts.
Gli affettati	*servono*	*a Marco.*
Cold cuts	are needed	by Marco.

In English, people need things. In Italian, things are necessary to people.

	SERVIRE	TO NEED
I need	*mi*	*serve/servono*
you need (familiar)	*ti*	*serve/servono*
he needs	*gli*	*serve/servono*
she needs	*le*	*serve/servono*
you need (polite)	*Le*	*serve/servono*
we need	*ci*	*serve/servono*
you need (familiar or polite)	*vi*	*serve/servono*
they need, you need (polite)	*gli*	*serve/servono*

If the thing you need or needed is singular use *serve* (present) or *è servito* (past), etc.; if it is plural use *servono* (present) or *sono serviti/e* (past).

Vi serve della frutta?
    Do you need any fruit?

Ti servono degli affettati?
    Do you need any cold cuts?

Ci servono dei surgelati.
    We need frozen foods.

VOCABOLARIO

supermercato	supermarket
fare la spesa	to go grocery shopping
lista della spesa	shopping list
cassa	cash register
Che cosa ci serve?	What do we need?
pasta	pasta
sale (m.)	salt
pepe (m.)	pepper
olio	oil
aceto	vinegar
zucchero	sugar
senape (f.)	mustard
ketchup (m.)	ketchup
miele (m.)	honey
dado di manzo	beef bouillon cube
dado di pollo	chicken bouillon cube
marmellata	jam
pane (m.)	bread
pane tostato	toast
latte (m.)	milk
burro	butter
una dozzina di uova	a dozen eggs
surgelati (m., pl.)	frozen food
affettati (m., pl.)	cold cuts
cinquecento grammi di mortadella	five hundred grams of mortadella
cinquecento grammi di salame	five hundred grams of salami

salame (m.)	salami
formaggio	cheese
prosciutto	prosciutto
carne (f.)	meat
carne (f.) **in scatola**	canned meat
tonno	tuna
pollo	chicken
dentifricio	toothpaste
tovagliolo	napkin
carta igienica	toilet paper
detersivo	detergent

ESERCIZI

A. *Eliminare la parola che non appartiene al gruppo.*

1. *olio / mela / sale*
2. *salame / burro / prosciutto*
3. *pollo / zucchero / tonno*
4. *grande / ottimo / pessimo*
5. *pera / arancia / senape*

B. *Rimettere le seguenti parole in ordine.*

1. *vino / del / migliore / mondo / è / questo / il*
2. *formaggio / è / ottimo / il / italiano*
3. *anche / degli / affettati / ci / servono*
4. *grammi / mortadella / vorrei / cinquecento / di*
5. *anche / prendiamo / miele / olio / dell' / e / del /?*

C. *Completare usando il comparativo appropriato. Scegliere tra "migliore, meglio, peggiore, maggiore, peggio."*

1. *È buono questo formaggio!*
   Sì, ma questo è _____.
2. *Daniele parla molto bene l'italiano!*
   Sì, ma Laura lo parla _____.

3. *Questa carne è cattiva!*
   Sì, e questa è ancora _____.
4. *Mio figlio è già grande: ha dodici anni.*
   Mio figlio è _____ del tuo: ha già sedici anni.
5. *John sta male: ha il raffreddore.*
   Sì, ma suo fratello sta ancora _____: ha la febbre e l'influenza.

NOTA CULTURALE

Today grocery shopping in Italy, like in North America, is done mainly on a weekly basis in large supermarkets. Many Italians, however, particularly those in small towns, still prefer to do their grocery shopping daily at the local *generi alimentari* (grocery store). In general, these small stores don't carry meat, poultry, fruits, or vegetables. To buy meat, Italians go to the *macelleria* (butcher's shop); for fruits and vegetables, to the *frutta e verdura* (fruit and vegetable stand).

CHIAVE PER GLI ESERCIZI

A. 1. *mela* 2. *burro* 3. *zucchero* 4. *grande* 5. *senape*
B. 1. *Questo vino è il migliore del mondo.* 2. *Il formaggio italiano è ottimo.*
   3. *Ci servono anche degli affettati.* 4. *Vorrei cinquecento grammi di mortadella.* 5. *Prendiamo anche del miele e dell'olio?*
C. 1. *migliore* 2. *meglio* 3. *peggiore* 4. *maggiore* 5. *peggio*

LEZIONE 30
I CAPELLI. Hair.

A. DIALOGO

1. Un barbiere in casa.

GINO: **Ciao, mamma. Come stai? È andato tutto bene al salone?**

MAMMA: **Ho capito! Cosa vuoi?**

GINO: **Devo uscire. Ho già fatto lo sciampo. Mi sono fatto la barba. Mi taglieresti i capelli?**

MAMMA: **Certo. Come li vuoi?**

GINO: **Vorrei solo una spuntatina.**

MAMMA: **Dovresti portarli più corti, con le basette sopra l'orecchio. Io sarei più contenta.**

GINO: **No, li preferisco lunghi.**

MAMMA: **Come vuoi tu!**

GINO: **Me li asciugheresti pure?**

MAMMA: **Sì, ma avrei anch'io un favore da chiederti.**

A barber at home.

GINO: Hi, mom. How are you? Did everything go well at the salon?

MOTHER: Okay, what do you want?

GINO: I have to go out. I have already washed my hair and shaved. Would you cut my hair?

MOTHER: Of course. How would you like it cut?

GINO: I would just like a trim.

MOTHER: You should keep it shorter, with your sideburns above the ears. I would be happier.

GINO: No, I prefer it long.

MOTHER: Whatever you like!

GINO: Would you dry it too?

MOTHER: Yes, but I would like to ask you a favor, too.

---

2. *Dal parrucchiere.*

PARRUCCHIERE: **In che cosa possiamo servirLa?**

SIGNORA CARLI: **Vorrei tingermi i capelli biondi.**

PARRUCCHIERE: **Le suggerirei questa tintura.**

SIGNORA CARLI: **Ne avrebbe una più scura?**

PARRUCCHIERE: **Ecco.**

SIGNORA CARLI: **Questa va bene. Potrebbe anche farmi la permanente?**

PARRUCCHIERE: **Certo. Mentre aspetta, vorrebbe una manicure?**

SIGNORA CARLI: **Sì, perché no?**

At the beauty parlor.

HAIRDRESSER: How may I help you?

MRS. CARLI: I'd like to dye my hair blonde.

HAIRDRESSER: I suggest this shade.

MRS. CARLI: Would you have a darker one?

HAIRDRESSER: Here you are.

MRS. CARLI: This one's fine. Could you also give me a perm?

HAIRDRESSER: Of course. While you wait, would you like a manicure?

MRS. CARLI: Yes, why not?

B. GRAMMATICA E SUOI USI

1. THE PRESENT CONDITIONAL

The present conditional (*il condizionale presente*) is generally translated into English with "would" and is used to make a request more polite.

Vorrei solo una spuntatina.
   I'd like just a trim.

Vorrei del caffè.
   I'd like some coffee.

The conditional also expresses an action or an event that may occur in the future—but probably won't, as it is subject to certain conditions. The conditions are not always stated.

Farei i compiti, ma non ho tempo.
   I'd do the homework, but I don't have time.

Andreste al cinema, ma non avete soldi.
   You'd go to the movies, but you don't have any money.

Conditional sentences describe the consequences of hypothetical situations, usually introduced by "if" clauses.

Se avessi soldi, comprerei questo vestito.
   If I had money, I'd buy this suit.

Andremmo dal barbiere se potessimo.
   We'd go to the barber, if we could.

The "if" clause is not always expressed.

Lo farei. (al tuo posto)
   I'd do it. (if I were in the same situation)

Finally, the conditional is used to express doubt.

Non so se andrebbero senza te.
   I don't know if they would go without you.

272

The present conditional is formed using the future stem and conditional personal endings. The endings are the same for all three conjugations: *-ei, -esti, -ebbe, -emmo, -este, -ebbero.*

INFINITIVE	FUTURE	CONDITIONAL
parlare	*parlerò*	*parlerei*

	PARLARE	TO SPEAK
I would speak	*io*	*parlerei*
you would speak (familiar)	*tu*	*parleresti*
he would speak	*lui*	*parlerebbe*
she would speak	*lei*	*parlerebbe*
you would speak (polite)	*Lei*	*parlerebbe*
we would speak	*noi*	*parleremmo*
you would speak (familiar or polite)	*voi*	*parlereste*
they would speak	*loro*	*parlerebbero*
you would speak (polite)	*Loro*	*parlerebbero*

Gli parlerei, ma non è a casa.
   I would speak to him, but he's not at home.

Mi taglieresti i capelli?
   Would you cut my hair?

	PRENDERE	TO TAKE
I would take	*io*	*prenderei*
you would take (familiar)	*tu*	*prenderesti*
he would take	*lui*	*prenderebbe*
she would take	*lei*	*prenderebbe*
you would take (polite)	*Lei*	*prenderebbe*
we would take	*noi*	*prenderemmo*
you would take (familiar or polite)	*voi*	*prendereste*
they would take	*loro*	*prenderebbero*
you would take (polite)	*Loro*	*prenderebbero*

Prendereste un caffè?
   Would you like some coffee?

Io non le scriverei.
   I wouldn't write to her.

FINIRE		TO FINISH
I would finish	*io*	*finirei*
you would finish (familiar)	*tu*	*finiresti*
he would finish	*lui*	*finirebbe*
she would finish	*lei*	*finirebbe*
you would finish (polite)	*Lei*	*finirebbe*
we would finish	*noi*	*finiremmo*
you would finish (familiar or polite)	*voi*	*finireste*
they would finish	*loro*	*finirebbero*
you would finish (polite)	*Loro*	*finirebbero*

Le suggerirei questa tintura.
   I would suggest this tint.

Preferirei i capelli più corti.
   I would prefer shorter hair.

2. THE PRESENT CONDITIONAL OF *AVERE* AND *ESSERE*

AVERE		TO HAVE
I would have	*io*	*avrei*
you would have (familiar)	*tu*	*avresti*
he would have	*lui*	*avrebbe*
she would have	*lei*	*avrebbe*
you would have (polite)	*Lei*	*avrebbe*
we would have	*noi*	*avremmo*
you would have (familiar or polite)	*voi*	*avreste*
they would have	*loro*	*avrebbero*
you would have (polite)	*Loro*	*avrebbero*

Avrebbe una tinta più scura?
   Would you have a darker shade?

Avresti lo sciampo?
   Would you have shampoo?

Avreste una spazzola?
   Would you have a brush?

274

	ESSERE	TO BE
I would be	io	sarei
you would be (familiar)	tu	saresti
he would be	lui	sarebbe
she would be	lei	sarebbe
you would be (polite)	Lei	sarebbe
we would be	noi	saremmo
you would be (familiar or polite)	voi	sareste
they would be	loro	sarebbero
you would be (polite)	Loro	sarebbero

Sarei più contenta.
I would be happier.

A quest'ora saresti a Roma.
By now, you would be in Rome.

3. THE PRESENT CONDITIONAL OF VERBS ENDING IN -*CARE*, -*GARE*, -*CIARE*, AND -*GIARE*

As in the future tense, verbs ending in -*care* and -*gare* add an *h* after the *c* or *g* in order to retain the hard consonant sounds, and verbs ending in -*ciare* and -*giare* drop the final *i* from their stem in all forms of the present conditional.

INFINITIVE	FUTURE	CONDITIONAL
cominciare (to start)	*comincerò, comincerai . . .*	*comincerei, cominceresti . . .*
mangiare (to eat)	*mangerò, mangerai . . .*	*mangerei, mangeresti . . .*
cercare (to look for)	*cercherò, cercherai . . .*	*cercherei, cercheresti . . .*
pagare (to pay)	*pagherò, pagherai . . .*	*pagherei, pagheresti . . .*
asciugare (to dry)	*asciugherò, asciugherai . . .*	*asciugherei, asciugheresti . . .*

Mi asciugheresti i capelli?
Would you dry my hair?

Hai sempre fame. Mangeresti sempre.
You're always hungry. You would eat all the time.

4. THE PRESENT CONDITIONAL OF *DOVERE, POTERE, AND VOLERE*

The present conditional of *dovere* ("to have to"), *potere* ("to be able to"), and *volere* ("to want") is often used to make a request more polite. All three verbs have irregular forms in the present conditional.

dovere	*dovrei, dovresti, dovrebbe, dovremmo, dovreste, dovrebbero*
potere	*potrei, potresti, potrebbe, potremmo, potreste, potrebbero*
volere	*vorrei, vorresti, vorrebbe, vorremmo, vorreste, vorrebbero*

Vorrei tingermi i capelli.
I would like to dye my hair.

Potrebbe farmi una permanente?
Could you give me a perm?

Dovremmo tagliarci i capelli.
We should cut our hair.

VOCABOLARIO

barbiere (m.)	barber
parrucchiere (m.)	beauty parlor
salone (m.)	salon
Vorrei tagliarmi i capelli.	I would like a haircut.
Vorrei tagliarmi i capelli a zero.	I would like a crewcut.
Potrebbe farmi la permanente?	Could you give me a perm?
Vorrei farmi la messa in piega.	I would like my hair set.
Come vuole i capelli?	How do you like your hair?

Vorrei solo una spuntatina.	I would just like a trim.
Non troppo corti davanti *(di dietro).*	Not too short in front (in the back).
con le basette sopra l'orecchio	with the sideburns above the ears
portare i capelli corti *(lunghi)*	to have short (long) hair
avere i capelli ricci *(lisci, ondulati)*	to have curly (straight, wavy) hair
avere i capelli biondi *(castani)*	to have blond (brown) hair
Vorrei farmi la barba.	I would like a shave.
Niente dopobarba, per favore.	No aftershave, please.
Niente lacca, per favore.	No hairspray, please.
avere i baffi	to have a moustache
Vorrei tingermi i capelli biondi.	I would like to dye my hair blond.
Le suggerirei questa tintura.	I suggest this color.
Avrebbe una tintura più scura?	Would you have a darker shade?
Vorrei una manicure.	I would like a manicure.
Mi faccia lo sciampo.	I would like a shampoo.
rossetto	lipstick
trucco	makeup
farsi lo sciampo	to shampoo
farsi la barba	to shave
sapone (m.) **per la barba**	shaving cream
rasoio	razor
asciugarsi i capelli	to dry one's hair
balsamo per i capelli	hair conditioner
pettinarsi	to comb one's hair
pettine (m.)	comb
spazzola	brush
tingersi le unghie	to paint one's nails
smalto per le unghie	nail polish

ESERCIZI

A. *Fare delle richieste basate sulle seguenti situazioni. Usare il condizionale.* (Make requests based on the following situations. Use the conditional.)

1. You are at a barbershop. Tell the barber that you would like a shave.
2. You are at the barbershop. Tell the barber that you would like a trim.
3. You are at a beauty parlor. Ask the hairdresser if he/she could give you a perm.
4. You are at a beauty parlor. Tell the hairdresser that you would like to dye your hair blond.
5. You are at a barbershop. Tell the barber that you would like a haircut.

B. *Riscrivere la frase mettendo il verbo sottolineato al condizionale.* (Rewrite each sentence by putting the underlined verb in the conditional.)

1. *Gino, i capelli devi portarli più corti!*
2. *Mamma, ho un favore da chiederti.*
3. *La signora Carli vuole una manicure.*
4. *Loro vogliono tagliarsi i capelli.*
5. *Io non scrivo a Gianni.*

C. *Scrivere la forma coretta del verbo nella schema.*

	INFINITO	*FUTURO*	*CONDIZIONALE*
ESEMPIO:	*parlare*	*parlerò*	*parlerei*
1.	*prendere*		
2.		*finirò*	
3.			*sarei*
4.	*cercare*		
5.	*cominciare*		
6.		*mangerò*	
7.		*potrò*	

278

NOTA CULTURALE

Italian hairdressers are among the leaders in hairstyle fashion. With some exceptions, barbers and hairdressers in Italy are closed Sundays and Mondays. From Tuesday through Friday, they are usually open from 9:00 A.M. to 12:30 P.M. and from 2:30 P.M. to 7:30 P.M. On Saturdays they remain open all day. Appointments are usually not necessary. Only well-established hairdressers may require one. Prices and tipping practices vary depending on the type of establishment and are more or less as in America.

CHIAVE PER GLI ESERCIZI

A. 1. *Vorrei farmi la barba.* 2. *Vorrei una spuntatina.* 3. *Potrebbe farmi la permanente?* 4. *Vorrei tingermi i capelli biondi.* 5. *Vorrei tagliarmi i capelli.*

B. 1. *Gino, i capelli dovresti portarli più corti!* 2. *Mamma, avrei un favore da chiederti.* 3. *La signora Carli vorrebbe una manicure.* 4. *Loro vorrebbero tagliarsi i capelli.* 5. *Io non scriverei a Gianni.*

C. 1. *prenderò, prenderei* 2. *finire, finirei* 3. *essere, sarò* 4. *cercherò, cercherei* 5. *comincerò, comincerei* 6. *mangiare, mangerei* 7. *potere, potrei*

SESTO RIPASSO

A. *Completare con l'articolo determinativo appropriato, poi cambiare al plurale.*

1. _____ *regista* (m.)　　　　_____
2. _____ *pianista* (f.)　　　　_____
3. _____ *atleta* (m.)　　　　_____
4. _____ *programma*　　　　_____
5. _____ *cinema*　　　　_____
6. _____ *problema*　　　　_____

B. *Completare con il passato prossimo o l'imperfetto.*

1. *Quando io* _____ *(essere) giovane,* _____ *(andare) spesso ai concerti dei Rolling Stones.*

2. Noi _____ (stare) per uscire quando _____ (arrivare) Paolo.

3. Che ore _____ (essere) quando _____ (venire) Stefania?

4. Io mentre mi _____ (fare) la barba, _____ (ascoltare) la radio.

5. Teresa e Anna _____ (volere) venire all'opera, ma non _____ (potere).

C. Completare in modo opportuno.

1. Le fragole sono più buone _____ ciliege.

2. Oggi ci sono meno mele _____ pere.

3. Quest'uva è dolcis _____ .

4. Questa è la frutta più fresca _____ mondo!

5. Questo è un buon albergo!
   Sì, ma il mio albergo è _____ di questo: è più elegante e più comodo.

6. Simona è già grande: ha quindici anni.
   Sì, ma Monica è _____: ha già diciannove anni.

D. Formare delle frasi con le seguenti parole. Usare il condizionale. (Using the present conditional, form a complete sentence out of each group of words below.)

1. Io / volere / tingermi / capelli

2. Noi / andare / Italia / ma / non / avere / soldi

3. Lei / comprare / questo / vestito / ma / costare / troppo

4. Tu / dovere / portare / capelli / più / corti

5. Loro / mangiare / pizza / ma / non / avere / fame

E. Accoppiare le parole nella colonna a sinistra con quelle nella colonna a destra.

1. Quando lui ha telefonato, io   a. straricco.

2. Oggi la frutta è   b. avevi già fatto colazione.

3. Signora, desidera   c. tagliarmi i capelli.

4. Quando lei è arrivata, tu   d. dei fagiolini?

5. Oggi vorrei andare a   e. ero già uscito.

6. Quel signore è   f. molto fresca.

A. 1. *il regista, i registi* 2. *la pianista, le pianiste* 3. *l'atleta, gli atleti* 4. *il programma, i programmi* 5. *il cinema, i cinema* 6. *il problema, i problemi*

B. 1. *ero, andavo* 2. *stavamo, è arrivato* 3. *erano, è venuta* 4. *facevo, ascoltavo* 5. *volevano, hanno potuto.*

C. 1. *delle* 2. *che* 3. *dolcissima* 4. *del* 5. *più buono/migliore* 6. *maggiore/più grande*

D. 1. *Io vorrei tingermi i capelli.* 2. *Noi andremmo in Italia, ma non abbiamo soldi.* 3. *Lei comprerebbe questo vestito, ma costa troppo.* 4. *Tu dovresti portare i capelli più corti.* 5. *Loro mangerebbero una pizza, ma non hanno fame.*

E. 1—e; 2—f; 3—d; 4—b; 5—c; 6—a

DA LEGGERE

L'ITALIANO E I DIALETTI

In Italia si parla la lingua italiana. L'italiano, però, non si parla nella stessa[1] maniera[2] in tutte le regioni. Ci sono diversità[3] nell'intonazione[4] e nella pronuncia. Un romano, per esempio, anche quando parla un italiano corretto, pronuncia le parole in una certa maniera che ci fa capire che è di Roma. In Italia ci sono anche molti dialetti,[5] diversi fra loro: il friulano, il lombardo, il piemontese, il napoletano, il calabrese, il siciliano, ecc. Infatti, se un milanese va in Calabria e parla il dialetto lombardo, non sarà capito facilmente; così come sarà pure difficile capire un calabrese a Milano. Il fiorentino, parlato a Firenze, è il dialetto che, per una serie di ragioni, si è affermato[6] sugli altri dialetti ed è diventato la lingua nazionale.

Molte parole che provengono[7] dal dialetto—come "mozzarella" (che proviene dal napoletano), "panettone"[8] (dal milanese), "grissini"[9] (dal piemontese) o "cassata"[10] (dal siciliano)—sono entrate perfino[11] a far parte della lingua nazionale. Anche la lingua nazionale, però, ha influenzato i dialetti. A Roma, per esempio, la parola "calzini"[12] sta sostituendo sempre più la voce[13] dialettale[14] "pedalini";[15] così come nel Nord Italia, per esempio, la parola italiana "patata"[16] sta prendendo il posto della parola dialettale "pom da tera."[17]

VOCABOLARIO

1. *stesso, -a* — same
2. *maniera* — manner, way
3. *diversità* — difference
4. *intonazione* (f.) — intonation
5. *dialetto* — dialect
6. *affermarsi* — to assert oneself
7. *provenire* — to come from, to originate
8. *panettone* (m.) — Milanese sweet cake
9. *grissino* — a thin breadstick
10. *cassata* — a type of Sicilian ice-cream cake
11. *perfino* — also, even
12. *calzini* (m., pl.) — socks
13. *voce* (f.) — word, voice
14. *dialettale* — of the dialect
15. *pedalini* (m., pl.) — socks (dialect)
16. *patata* — potato
17. *pom da tera* — potato (dialect)

LEZIONE 31

I SOLDI.   Money.

A. DIALOGO

All'ufficio di cambio.

RAGIONIER RISI: Buon giorno, signorina. Mi dica?

SIGNORINA MELI: Vorrei cambiare questi dollari in lire italiane, per piacere. Sono trecento dollari americani . . .

RAGIONIER RISI: Bene.

SIGNORINA MELI: Quanto è il cambio oggi? È alto?

RAGIONIER RISI: Beh, oggi non è molto alto né per i soldi in contanti né per i traveler's checks. Avrebbe dovuto cambiarli ieri; il cambio era più alto.

SIGNORINA MELI: Peccato! Sarei venuta ieri, ma non ho potuto. Quant'è la commissione?

RAGIONIER RISI: Due per cento.

SIGNORINA MELI: Ecco a Lei trecento dollari in contanti.

RAGIONIER RISI: Avrebbe un documento, per favore?

SIGNORINA MELI: Sì, ecco il passaporto.

RAGIONIER RISI: Grazie mille. Metta qui la data e la controfirma.

SIGNORINA MELI: Scusi, mi potrebbe dare delle banconote di piccolo taglio e degli spiccioli?

RAGIONIER RISI: Per ottenere i soldi deve andare allo sportello accanto. Presenti questa ricevuta.

At the exchange office.

MR. RISI: Good morning, Miss. May I help you?

MISS MELI: I'd like to change these dollars into lire, please. It's three hundred American dollars . . .

283

MR. RISI: Okay.

MISS MELI: What's the exchange rate today? Is it high?

MR. RISI: Well, today it isn't very high, for cash or for traveler's checks. You should have changed them yesterday; the exchange rate was higher.

MISS MELI: Too bad! I would have come yesterday, but I couldn't. How much is the commission?

MR. RISI: Two percent.

MISS MELI: Here's three hundred dollars in cash.

MR. RISI: Do you have any identification, please?

MISS MELI: Yes, here is my passport.

MR. RISI: Thanks a million. Put the date and your countersignature here.

MISS MELI: Pardon me, could you give me some small bills and some change?

MR. RISI: To get the money, you have to go to the next window. Show this receipt.

B. GRAMMATICA E SUOI USI

1. THE PRESENT CONDITIONAL OF IRREGULAR VERBS

Verbs that have irregular future forms are also irregular in the conditional.

to give	*dare*	*darei, daresti, darebbe, daremmo, dareste, darebbero*
to do	*fare*	*farei, faresti, farebbe, faremmo, fareste, farebbero*
to stay	*stare*	*starei, staresti, starebbe, staremmo, stareste, starebbero*
to go	*andare*	*andrei, andresti, andrebbe, andremmo, andreste, andrebbero*
to have to	*dovere*	*dovrei, dovresti, dovrebbe, dovremmo, dovreste, dovrebbero*

to see	vedere	vedrei, vedresti, vedrebbe, vedremmo, vedreste, vedrebbero
to know	sapere	saprei, sapresti, saprebbe, sapremmo, sapreste, saprebbero
to be able	potere	potrei, potresti, potrebbe, potremmo, potreste, potrebbero
to drink	bere	berrei, berresti, berrebbe, berremmo, berreste, berrebbero
to come	venire	verrei, verresti, verrebbe, verremmo, verreste, verrebbero
to want	volere	vorrei, vorresti, vorrebbe, vorremmo, vorreste, vorrebbero

2. THE PAST CONDITIONAL

The past conditional (*il condizionale passato*) has the same basic uses as the present conditional. It is used to express an unfulfilled request.

Avrebbe voluto un caffè.
He'd have liked some coffee.

The past conditional also expresses an action or an event which had the possibility to fulfill itself, but didn't.

Sarei andato al cinema, ma non avevo soldi.
I'd have gone to the movies, but I had no money.

The past conditional is used in conditional sentences about the past, describing hypothetical situations, i.e., situations that did not occur.

Saremmo andati al concerto, ma pioveva.
We'd have gone to the concert, but it was raining.

Finally, it expresses doubt.

Non so se avrebbero pagato.
I don't know if they would have paid.

The past conditional is formed by using the present conditional of *avere* or *essere* and the past participle of the main verb.

	PARLARE	TO SPEAK
I would have spoken	io	*avrei parlato*
you would have spoken (familiar)	tu	*avresti parlato*
he would have spoken	lui	*avrebbe parlato*
she would have spoken	lei	*avrebbe parlato*
you would have spoken (polite)	Lei	*avrebbe parlato*
we would have spoken	noi	*avremmo parlato*
you would have spoken (familiar or polite)	voi	*avreste parlato*
they would have spoken	loro	*avrebbero parlato*
you would have spoken (polite)	Loro	*avrebbero parlato*

	ANDARE	TO GO
I would have gone	io	*sarei andato/a*
you would have gone (familiar)	tu	*saresti andato/a*
he would have gone	lui	*sarebbe andato*
she would have gone	lei	*sarebbe andata*
you would have gone (polite)	Lei	*sarebbe andato/a*
we would have gone	noi	*saremmo andati/e*
you would have gone (familiar or polite)	voi	*sareste andati/e*
they would have gone	loro	*sarebbero andati/e*
you would have gone (polite)	Loro	*sarebbero andati/e*

In general, the Italian past conditional is the equivalent of the English "would have" plus the past participle. However, when expressing a future action from the viewpoint of the past, English uses the present conditional, while Italian uses the past conditional.

Ha detto che sarebbe venuto.
He said he would come.

3. THE PAST CONDITIONAL OF *DOVERE, POTERE,* AND *VOLERE*

Remember also the following constructions with *dovere, potere,* and *volere:*

The past conditional of *dovere* plus an infinitive = "should have/ought to have" plus the past participle.

The past conditional of *potere* plus an infinitive = "could have/might have" plus the past participle.

The past conditional of *volere* plus an infinitive = "I would have liked" plus an infinitive.

Avrebbe dovuto cambiarli ieri.
You should have changed them yesterday.

Avresti potuto studiare.
You could have studied.

Avremmo voluto andare in Italia.
We'd have liked to go to Italy.

VOCABOLARIO

ufficio del cambio	currency exchange office
sportello dei cambi	exchange window
listino dei cambi	exchange list
tasso del cambio	exchange rate
Vorrei cambiare dollari in lire.	I would like to change dollars into lire.
Quanto è il cambio oggi?	What is the exchange rate today?
A quanto sta il dollaro oggi?	How much is the dollar worth today?
Il cambio è alto.	The exchange rate is high.
Il cambio è basso.	The exchange rate is low.
Sono trecento dollari americani.	It's three hundred American dollars.
Quant'è la commissione?	How much is the commission?
Metta qui la data e la controfirma.	Put the date and your countersignature here.

Presenti questa ricevuta.	Show this receipt.
Il totale è . . .	The total is . . .
Ecco a Lei trecento dollari in contanti.	Here's three hundred dollars in cash.
Vorrei cambiare un traveler's cheque.	I'd like to cash a traveler's check.
soldi in contanti	cash
valuta	currency
valuta estera	foreign currency
banconota	banknote
moneta	coin
borsa	stock market
Mi dica.	May I help you?
lira	lira
dollaro	dollar
marco	mark
franco	franc
fiorino	florin
peseta	peseta
peso	peso
sterlina	pound, sterling
yen	yen

ESERCIZI

A. *Fare delle richieste basate sulle seguenti situazioni. Usare il condizionale.*

1. You're at the currency exchange office. Ask Mr. Risi if he could give you some small bills.
2. You've only got a 1,000 lire bill, and need change to make a telephone call. You walk up to a stranger and say:
3. You're at the currency exchange office. Say that you would like to exchange 300 dollars into lire.
4. You're a clerk at a currency exchange office. Ask Miss Meli if she has any identification.

B. *Completare con le forme del condizionale presente.*

1. *fare*	2. *andare*	3. *sapere*	4. *venire*	5. *vedere*
noi _____	*io* _____	*tu* _____	*lui* _____	*noi* _____
tu _____	*noi* _____	*voi* _____	*tu* _____	*io* _____
loro _____	*tu* _____	*noi* _____	*loro* _____	*lui* _____
io _____	*lei* _____	*loro* _____	*io* _____	*tu* _____
voi _____	*loro* _____	*io* _____	*noi* _____	*voi* _____
lui _____	*voi* _____	*lei* _____	*voi* _____	*loro* _____

C. *Rispondere alle seguenti domande giustificandosi, come nell'esempio.*
(Answer each question justifying your answer, as in the example. Hint: Use the past conditional.)

ESEMPIO: *Perché non hai cambiato i soldi?*
   Avrei cambiato i soldi, ma non ho potuto.

1. *Perché non sei andato all'ufficio di cambio?*
2. *Perché non sei andato dal dottore?*
3. *Perché non hai preso la medicina?*
4. *Perché non sei venuto ieri a cambiare i soldi?*
5. *Perché non hai finito il lavoro?*

NOTA CULTURALE

Money can be exchanged at a bank or an official exchange bureau (*ufficio di cambio*). In major tourist centers money can also be exchanged in stores. In major cities instant exchange machines are very common: once you have chosen the language of communication, you need only push the button with the image of the currency you want to exchange (more than 20 currencies available), insert the money, and confirm the operation. When you insert the money, the machine will indicate in a display window how much you've inserted and the equivalent in lire. You can cancel the transaction at any time. Once you finish the transaction, the machine will give you the lire and a receipt with all the details. When you change money, normally you pay a commission (3,000 to 5,000 lire) and, if a large amount is involved, a tax (*bollo*).

A. 1. *Signor Risi, potrebbe darmi dei biglietti di piccolo taglio?* 2. *Potrebbe cambiare 1.000 lire?* 3. *Vorrei cambiare trecento dollari in lire.* 4. *Signorina Meli, avrebbe un documento?*

B. 1. *faremmo, faresti, farebbero, farei, fareste, farebbe* 2. *andrei, andremmo, andresti, andrebbe, andrebbero, andreste* 3. *sapresti, sapreste, sapremmo, saprebbero, saprei, saprebbe* 4. *verrebbe, verresti, verrebbero, verrei, verremmo, verreste* 5. *vedremmo, vedrei, vedrebbe, vedresti, vedreste, vedrebbero*

C. 1. *Sarei andato/a all'ufficio di cambio, ma non ho potuto.* 2. *Sarei andato/a dal dottore, ma non ho potuto.* 3. *Avrei preso la medicina, ma non ho potuto.* 4. *Sarei venuto/a ieri a cambiare i soldi, ma non ho potuto.* 5. *Avrei finito il lavoro, ma non ho potuto.*

LEZIONE 32

A. DIALOGO

Alla tabaccheria.

MARK: **Un pacchetto di Nazionali, per favore.**

TABACCAIA: **Con filtro o senza filtro?**

MARK: **Con filtro.**

TABACCAIA: **Altro?**

MARK: **Sì, una scatola di cerini . . . Qui si vendono biglietti per l'autobus?**

TABACCAIA: **Quanti ne vuole?**

MARK: **Soltanto uno. Dove si può trovare della carta da lettere?**

TABACCAIA: **Anche qui si vende carta da lettere.**

MARK: **Davvero?**

TABACCAIA: **Sì, qui in Italia dai tabaccai si vende un po' di tutto. Si possono comprare sigarette, fiammiferi, accendini, francobolli, cartoline . . . Moduli per cambiali, carta e marche da bollo . . . Articoli da regalo come profumi, giocattoli . . .**

MARK: **Si vendono anche rullini?**

TABACCAIA: **Sì.**

MARK: **Allora della carta da lettere e un rullino a colori da 24 pose.**

TABACCAIA: **Ecco a Lei.**

MARK: **Un'ultima cosa . . . Dove si può trovare un telefono pubblico?**

TABACCAIA: **Il telefono è proprio qui. Le servono dei gettoni o una carta telefonica?**

At the tobacco shop.

MARK: A pack of *Nazionali,* please.

TOBACCONIST: Filtered or nonfiltered?

MARK: Filtered.

TOBACCONIST: Anything else?

MARK: Yes, a box of matches . . . Do you sell bus tickets here?

TOBACCONIST: How many would you like?

MARK: Only one. Where can I find some writing paper?

TOBACCONIST: We also sell writing paper.

MARK: Really?

TOBACCONIST: Yes, here in Italy, we sell a little bit of everything in tobacco shops. You can buy cigarettes, matches, lighters, stamps, postcards . . . promissory notes, stamped paper, and revenue stamps . . . Gift items such as perfumes, toys . . .

MARK: Do you also sell film?

TOBACCONIST: Yes.

MARK: Then I would like some writing paper and a roll of 24-exposure color film.

TOBACCONIST: Here you are.

MARK: One more thing . . . Where can I find a public phone?

TOBACCONIST: The phone is right here. Do you need some telephone tokens or a telephone card?

B. GRAMMATICA E SUOI USI

1. THE IMPERSONAL *SI*

We have already seen that *si* can be used as a reflexive pronoun.* But *si* may also be used as an impersonal pronoun. It then corresponds to the

* Please see lesson 12.

English impersonal subjects "one, we, they, people, you" and is usually accompanied by the third person singular of the verb.

Dove si può trovare un telefono?
Where can one find a telephone?

Qui si vende carta da lettere.
We sell writing paper here.

When the object is plural, *si* is followed by the third person plural of the verb.

Qui si vendono biglietti per l'autobus.
We sell bus tickets here.

Si vendono anche rullini?
Do you also sell film?

In negative sentences *si* follows *non* and precedes the verb.

Qui non si parla inglese.
We don't speak English here.

2. IDIOMATIC USE OF *DA*

The preposition *da* is often used to indicate the purpose of a specific thing. For instance, *carta da lettere* is paper used for writing.

Vendiamo carta da bollo.
We sell government-stamped paper.

Vorrei della carta da lettere.
I'd like some writing paper.

Ha una marca da bollo da 200 lire?
Do you have a 200 lire tax stamp?

Un rullino da 24 pose, per favore.
A 24-exposure roll of film, please.

"Tabacchi"/tabaccheria	tobacco shop
tabaccaio/a	tobacconist
Vorrei un pacchetto di sigarette.	I'd like a pack of cigarettes.
Vorrei una stecca di sigarette.	I'd like a carton of cigarettes.
sigarette con filtro	filtered cigarettes
sigarette senza filtro	nonfiltered cigarettes
scatola di cerini	box of (wax) matches
sigarette estere	imported cigarettes
sigarette lunghe	king-size cigarettes
fiammifero	matches
fiammiferi svedesi	safety matches
accendino/accendisigari	lighter
pipa	pipe
tabacco	tobacco
fumo	smoke
fumare	to smoke
vietato fumare	no smoking
biglietto per l'autobus	bus ticket
carta da bollo	government-stamped paper
marca da bollo	tax stamp
modulo per cambiale	promissory note
carta da lettere	stationery
rullino	a roll (of film)
rullino a colori da 24 pose	a roll of 24-exposure color film
articoli da regalo	gift items
profumo	perfume
giocattolo	toy
telefono pubblico	public phone
Dove si può trovare . . . ?	Where can I find . . . ?
soltanto	only
Un'ultima cosa.	One last thing.
Davvero?	Really?
un po' di tutto	a bit of everything

ESERCIZI

A. *Rispondere affermativamente alle seguenti domande, usando il pronome impersonale "si."*

1. *Qui vendono un po' di tutto?*
2. *Qui vendono biglietti per l'autobus?*
3. *Qui vendono carta da lettere?*
4. *Qui parlano italiano?*
5. *Qui molti parlano due lingue?*

B. *Nelle seguenti frasi riconoscere la funzione del pronome "si," come nell'esempio.* (In the following sentences indicate the function of the pronoun *si*, as in the example.)

	RIFLESSIVO	IMPERSONALE
ESEMPIO: *In Italia si mangia bene.*	_____	√ _____
1. *Maria la mattina si alza alle sei.*	_____	_____
2. *Qui non si parla inglese.*	_____	_____
3. *In Italia Susan si diverte molto.*	_____	_____
4. *Dove si può trovare un telefono?*	_____	_____
5. *Qui si vendono anche francobolli.*	_____	_____

C. *Accoppiare le parole della colonna a sinistra con quelle della colonna a destra.*

1. *un fiammifero*
2. *un giocattolo*
3. *carta da lettere*
4. *un rullino*
5. *un accendino*

a. stationery
b. a match
c. a lighter
d. a toy
e. a roll of film

NOTA CULTURALE

In Italy many large industries, such as tobacco, transportation, and telecommunications, are government run. As a result, several goods and services can be offered at a single convenient location like a tobacco shop. These shops, in addition to selling cigarettes and small necessities, also sell telephone tokens and cards, postcards, toiletries, souvenirs, gifts, bus and subway tickets, etc. Tobacco shops are normally open from 9:00 or 9:30 A.M. to 1:00 P.M., and from 3:30 or 4:00 P.M. to 7:00 or 7:30 P.M. A few of them are open seven days a week and are designated by a black-and-white sign with a big T, reading: *Tabacchi.*

CHIAVE PER GLI ESERCIZI

A. 1. *Sì, qui si vende un po' di tutto.* 2. *Sì, qui si vendono biglietti per l'autobus.* 3. *Sì, qui si vende carta da lettere.* 4. *Sì, qui si parla italiano.* 5. *Sì, qui si parlano due lingue.*

B. 1. *riflessivo* 2. *impersonale* 3. *riflessivo* 4. *impersonale* 5. *impersonale*

C. 1—b; 2—d; 3—a; 4—e; 5—c

LEZIONE 33

UN GIRO DELLA CITTÀ.   A tour of the city.

A. DIALOGO

All'APT (Azienda Promozione Turismo) di Siena.

TURISTA: **Ha una pianta della città?**

IMPIEGATO: **Sì, ecco.**

TURISTA: **Grazie. Vorrei girare la città a piedi, ma ho paura che oggi piova. Le chiese sono aperte?**

IMPIEGATO: **Certo che sono aperte.**

TURISTA: **Vorrei vedere anche qualche museo, però dubito che siano aperti.**

IMPIEGATO: **Oggi è lunedì. Sono sicuro che i musei non sono aperti.**

TURISTA: **Spero che ci siano delle manifestazioni, delle mostre, qualche festa questa settimana?**

IMPIEGATO: **Sì, domani c'è una mostra di fiori. Sono certo che Le piacerà . . .**

TURISTA: **Ma quand'è il Palio? Spero che sia anche in questo periodo.**

IMPIEGATO: **No, no, il Palio è la prima settimana di luglio . . .**

TURISTA: **Peccato! Ci sono dei giri organizzati della città?**

IMPIEGATO: **Sì, certamente. Se desidera possiamo darLe tutte le informazioni necessarie.**

At the tourist information office in Siena.

TOURIST: Do you have a map of the city?

CLERK: Yes, here it is.

TOURIST: Thank you. I'd like to tour the city on foot, but I'm afraid that it will rain. Are churches open?

CLERK: Of course they're open.

TOURIST: I'd also like to see some museums, but I doubt they'll be open.

CLERK: Today is Monday. I'm sure that the museums won't be open.

TOURIST: I hope that there are some special events, some shows, some feasts this week?

CLERK: Yes, tomorrow there's a flower show. I am sure that you'll like it . . .

TOURIST: But when is the Palio? I hope that it's also during this period.

CLERK: No, no, the Palio is in the first week of July . . .

TOURIST: Too bad! Are there any organized tours of the city?

CLERK: Yes, certainly. If you'd like, we could give you all the necessary information.

B. GRAMMATICA E SUOI USI

1. THE SUBJUNCTIVE

The present, present perfect, future, and imperfect tenses that you have already learned are tenses of the indicative mood. This mood is used to make statements and ask questions; it usually expresses certainty and reality.

There is another mood, called the subjunctive (*il congiuntivo*), which expresses uncertainty, doubt, opinion, hope, fear, possibility, belief, etc. The subjunctive is used only occasionally in English.

If I were you . . .
However that may be . . .
I fear lest he come.

In Italian, however, the subjunctive is used much more frequently. It comprises four tenses: the present, the imperfect, the past, and the past perfect.* It is mainly used in dependent clauses introduced by *che*.

* Where Italian uses one of the subjunctive tenses, English commonly uses an indicative counterpart.

(Dependent clauses are sentences introduced by a conjunction such as "that, when, because . . ." and do not have a complete meaning by themselves.)

2. FORMATION OF THE PRESENT SUBJUNCTIVE

The present subjunctive (*il congiuntivo presente*) of regular verbs is formed by dropping -*are*/-*ere*/-*ire* from the infinitive and adding the appropriate subjunctive endings. Note that -*ere* and -*ire* verbs have the same endings, and that verbs ending in -*isc* follow the same pattern as in the indicative present: add -*isc* before the endings in all but the *noi* and *voi* forms.

	PARLARE	TO SPEAK
that I speak	*che io*	*parli*
that you speak (familiar)	*che tu*	*parli*
that he speak	*che lui*	*parli*
that she speak	*che lei*	*parli*
that you speak (polite)	*che Lei*	*parli*
that we speak	*che noi*	*parliamo*
that you speak (familiar or polite)	*che voi*	*parliate*
that they speak	*che loro*	*parlino*
that you speak (polite)	*che Loro*	*parlino*

	VEDERE	TO SEE
that I see	*che io*	*veda*
that you see (familiar)	*che tu*	*veda*
that he see	*che lui*	*veda*
that she see	*che lei*	*veda*
that you see (polite)	*che Lei*	*veda*
that we see	*che noi*	*vediamo*
that you see (familiar or polite)	*che voi*	*vediate*
that they see	*che loro*	*vedano*
that you see (polite)	*che Loro*	*vedano*

	PARTIRE	TO LEAVE
that I leave	*che io*	*parta*
that you leave (familiar)	*che tu*	*parta*
that he leave	*che lui*	*parta*
that she leave	*che lei*	*parta*
that you leave (polite)	*che Lei*	*parta*
that we leave	*che noi*	*partiamo*
that you leave (familiar or polite)	*che voi*	*partiate*
that they leave	*che loro*	*partano*
that you leave (polite)	*che Loro*	*partano*

	FINIRE	TO FINISH
that I finish	*che io*	*finisca*
that you finish (familiar)	*che tu*	*finisca*
that he finish	*che lui*	*finisca*
that she finish	*che lei*	*finisca*
that you finish (polite)	*che Lei*	*finisca*
that we finish	*che noi*	*finiamo*
that you finish (familiar or polite)	*che voi*	*finiate*
that they finish	*che loro*	*finiscano*
that you finish (polite)	*che Loro*	*finiscano*

Dubito che oggi aprano.
I doubt that they'll open today.

Voglio che finiate il lavoro.
I want you to finish the work.

Remember that verbs ending in *-care* and *-gare* add an *h* before all endings of the present subjunctive. Verbs ending in *-ciare* and *-giare* drop the *i* from their stems in the present subjunctive.

Dubito che lui paghi il conto.
I doubt that he'll pay the bill.

Spero che tu mangi bene.
I hope that you eat well.

3. THE PRESENT SUBJUNCTIVE OF *AVERE* AND *ESSERE*

	AVERE	TO HAVE
that I have	che io	abbia
that you have (familiar)	che tu	abbia
that he have	che lui	abbia
that she have	che lei	abbia
that you have (polite)	che Lei	abbia
that we have	che noi	abbiamo
that you have (familiar or polite)	che voi	abbiate
that they have	che loro	abbiano
that you have (polite)	che Loro	abbiano

	ESSERE	TO BE
that I be	che io	sia
that you be (familiar)	che tu	sia
that he be	che lui	sia
that she be	che lei	sia
that you be (polite)	che Lei	sia
that we be	che noi	siamo
that you be (familiar or polite)	che voi	siate
that they be	che loro	siano
that you be (polite)	che Loro	siano

Credo che la festa sia oggi.
> I believe that the feast is today.

Spero che tu abbia abbastanza soldi.
> I hope that you have enough money.

4. USES OF THE SUBJUNCTIVE I

The subjunctive is used after verbs expressing hope, wish, desire, command, or doubt, such as *sperare* ("to hope"), *desiderare* ("to desire"), *volere* ("to want"), and *dubitare* ("to doubt").

Spero che lui vada via.
I hope that he goes away.

Dubito che loro vengano.
I doubt that they'll come.

The subjunctive is also used after verbs expressing an opinion, like *pensare* ("to think") and *credere* ("to believe").

Credo che lei non possa venire.
I believe that she cannot come.

But verbs or expressions that express a certainty or fact like *essere sicuro* ("to be sure"), *essere certo* ("to be certain"), and *sapere* ("to know") require the indicative.

Sono certo che Le piacerà.
I'm certain that you will like it.

Sono sicuro che i musei non aprono.
I'm sure that the museums will not open.

Now, compare these two sentences:

Non so se i musei siano aperti.
I don't know if the museums are open.

So che i musei sono aperti.
I know that the museums are open.

The first sentence requires the subjunctive because *non so* expresses uncertainty; the second sentence, on the other hand, implies a fact or certainty (*So che*) and is, therefore, in the indicative.

VOCABOLARIO

APT (Azienda Promozione Turismo)	tourist office
Azienda Autonoma Soggiorno	City Tourist Board
Ente Provinciale per il Turismo	Provincial Tourist Office
ENIT	Italian State Tourist Office

ufficio turistico	tourist office
Dove si trova l'ufficio informazioni turistiche?	Where is the tourist information office?
Mi potrebbe dare alcune informazioni?	Could you give me some information?
Mi serve un'informazione.	I need some information.
Possiamo darLe tutte le informazioni necessarie.	We can give you all the necessary information.
Non mi posso orientare.	I can't find my way around.
Sono straniero*(a)*.	I'm a foreigner.
Ha una pianta della città?	Do you have a map of the city?
Ha una guida turistica?	Do you have a guidebook?
Ha una carta stradale della regione?	Do you have a road map of the region?
Ha una carta geografica dell'Italia?	Do you have a map of Italy?
Ha un elenco degli alberghi della zona?	Do you have a list of the hotels in the area?
Ha un elenco dei ristoranti della zona?	Do you have a list of restaurants in the area?
Ci sono delle manifestazioni?	Are there any special events?
Ci sono delle mostre?	Are there any shows?
Quand'è la festa di . . . ?	When is the feast of . . . ?
È in questo periodo la festa di . . . ?	Is the feast of . . . during this period?
I musei sono aperti?	Are the museums open?
I musei sono chiusi?	Are the museums closed?
Dov'è il centro commerciale?	Where is the commercial center?
Quanto dista da qui il museo?	How far from here is the museum?
Come si fa ad arrivare al centro?	How do I get downtown?
girare la città	to tour the city
turista (m./f.)	tourist
pensare	to think
credere	to believe
avere paura	to be afraid
sperare	to hope

dubitare	to doubt
essere certo(a)	to be certain
essere sicuro(a)	to be sure

ESERCIZI

A. *Rispondere affermativamente alle domande iniziando la risposta con "Penso che . . ."*

1. *L'ufficio informazioni si trova qui vicino?*
2. *Ci sono dei giri organizzati della città oggi?*
3. *Quell'ufficio ha una pianta della città?*
4. *I musei aprono oggi?*
5. *Franco desidera andare alla mostra?*

B. *Completare le frasi usando il congiuntivo o l'indicativo.*

1. *Mi hanno detto che i musei _____ (aprire) alle dieci.*
2. *Ho paura che oggi _____ (piovere).*
3. *Tu pensi che io _____ (parlare) bene l'italiano?*
4. *Sono certo che la città ti _____ (piacere).*
5. *Credo che Marco _____ (preferire) bere il vino bianco.*

C. *Tradurre.*

1. Could you give me some information, please?
2. I believe that the churches are closed today.
3. Do you have a road map of Italy?
4. I doubt he will arrive today.

NOTA CULTURALE

Top seasonal events in Italy include carnival celebrations (Viareggio and Venice) in January and February; Epiphany celebrations in January (notable is the Epiphany Fair at *Piazza Navona* in Rome); Easter celebrations in Rome and Florence; the Florence May Music Festival (the oldest and most prestigious festival of the performing arts); Siena's *Palio,* a colorful horse race held in the medieval *Piazza del Campo* on July 2 and on August 16; the Maritime Republics' Regatta in June, held in turn in Venice, Genoa, Amalfi, and Pisa; and the Venice Film Festival in late August.

CHIAVE PER GLI ESERCIZI

A. 1. *Sì, penso che l'ufficio informazioni si trovi qui vicino.* 2. *Sì, penso che ci siano dei giri organizzati della città oggi.* 3. *Sì, penso che quell'ufficio abbia una pianta della città.* 4. *Sì, penso che i musei aprano oggi.* 5. *Sì, penso che Franco desideri andare alla mostra.*

B. 1. *aprono* 2. *piova* 3. *parli* 4. *piace/piacerà* 5. *preferisca*

C. 1. *Potrebbe darmi delle informazioni, per favore?* 2. *Credo che le chiese siano chiuse oggi.* 3. *Ha una carta stradale dell'Italia?* 4. *Dubito che lui arrivi oggi.*

LEZIONE 34

IN QUESTURA.   At the police station.

A. DIALOGO

Il portafoglio rubato.

SIGNORINA VERI: **Può aiutarmi, per favore?**

POLIZIOTTO: **Sì, dica?**

SIGNORINA VERI: **Ho perso il portafoglio!**

POLIZIOTTO: **Cosa c'era dentro?**

SIGNORINA VERI: **La mia carta di credito, alcuni documenti ed anche dei soldi . . .**

POLIZIOTTO: **Dove l'ha perso?**

SIGNORINA VERI: **Beh, non credo di averlo perso; penso che me l'abbiano rubato . . .**

POLIZIOTTO: **Allora è stata vittima di un furto?**

SIGNORINA VERI: **Credo di sì.**

POLIZIOTTO: **Ha visto il ladro?**

SIGNORINA VERI: **No, non ho visto nessun ladro. Non so chi sia stato.**

POLIZIOTTO: **È possibile che l'abbia lasciato da qualche parte?**

SIGNORINA VERI: **Sì, è possibile, sebbene io sia sempre attenta.**

POLIZIOTTO: **Forse è meglio che controlli prima di fare denuncia.**

SIGNORINA VERI: **Benché sia sicura, controllerò.**

POLIZIOTTO: **È necessario che mi dia il Suo indirizzo e il numero di telefono.**

SIGNORINA VERI: **Ecco.**

POLIZIOTTO: **Mi dispiace che non possiamo aiutarLa di più.**

The stolen wallet.

MISS VERI: Could you help me, please?

POLICEMAN: What can I do for you?

MISS VERI: I lost my wallet!

POLICEMAN: What was in it?

MISS VERI: My credit card, some documents, and also some money . . .

POLICEMAN: Where did you lose it?

MISS VERI: Well, I don't think I lost it; I think someone stole it from me . . .

POLICEMAN: Then you were the victim of a robbery?

MISS VERI: I think so.

POLICEMAN: Did you see the thief?

MISS VERI: No, I didn't see a thief. I don't know who it was.

POLICEMAN: Is it possible that you may have left it somewhere?

MISS VERI: Yes, it's possible, although I'm always careful.

POLICEMAN: Maybe it's better that you check before you file a complaint.

MISS VERI: Even though I'm sure, I'll check.

POLICEMAN: It's necessary that you leave me your address and telephone number.

MISS VERI: Here you are.

POLICEMAN: I regret that we're not able to help you more.

B. GRAMMATICA E SUOI USI

1. THE PRESENT SUBJUNCTIVE OF IRREGULAR VERBS

Some common verbs have irregular present subjunctive forms.

| to go | *andare* | *vada, vada, vada, andiamo, andiate, vadano* |
| to drink | *bere* | *beva, beva, beva, beviamo, beviate, bevano* |

to give	dare	dia, dia, dia, diamo, diate, diano
to say	dire	dica, dica, dica, diciamo, diciate, dicano
to have to	dovere	debba, debba, debba, dobbiamo, dobbiate, debbano
to do, to make	fare	faccia, faccia, faccia, facciamo, facciate, facciano
to be able to	potere	possa, possa, possa, possiamo, possiate, possano
to know	sapere	sappia, sappia, sappia,
		sappiamo, sappiate, sappiano
to stay	stare	stia, stia, stia, stiamo, stiate, stiano
to go out	uscire	esca, esca, esca, usciamo, usciate, escano
to come	venire	venga, venga, venga, veniamo, veniate, vengano
to want	volere	voglia, voglia, voglia, vogliamo, vogliate, vogliano

È meglio che Lei faccia denuncia.

It's better that you file a complaint.

È necessario che mi dia l'indirizzo.

It's necessary that you give me your address.

Mi dispiace che non possiamo aiutarla.

I regret that we're not able to help you.

2. THE PRESENT PERFECT SUBJUNCTIVE

The present perfect subjunctive (*il congiuntivo passato*) is formed with the present subjunctive of *avere* or *essere* and the past participle of the main verb.

	PARLARE	TO SPEAK
that I spoke	che io	abbia parlato
that you spoke (familiar)	che tu	abbia parlato
that he spoke	che lui	abbia parlato
that she spoke	che lei	abbia parlato
that you spoke (polite)	che Lei	abbia parlato
that we spoke	che noi	abbiamo parlato
that you spoke (familiar or polite)	che voi	abbiate parlato
that they spoke	che loro	abbiano parlato
that you spoke (polite)	che Loro	abbiano parlato

PARTIRE		TO LEAVE
that I left	che io	sia partito/a
that you left (familiar)	che tu	sia partito/a
that he left	che lui	sia partito
that she left	che lei	sia partita
that you left (polite)	che Lei	sia partito/a
that we left	che noi	siamo partiti/e
that you left (familiar or polite)	che voi	siate partiti/e
that they left	che loro	siano partiti/e
that you left (polite)	che Loro	siano partiti/e

Penso che me l'abbiano rubato.
    I think that they stole it from me.

È possibile che io l'abbia lasciato a casa.
    It's possible that I have left it at home.

3. THE PRESENT PERFECT SUBJUNCTIVE OF *AVERE* AND *ESSERE*

As in all compound tenses, the auxiliary of *avere* is *avere,* and the auxiliary of *essere* is *essere.*

AVERE		TO HAVE
that I had	che io	abbia avuto
that you had (familiar)	che tu	abbia avuto
that he had	che lui	abbia avuto
that she had	che lei	abbia avuto
that you had (polite)	che Lei	abbia avuto
that we had	che noi	abbiamo avuto
that you had (familiar or polite)	che voi	abbiate avuto
that they had	che loro	abbiano avuto
that you had (polite)	che Loro	abbiano avuto

	ESSERE	TO BE
that I was	*che io*	*sia stato/a*
that you were (familiar)	*che tu*	*sia stato/a*
that he was	*che lui*	*sia stato*
that she was	*che lei*	*sia stata*
that you were (polite)	*che Lei*	*sia stato/a*
that we were	*che noi*	*siamo stati/e*
that you were (familiar or polite)	*che voi*	*siate stati/e*
that they were	*che loro*	*siano stati/e*
that you were (polite)	*che Loro*	*siano stati/e*

Non so chi sia stato.
   I don't know who it was.

Credo che Lei abbia avuto molta paura.
   I believe that you were really scared.

4. USE OF THE PRESENT AND PRESENT PERFECT SUBJUNCTIVE

If the verb in the main clause is in the present indicative:

Use the present subjunctive in the dependent clause if the action of the dependent clause is simultaneous with or follows the action of the main clause.

Credo che loro vengano oggi.
   I believe that they're coming today.

Spero che la polizia prenda il ladro.
   I hope that the police catch the thief.

Use the present perfect subjunctive in the dependent clause if the action of the dependent clause precedes the action of the main clause.

Spero che sia arrivato ieri.
   I hope that he arrived yesterday.

Credo che qualcuno me l'abbia rubato.
   I believe that someone stole it from me.

5. USES OF THE SUBJUNCTIVE II

The subjunctive is used in dependent clauses after impersonal expressions consisting of *essere* and an adjective or an adverb—*è necessario* ("it is necessary"), *è meglio* ("it is better"), *è possibile* ("it is possible"), *è probabile* ("it is probable")—or other impersonal expressions like *bisogna* ("it is necessary"), unless they state a fact or a certainty.

È possibile che l'abbia lasciato da qualche parte.
It's possible that I left it somewhere.

È necessario che tu mi dia l'indirizzo.
It's necessary that you give me your address.

However, impersonal expressions of certainty, like *è certo* ("it is certain"), *è sicuro* ("it is sure"), and *è vero* ("it is true"), require the indicative.

È vero che ho perso il portafoglio.
It's true that I lost my wallet.

Sono sicuro che lui è il ladro.
I'm sure that he is the thief.

The subjunctive is also used after certain conjunctions like *sebbene* ("even though"), *benché* ("although"), *affinché* ("so that"), *prima che* ("before"), *purché* ("provided that, as long as"), and *nel caso che* ("in the event that").

Ho perso il portafoglio, sebbene io sia sempre attenta.
I lost my wallet, even though I'm always very careful.

Puoi andare al cinema purché ritorni prima delle dieci.
You can go to the movies as long as you return by ten.

If the subject of both verbs in the sentence is the same, use *di* with the infinitive instead of the subjunctive.

Non credo di averlo perso.
I don't think that I lost it.

Carlo crede di conoscere il ladro.
Carlo believes that he knows the thief.

6. USE OF *NESSUNO*

When acting as an adjective, *nessuno* ("no, any") precedes a singular noun and agrees with it in gender. It follows the same pattern as the indefinite article (*un, un', uno, una*).

Non ho visto nessun ladro.
I didn't see any thieves./I saw no thieves.

Non ho perso nessuna carta di credito.
I didn't lose any credit cards.

When acting as a pronoun, it has only one form: *nessuno* ("anyone, no one").

Hai visto la ragazza?
Did you see the girl?

No, non ho visto nessuno.
No, I didn't see anyone./No, I saw no one (nobody).

VOCABOLARIO

questura	police station
Dov'è la stazione della polizia?	Where is the police station?
Dov'è il commissariato?	Where is the police station?
andare al commissariato	to go to the police station
questore (m.)	chief of police
poliziotto	policeman
carabiniere (m.)	(see cultural note)
vigile (m.) **urbano**	municipal (traffic) policeman
guardia comunale	municipal (traffic) policeman
polizia stradale	traffic police
tribunale (m.)	tribunal, court
pretura	magistrate's court
giudice (m.)	judge
ladro	thief

312

vittima	victim
scippatore (m.)	bag snatcher
scippo	bag snatching
crimine (m.)	crime
rubare	to steal
Mi hanno rubato il portafoglio!	They stole my wallet!
Mi hanno derubato.	I have been robbed.
essere vittima di un furto	to be a victim of a robbery
fare denuncia	to file a complaint
denunciare	to file a complaint
multa	ticket, fine
contravvenzione (f.)	ticket, fine
è possibile	it's possible
è probabile	it's probable
è meglio	it's better
è necessario	it's necessary
è certo	it's certain
è sicuro	it's sure
è vero	it's true

ESERCIZI

A. *Tradurre.*

1. John believes he knows the thief.
2. It's necessary that you (singular, familiar) give me your address.
3. I regret that they are not able to come.
4. It's better that you (singular, formal) file a complaint.
5. I think Paul wants to tour the city.

B. *Rispondere alle seguenti domande usando il congiuntivo passato.*

1. *È andata in questura la signorina Veri?*
   No, non penso che _____.
2. *Ti hanno rubato il portafoglio?*
   Sì, credo che _____.

3. *Sandra ha lasciato il libro a casa?*
   Sì, è probabile che _____.
4. *Sono arrivati i carabinieri?*
   Sì, è possibile che _____.
5. *Sono partiti i signori Rossi?*
   No, dubito che _____.
6. *Gianni è stato malato?*
   No, non credo che _____.

C. *Usare le seguenti parole per completare le frasi.*

sebbene   nel caso che   prima che   affinché   purché

1. *Vengo anch'io alla stazione della polizia,* _____ *venga anche tu.*
2. _____ *il questore esca, dovrei dirgli una cosa importante.*
3. *I miei genitori lavorano* _____ *io possa studiare.*
4. _____ *sia ricca, la signorina Veri non spende molto.*
5. _____ *cominci a piovere resteremo a casa.*

NOTA CULTURALE

The Italian police system consists of the police force and the *carabinieri*. The *carabinieri* are members of an Italian army corps that collaborates with the police force and has similar powers. In general, in small towns, the *carabinieri* carry out normal police duties, and the *guardie comunali* or *vigili urbani* direct traffic and issue parking tickets. The *polizia stradale* has traffic jurisdiction outside the towns.

CHIAVE PER GLI ESERCIZI

A. 1. *John crede di conoscere il ladro.* 2. *È necessario che tu mi dia il tuo indirizzo.* 3. *Mi dispiace che loro non possano venire.* 4. *È meglio che Lei faccia denuncia.* 5. *Credo che Paul voglia fare un giro della città.*

B. 1. *No, non penso che sia andata in questura.* 2. *Sì, credo che mi abbiano rubato il portafoglio.* 3. *Sì, è probabile che Sandra abbia lasciato il libro a casa.* 4. *Sì, è possibile che i carabinieri siano arrivati.* 5. *No, dubito che i signori Rossi siano partiti.* 6. *No, non credo che sia stato malato.*

C. 1. *purché* 2. *Prima che* 3. *affinché* 4. *Sebbene* 5. *Nel caso che*

LEZIONE 35

A. DIALOGO

Un mal di testa.

FARMACISTA: **In che cosa posso servirLa?**

CLIENTE: **Ho un forte mal di testa: il più forte mal di testa che abbia mai avuto. Vorrei un antidolorifico.**

FARMACISTA: **Potrei darLe questo, ma occorre la ricetta.**

CLIENTE: **Ne ha uno per cui la ricetta non è necessaria?**

FARMACISTA: **Sì, Le consiglio questo.**

CLIENTE: **Fa male allo stomaco?**

FARMACISTA: **No, è l'unico prodotto che non faccia male. È proprio questo il motivo per cui glielo consiglio.**

CLIENTE: **Dottore, La ringrazio. Lei è la sola persona nella quale abbia fiducia. Vorrei anche delle pillole per dormire.**

FARMACISTA: **Mi dispiace, ma per le pillole di cui ha bisogno ci vuole la ricetta.**

CLIENTE: **Va bene. Andrò dal medico.**

A headache.

PHARMACIST: How may I help you?

CLIENT: I have a bad headache: the worst headache I've ever had. I'd like a pain reliever.

PHARMACIST: I could give you this one, but you need a prescription.

CLIENT: Do you have one for which a prescription isn't necessary?

PHARMACIST: Yes, I suggest this one.

CLIENT: Will it upset my stomach?

PHARMACIST: No, it's the only product that won't harm you. It's precisely for this reason that I'm suggesting it.

CLIENT: Thank you, Doctor. You're the only person I trust. I'd also like some sleeping pills.

PHARMACIST: I'm sorry, but for the pills you need, it's necessary to have a prescription.

CLIENT: Okay. I'll go to the doctor.

B. GRAMMATICA E SUOI USI

1. RELATIVE PRONOUNS

A relative pronoun (*pronome relativo*) links a dependent clause to a noun or pronoun in a main clause. A dependent clause that starts with a relative pronoun is called a relative clause. The noun or pronoun to which the relative pronoun refers is called the antecedent.

È l'unico prodotto che non faccia male allo stomaco.
It's the only product that doesn't upset your stomach.

| Main clause: | *È l'unico prodotto* | It's the only product |
| Relative clause: | *che non faccia male allo stomaco* | that doesn't upset your stomach |

Here, the relative pronoun *che* ("that") refers back to *prodotto* ("product"), its antecedent.

La ragazza che vedi è mia sorella.
The girl whom you see is my sister.

| Main clause: | *La ragazza . . . è mia sorella.* | The girl . . . is my sister |
| Relative clause: | *che vedi* | whom you see |

Here, the relative pronoun *che* ("whom") refers back to *ragazza* ("girl"), its antecedent.

When the antecedent is a definite person, animal, or thing, *che, cui,* or a form of *il quale* should be used.

ANTECEDENT	SUBJECT OR DIRECT OBJECT	OBJECT OF A PREPOSITION
definite person, animal, or thing	*che*	*cui*
	il quale, la quale, i quali, le quali	

Che is invariable and is never used with a preposition.

Cui is invariable and is always used with a preposition.

Il quale has four forms—masculine and feminine singular, and masculine and feminine plural—and can be used with articles or articles plus prepositions. It can replace either *che* or *cui*. It is used mainly in formal speech, writing, and for clarity.

È una medicina che (la quale) non fa male allo stomaco.
It's medicine that doesn't upset your stomach.

Le pillole che (le quali) prendo sono pillole per dormire.
The pills that I take are sleeping pills.

Per le pillole di cui (delle quali) ha bisogno ci vuole la ricetta.
The pills which you need require a prescription.

Questo è il motivo per cui (per il quale) Le consiglio queste pillole.
This is why (the reason for which) I suggest these pills.

Lei è la sola persona nella quale (in cui) io abbia fiducia.
You are the only person whom I trust.

La ragazza con la quale (con cui) esco è italiana.
The girl with whom I go out is Italian.

When the andecedent is indefinite (unknown), other relative pronouns should be used.

Chi is invariable and used when referring to people. It means: "he/she who," "whoever," "the one who" and takes a verb in the third person singular form.

Chi sta bene non va dal dottore.
He who feels well doesn't go to the doctor.

Chi ha bisogno di una medicina va in farmacia.
The one who needs medicine goes to the pharmacy.

Quello che, quel che, and *ciò che* are invariable and interchangeable. They are used when referring to a thing and mean "what" or "that which."

Non capisco quello che dice.
I don't understand what (that which) he is saying.

Ciò che scrivi è sbagliato.
What (that which) you're writing is wrong.

2. USES OF THE SUBJUNCTIVE III

The subjunctive is also used after a relative superlative plus *che,* and after words like *il primo* ("the first") plus *che, l'ultimo* ("the last") plus *che, il solo* ("the only") plus *che.*

È il più forte mal di testa che abbia mai avuto.
It's the strongest headache that I've ever had.

È il solo prodotto che non faccia male allo stomaco.
It's the only product that doesn't upset your stomach.

VOCABOLARIO

farmacia	pharmacy
farmacia di turno	pharmacy "on duty" (open on a holiday or at night)
farmacista (m./f.)	pharmacist
Vorrei un antidolorifico.	I would like a pain reliever.
Mi serve dello sciroppo per la tosse.	I need some cough syrup.
Mi dia qualcosa per la tosse.	Please, give me something for my cough.
Ha dello spirito?	Do you have rubbing alcohol?
Ha della garza?	Do you have any gauze?
Vorrei un digestivo.	I would like a digestive.
Ha un disinfettante?	Do you have a disinfectant?
Vorrei una pomata per l'irritazione della pelle.	I would like an ointment for skin rash.

pomata contro le scottature	suntan lotion
Ci vuole/Occorre la ricetta?	Is a prescription necessary?
Le consiglio questa medicina.	I suggest this medicine.
Non fa male allo stomaco.	It doesn't upset your stomach.
pasticca per la tosse	cough drop
gocce (f., pl.)	drops
pillola per dormire	sleeping pill
sedativo/calmante (m.)	sedative
cerotto	bandage
fazzolettino di carta	tissue
puntura/iniezione (f.)	injection
supposta	suppository
termometro	thermometer
siringa	syringe
vitamina	vitamin
bruciore (m.) allo stomaco	heartburn
prurito	itchiness
penicillina	penicillin
indicazioni per l'uso	usage instructions
dose (f.)	dosage
prodotto	product
avere fiducia in . . .	to trust . . .

ESERCIZI

A. *Tradurre.*

1. Do you have any bandages?
2. I would like a digestive.
3. Is a prescription necessary?
4. Do you have a suntan lotion?
5. He is the only doctor I trust.

B. *Rimettere le parole in ordine.*

1. *questa / medicina / l' / unica / è / non / male / che / faccia*
2. *Lucia / la / è / persona / sola / nella / quale / fiducia / io / abbia*

3. *questa / più / buona / la / è / pomata / che / io / conosca*
4. *dello / per / vorrei / sciroppo / tosse / la*
5. *dia / mi / antidolorifico / un / piacere / per*

C. *Completare con il pronome relativo appropriato: "che, cui, chi, quello che."*

1. *La medicina* _____ *ho comprato è molto buona.*
2. *Ecco la farmacia di* _____ *ti ho parlato.*
3. _____ *sta bene non va dal dottore.*
4. *Tu non hai capito* _____ *ti ho detto.*
5. *Gli amici con* _____ *sono uscito ieri sono tutti italiani.*

NOTA CULTURALE

In Italy most pharmacies are open from 8:30 A.M. to 1:00 P.M., and 4:00 to 8:00 P.M.; some are open all night. Pharmacies alternate staying open on Sundays. They can be identified by a green or red cross sign lighted at night. A list of pharmacies open on Sundays (*farmacia di turno*) and their working hours is posted in each pharmacy.

Baby food, baby formula, and diapers may be bought in large supermarkets as well as in pharmacies.

Pharmacists are addressed as doctors.

CHIAVE PER GLI ESERCIZI

A. 1. *Ha dei cerotti?* 2. *Vorrei un digestivo.* 3. *Ci vuole/Occorre/È necessaria la ricetta?* 4. *Ha una pomata contro le scottature?* 5. *È il solo dottore in cui abbia fiducia.*

B. 1. *Questa medicina è l'unica che non faccia male.* 2. *Lucia è la sola persona nella quale io abbia fiducia.* 3. *Questa è la pomata più buona che io conosca.* 4. *Vorrei dello sciroppo per la tosse.* 5. *Mi dia un antidolorifico, per piacere.*

C. 1. *che*   2. *cui*   3. *chi*   4. *quello che*   5. *cui*

SETTIMO RIPASSO

A. *Trasformare le seguenti frasi in frasi impersonali usando il pronome "si."* (Rewrite the following sentences using the impersonal pronoun *si.*)

1. *Qui vendiamo sigarette e francobolli.*
2. *In Canada molti parlano due lingue.*
3. *In questa casa nessuno può fumare.*
4. *A casa mia mangiamo molta verdura.*
5. *Con il pesce tutti bevono il vino bianco.*
6. *Oggi diamo 1.230 lire per i soldi in contanti.*

B. *Completare le seguenti frasi usando il condizionale di un verbo appropriato, scegliendo tra i seguenti.* (Complete with the correct form of the conditional, choosing the verbs from the list below.)

essere   venire   volere   potere   avere

1. *Io _____ cambiare questi dollari in lire italiane.*
2. *Signore, _____ un documento, per favore?*
3. *Loro _____ venuti ieri, ma non hanno potuto.*
4. *Scusi, mi _____ dare delle banconote di piccolo taglio?*
5. *_____ al cinema, ma oggi non posso.*

C. *Completare con un verbo all'indicativo o al congiuntivo.*

1. *Il ragionier Risi è italiano?*
   Sì, mi ha detto che _____ italiano.
2. *Silvana lavora in banca o in una farmacia?*
   So che _____ in una farmacia.
3. *Quante case hanno i signori Verdi?*
   Penso che _____ due case.
4. *Le devo dare il mio indirizzo, signorina?*
   Sì, è necessario che me lo _____.
5. *Gianfranco è andato dal dottore oggi?*
   Sì, credo che ci _____.
6. *Le chiese sono aperte oggi?*
   No, dubito che _____ aperte.

D. *Completare con il pronome relativo appropriato.*

1. *L'impiegato _____ lavora all'ufficio di cambio sa bene l'inglese.*
2. *I giocattoli _____ ho comprato sono molto belli.*

3. *Domani c'è quella mostra _____ ti ho parlato.*

4. *_____ ha visto il ladro dovrebbe telefonare subito ai carabinieri.*

5. *Ho un forte mal di testa. Non ho sentito _____ hai detto.*

6. *Maria è l'unica persona nella _____ abbiamo fiducia.*

CHIAVE PER GLI ESERCIZI

A. 1. *Qui si vendono sigarette e francobolli.* 2. *In Canada si parlano due lingue.* 3. *In questa casa non si può fumare.* 4. *A casa mia si mangia molta verdura.* 5. *Con il pesce si beve il vino bianco.* 6. *Oggi si danno 1.230 lire per i soldi in contanti.*

B. 1. *vorrei* 2. *avrebbe* 3. *sarebbero* 4. *potrebbe* 5. *Verrei*

C. 1. *è* 2. *lavora* 3. *abbiano* 4. *dia* 5. *sia andato* 6. *siano*

D. 1. *che/il quale* 2. *che/i quali* 3. *di cui/della quale* 4. *Chi* 5. *quello che/ ciò che* 6. *quale*

LEZIONE 36

NOLEGGIARE UNA MACCHINA.   Renting a car.

A. DIALOGO

All'autonoleggio.

SIGNORA SMITH: **Vorrei noleggiare una macchina.**

IMPIEGATO: **Che tipo di auto preferisce?**

SIGNORA SMITH: **Una macchina con il cambio automatico. Vuole vedere la patente internazionale?**

IMPIEGATO: **Mi dispiace, ma le macchine con il cambio automatico sono tutte esaurite.**

SIGNORA SMITH: **Ma l'ho ordinata un mese fa! Speravo proprio che fosse pronta.**

IMPIEGATO: **Non credevamo che Lei partisse oggi. Questa Fiat Uno non ha il cambio automatico, ma è una bella macchina. E non Le verrà a costare molto: cinquantamila lire al giorno.**

SIGNORA SMITH: **Pensavo che costasse di meno. Guardi, desidererei che Lei mi facesse un favore?**

IMPIEGATO: **Sì, dica.**

SIGNORA SMITH: **Potrebbe procurarmene una con il cambio automatico al più presto?**

IMPIEGATO: **Certo, torni dopodomani.**

SIGNORA SMITH: **Un'altra cosa. Vorrei che Lei mi procurasse anche una carta stradale dell'Italia.**

At a car rental agency.

MRS. SMITH: I'd like to rent a car.

CLERK: What type would you prefer?

MRS. SMITH: An automatic car. Would you like to see my International Driver's License?

CLERK: I'm sorry, but there are no more automatic cars.

MRS. SMITH: But I reserved it a month ago! I really hoped that you'd have one ready.

CLERK: We didn't think that you were leaving today. This Fiat Uno is not automatic, but it's a beautiful car. And it won't cost you much: fifty thousand lire a day.

MRS. SMITH: I thought it was cheaper. Look, would you do me a favor?

CLERK: Yes, go ahead.

MRS. SMITH: Could you find me one with automatic transmission as soon as possible?

CLERK: Of course, come back the day after tomorrow.

MRS. SMITH: One more thing. I'd also appreciate it if you would furnish me with a road map of Italy.

B. GRAMMATICA E SUOI USI

1. THE IMPERFECT SUBJUNCTIVE

The imperfect subjunctive (*il congiuntivo imperfetto*) is formed by dropping the *-re* from the infinitive and replacing it with the appropriate imperfect subjunctive personal ending: *-ssi, -sse, -ssimo, -ste,* or *-ssero*.

	PARLARE	TO SPEAK
that I spoke	*che io*	*parlassi*
that you spoke (familiar)	*che tu*	*parlassi*
that he spoke	*che lui*	*parlasse*
that she spoke	*che lei*	*parlasse*
that you spoke (polite)	*che Lei*	*parlasse*
that we spoke	*che noi*	*parlassimo*
that you spoke (familiar or polite)	*che voi*	*parlaste*
that they spoke	*che loro*	*parlassero*
that you spoke (polite)	*che Loro*	*parlassero*

	VEDERE	TO SEE
that I saw	che io	vedessi
that you saw (familiar)	che tu	vedessi
that he saw	che lui	vedesse
that she saw	che lei	vedesse
that you saw (polite)	che Lei	vedesse
that we saw	che noi	vedessimo
that you saw (familiar or polite)	che voi	vedeste
that they saw	che loro	vedessero
that you saw (polite)	che Loro	vedessero

	PARTIRE	TO LEAVE
that I left	che io	partissi
that you left (familiar)	che tu	partissi
that he left	che lui	partisse
that she left	che lei	partisse
that you left (polite)	che Lei	partisse
that we left	che noi	partissimo
that you left (familiar or polite)	che voi	partiste
that they left	che loro	partissero
that you left (polite)	che Loro	partissero

Non credevamo che Lei partisse oggi.
We didn't think that you were leaving today.

Vorrei che vedesse questa Fiat Uno.
I would like you to see this Fiat Uno.

Pensavo che costasse di meno.
I thought it would cost me less.

"Con chi parlava Carlo al telefono?"
With whom was Carlo talking on the phone?

"Non so. Penso che parlasse con un suo amico."
I don't know. I think he was speaking with one of his friends.

2. THE IMPERFECT SUBJUNCTIVE OF *AVERE* AND *ESSERE*

Avere is regular in the imperfect subjunctive, while *essere* is irregular.

	AVERE	TO HAVE
that I had	*che io*	*avessi*
that you had (familiar)	*che tu*	*avessi*
that he had	*che lui*	*avesse*
that she had	*che lei*	*avesse*
that you had (polite)	*che Lei*	*avesse*
that we had	*che noi*	*avessimo*
that you had (familiar or polite)	*che voi*	*aveste*
that they had	*che loro*	*avessero*
that you had (polite)	*che Loro*	*avessero*

Volevo una macchina che avesse il cambio automatico.
   I wanted a car that had automatic transmission.

Pensavo che tu avessi vent' anni.
   I thought you were twenty years old.

	ESSERE	TO BE
that I was	*che io*	*fossi*
that you were (familiar)	*che tu*	*fossi*
that he was	*che lui*	*fosse*
that she was	*che lei*	*fosse*
that you were (polite)	*che Lei*	*fosse*
that we were	*che noi*	*fossimo*
that you were (familiar or polite)	*che voi*	*foste*
that they were	*che loro*	*fossero*
that you were (polite)	*che Loro*	*fossero*

Speravo che la macchina fosse pronta.
   I hoped that the car would be ready.

Credevamo che voi foste felici.
   We believed you were happy.

3. THE IMPERFECT SUBJUNCTIVE OF IRREGULAR VERBS

Four very common verbs have irregular imperfect subjunctive forms.
Notice that the stems are irregular, but the endings are regular.

	FARE	TO DO, TO MAKE
that I did	*che io*	*facessi*
that you did (familiar)	*che tu*	*facessi*
that he did	*che lui*	*facesse*
that she did	*che lei*	*facesse*
that you did (polite)	*che Lei*	*facesse*
that we did	*che noi*	*facessimo*
that you did (familiar or polite)	*che voi*	*faceste*
that they did	*che loro*	*facessero*
that you did (polite)	*che Loro*	*facessero*

Desidererei che Lei mi facesse un favore.
I'd like you to do me a favor.

Speravamo che voi faceste questo lavoro.
We were hoping you'd do this work.

	BERE	TO DRINK
that I drank	*che io*	*bevessi*
that you drank (familiar)	*che tu*	*bevessi*
that he drank	*che lui*	*bevesse*
that she drank	*che lei*	*bevesse*
that you drank (polite)	*che Lei*	*bevesse*
that we drank	*che noi*	*bevessimo*
that you drank (familiar or polite)	*che voi*	*beveste*
that they drank	*che loro*	*bevessero*
that you drank (polite)	*che Loro*	*bevessero*

Preferirei che voi non beveste.
I would prefer that you don't drink.

Volevano che io bevessi la birra.
They wanted me to drink the beer.

		TO SAY, TO TELL
that I said	*che io*	*dicessi*
that you said (familiar)	*che tu*	*dicessi*
that he said	*che lui*	*dicesse*
that she said	*che lei*	*dicesse*
that you said (polite)	*che Lei*	*dicesse*
that we said	*che noi*	*dicessimo*
that you said (familiar or polite)	*che voi*	*diceste*
that they said	*che loro*	*dicessero*
that you said (polite)	*che Loro*	*dicessero*

Volevo che tu mi dicessi di sì.
   I wanted you to say yes to me.

Credevamo che Lei dicesse la verità.
   We believed you were telling the truth.

		TO BE, TO STAY
that I was, stayed	*che io*	*stessi*
that you were, stayed (familiar)	*che tu*	*stessi*
that he was, stayed	*che lui*	*stesse*
that she was, stayed	*che lei*	*stesse*
that you were, stayed (polite)	*che Lei*	*stesse*
that we were, stayed	*che noi*	*stessimo*
that you were, stayed (familiar or polite)	*che voi*	*steste*
that they were, stayed	*che loro*	*stessero*
that you were, stayed (polite)	*che Loro*	*stessero*

Pensavo che tu stessi bene.
   I thought you were fine.

Volevo che Maria stesse in Italia.
   I wanted Maria to stay in Italy.

328

4. FEMININE NOUNS ENDING IN -O

The following common nouns are abbreviated forms and are feminine even though they end in -o. They do not change in the plural.

l'auto	*le auto*	the car, the cars
la moto	*le moto*	the motorcycle, the motorcycles
la radio	*le radio*	the radio, the radios
la foto	*le foto*	the photo, the photos

In quell'autonoleggio hanno delle auto con il cambio automatico.
In that car rental agency they have cars with automatic transmission.

In quell'autonoleggio noleggiano anche moto.
In that car rental agency they also rent motorcycles.

Ho comprato due radio.
I bought two radios.

Avete fatto delle foto?
Did you take some pictures?

VOCABOLARIO

noleggiare una macchina	to rent a car
autonoleggio	car rental agency
Che tipo di macchina preferisce?	What kind of car do you like?
utilitaria	compact car
un pulmino	a mini van
una macchina con le marce	standard transmission car
cambio automatico	automatic transmission
una macchina per cinque persone	a five-seater car
Quant'è il noleggio per una settimana?	How much is the rental for a week?
pagamento anticipato	payment in advance
tassa governativa	government tax
cancellazione (f.)	cancellation

assicurazione (f.)	insurance
L'assicurazione è inclusa nel prezzo?	Is the insurance included in the price?
Carta Verde	green card insurance
assicurazione contro ogni rischio	full insurance coverage
assicurazione contro i danni	collision damage waiver
assicurazione medica	medical insurance
Quanti chilometri fa con un pieno?	How many kilometers with a fill up?
Consuma molta benzina?	Does it use a lot of gas?
C'è abbastanza benzina?	Is there enough gas?
buono benzina	gas coupon
carta carburante turistica	highway toll card
pacchetto di agevolazione turistica	Incentive Tourist Package
pacchetto Italia Nord	Tourist Package for the North of Italy
pacchetto Italia Sud	Tourist Package for the South of Italy
tagliando Km. 1.000	1,000 kilometers coupon
ispezione (f.)	inspection
Quant'è grande il portabagagli?	How big is the trunk?
Ha un portabagagli (una rete portabagagli)?	Does it have a trunk/luggage rack?
A quanti cilindri è?	How many cylinders does it have?
Ha il mangianastri?	Does it have a cassette player?
chilometraggio illimitato	unlimited mileage
patente (f.) internazionale	International Driving Permit
Dov'è l'ACI (Automobile Club Italiano)?	Where is the ACI (Italian Automobile Association)?
l'auto (f.)	car
la moto	motorcycle
la radio	radio
la foto	photo

ESERCIZI

A. *Tradurre.*

1. Do you (singular, familiar) like driving standard cars?
2. How much is the rental for a week?
3. Is the insurance included in the price?
4. Does this car have a big trunk?
5. I would like you to see this compact car.

B. *Formare delle frasi con le seguenti parole.*

ESEMPIO: *Speravo / Luigi / venire / oggi*
           Speravo che Luigi venisse oggi.

1. *Io / credevo / Maria / partire / oggi*
2. *Pensavo / questa / macchina / costare / di / meno*
3. *Io / desidererei / tu / mi / fare / favore*
4. *Vorrei / voi / comprare / macchina*
5. *Io / pensavo / Barbara / essere / italiana*

C. *Completare con la forma appropriata del verbo fra parentesi.*

1. *Mio fratello vorrebbe che io gli _____ (dare) la mia macchina.*
2. *Io pensavo che quella macchina _____ (avere) il cambio automatico.*
3. *Sono sicuro che da bambino lui _____ (abitare) in quella casa.*
4. *Credevo che Anna e Roberto _____ (venire) con noi.*
5. *Volevo che tu mi _____ (dire) di sì.*

NOTA CULTURALE

Renting a car in Italy is easy: most of the large car rental companies (Hertz, Avis, and the Italian-based *Maggiore*) have branches in the major cities and towns. It is, however, difficult to find automatic-transmission cars. Rental prices are relatively high, and you must purchase insurance (about $11 a day) as well as pay a government tax of 19 percent. Luckily, most major credit cards will cover your insurance fee if you use the credit card in the rental transaction. Weekend and monthly rates are also available. To drive in Italy you need a valid International Driver's Licence and a passport.

CHIAVE PER GLI ESERCIZI

A. 1. *Ti piace guidare macchine con le marce? 2. Quant'è il noleggio per una settimana? 3. L'assicurazione è inclusa nel prezzo? 4. Questa macchina ha un portabagagli grande? 5. Vorrei che tu vedessi questa utilitaria.*

B. 1. *Io credevo che Maria partisse oggi. 2. Pensavo che questa macchina costasse di meno. 3. Io desidererei che tu mi facessi un favore. 4. Vorrei che voi compraste una macchina. 5. Io pensavo che Barbara fosse italiana.*

C. 1. *dessi* 2. *avesse* 3. *abitava* 4. *venissero* 5. *dicessi*

LEZIONE 37

IN UN NEGOZIO DI SCARPE.   In a shoe store.

A. DIALOGO

Un paio di scarpe perfette.

CLIENTE: **Vorrei un paio di scarpe.**

COMMESSA: **Di che colore?**

CLIENTE: **Nere.**

COMMESSA: **Che numero porta?**

CLIENTE: **Il quarantatrè.**

COMMESSA: **Provi queste.**

CLIENTE: **Mi vanno troppo strette. Ma queste sono quarantadue, non quarantatrè.**

COMMESSA: **Scusi, credevo che avesse detto quarantadue. Ecco il quarantatrè. Le vanno bene? Le piacciono?**

CLIENTE: **Sì, sono belle. E mi vanno anche bene. Quanto costano?**

COMMESSA: **Duecentocinquantamila lire.**

CLIENTE: **Troppo care! Se fossi ricco le comprerei. Ha qualcosa di meno caro?**

COMMESSA: **Se desidera, posso farLe vedere qualcos'altro. Vuole provare queste marroni?**

CLIENTE: **Sono comode. Se le avesse in nero, le prenderei.**

COMMESSA: **Un attimo che gliele prendo. Ecco.**

CLIENTE: **Le compro. Vorrei anche un paio di scarponi da sci.**

COMMESSA: **Non ne abbiamo.**

CLIENTE: **Ne ho visto un paio in vetrina.**

COMMESSA: **Scusi, non sapevo che fossero arrivati.**

A perfect pair of shoes.

CLIENT: I would like a pair of shoes.

SALESPERSON: What color?

CLIENT: Black.

SALESPERSON: What size do you wear?

CLIENT: Forty-three.

SALESPERSON: Try these on.

CLIENT: They're too tight. But these are size forty-two, not forty-three.

SALESPERSON: I apologize. I thought that you had said forty-two. Here's size forty-three. Do they fit well? Do you like them?

CLIENT: Yes, they're beautiful. And they fit well too. How much do they cost?

SALESPERSON: Two hundred fifty thousand lire.

CLIENT: Too expensive! If I were rich, I would buy them. Do you have anything less expensive?

SALESPERSON: If you want, I can show you something else. Would you like to try on these brown ones?

CLIENT: They're comfortable. If you had them in black, I would buy them.

SALESPERSON: One moment, I'll get them. Here you are.

CLIENT: I'll buy them. I would also like a pair of ski boots.

SALESPERSON: We don't have any.

CLIENT: I saw a pair in the window.

SALESPERSON: I apologize, I didn't know that they had arrived.

B. GRAMMATICA E SUOI USI

1. THE PAST PERFECT SUBJUNCTIVE

The past perfect subjunctive (*il trapassato del congiuntivo*) consists of the imperfect subjunctive of *avere* or *essere* plus the past participle of the main verb.

	PARLARE	TO SPEAK
that I had spoken	*che io*	*avessi parlato*
that you had spoken (familiar)	*che tu*	*avessi parlato*
that he had spoken	*che lui*	*avesse parlato*
that she had spoken	*che lei*	*avesse parlato*
that you had spoken (polite)	*che Lei*	*avesse parlato*
that we had spoken	*che noi*	*avessimo parlato*
that you had spoken (familiar or polite)	*che voi*	*aveste parlato*
that they had spoken	*che loro*	*avessero parlato*
that you had spoken (polite)	*che Loro*	*avessero parlato*

	PARTIRE	TO LEAVE
that I had left	*che io*	*fossi partito/a*
that you had left (familiar)	*che tu*	*fossi partito/a*
that he had left	*che lui*	*fosse partito*
that she had left	*che lei*	*fosse partita*
that you had left (polite)	*che Lei*	*fosse partito/a*
that we had left	*che noi*	*fossimo partiti/e*
that you had left (familiar or polite)	*che voi*	*foste partiti/e*
that they had left	*che loro*	*fossero partiti/e*
that you had left (polite)	*che Loro*	*fossero partiti/e*

Credevo che Lei avesse detto quarantadue.
   I thought that you had said forty-two.

Non sapevo che fossero già arrivati.
   I didn't know that they had already arrived.

2. USE OF THE IMPERFECT AND PAST PERFECT SUBJUNCTIVE

If the main clause is in one of the past tenses (*passato prossimo, imperfetto, trapassato prossimo*) or in the conditional (present or past), use the imperfect subjunctive if the action of the dependent clause is simultaneous with or follows the action of the main clause.

Credevo che le scarpe Le andassero bene.
I thought that the shoes fit you well.

Speravo che il colore Le piacesse.
I hoped that you liked the color.

Use the past perfect subjunctive if the action of the dependent clause precedes the action of the main clause.

Credevo che tu avessi già provato le scarpe.
I thought that you had already tried on the shoes.

Speravo che fosse già andata a comprarsi le scarpe.
I hoped that she had already gone to buy her shoes.

3. THE "IF" CLAUSE OF REALITY AND POSSIBILITY/IMPOSSIBILITY

As explained in lessons 30 and 31, a conditional sentence includes an "if" clause and a conclusion. The "if" clause can express (1) reality, (2) possibility/impossibility, or (3) impossibility, unreality. In this lesson we will discuss the first two cases.

The "if" clause of reality expresses a state or action that may really exist or occur. In this case the indicative is used in both the "if" clause and the conclusion.

Se desidera, posso farLe vedere qualcos'altro.
If you want, I can show you something else.
(You may indeed want me to.)

Se non compro le scarpe oggi, non le comprerò mai.
If I don't buy shoes today, I'll never buy them.
(I may indeed not buy them today.)

The "if" clause of possibility/impossibility presents a hypothetical situation in the present, that is, a state or action that the speaker knows or believes to be impossible or unlikely to occur. In this case the imperfect subjunctive is used in the "if" clause and the present conditional in the conclusion.

Se fossi ricco, le comprerei.
   If I were rich, I would buy them. (But I'm not rich.)

Se le avesse in nero, le prenderei.
   If you had them in black, I would take them.
   (But you probably don't have them in black.)

4. THE PLURAL OF MONOSYLLABIC NOUNS

Monosyllabic nouns like *sci, tè,* and *re* do not change in the plural.

il re	*i re*	king, kings
lo sci	*gli sci*	ski, skis
il tè	*i tè*	tea, teas

Gli sci sono nuovi.
   The skis are new.

Due tè, per favore.
   Two teas, please.

VOCABOLARIO

negozio di scarpe	shoe store
calzoleria	shoe repair store
scarpe da uomo	men's shoes
scarpe da donna	women's shoes
un paio di scarpe	a pair of shoes
sandali (m., pl.)	sandals
stivali (m., pl.)	boots
stivaletto	ankle boot
pantofola	slipper
zoccolo	clog

scarpe da tennis	tennis shoes
scarponi (m., pl.) da sci	ski boots
scarpe di camoscio	suede shoes
tacco alto	high heel
tacco basso	low heel
tacco a spillo	stiletto/spike heel
Di che colore?	What color?
Le ha in nero?	Do you have them in black?
Le ha in marrone?	Do you have them in brown?
Che numero porta?	What size do you wear?
Il quaranta.	Size forty.
provare una scarpa	to try on a shoe
Sono comode.	They're comfortable.
Mi stanno strette.	They're tight.
Mi stanno larghe.	They're big on me.
soletta	insole
calzascarpe (m.)	shoehorn
Ha qualcosa di meno caro?	Do you have something less expensive?
Un attimo che gliele prendo.	One moment. I'll get them.
Posso farLe vedere qualcos'altro?	May I show you something else?
calzolaio	shoemaker
mettersi le scarpe	to put on one's shoes
togliersi le scarpe	to take off one's shoes
allacciarsi le scarpe	to tie one's shoes
lucidare le scarpe	to clean one's shoes
lucido per scarpe	shoe polish
spazzola per scarpe	shoe brush
lacci (m., pl.) per le scarpe	shoe laces

ESERCIZI

A. *Trasformare queste frasi in frasi ipotetiche, come nell'esempio.* (Change each sentence to a hypothetical statement, as in the example.)

ESEMPIO: *Se piove, non esco.*
Se piovesse, non uscirei.

1. *Se ha delle scarpe nere, le compro.*
2. *Se tu vai al negozio di scarpe, vengo anch'io.*
3. *Se hanno i soldi, vanno in Italia.*
4. *Se ho il tempo, vado a comprare delle scarpe da tennis.*
5. *Se mi telefona Marco, gli dico di venire qui.*
6. *Se ho fame, mangio.*

B. *Completare con un verbo al trapassato del congiuntivo.*

1. *Io sapevo che le scarpe erano arrivate.*
   Oh, io pensavo che non _____.
2. *Io sapevo che loro avevano comprato quegli stivali.*
   Oh, io pensavo che non li _____.
3. *Io sapevo che lui era andato dal calzolaio.*
   Oh, io pensavo che _____ dal dentista.
4. *Io sapevo che Monica aveva già visto il film.*
   Oh, io pensavo che non l'_____.
5. *Io sapevo che Diana era già partita.*
   Oh, io pensavo che non _____.

C. *Tradurre.*

1. I would like a pair of women's shoes.
2. What size do you wear?
3. Could I try these slippers on?
4. Do you have any suede shoes?
5. Do you have any shoe polish?
6. These shoes don't fit me well. They aren't comfortable.

Italy is a shopper's paradise. Leather and silk are traditional good buys and are somewhat less expensive than in America. Among the better-known designers, try Ferragamo and Gucci for leather goods, shoes, and scarves. Bruno Magli is another exceptional choice for shoes.

Milan's *Via Montenapoleone, Via de' Tornabuoni* in Florence, Rome's *Via Condotti,* and the *Piazza San Marco* in Venice offer the finest shopping, but many other cities have specialties of interest.

Stores in Italy generally do not give refunds, and they often cannot exchange goods for a different size due to a limited inventory. Bargaining is common, though many stores have a fixed price policy. Look for sales in August and after Christmas, when you'll see signs advertising *saldi, sconti, occasioni, liquidazione,* or *vendita promozionale.*

Shoe sizes differ in Italy: women should add 30 or 30½ to their American shoe size to obtain the Italian counterpart; men should add 33.

CHIAVE PER GLI ESERCIZI

A. 1. *Se avesse delle scarpe nere, le comprerei.* 2. *Se tu andassi al negozio di scarpe, verrei anch'io.* 3. *Se avessero i soldi, andrebbero in Italia.* 4. *Se avessi il tempo, andrei a comprare delle scarpe da tennis.* 5. *Se mi telefonasse Marco, gli direi di venire qui.* 6. *Se avessi fame, mangerei.*

B. 1. *Oh, io pensavo che non fossero arrivate.* 2. *Oh, io pensavo che non li avessero comprati.* 3. *Oh, io pensavo che fosse andato dal dentista.* 4. *Oh, io pensavo che non l'avesse visto.* 5. *Oh, io pensavo che non fosse partita.*

C. 1. *Vorrei un paio di scarpe da donna.* 2. *Che numero porta/porti?* 3. *Potrei provare queste pantofole?* 4. *Ha delle scarpe di camoscio?* 5. *Ha del lucido per scarpe?* 6. *Queste scarpe non mi vanno bene. Non sono comode.*

LEZIONE 38

IN UFFICIO.   At the office.

A. DIALOGO

Prima della riunione.

DIRETTORE: È pronta la documentazione per la riunione?

SEGRETARIA: Sì, ho quasi finito. Ho fatto le fotocopie. Devo solo battere a macchina alcune pagine.

DIRETTORE: Finirà per le due?

SEGRETARIA: Sì, per le due avrò finito. Se avessi avuto un computer più veloce, avrei fatto più in fretta.

DIRETTORE: Se ci danno questo contratto, Le compreremo un altro computer. Ha risposto Diodati?

SEGRETARIA: Sì, ha mandato un fax. Verrà alle tre.

DIRETTORE: Alle tre la riunione sarà quasi finita!

SEGRETARIA: Se lo avesse saputo prima, sarebbe venuto subito.

DIRETTORE: Ha ragione. Se io glielo avessi detto subito, ora sarebbe già qui. Signorina, si assicuri che il videoregistratore nella sala delle riunioni funzioni bene.

SEGRETARIA: Okay. Ecco le cartelle con tutta la documentazione.

DIRETTORE: Grazie. Le metta sulla mia scrivania.

Before the meeting.

MANAGER: Is the file for the meeting ready?

SECRETARY: Yes, I'm almost finished. I've made the photocopies. I just have to type a few pages.

MANAGER: Will you have finished by two?

SECRETARY: Yes, by two I'll be done. If I had had a faster computer, I would have finished much sooner.

MANAGER: If they give us this contract, we'll buy you another computer. Has Diodati replied?

SECRETARY: Yes, he sent a fax. He'll come at three.

MANAGER: By three the meeting will be almost finished!

SECRETARY: If he had known about it sooner, he would have come right away.

MANAGER: You're right. If I had told him right away, by now he would be here. Miss, make sure that the VCR in the meeting room works properly.

SECRETARY: Okay. Here are the folders with all the files.

MANAGER: Thank you. Put them on my desk.

B. GRAMMATICA E SUOI USI

1. THE "IF" CLAUSE OF IMPOSSIBILITY/UNREALITY

The "if" clause of impossibility presents a hypothetical situation in the past. In these sentences the condition cannot be fulfilled because it would have to have occurred in the past. To express impossibility or unreality in the past, the past perfect subjunctive is used in the "if" clause, and the past conditional in the conclusion.

Se avessi avuto un computer più veloce, avrei fatto dei miracoli.
If I had had a faster computer, I would have performed miracles.

Se lo avesse saputo prima, sarebbe venuto.
If he had known sooner, he would have come.

In the conclusion, the present conditional may also be used if the conclusion is in the present or future.

Se lo avessi avvisato prima, ora sarebbe già qui.
If I had told him sooner, he would already be here by now.

2. THE FUTURE PERFECT

The future perfect tense (*il futuro anteriore*) is formed by adding the past participle to the future of *avere* or *essere*. It is used to express a future action or event that will have taken place before another action.

Dopo che avrò studiato, ti telefonerò.
After studying, I'll phone you.

Appena sarò arrivato, ti telefonerò.
As soon as I arrive, I'll phone you.

	PARLARE	TO SPEAK
I will have spoken	*io*	*avrò parlato*
you will have spoken (familiar)	*tu*	*avrai parlato*
he will have spoken	*lui*	*avrà parlato*
she will have spoken	*lei*	*avrà parlato*
you will have spoken (polite)	*Lei*	*avrà parlato*
we will have spoken	*noi*	*avremo parlato*
you will have spoken (familiar or polite)	*voi*	*avrete parlato*
they will have spoken	*loro*	*avranno parlato*
you will have spoken (polite)	*Loro*	*avranno parlato*

Avrà finito per le due?
Will you have finished by two?

Quando arriverai, avrò già letto gli appunti.
When you arrive, I will have already read the notes.

	ANDARE	TO GO
I will have gone	*io*	*sarò andato/a*
you will have gone (familiar)	*tu*	*sarai andato/a*
he will have gone	*lui*	*sarà andato*
she will have gone	*lei*	*sarà andata*
you will have gone (polite)	*Lei*	*sarà andato/a*
we will have gone	*noi*	*saremo andati/e*
you will have gone (familiar or polite)	*voi*	*sarete andati/e*
they will have gone	*loro*	*saranno andati/e*
you will have gone (polite)	*Loro*	*saranno andati/e*

Alle sei, saremo già partite per la riunione.
At six, we will have already left for the meeting.

Quando arriverai, lui sarà già andato via.
When you arrive, he will already have left.

The future perfect can also indicate probability in the past, which is usually expressed in English with "probably" or "must have" plus past participle.

Dov'è la segretaria?
Where is the secretary?

Non lo so. Sarà uscita per un minuto.
I don't know. She must have stepped out for a minute.

VOCABOLARIO

ufficio	office
segretaria	secretary
capoufficio	head clerk, manager
scrivania	desk
gomma	eraser
matita	pencil
pennarello	marker
evidenziatore (m.)	highlighter
bianchetto	correction fluid
spillatrice (f.)/**cucitrice** (f.)	stapler
graffetta	paper clip
puntina	thumb tack
tagliacarte (m.)	letter opener
taglierina	paper cutter
forbici (f., pl.)	scissors
riga	ruler
blocchetto	paper pad
promemoria (m.)	memo
carta carbone	carbon paper
documentazione (f.)	documentation, file

cartella	folder, file
pratica	dossier
casellario	filing cabinet
macchina da scrivere	typewriter
battere a macchina	to type
computer (m.)	computer
elaboratore (m.) di testi	word processor
fotocopiare	to photocopy
fare una fotocopia	to make a photocopy
La fotocopiatrice non funziona.	The photocopier doesn't work.
mandare un fax	to send a fax
ricevere un fax	to receive a fax
videoregistratore (m.)	VCR
sala delle riunioni	meeting room
cassetta postale	mailbox
contratto	contract

ESERCIZI

A. *Rispondere affermativamente alle seguenti domande.*

1. *Se il direttore lo avesse saputo prima, sarebbe venuto?*
2. *Se tu avessi potuto, saresti andato al cinema?*
3. *Se tu avessi avuto i soldi, avresti comprato un computer?*
4. *Se lei avesse avvisato il capoufficio prima, lui sarebbe venuto alla riunione?*
5. *Se tu avessi avuto tempo, avresti fatto le fotocopie?*

B. *Eliminare la parola che non appartiene al gruppo.*

1. *macchina da scrivere / fotocopiatrice / automobile*
2. *capoufficio / segretaria / cameriere*
3. *matita / rasoio / gomma*
4. *accendino / spillatrice / graffetta*
5. *pennarello / fiammifero / evidenziatore*

C. *Rimettere le parole in ordine.*

1. *riunione / è / la / pronta / documentazione / la / per*
2. *battere / devo / questa / a / lettera / macchina*
3. *fotocopiatrice / non / questa / funziona*
4. *cartelle / sono / le / mia / sulla / scrivania*
5. *mandato / fax / un / ieri / ho / al / Rossi / signor*

NOTA CULTURALE

The office machines and data processing industry, one of Italy's main export earners, is centered in the Piedmont city of Ivrea, north of Turin. It is here that the Olivetti company, one of the leaders in its field, is headquartered. What distinguishes Olivetti on the world market is its genius for design.

CHIAVE PER GLI ESERCIZI

A. 1. *Sì, se il direttore lo avesse saputo prima, sarebbe venuto.* 2. *Sì, se io avessi potuto, sarei andato al cinema.* 3. *Sì, se io avessi avuto i soldi, avrei comprato un computer.* 4. *Sì, se lei avesse avvisato il capoufficio prima, lui sarebbe venuto alla riunione.* 5. *Sì, se io avessi avuto tempo, avrei fatto le fotocopie.*
B. 1. *automobile* 2. *cameriere* 3. *rasoio* 4. *accendino* 5. *fiammifero*
C. 1. *La documentazione per la riunione è pronta.* 2. *Devo battere a macchina questa lettera.* 3. *Questa fotocopiatrice non funziona.* 4. *Le cartelle sono sulla mia scrivania.* 5. *Ieri ho mandato un fax al signor Rossi.*

LEZIONE 39

ALL'AGENZIA IMMOBILIARE.   At a real estate agency.

A. DIALOGO

Cerchiamo un appartamento.

SIGNORINA JONES: **Buon giorno. Cerco un appartamento in affitto.**

AGENTE: **Come lo desidera? Piccolo? Grande?**

SIGNORINA JONES: **Siamo due studentesse. Andrebbe bene un appartamento non troppo piccolo. Due stanze, forse . . . Preferibilmente vicino al centro.**

AGENTE: **Beh, ne avevo uno che avrebbe fatto per Lei, ma è stato affittato proprio stamattina . . . Questo qui, comunque, potrebbe piacerLe: è a pochi secondi dal centro; ha due stanze; la cucina e il bagno sono arredati; c'è anche un bel ripostiglio . . . E il palazzo è abitato da persone perbene.**

SIGNORINA JONES: **Quant'è l'affitto?**

AGENTE: **Un milione e mezzo al mese.**

SIGNORINA JONES: **Beh, dovremmo farcela. Tanto l'affitto sarà pagato dai nostri genitori . . . A che piano è? C'è l'ascensore?**

AGENTE: **È al secondo piano; sì, l'ascensore c'è.**

SIGNORINA JONES: **Qual è l'indirizzo?**

AGENTE: **Corso Mazzini 81/D, interno 13.**

Let's look for an apartment.

MISS JONES: Good morning. I'm looking for an apartment to rent.

AGENT: What kind would you like? Small? Big?

MISS JONES: We're two students. We'd like an apartment which is not too small. Two rooms, perhaps . . . Preferably close to downtown.

AGENT: Well, I had one that would have been perfect for you, but it was just rented this morning . . . You should like this one, however: it's only a few seconds away from downtown; it has two rooms; the kitchen and the bathroom are furnished; it also has a closet . . . And nice people live in the building.

MISS JONES: How much is the rent?

AGENT: A million and a half lire a month.

MISS JONES: Well, we should manage. The rent will be paid by our parents, anyway . . . On which floor is the apartment? Is there an elevator?

AGENT: It's on the third floor, and there is an elevator.

MISS JONES: What's the address?

AGENT: Corso Mazzini 81/D, Apartment 13.

B. GRAMMATICA E SUOI USI

THE PASSIVE FORM

In active constructions, the subject performs the action of the verb.

Io affitto un appartamento.
I rent an apartment.

In passive constructions, however, the subject does not perform, but receives the action. In other words, the passive form indicates that something is/was/will be done to someone or something.

L'affitto sarà pagato dai miei genitori.
My rent will be paid by my parents.

The meaning of an active sentence and its corresponding passive sentence is the same. The passive form is possible only with transitive verbs.

The passive form is more common in English than in Italian. In Italian, the passive form consists of the verb *essere* plus the past participle of the main verb. Compare the active and passive forms below.

I miei genitori pagano l'affitto.
My parents pay the rent.

L'affitto è pagato dai miei genitori.
   The rent is paid by my parents.

I miei genitori hanno pagato l'affitto.
   My parents paid the rent.

L'affitto è stato pagato dai miei genitori.
   The rent was paid by my parents.

I miei genitori pagheranno l'affitto.
   My parents will pay the rent.

L'affitto sarà pagato dai miei genitori.
   The rent will be paid by my parents.

Note that in the passive form, the verb *essere* should be in the same tense as the verb in its corresponding active sentence. For example:

ACTIVE FORM	PASSIVE FORM
mangia	*è mangiata*
è mangiata	*è stata mangiata*
mangerà	*sarà mangiata*

The past participle agrees in gender and number with the subject.

L'affitto è pagato dai miei genitori.
   The rent is paid by my parents.

La casa è abitata da una famiglia americana.
   The house is inhabited by an American family.

I contratti sono firmati dalle ragazze.
   The contracts are signed by the girls.

The agent (the person by whom the action is done) is introduced by the preposition *da* plus an article (if necessary).

L'appartamento è stato venduto dall'agente.
   The apartment was sold by the agent.

La stanza è stata arredata da Carlo.
   The room was decorated by Carlo.

349

agenzia immobiliare	real estate agency
agente (m./f.) immobiliare	real estate agent
proprietario	landlord
inquilino	tenant
vicino di casa	neighbor
portinaio/portiere (m.)	doorman
palazzina	a small apartment building
condominio	condominium
villa	villa
Cerco un appartamento in affitto.	I'm looking for an apartment to rent.
affittare un appartamento	to rent an apartment
appartamento ammobiliato	furnished apartment
La stanza è arredata.	The room is furnished.
La camera è ammobiliata.	The room is furnished.
L'appartamento offre tutte le comodità.	The apartment offers all amenities.
È a pochi minuti dal centro.	It's a few minutes away from downtown.
armadio/guardaroba	closet
ascensore (m.)	elevator
affitto	rent
affittasi	for rent
dare in affitto	to let, to rent
Ha camere da affittare?	Do you have rooms for rent?
Quant'è l'affitto?	How much is the rent?
Un milione al mese.	A million a month.
Dovremmo farcela.	We should manage.
Dovrebbe dare un mese anticipato.	You should pay one month rental in advance.
A che piano è l'appartamento?	On what floor is the apartment?
È al secondo piano.	It's on the third floor.
Qual è l'indirizzo?	What's the address?
È in Corso Mazzini 81.	It's on Corso Mazzini 81.
Interno 13.	Apt. 13.
quartiere (m.)	neighborhood

È in periferia.   It's in the suburbs.
preferibilmente   preferably

ESERCIZI

A. *Cambiare le seguenti frasi al passivo.*

1. *Marianna arreda la casa.*
2. *L'agente immobiliare ha venduto il mio appartamento.*
3. *I miei genitori pagheranno l'affitto.*
4. *La segretaria ha fatto le fotocopie.*
5. *Mio padre pulisce sempre la casa.*

B. *Accoppiare le parole della colonna a sinistra con quelle della colonna a destra.*

1. *L'agente ha venduto l'appartamento.*   a. elevator
2. *Qual è il Suo indirizzo?*   b. The apartment was sold by the agent
3. *periferia*   c. What's your address?
4. *ascensore*   d. tenant
5. *Dovremmo farcela.*   e. We should manage.
6. *Quant'è l'affitto?*   f. The agent sold the apartment.
7. *affittacamere*   g. neighbor
8. *L'appartamento è stato venduto dall'agente.* h. How much is the rent?
9. *vicino di casa*   i. suburbs
10. *inquilino*   j. landlord

C. *Completare in modo opportuno.*

1. *Noi _____ un appartamento in affitto.*
2. *Il mio _____ di casa si chiama Roberto.*
3. *Quell____villa è molt _____ bell _____.*
4. *Quant'____ ____affitto?*
5. *Voi abit____ _____ periferia?*
6. *Cerco un appartamento ammo____.*

351

NOTA CULTURALE

Italy offers a good choice of accommodations for rental purposes. Rental prices of houses, apartments, and villas vary according to location, size, and time of the year. A fully furnished accommodation is ideal for families and for extended vacations. Tourist villages offer all sorts of amenities from valet parking to sports facilities, babysitting, entertainment, swimming pools, private beaches, etc.

In general, it's not very hard to find rental accommodation, and the prices are reasonable. However, in high season and in tourist cities, accommodations could be very expensive, and reservations should be made well in advance through the local tourist offices or rental agencies.

CHIAVE PER GLI ESERCIZI

A. 1. *La casa è arredata da Marianna.* 2. *Il mio appartamento è stato venduto dall'agente immobiliare.* 3. *L'affitto sarà pagato dai miei genitori.* 4. *Le fotocopie sono state fatte dalla segretaria.* 5. *La casa è sempre pulita da mio padre.*

B. 1—f; 2—c; 3—i; 4—a; 5—e; 6—h; 7—j; 8—b; 9—g; 10—d

C. 1. *Noi cerchiamo un appartamento in affitto.* 2. *Il mio vicino di casa si chiama Roberto.* 3. *Quella villa è molto bella.* 4. *Quant'è l'affitto?* 5. *Voi abitate in periferia?* 6. *Cerco un appartamento ammobiliato.*

LEZIONE 40
LA CULTURA ITALIANA.   Italian culture.

A. DAL LIBRO DI STORIA

Il Rinascimento italiano.

In Italia, durante il Rinascimento, molti Signori ebbero una grande sensibilità artistica: finanziarono, favorirono e seguirono la realizzazione di palazzi, chiese, ville, sculture, affreschi. Con il loro contributo nacque l'età del Rinascimento e rifiorì l'arte, la cultura, l'artigianato, il commercio.

Firenze divenne il centro europeo del Rinascimento. Qui Lorenzo il Magnifico ospitò i più grandi artisti del tempo, fece costruire palazzi e ville e fondò una scuola di scultura. Altri personaggi famosi del periodo furono: Michelangelo per la scultura, Botticelli per la pittura, Leon Battista Alberti per l'architettura e Machiavelli per la letteratura. Grande rappresentante del Rinascimento fu anche Leonardo da Vinci: disegnò macchine volanti, studiò nuove tecniche di pittura murale, dipinse e si interessò di anatomia.

(Adapted from *"Il libro dei perché." Firenze: Giunti Marzocco, 1988*)

The Italian Renaissance

In Italy, during the Renaissance, many heads of state exhibited a great artistic sensibility: they financed, favored, and oversaw the creation of buildings, churches, villas, sculptures, and frescoes. Thanks to their contributions, the Renaissance was born, and art, culture, craftmanship, and commerce flourished.

Florence became the European center of the Renaissance. In this city, Lorenzo the Magnificent welcomed the greatest artists of the period, commissioned buildings and villas, and founded a school of sculpture. Other famous artists of this period were: Michelangelo for his sculptures, Botticelli for his paintings, Leon Battista Alberti for architecture, and Machiavelli for literature. Another prominent representative of the Renaissance was Leonardo da Vinci: he designed flying machines, studied new techiniques of mural painting, painted, and was interested in anatomy.

B. GRAMMATICA E SUOI USI

1. THE HISTORICAL PAST

Like the present perfect (*passato prossimo*), the historical past, or the *passato remoto* (which corresponds to the English preterite "I spoke, he repeated"), is used to indicate a completed action. Thus, there is no substantial difference between the two tenses, and the choice between them is often subjective. However, the historical past is used mainly in writing (especially in narrative works and when relating or narrating historical events or stories of the distant past), and rarely in speech. Its use with the imperfect follows the same rules as the present perfect.

The historical past is not a compound tense: it consists of only one word. It is formed by dropping the ending of the infinitive and adding the appropriate personal endings to the stem.

	PARLARE	TO SPEAK
I spoke	io	*parlai*
you spoke (familiar)	tu	*parlasti*
he spoke	lui	*parlò*
she spoke	lei	*parlò*
you spoke (polite)	Lei	*parlò*
we spoke	noi	*parlammo*
you spoke (familiar or polite)	voi	*parlaste*
they spoke	loro	*parlarono*
you spoke (polite)	Loro	*parlarono*

Lorenzo il Magnifico ospitò i più grandi artisti del tempo.
Lorenzo the Magnificent welcomed the greatest artists of the period.

Loro fondarono una scuola di scultura.
They founded a school of sculpture.

Leonardo disegnò macchine volanti.
Leonardo designed flying machines.

RIPETERE		TO REPEAT
I repeated	io	ripetei (ripetetti)
you repeated (familiar)	tu	ripetesti
he repeated	lui	ripetè (ripetette)
she repeated	lei	ripetè (ripetette)
you repeated (polite)	Lei	ripetè (ripetette)
we repeated	noi	ripetemmo
you repeated (familiar or polite)	voi	ripeteste
they repeated	loro	ripeterono (ripetettero)
you repeated (polite)	Loro	ripeterono (ripetettero)

Lorenzo il Magnifico credè nell'arte.
Lorenzo the Magnificent believed in art.

Il ragazzo ripetè la parola.
The boy repeated the word.

DORMIRE		TO SLEEP
I slept	io	dormii
you slept (familiar)	tu	dormisti
he slept	lui	dormì
she slept	lei	dormì
you slept (polite)	Lei	dormì
we slept	noi	dormimmo
you slept (familiar or polite)	voi	dormiste
they slept	loro	dormirono
you slept (polite)	Loro	dormirono

L'artista non finì mai la sua scultura.
The artist never finished his sculpture.

Lorenzo il Magnifico favorì gli artisti.
Lorenzo the Magnificent favored artists.

Loro seguirono la costruzione del palazzo.
They oversaw the construction of the building.

355

2. THE HISTORICAL PAST OF *AVERE* AND *ESSERE*

	AVERE	TO HAVE
I had	*io*	*ebbi*
you had (familiar)	*tu*	*avesti*
he had	*lui*	*ebbe*
she had	*lei*	*ebbe*
you had (polite)	*Lei*	*ebbe*
we had	*noi*	*avemmo*
you had (familiar or polite)	*voi*	*aveste*
they had	*loro*	*ebbero*
you had (polite)	*Loro*	*ebbero*

Molti signori ebbero una grande sensibilità artistica.
Many heads of state had a great artistic sensitivity.

Lorenzo il Magnifico ebbe molti amici artisti.
Lorenzo the Magnificent had many artist friends.

	ESSERE	TO BE
I was	*io*	*fui*
you were (familiar)	*tu*	*fosti*
he was	*lui*	*fu*
she was	*lei*	*fu*
you were (polite)	*Lei*	*fu*
we were	*noi*	*fummo*
you were (familiar or polite)	*voi*	*foste*
they were	*loro*	*furono*
you were (polite)	*Loro*	*furono*

Leonardo fu un rappresentante del Rinascimento.
Leonardo was a representative of the Renaissance.

Artisti del Rinascimento furono: Michelangelo, Alberti e Machiavelli.
Artists of the Renaissance were: Michelangelo, Alberti, and Machiavelli.

356

3. THE HISTORICAL PAST OF IRREGULAR VERBS

Many verbs have irregular forms in the historical past. The following verbs are irregular in all their forms.

fare	*feci, facesti, fece, facemmo, faceste, fecero*
dire	*dissi, dicesti, disse, dicemmo, diceste, dissero*
dare	*diedi (detti), desti, diede (dette), demmo, deste, diedero (dettero)*
bere	*bevvi, bevesti, bevve, bevemmo, beveste, bevvero*
stare	*stetti, stesti, stette, stemmo, steste, stettero*

Lorenzo il Magnifico diede aiuto a molti artisti.
Lorenzo the Magnificent helped many artists.

L'artista disse: "Il lavoro è finito."
The artist said: "The work is finished."

The following verbs are irregular only in the *io, lui/lei/Lei,* and *loro/Loro* forms. Once you learn the irregular stem of the verb (*chiedere* → *chies-, leggere* → *less-*), you add the following endings, respectively: *-i, -e, -ero.* Here is an example, *prendere:*

regular forms (regular stem: *prend-*):

tu prendesti
noi prendemmo
voi prendeste

irregular forms (irregular stem: *pres-*):

io presi
lui/lei/Lei prese
loro/Loro presero

Here are some common verbs that follow this pattern:

chiedere	*chiesi, chiedesti, chiese, chiedemmo, chiedeste, chiesero*
chiudere	*chiusi, chiudesti, chiuse, chiudemmo, chiudeste, chiusero*
conoscere	*conobbi, conoscesti, conobbe, conoscemmo, conosceste, conobbero*

decidere	*decisi, decidesti, decise, decidemmo, decideste, decisero*
leggere	*lessi, leggesti, lesse, leggemmo, leggeste, lessero*
mettere	*misi, mettesti, mise, mettemmo, metteste, misero*
nascere	*nacqui, nascesti, nacque, nascemmo, nasceste, nacquero*
prendere	*presi, prendesti, prese, prendemmo, prendeste, presero*
rispondere	*risposi, rispondesti, rispose, rispondemmo, rispondeste, risposero*
sapere	*seppi, sapesti, seppe, sapemmo, sapeste, seppero*
scegliere	*scelsi, scegliesti, scelse, scegliemmo, sceglieste, scelsero*
scrivere	*scrissi, scrivesti, scrisse, scrivemmo, scriveste, scrissero*
vedere	*vidi, vedesti, vide, vedemmo, vedeste, videro*
venire	*venni, venisti, venne, venimmo, veniste, vennero*
vivere	*vissi, vivesti, visse, vivemmo, viveste, vissero*
volere	*volli, volesti, volle, volemmo, voleste, vollero*

Firenze divenne il centro del Rinascimento.
Florence became the center of the Renaissance.

Leonardo dipinse "L'Ultima Cena."
Leonardo painted "The Last Supper."

Michelangelo nacque nel 1475.
Michelangelo was born in 1475.

4. THE PAST PERFECT

Just like the pluperfect, the past perfect (*il trapassato remoto*) is used to indicate an event that had happened just before another past event. It is used mainly in literary Italian. It is formed by adding the past participle to the historical past of *avere* or *essere*.

	PARLARE	TO SPEAK
I had spoken	*io*	*ebbi parlato*
you had spoken (familiar)	*tu*	*avesti parlato*
he had spoken	*lui*	*ebbe parlato*
she had spoken	*lei*	*ebbe parlato*
you had spoken (polite)	*Lei*	*ebbe parlato*
we had spoken	*noi*	*avemmo parlato*
you had spoken (familiar or polite)	*voi*	*aveste parlato*
they had spoken	*loro*	*ebbero parlato*
you had spoken (polite)	*Loro*	*ebbero parlato*

Dopo che ebbe finito il lavoro, uscì.

After he had finished his work, he left.

Dopo che ebbe mangiato, andò a dormire.

After he had eaten, he went to bed.

	ANDARE	TO GO
I had gone	*io*	*fui andato/a*
you had gone (familiar)	*tu*	*fosti andato/a*
he had gone	*lui*	*fu andato*
she had gone	*lei*	*fu andata*
you had gone (polite)	*Lei*	*fu andato/a*
we had gone	*noi*	*fummo andati/e*
you had gone (familiar or polite)	*voi*	*foste andati/e*
they had gone	*loro*	*furono andati/e*
you had gone (polite)	*Loro*	*furono andati/e*

Dopo che fu andato a Firenze, andò a Roma.

After he had gone to Florence, he went to Rome.

Dopo che furono arrivati, telefonarono a casa.

After they had arrived, they phoned home.

To use the past perfect, four conditions need to be present at the same time:

1. The verb must appear in a dependent clause.
2. The verb must be introduced by a temporal conjunction such as *quando, appena,* or *dopo che.*
3. Its action must take place before the action of the main verb.
4. The action of the main verb must be in the historical past.

cultura	culture
architettura	architecture
artigianato	craftmanship
pittura/quadro	painting
pittura murale	mural painting
scultura	sculpture
anatomia	anatomy
affresco	fresco
letteratura	literature
capolavoro	masterpiece
artista (m./f.)	artist
architetto	architect
pittore (m.)	painter
scultore (m.)	sculptor
scrittore (m.)	writer
dipingere	to paint
disegnare	to draw
scolpire	to sculpt, to carve
inventare	to invent
critica d'arte	art criticism
critico d'arte	art critic
opera d'arte	work of art
storia dell'arte	art history
interessarsi di pittura	to be interested in painting
interessarsi di letteratura	to be interested in literature
finanziare un progetto	to finance a project
seguire la realizzazione di un progetto	to oversee the creation of a project
favorire un progetto	to favor a project
tecnica	technique
sensibilità artistica	artistic sensitivity
contributo artistico	artistic contribution
Rinascimento	Renaissance
personaggio famoso	famous person
rappresentante (m./f.)	representative
età/periodo	period

ESERCIZI

A. *Dare la terza persona singolare del passato remoto dei seguenti verbi.* (Give the third person singular of the historical past of each verb.)

1. *essere*
2. *parlare*
3. *dormire*
4. *ripetere*
5. *nascere*

B. *Dare la terza persona plurale del passato remoto dei seguenti verbi.*

1. *rispondere*
2. *prendere*
3. *dire*
4. *fare*
5. *scrivere*

C. *Completare con la forma appropriata del passato remoto, scegliendo tra i seguenti verbi.*

avere   vedere   interessarsi
studiare   dipingere   ospitare

1. *Quel pittore _____ nuove tecniche di pittura murale.*
2. *Leonardo da Vinci _____ quadri bellissimi.*
3. *Leonardo da Vinci _____ anche di anatomia.*
4. *In Italia durante il Rinascimento molti Signori _____ una grande sensibilità artistica.*
5. *L'età del Rinascimento _____ rifiorire l'arte, la scultura, l'artigianato, il commercio.*
6. *A Firenze Lorenzo De' Medici _____ i più grandi artisti del tempo.*

NOTA CULTURALE

When you think of the Italian Renaissance, you can't help thinking of the city of Florence and the Medici family. This family ruled almost without interruption until the eighteenth century. The most famous of them, Lorenzo De' Medici, was not only an astute politician, but also a highly educated man and a great patron of the arts. In the late fifteenth century, he gathered around him a court of poets, artists, philosophers, architects, and musicians, and organized all kinds of cultural events, festivals, and tournaments. It was Florence's golden period of creativity.

CHIAVE PER GLI ESERCIZI

A. 1. *fu* 2. *parlò* 3. *dormì* 4. *ripeté/ripetette* 5. *nacque*
B. 1. *risposero* 2. *presero* 3. *dissero* 4. *fecero* 5. *scrissero*
C. 1. *studiò* 2. *dipinse* 3. *si interessò* 4. *ebbero* 5. *vide* 6. *ospitò*

OTTAVO RIPASSO

A. *Rispondere alle domande affermativamente.*

1. *Se tu avessi i soldi, compreresti questo appartamento?*
2. *Se tu potessi, andresti al concerto?*
3. *Se tu potessi, finiresti il lavoro stasera?*
4. *Se il direttore lo avesse saputo prima, sarebbe venuto?*
5. *Se venisse Gianni, verreste anche voi alla festa?*

B. *Completare le seguenti frasi con un verbo al congiuntivo imperfetto.*

1. *Tu sai chi era quella signora?*
   Credo che _____ la segretaria dell'ingegner Diodati.
2. *Con chi parlava Diana al telefono?*
   Non so. Penso che _____ con il direttore.
3. *Questo computer costa duemila dollari.*
   Oh, credevo che _____ molto di più.
4. *Giulio parte domani.*
   Oh, pensavo che _____ oggi.
5. *Quando devo finire questo lavoro?*
   Vorrei che Lei lo _____ per domani.

C. *Abbinare le domande con la situazione appropriata.* (Match each question with its situation.)

1. *All'autonoleggio*
2. *In un negozio di scarpe*

a. *Signorina, mi potrebbe battere a macchina questa lettera?*

3. *A scuola*
4. *All'agenzia immobiliare*
5. *In ufficio*

b. *Quant'è l'affitto?*
c. *Che tipo di auto preferisce?*
d. *Che numero porta?*
e. *Professore, Leonardo da Vinci si interessò anche di anatomia?*

D. *Abbinare il pronome con il verbo.*

1. *tu*
2. *lei*
3. *noi*
4. *loro*
5. *io*
6. *voi*

a. *prendemmo*
b. *sapeste*
c. *partii*
d *avesti*
e. *comprò*
f. *misero*

E. *Tradurre.*

1. This apartment was rented yesterday.
2. Botticelli was an Italian painter.
3. We would like to rent a car.
4. Do you have something less expensive?
5. Today the photocopier doesn't work.
6. They live on the second floor.

CHIAVE PER GLI ESERCIZI

A. 1. *Sì, se io avessi i soldi, comprerei questo appartamento.* 2. *Sì, se io potessi, andrei al concerto.* 3. *Sì, se io potessi, finirei il lavoro stasera.* 4. *Sì, se il direttore lo avesse saputo prima, sarebbe venuto.* 5. *Sì, se venisse Gianni, verremmo anche noi alla festa.*

B. 1. *fosse* 2. *parlasse* 3. *costasse* 4. *partisse* 5. *finisse*

C. 1—c; 2—d; 3—e; 4—b; 5—a

D. 1—d; 2—e; 3—a; 4—f; 5—c; 6—b

E. 1. *Questo appartamento è stato affittato ieri.* 2. *Botticelli era un pittore italiano.* 3. *Noi vorremmo noleggiare una macchina.* 4. *Ha qualcosa di meno caro?* 5. *Oggi la fotocopiatrice non funziona.* 6. *Abitano al primo piano.*

DA LEGGERE

LE PAROLE STRANIERE

Nell'italiano moderno le parole straniere[1] aumentano[2] sempre di più e molte di loro hanno ormai[3] sostituito la corrispondente parola italiana. Questo è dovuto naturalmente agli scambi[4] ormai sempre più frequenti fra paese e paese e alla diffusione[5] dei mezzi di comunicazione,[6] cinema, televisione, radio e giornali.

La maggior parte delle parole straniere usate in Italia proviene dalla lingua inglese. I motivi sono innanzitutto[7] da ricercare[8] nell'importanza politica ed economica che hanno oggi gli Stati Uniti. Infatti, oggi quasi tutti i rapporti[9] economici, scientifici e commerciali sono realizzati in inglese.

In Italia oggi il termine[10] *okay,* per esempio, ha quasi soppiantato[11] le parole italiane *va bene* o *d'accordo.* Gli italiani la mattina, dopo il *jogging,* passano al *bar* a mangiare un *toast* oppure[12] uno *yogurt;* poi vanno in centro a fare lo *shopping* per comprare dei *blue jeans,* una *T-shirt,* o forse delle *sneakers;* durante la pausa del *lunch* vanno ad un *fast food* e ordinano un *hamburger* o un *hot dog* con senape[13] e *ketchup;* la sera in televisione guardano una *soap opera,* oppure le *news,* o anche un *talk show;* il *week-end* giocano a *tennis,* a *squash,* a *poker,* o incontrano gli amici al *night-club* per ascoltare gli ultimi *hit* delle loro *rockstar.*

L'inglese in Italia è dunque[14] *in.* Questo *trend* è normale e logico e in tempi di continui scambi di informazione rende la comunicazione certamente più facile.

VOCABOLARIO

1. *straniere* — foreign
2. *aumentare* — to augment, to increase
3. *ormai* — by now, already
4. *scambio* — exchange
5. *diffusione* (f.) — diffusion, spreading
6. *mezzi* (m., pl.) *di comunicazione* (f.) — means of communication
7. *innanzitutto* — first of all
8. *ricercare* — to seek out
9. *rapporto* — relation
10. *termine* (m.) — term, word
11. *soppiantare* — to supplant, to oust
12. *oppure* — or, or else
13. *senape* (f.) — mustard
14. *dunque* — then, consequently

APPENDIXES

A. CONTINENTS, COUNTRIES, CITIES, AND LANGUAGES

ITALIAN–ENGLISH

CONTINENTI	CONTINENTS
Africa	Africa
Asia	Asia
Australia	Australia
Europa	Europe
America del Nord	North America
America del Sud	South America

NAZIONI	COUNTRIES
Argentina	Argentina
Belgio	Belgium
Bermude (f., pl.)	Bermuda
Brasile (m.)	Brazil
Canada	Canada
Cina	China
Confederazione Stati Indipendenti	Commonwealth of Independent States
Danimarca	Denmark
Egitto	Egypt
Francia	France
Galles	Wales
Germania	Germany
Giappone (m.)	Japan
Gran Bretagna	Great Britain
Grecia	Greece
India	India
Inghilterra	England
Irlanda	Ireland
Islanda	Iceland
Italia	Italy
Messico	Mexico
Norvegia	Norway
Nuova Zelanda	New Zeland
Olanda	Holland
Polonia	Poland
Portogallo	Portugal
Romania	Romania
Russia	Russia
Scozia	Scotland
Spagna	Spain
Stati Uniti	United States

Svezia	Sweden
Svizzera	Switzerland
Turchia	Turkey
Ungheria	Hungary

CITTÀ — CITIES

Bruxelles	Brussels
Firenze	Florence
Francoforte	Frankfurt
Genova	Genoa
Ginevra	Geneva
Lisbona	Lisbon
Londra	London
Milano	Milan
Mosca	Moscow
Napoli	Naples
Padova	Padua
Parigi	Paris
Praga	Prague
Roma	Rome
Varsavia	Warsaw
Venezia	Venice

LINGUE — LANGUAGES

cinese	Chinese
finlandese	Finnish
francese	French
giapponese	Japanese
greco	Greek
inglese	English
italiano	Italian
arabo	Arabic
polacco	Polish
portoghese	Portuguese
russo	Russian
spagnolo	Spanish
svedese	Swedish
tedesco	German
turco	Turkish

B. GRAMMAR SUMMARY

1. SUBJECT PRONOUNS

	SINGULAR			PLURAL
I	*io*	we	*noi*
you (familiar)	*tu*	you (familiar or polite)	*voi*
he, she	*lui, lei*	they	*loro*
you (polite)	*Lei*	you (polite)	*Loro*

2. DISJUNCTIVE PRONOUNS

	SINGULAR			PLURAL
me	*me*	us	*noi*
you (familiar)	*te*	you (familiar or polite)	*voi*
him	*lui*	them	*loro*
her	*lei*		
you (polite)	*Lei*	you (polite)	*Loro*

3. REFLEXIVE PRONOUNS

	SINGULAR			PLURAL
myself	*mi*	ourselves	*ci*
yourself (familiar)	*ti*	yourselves (familiar or polite)	*vi*
him/her/it/oneself	*si*	themselves	*si*
yourself (polite)	*si*	yourselves (polite)	*si*

4. DIRECT OBJECT PRONOUNS

	SINGULAR			PLURAL
me	*mi*	us	*ci*
you (familiar)	*ti*	you (familiar or polite)	*vi*
him, it (m.n.)	*lo*	them (m.)	*li*
her, it (f.n.)	*la*	them (f.)	*le*
you (polite)	*La*	you (polite m.)	*Li*
		you (polite f.)	*Le*

5. INDIRECT OBJECT PRONOUNS

	SINGULAR		PLURAL
to me	*mi*	to us	*ci*
to you (familiar)	*ti*	to you (familiar or polite)	*vi*
to him, it (m.m.)	*gli*	to them	*loro, gli*
to her, it (f.n.)	*le*		
to you (polite)	*Le*	to you (polite)	*Loro, gli*

6. DOUBLE OBJECT PRONOUNS

IND. OBJ.	+ LO	+ LA	+ LI	+ LE	+ NE
mi	*me lo*	*me la*	*me li*	*me le*	*me ne*
ti	*te lo*	*te la*	*te li*	*te le*	*te ne*
gli/le/Le	*glielo*	*gliela*	*glieli*	*gliele*	*gliene*
ci	*ce lo*	*ce la*	*ce li*	*ce le*	*ce ne*
vi	*ve lo*	*ve la*	*ve li*	*ve le*	*ve ne*
gli	*glielo*	*gliela*	*glieli*	*gliele*	*gliene*
loro	*lo . . . loro*	*la . . . loro*	*li . . . loro*	*le . . . loro*	*ne . . . loro*

7. PLURAL OF NOUNS AND ADJECTIVES

GENDER	SINGULAR ENDING	PLURAL ENDING
MASCULINE	*-o*	*-i*
MASCULINE/FEMININE	*-e*	*-i*
FEMININE	*-a*	*-e*

8. INDEFINITE ARTICLES

MASCULINE	FEMININE
Before a consonant:	Before a consonant:
un	*una*
Before *s* plus consonant, or *z*:	Before *s* plus consonant, or *z*:
uno	*una*
Before a vowel:	Before a vowel:
un	*un'*

9. DEFINITE ARTICLES

	SINGULAR	PLURAL
Before masculine nouns beginning with a:		
consonant	*il*	*i*
s plus consonant, or with *z*	*lo*	*gli*
vowel	*l'*	*gli*
Before feminine nouns beginning with a:		
consonant	*la*	*le*
vowel	*l'*	*le*

369

10. PREPOSITIONS PLUS DEFINITE ARTICLES

PREPOSITIONS	+ LO	+ L'	+ GLI	+ IL	+ I	+ LA	+ LE
di	dello	dell'	degli	del	dei	della	delle
a	allo	all'	agli	al	ai	alla	alle
da	dallo	dall'	dagli	dal	dai	dalla	dalle
in	nello	nell'	negli	nel	nei	nella	nelle
su	sullo	sull'	sugli	sul	sui	sulla	sulle
con				col	coi		

11. POSSESSIVE ADJECTIVES

	MASCULINE SINGULAR	MASCULINE PLURAL	FEMININE SINGULAR	FEMININE PLURAL
my	il mio	i miei	la mia	le mie
your (familiar)	il tuo	i tuoi	la tua	le tue
his, her, its	il suo	i suoi	la sua	le sue
your (polite)	il Suo	i Suoi	la Sua	le Sue
our	il nostro	i nostri	la nostra	le nostre
your (familiar/polite)	il vostro	i vostri	la vostra	le vostre
their	il loro	i loro	la loro	le loro
your (polite)	il Loro	i Loro	la Loro	le Loro

12. COMPARATIVES

più . . . di/che	more . . . than
meno . . . di/che	less . . . than
così . . . come	as . . . as
tanto . . . quanto	as much . . . as

13. IRREGULAR COMPARATIVES AND SUPERLATIVES

ADJECTIVE	COMPARATIVE	RELATIVE SUPERLATIVE	ABSOLUTE SUPERLATIVE
buono good	migliore better	il migliore the best	ottimo very good
cattivo bad	peggiore worse	il peggiore the worst	pessimo very bad
grande big	maggiore bigger, greater	il maggiore the biggest, the greatest	massimo very big, great
piccolo small	minore smaller	il minore smallest	minimo very small

14. THE IRREGULAR ADJECTIVE: *BELLO* (BEAUTIFUL)

	SINGULAR	PLURAL
Before masculine nouns beginning with a:		
consonant	*bel*	*bei*
s plus consonant, or with *z*	*bello*	*begli*
vowel	*bell'*	*begli*
Before feminine nouns beginning with a:		
consonant	*bella*	*belle*
vowel	*bell'*	*belle*

When *bello* follows a noun for emphasis, it has the following four forms.

	SINGULAR	PLURAL
MASCULINE	*bello*	*belli*
FEMININE	*bella*	*belle*

15. THE ADJECTIVE: *BUONO* (GOOD)

When *buono* follows the noun it modifies, it has the following four forms.

	SINGULAR	PLURAL
MASCULINE	*buono*	*buoni*
FEMININE	*buona*	*buone*

When it precedes the noun it modifies, the singular forms of *buono* resemble those of the indefinite articles and follow the same rules.

MASCULINE
Before most nouns:

buon

Before nouns beginning with
s plus consonant, or with *z:*
buono

FEMININE
Before nouns beginning with a
consonant:
buona

Before nouns beginning with a vowel:
buon'

16. THE ADJECTIVE: *GRANDE* (BIG)

Grande may precede or follow the noun it modifies. When it follows the noun, it has two forms: *grande* (m., f. singular) and *grandi* (m., f. plural). When it precedes the noun, however, there are several possibilities.

SINGULAR
Before masculine and feminine nouns
beginning with a consonant:
gran or *grande*
Before masculine and feminine nouns
beginning with a vowel:
grand' or *grande*

PLURAL

For all masculine and feminine nouns:
grandi

371

17. RELATIVE PRONOUNS

RELATIVE PRONOUN	RULES OF USAGE
che	invariable, replaces subject or direct object, never used with a preposition
cui	invariable, replaces object of a preposition
il quale, la quale, i quali, le quali	may replace subject, direct object, or object of a preposition (in which case both preposition and definite article must be used); agrees with person, animal, or thing to which it refers

18. ABBREVIATIONS OF TITLES

TITLE	ABBREVIATION	TRANSLATION
signore	*sig.*	Mr.
signora	*sig.a*	Mrs.
signorina	*sig.na*	Miss
professore	*prof.*	Prof. (m.)
professoressa	*prof.essa*	Prof. (f.)
dottore	*dott.*	Dr. (m.)
dottoressa	*dott.essa*	Dr. (f.)
ingegnere	*ing.*	engineer
avvocato	*avv.*	lawyer

19. DOUBLE NEGATIVES

non . . . più	no more, no longer
non . . . ancora	not yet
non . . . affatto	not at all
non . . . niente/nulla	nothing
non . . . nessuno	no one, nothing
non . . . mai	never
non . . . né . . . né	neither . . . nor

C. VERB CHARTS

REGULAR VERBS

The following charts cover the first, second, and third conjugations from left to right.

PARLARE	RIPETERE	PARTIRE	CAPIRE

GERUNDIO PRESENTE

parlando	ripetendo	partendo	capendo

GERUNDIO PASSATO

avendo parlato	avendo ripetuto	essendo partito (-a, -i, -e)	avendo capito

PARTICIPIO PRESENTE

parlante	ripetente	partente	

PARTICIPIO PASSATO

parlato	ripetuto	partito	capito

INDICATIVO PRESENTE

io parlo	io ripeto	io parto	io capisco
tu parli	tu ripeti	tu parti	tu capisci
lui parla	lui ripete	lui parte	lui capisce
lei parla	lei ripete	lei parte	lei capisce
Lei parla	Lei ripete	Lei parte	Lei capisce
noi parliamo	noi ripetiamo	noi partiamo	noi capiamo
voi parlate	voi ripetete	voi partite	voi capite
loro parlano	loro ripetono	loro partono	loro capiscono
Loro parlano	Loro ripetono	Loro partono	Loro capiscono

INDICATIVO IMPERFETTO

io parlavo	io ripetevo	io partivo	io capivo
tu parlavi	tu ripetevi	tu partivi	tu capivi
lui parlava	lui ripeteva	lui partiva	lui capiva
lei parlava	lei ripeteva	lei partiva	lei capiva
Lei parlava	Lei ripeteva	Lei partiva	Lei capiva
noi parlavamo	noi ripetevamo	noi partivamo	noi capivamo
voi parlavate	voi ripetevate	voi partivate	voi capivate
loro parlavano	loro ripetevano	loro partivano	loro capivano
Loro parlavano	Loro ripetevano	Loro partivano	Loro capivano

PASSATO REMOTO

io parlai	io ripetei	io partii	io capii
tu parlasti	tu ripetesti	tu partisti	tu capisti

lui parlò	lui ripetè	lui partì	lui capì
lei parlò	lei ripetè	lei partì	lei capì
Lei parlò	Lei ripetè	Lei partì	Lei capì
noi parlammo	noi ripetemmo	noi partimmo	noi capimmo
voi parlaste	voi ripeteste	voi partiste	voi capiste
loro parlarono	loro ripeterono	loro partirono	loro capirono
Loro parlarono	Loro ripeterono	Loro partirono	Loro capirono

FUTURO

io parlerò	io ripeterò	io partirò	io capirò
tu parlerai	tu ripeterai	tu partirai	tu capirai
lui parlerà	lui ripeterà	lui partirà	lui capirà
lei parlerà	lei ripeterà	lei partirà	lei capirà
Lei parlerà	Lei ripeterà	Lei partirà	Lei capirà
noi parleremo	noi ripeteremo	noi partiremo	noi capiremo
voi parlerete	voi ripeterete	voi partirete	voi capirete
loro parleranno	loro ripeteranno	loro partiranno	loro capiranno
Loro parleranno	Loro ripeteranno	Loro partiranno	Loro capiranno

PASSATO PROSSIMO

io ho parlato	io ho ripetuto	io sono partito/a	io ho capito
tu hai parlato	tu hai ripetuto	tu sei partito/a	tu hai capito
lui ha parlato	lui ha ripetuto	lui è partito	lui ha capito
lei ha parlato	lei ha ripetuto	lei è partita	lei ha capito
Lei ha parlato	Lei ha ripetuto	Lei è partito/a	Lei ha capito
noi abbiamo parlato	noi abbiamo ripetuto	noi siamo partiti/e	noi abbiamo capito
voi avete parlato	voi avete ripetuto	voi siete partiti/e	voi avete capito
loro hanno parlato	loro hanno ripetuto	loro sono partiti/e	loro hanno capito
Loro hanno parlato	Loro hanno ripetuto	Loro sono partiti/e	Loro hanno capito

TRAPASSATO PROSSIMO

io avevo parlato	io avevo ripetuto	io ero partito/a	io avevo capito
tu avevi parlato	tu avevi ripetuto	tu eri partito/a	tu avevi capito
lui aveva parlato	lui aveva ripetuto	lui era partito	lui aveva capito
lei aveva parlato	lei aveva ripetuto	lei era partita	lei aveva capito
Lei aveva parlato	Lei aveva ripetuto	Lei era partito/a	Lei aveva capito
noi avevamo parlato	noi avevamo ripetuto	noi eravamo partiti/e	noi avevamo capito
voi avevate parlato	voi avevate ripetuto	voi eravate partiti/e	voi avevate capito
loro avevano parlato	loro avevano ripetuto	loro erano partiti/e	loro avevano capito
Loro avevano parlato	Loro avevano ripetuto	Loro erano partiti/e	Loro avevano capito

TRAPASSATO REMOTO

io ebbi parlato	io ebbi ripetuto	io fui partito/a	io ebbi capito
tu avesti parlato	tu avesti ripetuto	tu fosti partito/a	tu avesti capito
lui ebbe parlato	lui ebbe ripetuto	lui fu partito	lui ebbe capito
lei ebbe parlato	lei ebbe ripetuto	lei fu partita	lei ebbe capito
Lei ebbe parlato	Lei ebbe ripetuto	Lei fu partito/a	Lei ebbe capito
noi avemmo parlato	noi avemmo ripetuto	noi fummo partiti/e	noi avemmo capito
voi aveste parlato	voi aveste ripetuto	voi foste partiti/e	voi aveste capito
loro ebbero parlato	loro ebbero ripetuto	loro furono partiti/e	loro ebbero capito
Loro ebbero parlato	Loro ebbero ripetuto	Loro furono partiti/e	Loro ebbero capito

FUTURO ANTERIORE

io avrò parlato	io avrò ripetuto	io sarò partito/a	io avrò capito
tu avrai parlato	tu avrai ripetuto	tu sarai partito/a	tu avrai capito
lui avrà parlato	lui avrà ripetuto	lui sarà partito	lui avrà capito
lei avrà parlato	lei avrà ripetuto	lei sarà partita	lei avrà capito
Lei avrà parlato	Lei avrà ripetuto	Lei sarà partito/a	Lei avrà capito
noi avremo parlato	noi avremo ripetuto	noi saremo partiti/e	noi avremo capito
voi avrete parlato	voi avrete ripetuto	voi sarete partiti/e	voi avrete capito
loro avranno parlato	loro avranno ripetuto	loro saranno partiti/e	loro avranno capito
Loro avranno parlato	Loro avranno ripetuto	Loro saranno partiti/e	Loro avranno capito

CONGIUNTIVO PRESENTE

che io parli	che io ripeta	che io parta	che io finisca
che tu parli	che tu ripeta	che tu parta	che tu finisca
che lui parli	che lui ripeta	che lui parta	che lui finisca
che lei parli	che lei ripeta	che lei parta	che lei finisca
che Lei parli	che Lei ripeta	che Lei parta	che Lei finisca
che noi parliamo	che noi ripetiamo	che noi partiamo	che noi finiamo
che voi parliate	che voi ripetiate	che voi partiate	che voi finiate
che loro parlino	che loro ripetano	che loro partano	che loro finiscano
che Loro parlino	che Loro ripetano	che Loro partano	che Loro finiscano

CONGIUNTIVO IMPERFETTO

che io parlassi	che io ripetessi	che io partissi	che io capissi
che tu parlassi	che tu ripetessi	che tu partissi	che tu capissi
che lui parlasse	che lui ripetesse	che lui partisse	che lui capisse
che lei parlasse	che lei ripetesse	che lei partisse	che lei capisse
che Lei parlasse	che Lei ripetesse	che Lei partisse	che Lei capisse
che noi parlassimo	che noi ripetessimo	che noi partissimo	che noi capissimo
che voi parlaste	che voi ripeteste	che voi partiste	che voi capiste
che loro parlassero	che loro ripetessero	che loro partissero	che loro capissero
che Loro parlassero	che Loro ripetessero	che Loro partissero	che Loro capissero

CONGIUNTIVO PASSATO

che io abbia parlato	che io abbia ripetuto	che io sia partito/a	che io abbia capito
che tu abbia parlato	che tu abbia ripetuto	che tu sia partito/a	che tu abbia capito
che lui abbia parlato	che lui abbia ripetuto	che lui sia partito	che lui abbia capito
che lei abbia parlato	che lei abbia ripetuto	che lei sia partita	che lei abbia capito
che Lei abbia parlato	che Lei abbia ripetuto	che Lei sia partito/a	che Lei abbia capito
che noi abbiamo parlato	che noi abbiamo ripetuto	che noi siamo partiti/e	che noi abbiamo capito
che voi abbiate parlato	che voi abbiate ripetuto	che voi siate partiti/e	che voi abbiate capito
che loro abbiano parlato	che loro abbiano ripetuto	che loro siano partiti/e	che loro abbiano capito
che Loro abbiano parlato	che Loro abbiano ripetuto	che Loro siano partiti/e	che Loro abbiano capito

CONGIUNTIVO TRAPASSATO

che io avessi parlato	che io avessi ripetuto	che io fossi partito/a	che io avessi capito
che tu avessi parlato	che tu avessi ripetuto	che tu fossi partito/a	che tu avessi capito

che lui avesse parlato	che lui avesse ripetuto	che lui fosse partito	che lui avesse capito
che lei avesse parlato	che lei avesse ripetuto	che lei fosse partita	che lei avesse capito
che Lei avesse parlato	che Lei avesse ripetuto	che Lei fosse partito/a	che Lei avesse capito
che noi avessimo parlato	che noi avessimo ripetuto	che noi fossimo partiti/e	che noi avessimo capito
che voi aveste parlato	che voi aveste ripetuto	che voi foste partiti/e	che voi aveste capito
che loro avessero parlato	che loro avessero ripetuto	che loro fossero partiti/e	che loro avessero capito
che Loro avessero parlato	che Loro avessero ripetuto	che Loro fossero partiti/e	che Loro avessero capito

CONDIZIONALE PRESENTE

io parlerei	io prenderei	io partirei	io capirei
tu parleresti	tu prenderesti	tu partiresti	tu capiresti
lui parlerebbe	lui prenderebbe	lui partirebbe	lui capirebbe
lei parlerebbe	lei prenderebbe	lei partirebbe	lei capirebbe
Lei parlerebbe	Lei prenderebbe	Lei partirebbe	Lei capirebbe
noi parleremmo	noi prenderemmo	noi partiremmo	noi capiremmo
voi parlereste	voi prendereste	voi partireste	voi capireste
loro parlerebbero	loro prenderebbero	loro partirebbero	loro capirebbero
Loro parlerebbero	Loro prenderebbero	Loro partirebbero	Loro capirebbero

CONDIZIONALE PASSATO

io avrei parlato	io avrei ripetuto	io sarei partito/a	io avrei capito
tu avresti parlato	tu avresti ripetuto	tu saresti partito/a	tu avresti capito
lui avrebbe parlato	lui avrebbe ripetuto	lui sarebbe partito	lui avrebbe capito
lei avrebbe parlato	lei avrebbe ripetuto	lei sarebbe partita	lei avrebbe capito
Lei avrebbe parlato	Lei avrebbe ripetuto	Lei sarebbe partito/a	Lei avrebbe capito
noi avremmo parlato	noi avremmo ripetuto	noi saremmo partiti/e	noi avremmo capito
voi avreste parlato	voi avreste ripetuto	voi sareste partiti/e	voi avreste capito
loro avrebbero parlato	loro avrebbero ripetuto	loro sarebbero partiti/e	loro avrebbero capito
Loro avrebbero parlato	Loro avrebbero ripetuto	Loro sarebbero partiti/e	Loro avrebbero capito

IMPERATIVO

(tu) parla	(tu) ripeti	(tu) parti	(tu) capisci
(Lei) parli	(Lei) ripeta	(Lei) parta	(Lei) capisca
(noi) parliamo	(noi) ripetiamo	(noi) partiamo	(noi) capiamo
(voi) parlate	(voi) ripetete	(voi) partite	(voi) capite
(Loro) parlino	(Loro) ripetano	(Loro) partano	(Loro) capiscano

AUXILIARY VERBS

AVERE

GERUNDIO PRESENTE	GERUNDIO PASSATO	PARTICIPIO PRESENTE	PARTICIPIO PASSATO
avendo	avendo avuto	avente	avuto

INDICATIVO

PRESENTE	IMPERFETTO	PASSATO REMOTO	FUTURO
io ho	io avevo	io ebbi	io avrò
tu hai	tu avevi	tu avesti	tu avrai
lui ha	lui aveva	lui ebbe	lui avrà
lei ha	lei aveva	lei ebbe	lei avrà
Lei ha	Lei aveva	Lei ebbe	Lei avrà
noi abbiamo	noi avevamo	noi avemmo	noi avremo
voi avete	voi avevate	voi aveste	voi avrete
loro hanno	loro avevano	loro ebbero	loro avranno
Loro hanno	Loro avevano	Loro ebbero	Loro avranno

PASSATO PROSSIMO	TRAPASSATO PROSSIMO	TRAPASSATO REMOTO	FUTURO ANTERIORE
io ho avuto	io avevo avuto	io ebbi avuto	io avrò avuto
tu hai avuto	tu avevi avuto	tu avesti avuto	tu avrai avuto
lui ha avuto	lui aveva avuto	lui ebbe avuto	lui avrà avuto
lei ha avuto	lei aveva avuto	lei ebbe avuto	lei avrà avuto
Lei ha avuto	Lei aveva avuto	Lei ebbe avuto	Lei avrà avuto
noi abbiamo avuto	noi avevamo avuto	noi avemmo avuto	noi avremo avuto
voi avete avuto	voi avevate avuto	voi aveste avuto	voi avrete avuto
loro hanno avuto	loro avevano avuto	loro ebbero avuto	loro avranno avuto
Loro hanno avuto	Loro avevano avuto	Loro ebbero avuto	Loro avranno avuto

CONGIUNTIVO

PRESENTE	IMPERFETTO	PASSATO	TRAPASSATO
che io abbia	che io avessi	che io abbia avuto	che io avessi avuto
che tu abbia	che tu avessi	che tu abbia avuto	che tu avessi avuto
che lui abbia	che lui avesse	che lui abbia avuto	che lui avesse avuto
che lei abbia	che lei avesse	che lei abbia avuto	che lei avesse avuto
che Lei abbia	che Lei avesse	che Lei abbia avuto	che Lei avesse avuto
che noi abbiamo	che noi avessimo	che noi abbiamo avuto	che noi avessimo avuto
che voi abbiate	che voi aveste	che voi abbiate avuto	che voi aveste avuto
che loro abbiano	che loro avessero	che loro abbiano avuto	che loro avessero avuto
che Loro abbiano	che Loro avessero	che Loro abbiano avuto	che Loro avessero avuto

CONDIZIONALE

PRESENTE	PASSATO	IMPERATIVO
io avrei	io avrei avuto	(tu) abbi
tu avresti	tu avresti avuto	(Lei) abbia

lui avrebbe	*lui avrebbe avuto*	*(noi) abbiamo*
lei avrebbe	*lei avrebbe avuto*	*(voi) abbiate*
Lei avrebbe	*Lei avrebbe avuto*	*(Loro) abbiano*
noi avremmo	*noi avremmo avuto*	
voi avreste	*voi avreste avuto*	
loro avrebbero	*loro avrebbero avuto*	
Loro avrebbero	*Loro avrebbero avuto*	

ESSERE

GERUNDIO PRESENTE	GERUNDIO PASSATO	PARTICIPIO PRESENTE	PARTICIPIO PASSATO
essendo	*essendo stato (-a, -i, -e)*	*ente*	*stato (-a, -i, -e)*

INDICATIVO

PRESENTE	IMPERFETTO	PASSATO REMOTO	FUTURO
io sono	*io ero*	*io fui*	*io sarò*
tu sei	*tu eri*	*tu fosti*	*tu sarai*
lui è	*lui era*	*lui fu*	*lui sarà*
lei è	*lei era*	*lei fu*	*lei sarà*
Lei è	*Lei era*	*Lei fu*	*Lei sarà*
noi siamo	*noi eravamo*	*noi fummo*	*noi saremo*
voi siete	*voi eravate*	*voi foste*	*voi sarete*
loro sono	*loro erano*	*loro furono*	*loro saranno*
Loro sono	*Loro erano*	*Loro furono*	*Loro saranno*

PASSATO PROSSIMO	TRAPASSATO PROSSIMO	TRAPASSATO REMOTO	FUTURO ANTERIORE
io sono stato/a	*io ero stato/a*	*io fui stato/a*	*io sarò stato/a*
tu sei stato/a	*tu eri stato/a*	*tu fosti stato/a*	*tu sarai stato/a*
lui è stato	*lui era stato*	*lui fu stato*	*lui sarà stato*
lei è stata	*lei era stata*	*lei fu stata*	*lei sarà stata*
Lei è stato/a	*Lei era stato/a*	*Lei fu stato/a*	*Lei sarà stato/a*
noi siamo stati/e	*noi eravamo stati/e*	*noi fummo stati/e*	*noi saremo stati/e*
voi siete stati/e	*voi eravate stati/e*	*voi foste stati/e*	*voi sarete stati/e*
loro sono stati/e	*loro erano stati/e*	*loro furono stati/e*	*loro saranno stati/e*
Loro sono stati/e	*Loro erano stati/e*	*Loro furono stati/e*	*Loro saranno stati/e*

CONGIUNTIVO

PRESENTE	IMPERFETTO	PASSATO	TRAPASSATO
che io sia	*che io fossi*	*che io sia stato/a*	*che io fossi stato/a*
che tu sia	*che tu fossi*	*che tu sia stato/a*	*che tu fossi stato/a*
che lui sia	*che lui fosse*	*che lui sia stato*	*che lui fosse stato*
che lei sia	*che lei fosse*	*che lei sia stata*	*che lei fosse stata*
che Lei sia	*che Lei fosse*	*che Lei sia stato/a*	*che Lei fosse stato/a*
che noi siamo	*che noi fossimo*	*che noi siamo stati/e*	*che noi fossimo stati/e*
che voi siate	*che voi foste*	*che voi siate stati/e*	*che voi foste stati/e*
che loro siano	*che loro fossero*	*che loro siano stati/e*	*che loro fossero stati/e*
che Loro siano	*che Loro fossero*	*che Loro siano stati/e*	*che Loro fossero stati/e*

CONDIZIONALE

PRESENTE	PASSATO	IMPERATIVO
io sarei	io sarei stato/a	(tu) sii
tu saresti	tu saresti stato/a	(Lei) sia
lui sarebbe	lui sarebbe stato	(noi) siamo
lei sarebbe	lei sarebbe stata	(voi) siate
Lei sarebbe	Lei sarebbe stato/a	(Loro) siano
noi saremo	noi saremmo stati/e	
voi sareste	voi sareste stati/e	
loro sarebbero	loro sarebbero stati/e	
Loro sarebbero	Loro sarebbero stati/e	

COMMON IRREGULAR VERBS

Listed below are the irregular forms of some commonly used verbs.

ANDARE   TO GO

present indicative	vado, vai, va, andiamo, andate, vanno
future indicative	andrò, andrai, andrà, andremo, andrete, andranno
present subjunctive	vada, vada, vada, andiamo, andiate, vadano
present conditional	andrei, andresti, andrebbe, andremmo, andreste, andrebbero
imperative	va', vada, andiamo, andate, vadano

BERE   TO DRINK

past participle	bevuto
present indicative	bevo, bevi, beve, beviamo, bevete, bevono
imperfect indicative	bevevo, bevevi, beveva, bevevamo, bevevate, bevevano
historical past	bevvi, bevesti, bevve, bevemmo, beveste, bevvero
future indicative	berrò, berrai, berrà, berremo, berrete, berranno
present subjunctive	beva, beva, beva, beviamo, beviate, bevano
imperfect subjunctive	bevessi, bevessi, bevesse, bevessimo, beveste, bevessero
present conditional	berrei, berresti, berrebbe, berremmo, berreste, berrebbero

CHIEDERE   TO ASK

past participle	chiesto
historical past	chiesi, chiedesti, chiese, chiedemmo, chiedeste, chiesero

CHIUDERE   TO CLOSE

past participle — *chiuso*

historical past — *chiusi, chiudesti, chiuse, chiudemmo, chiudeste, chiusero*

CONOSCERE   TO KNOW

past participle — *conosciuto*

historical past — *conobbi, conoscesti, conobbe, conoscemmo, conosceste, conobbero*

DARE   TO GIVE

present indicative — *do, dai, dà, diamo, date, danno*

historical past — *diedi, desti, diede, demmo, deste, diedero*

future indicative — *darò, darai, darà, daremo, darete, daranno*

present subjunctive — *dia, dia, dia, diamo, diate, diano*

imperfect subjunctive — *dessi, dessi, desse, dessimo, deste, dessero*

conditional present — *darei, daresti, darebbe, daremmo, dareste, darebbero*

imperative — *da', dia, diamo, date, diano*

DECIDERE   TO DECIDE

past participle — *deciso*

historical past — *decisi, decidesti, decise, decidemmo, decideste, decisero*

DIRE   TO SAY

past participle — *detto*

present indicative — *dico, dici, dice, diciamo, dite, dicono*

imperfect indicative — *dicevo, dicevi, diceva, dicevamo, dicevate, dicevano*

historical past — *dissi, dicesti, disse, dicemmo, diceste, dissero*

present subjunctive — *dica, dica, dica, diciamo, diciate, dicano*

imperfect subjunctive — *dicessi, dicessi, dicesse, dicessimo, diceste, dicessero*

imperative — *di', dica, diciamo, dite, dicano*

DOVERE   TO HAVE TO

present indicative — *devo, devi, deve, dobbiamo, dovete, devono*

future indicative — *dovrò, dovrai, dovrà, dovremo, dovrete, dovranno*

present subjunctive — *debba, debba, debba, dobbiamo, dobbiate, debbano*

present conditional — *dovrei, dovresti, dovrebbe, dovremmo, dovreste, dovrebbero*

FARE   TO DO

past participle   *fatto*

present indicative   *faccio, fai, fa, facciamo, fate, fanno*

imperfect indicative   *facevo, facevi, faceva, facevamo, facevate, facevano*

historical past   *feci, facesti, fece, facemmo, faceste, fecero*

future indicative   *farò, farai, farà, faremo, farete, faranno*

present subjunctive   *faccia, faccia, faccia, facciamo, facciate, facciano*

imperfect subjunctive   *facessi, facessi, facesse, facessimo, faceste, facessero*

present conditional   *farei, faresti, farebbe, faremmo, fareste, farebbero*

imperative   *fa', faccia, facciamo, fate, facciano*

LEGGERE   TO READ

past participle   *letto*

historical past   *lessi, leggesti, lesse, leggemmo, leggeste, lessero*

METTERE   TO PUT

past participle   *messo*

historical past   *misi, mettesti, mise, mettemmo, metteste, misero*

NASCERE   TO BE BORN

past participle   *nato*

historical past   *nacqui, nascesti, nacque, nascemmo, nasceste, nacquero*

PIACERE   TO LIKE

past participle   *piaciuto*

present indicative   *piaccio, piaci, piace, piacciamo, piacete, piacciono*

POTERE   TO BE ABLE TO

present indicative   *posso, puoi, può, possiamo, potete, possono*

future indicative   *potrò, potrai, potrà, potremo, potrete, potranno*

present subjunctive   *possa, possa, possa, possiamo, possiate, possano*

present conditional   *potrei, potresti, potrebbe, potremmo, potreste, potrebbero*

RISPONDERE   TO ANSWER

past participle   *risposto*

historical past   *risposi, rispondesti, rispose, rispondemmo, rispondeste, risposero*

SAPERE   TO KNOW
present indicative   *so, sai, sa, sappiamo, sapete, sanno*
historical past   *seppi, sapesti, seppe, sapemmo, sapeste,*
                                        seppero
future indicative   *saprò, saprai, saprà, sapremo, saprete,*
                                        sapranno
present subjunctive   *sappia, sappia, sappia, sappiamo, sappiate,*
                                        sappiano
present conditional   *saprei, sapresti, saprebbe, sapremmo,*
                                        sapreste, saprebbero
imperative   *sappi, sappia, sappiamo, sappiate, sappiano*

SCRIVERE   TO WRITE
past participle   *scritto*
historical past   *scrissi, scrivesti, scrisse, scrivemmo,*
                                        scriveste, scrissero

SEDERSI   TO SIT DOWN
present indicative   *mi siedo, ti siedi, si siede, ci sediamo,*
                                        vi sedete, si siedono

SPEGNERE   TO TURN OFF
past participle   *spento*
imperative   *spegni, spenga, spegniamo, spegnete,*
                                        spengano

STARE   TO STAY
present indicative   *sto, stai, sta, stiamo, state, stanno*
historical past   *stetti, stesti, stette, stemmo, steste, stettero*
future indicative   *starò, starai, starà, staremo, starete,*
                                        staranno
present subjunctive   *stia, stia, stia, stiamo, stiate, stiano*
imperfect subjunctive   *stessi, stessi, stesse, stessimo, steste, stessero*
present conditional   *starei, staresti, starebbe, staremmo, stareste,*
                                        starebbero
imperative   *sta', stia, stiamo, state, stiano*

USCIRE   TO GO OUT
present indicative   *esco, esci, esce, usciamo, uscite, escono*
present subjunctive   *esca, esca, esca, usciamo, usciate, escano*
imperative   *esci, esca, usciamo, uscite, escano*

VEDERE   TO SEE
past participle   *visto, veduto*
historical past   *vidi, vedesti, vide, vedemmo, vedeste, videro*
future indicative   *vedrò, vedrai, vedrà, vedremo, vedrete,*
                                        vedranno
present conditional   *vedrei, vedresti, vedrebbe, vedremmo,*
                                        vedreste, vedrebbero

VENIRE   TO COME

past participle	*venuto*
present indicative	*vengo, vieni, viene, veniamo, venite, vengono*
future indicative	*verrò, verrai, verrà, verremo, verrete, verranno*
present subjunctive	*venga, venga, venga, veniamo, veniate, vengano*
present conditional	*verrei, verresti, verrebbe, verremmo, verreste, verrebbero*
imperative	*vieni, venga, veniamo, venite, vengano*

VOLERE   TO WANT

present indicative	*voglio, vuoi, vuole, vogliamo, volete, vogliono*
future indicative	*vorrò, vorrai, vorrà, vorremo, vorrete, vorranno*
present subjunctive	*voglia, voglia, voglia, vogliamo, vogliate, vogliano*
present conditional	*vorrei, vorresti, vorrebbe, vorremmo, vorreste, vorrebbero*

D. LETTER WRITING

1. FORMAL INVITATIONS AND ACCEPTANCES

INVITATIONS   *INVITI FORMALI*

marzo 1993

Il signore e la signora Peretti hanno il piacere di annunciare il matrimonio della figlia Maria con il signor Giovanni Rossi, ed hanno l'onore di invitare la Signoria Vostra alla cerimonia che avrà luogo nella Chiesa di San Giuseppe il sei c.m. alle ore dodici. Dopo la cerimonia sarà offerto in onore degli sposi un ricevimento a casa dei genitori della sposa.

March 1993

Mr. and Mrs. Peretti take pleasure in announcing the wedding of their daughter Maria to Mr. Giovanni Rossi and have the honor of inviting you to the ceremony that will take place at the Church of St. Joseph, on the 6th of this month at 12 noon. There will be a reception for the newlyweds afterwards at the residence of the bride's parents.

---

9 marzo 1993

Abbiamo il piacere di invitare Lei e la Sua gentile signora a cena lunedì prossimo, alle ore venti.

March 9, 1993

We take pleasure in inviting you and your wife to dinner next Monday at 8 o'clock.

---

marzo 1993

Il signor Rossi e la Sua gentile signora sono cordialmente invitati al ricevimento in onore di Anna Martini, figlia di Maria e Paolo Martini, domenica sera 19 marzo, ore ventuno.

March 1993

Mr. and Mrs. Rossi are cordially invited to a party in honor of Anna Martini, daughter of Maria and Paolo Martini, on Sunday evening, March 19, at nine o'clock.

Il signor Parisi e signora ringraziano per il cortese invito, felici di partecipare al ricevimento del 19 marzo p.v.

Thank you for your kind invitation. We shall be honored to attend the reception on March 19th.

[Note: *p.v.* = *prossimo venturo,* which means "the next coming" (month). *c.m.* = *corrente mese,* which means "of this month" (the running month).]

I coniugi Rossi accettano il gentile invito per lunedì prossimo e ringraziano sentitamente.

Mr. and Mrs. Rossi will be honored to have dinner with Mr. and Mrs. De Marchi next Monday. With kindest regards.

Ringraziamo sentitamente per il cortese invito, spiacenti che impegni precedenti non ci permettano di poter accettare.

We thank you for your kind invitation and regret that we are unable to come owing to a previous engagement.

2. THANK YOU NOTES *BIGLIETTI DI RINGRAZIAMENTO*

Roma, 5 marzo 1993

Cara Anna,

poche righe soltanto per sapere come stai e per ringraziarti del bellissimo vaso che mi hai regalato. L'ho messo sul pianoforte e ti assicuro che è bellissimo.
Spero di vederti al ricevimento di Angela. Sono sicura che la festa sarà molto divertente.
Mi auguro che la tua famiglia stia bene, così posso assicurarti della mia. Ti saluto affettuosamente.

Maria

Rome, March 5, 1993

Dear Anna,

This is just to say hello and to thank you for the beautiful vase you sent me as a gift. I've put it on the piano and you can't imagine how nice it looks.
I hope to see you at Angela's party. I'm sure it's going to be a lot of fun.
I hope your family is all well. Everyone here is fine.

Affectionately,
Maria

385

Cavatorta & Co.,
969 Third Avenue
New York, N.Y. 10022

Ditta Marini e Figli
Via Nomentana 11
00100 Roma, Italia

Roma, 2 aprile 1993

Gentili Signori,

   con la presente abbiamo il piacere di presentarVi il signor Carlo Fontanesi, uno dei nostri agenti attualmente nelle principali città del Vostro paese. Inutile aggiungere che qualsiasi gentilezza usata al signor Fontanesi sarà da noi gradita come un personale favore.
   RingraziandoVi anticipatamente, inviamo distinti saluti.

Cavatorta & Co.
il Presidente

Cavatorta & Co.
969 Third Avenue
New York, N.Y. 10022

Marini & Sons
Via Nomentana 11
00100 Rome, Italia

April 2, 1993

Gentlemen:

   We have the pleasure of introducing to you the bearer of this letter, Mr. Carlo Fontanesi, one of our salesmen, who is visiting the principal cities of your country. It is needless to say that we shall consider any courtesy you extend to him as a personal favor.
   Thanking you in advance, we send our best regards.

Cavatorta & Co.
President

Milano,
3 marzo 1993

Signor Giulio Perri
direttore de "Il Mondo"
Via Montenapoleone 3
20100 Milano

Gentile Signore,

   accludo un assegno di L. 30.000 (trentamila) per un anno di abbonamento alla Sua rivista.

Distintamente,
Lucia Landi

Lucia Landi
Corso Vittorio Emanuele, 8
00100 Roma

March 3, 1993

Mr. Giulio Perri
Editor of *Il Mondo*
Via Montenapoleone 3
20100 Milan

Dear Sir:

   Enclosed please find a check for $25.00 for a year's subscription to your magazine.

Very truly yours,
Lucia Landi

Lucia Landi
8 Corso Vittorio Emanuele
00100 Rome

4. INFORMAL LETTERS   *LETTERE INFORMALI*

Caro Giuseppe,

   sono molto lieto di aver ricevuto la tua ultima lettera. Prima di tutto desidero darti la grande notizia. Ho finalmente deciso di fare un viaggio fino a Roma, dove intendo rimanere tutto il mese di maggio. Anna verrà con me. Lei è molto felice di avere finalmente l'occasione di conoscere te ed Elena. Perciò, se possibile, cercate di liberarvi dai vostri impegni.
   Gli affari vanno bene e spero che il buon vento continui. L'altro giorno ho visto Antonio che mi ha chiesto tue notizie.
   Ti sarei grato se potessi prenotarci una camera all'albergo Nazionale. Scrivici al più presto. Saluti ad Elena.

tuo Giovanni

387

Dear Giuseppe,

I was very happy to get your last letter. First of all, let me give you the big news. I have finally decided to make a trip to Rome, where I expect to spend all of May. Anna will come with me. She is extremely happy to be able to meet the two of you at last. Try, therefore, to be as free as you can then.

Business is good now, and I hope it will stay that way ("that the good wind will continue"). I saw Antonio the other day and he asked me about you.

I'd be grateful to you if you would try to reserve a room for us at the *Nazionale* Hotel. Write soon. Give my regards to Elena.

Yours,
Giovanni

5. FORMS OF SALUTATIONS

FORMAL

Signore	Sir
Signora	Madam
Signorina	Miss
Signor Professore	My dear Professor
Eccellentissimo	Your Excellency
Gentile Signor Rossi	My dear Mr. Rossi
Gentile Signora Rossi	My dear Mrs. Rossi
Gentile Signorina Rossi	My dear Miss Rossi

INFORMAL

Caro Antonio	My dear Anthony
Cara Anna	My dear Anna
Amore mio	My beloved, My dear
Carissimo Paolo	My very dear Paul
Carissima Giovanna	My very dear Jane

6. FORMS OF COMPLIMENTARY CLOSINGS

FORMAL

1. *Gradisca i miei più distinti saluti* (The *lei* form is used.) — Very truly yours. (Accept my most distinguished greetings.)

2. *Gradite i miei distinti saluti.* (The *voi* form is used.) — Very truly yours. (Accept my distinguished greetings.)

3. *Voglia gradire i miei sinceri saluti.* (The *lei* form is used.) — Yours truly. (Accept my sincere greetings.)

4. *Vogliate gradire i miei cordiali saluti.* (The *voi* form is used.) — Yours truly. (Accept my heartfelt greetings.)

388

INFORMAL

1. *Ricevete i nostri saluti.* — Very sincerely. (Receive our heartfelt greetings.)

2. *In attesa di vostre notizie, vi invio i miei sinceri e cordiali saluti.* — Sincerely yours. (Waiting for your news I send you my sincere and heartfelt greetings.)

3. *Sperando di ricevere presto tue notizie, t'invio cordialissimi saluti.* — Sincerely yours. (Waiting to hear from you soon I send you my most heartfelt greetings.)

4. *Affettuosissimo.* (Shortened to *Aff.mo*) — Affectionately yours. (m.) (Very affectionately.)

5. *Affettuosissima.* (Shortened to *Aff.ma*) — Affectionately yours. (f.) (Very affectionately.)

6. *Affezionatissimo* (*Aff.mo*) — Affectionately yours. (Very affectionately.)

7. *Vi invio cordiali saluti.* — Sincerely. (I send you heartfelt greetings.)

8. *T'invio cordiali saluti e abbracci.* — Sincerely. (I send you heartfelt greetings and embraces.)

9. *Con mille abbracci e baci.* — Love. (With a thousand embraces and kisses.)

10. *Abbracciandoti e baciandoti caramente.* — Love. (Embracing and kissing you dearly.)

7. FORM OF THE ENVELOPE

Paolo Bolla
Via Veneto 10
00100 Roma, Italy

Gent.mo Sig. Angelo Rossi
Piazza Roma 81/D
80100 Napoli

Maria Ferrero
Via Nomentana 27
00100 Roma

Gent.ma Sig.a Marcella Marini
Via Montenapoleone 35
20100 Milano

Anna Rossi
Piazza Vittorio *Emanuele 9*
50100 Firenze

Gent.ma Sig.na Silvana Tarri
Piazza Venezia 71
00100 Roma

GLOSSARY

ITALIAN–ENGLISH

A

a *to, at*
  a buon mercato *at a cheap price*
  A più tardi. *See you later.*
  A presto. *See you soon.*
  A domani. *See you tomorrow.*
  a destra *on the right*
  a sinistra *on the left*
  al mercato *at the market*
  all'agenzia immobiliare *at the real estate agency*
  alla questura *at the police station*
  all'ufficio di cambio *at the currency exchange office*
  andare a piedi *to go on foot*
abbassare *to lower*
  abbassare il volume *to lower the volume*
abbastanza *enough, rather*
  Sto abbastanza bene. *I'm well enough.*
abbigliamento *clothes, clothing*
  articoli di abbigliamento *articles of clothing*
  negozio di abbigliamento *clothing store*
abitare *to live*
  abitare al primo piano *to live on the second floor*
  abitare in Italia *to live in Italy*
  abitare a Roma *to live in Rome*
abito *outfit, suit, dress*
accanto *beside, near, by*
  Il museo è accanto alla pinacoteca. *The museum is beside the art gallery.*
  Siediti accanto a me. *Sit down beside me.*
accelerare *to accelerate*
accendere *to turn on, to light*
  accendere la televisione *to turn on the television*
  accendere la radio *to turn on the radio*
accendino *lighter*
accertamento *assurance; assessment, control*
accettazione *acceptance*
  banco d'accettazione *check-in counter*
accomodarsi *to sit down, to make oneself comfortable*
  Si accomodi. *Make yourself comfortable.*
aceto *vinegar*
acqua *water*
  acqua minerale *mineral water*
  acqua tonica *tonic water*
adesso *now*
addormentarsi *to fall asleep*
aereo *(n.) airplane*
aereo *(adj.) aerial*
  compagnia aerea *airline*
aeroporto *airport*
affare *(m.) business*
  viaggio d'affari *business trip*

affatto *at all*
  Non sono affatto stanco. *I'm not tired at all.*
affettati *cold cuts*
affittacamere *(m./f.) landlord, landlady*
affittare *to rent*
  affittare un appartamento *to rent an apartment*
  affittasi *for rent*
  Ha camere da affittare? *Do you have rooms for rent?*
affitto *rent*
  cercare un appartamento in affitto *to look for an apartment for rent*
  dare in affitto *to let, to rent*
affrancare *to put a stamp on*
  affrancare una lettera *to put a stamp on a letter*
affresco *fresco*
agente *(m./f.) agent*
  agente di viaggio *travel agent*
  agente immobiliare *real estate agent*
agenzia *agency*
  agenzia di viaggio *travel agency*
  agenzia immobiliare *real estate agency*
aggiustare *to fix*
  aggiustare la macchina *to fix the car*
aglio *garlic*
agosto *August*
albergo *hotel*
  albergo a tre stelle *three-star hotel*
  albergo di prima categoria *first-class hotel*
album *album*
  l'ultimo album *the latest album*
alcuni/e *some*
allacciare *to fasten, to tie*
  allacciarsi le scarpe *to tie one's shoes*
allenamento *training*
allenatore *(m.) coach*
allergico *allergic*
allora *then, so*
almeno *at least*
alto *tall, high*
altro *other*
alzarsi *to get up*
ambasciata *embassy*
ambulanza *ambulance*
  Ho bisogno di un'ambulanza. *I need an ambulance.*
americano *American*
amico *friend*
ammobiliato *furnished*
  appartamento ammobiliato *furnished apartment*
analisi *(f.) analysis, test*
  analisi del sangue *blood test*
  analisi dell'urina *urine test*
anatomia *anatomy*
anche *too, also*

andare *to go*
andare al lavoro *to go to work*
andare dal dottore *to go to the doctor*
andare a messa *to go to mass*
andare in centro *to go downtown*
andare al ristorante *to go to à restaurant*
andare al mare *to go to the shore*
andare alla spiaggia *to go to the beach*
andare a piedi *to walk*
andare al negozio *to go to the store*
andare al cinema *to go to the movies*
andare al concerto *to go to a concert*
andare in vacanza *to go on vacation*
andare alla posta *to go to the post office*
andare alla questura *to go to the police station*
andare a teatro *to go to the theater*
andare all'opera *to go to the opera*
Andiamo a prendere un caffè? *Shall we go for coffee?*
Andiamo a fare un giro. *Let's go for a ride.*
Va bene! *Okay!*
Va piano. *Go slow.*
Vada sempre dritto. *Go straight ahead.*
andata *departure, going*
biglietto di andata *one-way ticket*
biglietto di andata e ritorno *round-trip ticket*
anguria *watermelon*
anno *year*
l'anno scorso *last year*
Ho venti anni. *I'm 20 years old.*
annuncio *announcement, advertisement*
annunci economici *classified ads*
anticipato *in advance*
pagamento anticipato *advance payment*
antidolorifico *pain killer*
aperitivo *aperitif*
aperto *open*
concerto all'aperto *open-air concert*
appartamento *apartment*
appartamento ammobiliato *furnished apartment*
affittare un appartamento *to rent an apartment*
appetito *appetite*
Buon appetito! *Enjoy your meal!*
applaudire *to applaud*
appuntamento *appointment*
fissare un appuntamento *to make an appointment*
aprile *(m.) April*
aprire *to open*
Vorrei aprire un conto. *I'd like to open an account.*
arancia *orange*
spremuta d'arancia *freshly squeezed orange juice*
aranciata *orange drink*
arbitro *referee*
architetto *architect*
architettura *architecture*
aria *air*
aria condizionata *air conditioning*
armadio *wardrobe, armoire*
armadio a muro *closet*
arredare *to furnish*
La stanza è arredata. *The room is furnished.*
arrivare *to arrive*
A che ora arriva il treno? *At what time does the train arrive?*

arrivederci *Good-bye (familiar)*
arrivederLa *Good-bye (polite)*
arrivo *arrival*
arte *(f.) art*
Belle Arti *Fine Arts*
articolo *article, item*
articoli di regalo *gift items*
articoli di abbigliamento *articles of clothing*
artigianato *craftsmanship*
artista *(m./f.) artist*
artistico *artistic*
ascensore *(m.) elevator*
asciugare *to dry*
asciugarsi i capelli *to dry one's hair*
ascoltare *to listen, to hear*
ascoltare la radio *to listen to the radio*
ascoltare una canzone *to listen to a song*
aspettare *to wait, to wait for*
aspettare in fila *to wait in line*
aspettare l'autobus *to wait for the bus*
aspetto *waiting, wait; look, appearance*
sala d'aspetto *waiting room*
aspirina *aspirin*
assegno *check*
libretto degli assegni *checkbook*
riscuotere un assegno *to cash a check*
assicurare *to insure*
assicurare un pacco *to insure a parcel*
assicurazione *insurance*
assicurazione per il furto *antitheft insurance*
assicurazione medica *medical insurance*
assicurazione contro i danni *collision damage waiver*
assistente *(m./f.) assistant*
assistente di volo *flight attendant*
assistere *to assist; to attend*
assistere ad uno spettacolo *to attend a show*
assumere *to hire*
essere assunto *to be hired*
attento *attentive*
Sta' attento! *Be careful!*
attimo *instant, moment*
Un attimo, per favore. *One moment, please.*
attore *(m.) actor*
attrice *(f.) actress*
attualità *current event*
servizio di attualità *news report*
augurio *wish*
Tanti auguri! *Best wishes!*
autobus *(m.) bus*
aspettare l'autobus *to wait for the bus*
biglietto per l'autobus *bus ticket*
prendere l'autobus *to take the bus*
automatico *automatic*
cambio automatico *automatic transmission*
automobilismo *car racing*
autonoleggio *car rental office*
autonomo *autonomous*
Azienda Autonoma Soggiorno *City Tourist Board*
autunno *fall*
avere *to have*
avere sete *to be thirsty*
avere caldo *to be warm/hot*
avere una promozione *to get promoted*
avere occasione di *to have the opportunity to*

avere pazienza *to be patient*
avere fame *to be hungry*
avere un bel posto *to have a good job, position*
avere fretta *to be in a hurry*
avere un esaurimento nervoso *to have a nervous breakdown*
avere fiducia in *to trust*
avere la febbre *to have a fever*
avere mal di gola *to have a sore throat*
avere mal di stomaco *to have a stomachache*
avere paura *to be afraid*
avere i baffi *to have a mustache*
avere . . . anni *to be . . . years old*
avere bisogno di *to need*
avviso *notice, advertisement*
avviso economico *newspaper ad*
azienda *company, firm*
Azienda Autonoma Soggiorno *City Tourist Board*

B

baffi *(m., pl.) mustache*
avere i baffi *to have a mustache*
bagaglio *luggage*
bagno *bathroom*
fare il bagno *to go swimming*
farsi il bagno *to take a bath*
ballare *to dance*
ballare il liscio *to dance to a slow song*
ballare il rock *to dance to rock and roll*
ballerina *ballerina, ballet dancer*
balletto *ballet*
balsamo *balsam*
balsamo per i capelli *hair conditioner*
bambino *child, son*
banana *banana*
banca *bank*
bancarella *stand*
banco *desk, counter*
banco d'accettazione *check-in counter*
bancomat *instant teller*
banconota *bank note*
bar *bar, café*
barba *beard*
farsi la barba *to shave*
sapone per la barba *shaving cream*
barbiere *(m.) barber*
barista *(m./f.) bartender*
basetta *sideburn*
portare le basette *to wear sideburns*
basso *short, low*
battere *to beat*
battere a macchina *to type*
bello *beautiful*
Studio Belle Arti. *I study Fine Arts.*
È una bella giornata. *It's a beautiful day.*
bene *well*
Sto bene. *I am fine.*
Ti voglio bene. *I love you.*
benzina *gasoline*
benzina super *super gas*
benzina normale *regular gas*
benzina senza piombo *unleaded gas*

benzina verde *unleaded gas*
buono benzina *gas coupon*
fare benzina *to get gas*
benzinaio *gas station attendant*
bere *to drink*
bianchetto *correction fluid*
bianco *white*
bicchiere *(m.) glass*
bicchiere d'acqua minerale *glass of mineral water*
bigliettaio *ticket collector*
biglietteria *ticket booth*
biglietto *ticket*
biglietto di andata e ritorno *round-trip ticket*
biglietto di andata *one-way ticket*
biglietto di prima classe *first-class ticket*
biglietto per l'autobus *bus ticket*
biglietti di grosso taglio *big bills*
biglietti di piccolo taglio *small bills*
binario *train track*
Su quale binario arriva il treno? *Which track is the train arriving on?*
biondo *blond*
capelli biondi *blond hair*
birra *beer*
bis *encore*
concedere il bis *to give an encore*
chiedere il bis *to ask for an encore*
bisogno *need*
avere bisogno di *to need*
bistecca *steak*
Voglio la mia bistecca ben cotta. *I want my steak well-done.*
Voglio la mia bistecca al sangue. *I want my steak rare.*
blocchetto *writing pad*
blu *blue*
bolletta *bill; receipt*
pagare la bolletta *to pay the bill*
bollo *stamp*
carta da bollo *government-stamped paper*
marca da bollo *tax stamp*
borsa *purse, bag; stock market*
borsa a mano *hand luggage*
botteghino *ticket booth*
braccio *arm*
Mi sento le braccia pesanti. *My arms feel heavy.*
bruciore *burning sensation*
bruciore allo stomaco *heartburn*
bruno *brown, dark*
buca *hole*
buca delle lettere *mailbox*
buono *(n.) coupon, bond*
buono benzina *gas coupon*
buono *(adj.) good*
Buon viaggio! *Have a nice trip!*
Buon appetito! *Enjoy your meal!*
Buon giorno. *Good morning. Good afternoon.*
Buon compleanno! *Happy Birthday!*
Buon onomastico! *Happy Name Day! Happy Saint's Day!*
Buona notte. *Good night.*
Buona sera. *Good evening.*
a buon mercato *at a cheap price*

burro *butter*
busta *envelope*

C

cabina *cabin, booth*
    cabina telefonica *telephone booth*
caffè *(m.) coffee*
    caffè espresso *espresso coffee*
    caffè corretto *laced coffee*
    caffè macchiato *coffee with a dash of milk*
    caffè lungo *weak coffee*
    caffè ristretto *extra strong coffee*
    Andiamo a prendere un caffè? *Shall we go for a coffee?*
    caffellatte *(m.) coffee with milk*
calcio *soccer*
caldo *hot*
    Fa caldo. *It's hot.*
    avere caldo *to be warm/hot*
calmante *(n. m.) sedative*
calmante *(adj.) soothing*
calzascarpe *(m.) shoehorn*
calzolaio *shoemaker*
calzoleria *shoe repair store*
cambiale *(f.) promissory note*
cambiare *to change*
    cambiare casa *to move*
    cambiare canale *to change the channel*
    cambiare dollari in lire *to exchange dollars into lire*
    cambiare l'olio *to change the oil*
cambio *gear; exchange*
    cambio automatico *automatic transmission*
    Quanto è il cambio oggi? *What is the exchange rate today?*
    Il cambio è alto. *The exchange rate is high.*
camera *room, chamber*
    camera da letto *bedroom*
    Vorrei una camera con bagno. *I would like a room with a bathroom.*
    camera senza bagno *room without a bathroom*
    camera con doccia *room with a shower*
    camera singola *single room*
    camera doppia/matrimoniale *double room*
    Ha camere da affittare? *Do you have rooms for rent?*
    prenotare una camera *to reserve a room*
    Camera di Commercio *Chamber of Commerce*
cameriera *waitress*
cameriere *(m.) waiter*
camicetta *blouse*
camicia *shirt*
camoscio *suede*
    scarpe di camoscio *suede shoes*
campionato *championship*
canadese *Canadian*
canale *(m.) channel*
    cambiare canale *to change channels*
cancellazione *(f.) cancellation*
cantante *(m./f.) singer*
cantare *to sing*
cantautore *(m.) singer-songwriter*
cantina *wine cellar*

canzone *(f.) song*
capacità *ability, capacity*
    cercare qualcuno con capacità manageriali *to look for someone with managerial abilities*
capelli *hair*
    capelli corti *short hair*
    avere capelli lunghi *to have long hair*
    capelli ricci *curly hair*
    capelli lisci *straight hair*
    capelli ondulati *wavy hair*
    capelli biondi *blond hair*
    capelli castani *brown hair*
    tagliarsi i capelli *to get a haircut*
    tagliarsi i capelli a zero *to get a crew cut*
    asciugarsi i capelli *to dry one's hair*
    tingersi i capelli biondi *to dye one's hair blond*
    balsamo per i capelli *hair conditioner*
capire (isc) *to understand*
capolavoro *masterpiece*
capoufficio *head clerk, director, boss*
cappello *hat*
cappotto *coat*
cappuccino *cappuccino*
carabiniere *(m.) type of policeman*
carbone *(m.) charcoal*
    carta carbone *carbon paper*
carburante *(m.) gas, fuel*
carino *pretty, dear, kind*
carne *(f.) meat*
    carne in scatola *canned meat*
caro *dear; expensive*
    Ha qualcosa di meno caro? *Do you have something less expensive?*
carota *carrot*
carriera *career*
    fare carriera *to have a successful career*
carta *paper*
    carta d'imbarco *boarding pass*
    carta da lettere *writing paper*
    carta telefonica *telephone card*
    carta carbone *carbon paper*
    carta carburante turistica *highway toll card*
    carta da bollo *government-stamped paper*
    carta igienica *toilet paper*
    Carta Verde *green card insurance*
    carta geografica *map*
    carta stradale *road map*
cartella *folder, file*
cartolina *postcard*
cartoni animati *cartoons*
casa *house*
    a casa *at home, home*
    cambiare casa *to move*
    restare a casa *to stay home*
casella *box*
    casella postale *post-office box*
casellario *filing cabinet*
cassa *cash register*
    Si accomodi alla cassa. *Please go to the cashier's window.*
cassaforte *(f.) safe*
cassetta *cassette; box*
    cassetta di sicurezza *safety deposit box*
    cassetta postale *mailbox*

cassiere/a *(m./f.) cashier, treasurer*
castano *brown*
   capelli castani *brown hair*
categoria *category*
   albergo di prima categoria *first-class hotel*
CD *CD (compact disc)*
   l'ultimo CD *the latest CD*
cenare *to have supper*
cento *hundred*
   Il tasso di interesse è al dieci per cento. *The interest rate is ten percent.*
centralinista *(m./f.) operator*
centralino (place) *operator, telephone exchange*
   Chiama il centralino. *Call the operator.*
centro *center*
   andare in centro *to go downtown*
   centro commerciale *commercial center*
cercare *to look for*
   cercare lavoro *to look for a job*
   cercare un appartamento in affitto *to look for an apartment for rent*
cerino *wax match*
   scatola di cerini *box of (wax) matches*
cerotto *bandage*
certamente *certainly*
certo *certain*
   essere certo *to be certain*
cetriolo *cucumber*
che *what, which; that, whom*
   Che bel giorno! *What a beautiful day!*
   Che giorno è oggi? *What day is today?*
   Che tempo fa? *What's the weather like?*
   Che ora è? *What time is it?*
   Che taglia porta? *What size do you wear?*
   La ragazza che vedo è bella. *The girl (whom) I see is beautiful.*
chi *who, whom*
   Pronto! Chi parla? *Hello! Who's speaking?*
chiamare *to call*
   Chiamate un medico. *Call a doctor.*
   Chiama il centralino. *Call the operator.*
chiamarsi *to be called*
   Come ti chiami/si chiama? *What's your name? (familiar/polite)*
   Mi chiamo Antonio. *My name is Anthony.*
chiave *(f.) key; wrench*
   chiavi della camera *room keys*
chiedere *to ask*
   chiedere il bis *to ask for an encore*
   chiedere indicazioni *to ask for directions*
chiesa *church*
chilo *kilo*
   Cinquemila lire al chilo. *Five thousand lire a kilo.*
chilometraggio *mileage*
   chilometraggio illimitato *unlimited mileage*
chilometro *kilometer*
chitarra *guitar*
   suonare la chitarra *to play the guitar*
chiuso *closed*
ci *(adv.) here, there*
   Ci vado domani. *I'm going there tomorrow.*
   Ci sono delle mostre? *Are there any shows?*

ci *(pron.) us; to us; each other; it, about/of it*
   Ci penso io. *I'll take care of it.*
   Ci vuole la ricetta? *Is a prescription necessary?*
ciao *(familiar) Hi! Hello! Bye!*
ciclismo *cycling*
ciliegia *cherry*
cilindro *cylinder*
   A quanti cilindri è la macchina? *How many cylinders does the car have?*
cinema *(m.) movie theater*
   andare al cinema *to go to the movies*
cinese *Chinese*
cinquecento *five hundred*
cintura *belt*
   cintura di sicurezza *seat belt*
cioccolato *chocolate*
   gelato al cioccolato *chocolate ice cream*
cipolla *onion*
circa *approximately, around*
   È distante circa un chilometro. *It's approximately a kilometer away.*
città *city*
   girare la città *to tour the city*
   pianta della città *map of the city*
classe *(f.) class*
   viaggiare in prima classe *to travel first class*
   classe turistica *economy class*
classico *classical*
   musica classica *classical music*
codice *(m.) code*
   codice postale *postal code*
cognato/a *brother-/sister-in-law*
colazione *breakfast*
   fare colazione *to have breakfast*
colore *(m.) color*
   Di che colore? *What color?*
   rullino a colori *color film*
coltello *knife*
come *how, as, like*
   Come ti chiami? *What's your name? (familiar)*
   Come passi il weekend? *How will you spend the weekend? (familiar)*
   Come stai? *How are you? (familiar)*
cominciare *to start*
commedia *comedy*
commesso *salesman*
commissariato *police station*
   andare al commissariato *to go to the police station*
commissione *(f.) commission; errand*
comodamente *comfortably*
comodità *commodity*
comodo *(n.) comfort, convenience, ease*
comodo *(adj.) comfortable, convenient, handy*
compagnia *company; society*
   compagnia aerea *airline*
compilare *to fill in*
   Deve compilare alcuni moduli. *You have to fill in some forms.*
compleanno *birthday*
   Buon compleanno! *Happy birthday!*
complesso *musical group*
compra *purchase*
   fare delle compre *to go shopping*

comprare *to buy*

comprare il giornale *to buy the newspaper*

compreso *included; understood*

Il servizio è compreso? *Is the service charge included?*

computer *computer*

comunale *municipal*

guardia comunale *municipal (traffic) policeman*

concedere *to concede, to allow*

concedere il bis *to give an encore*

concerto *concert*

concerto all'aperto *open-air concert*

andare al concerto *to go to a concert*

condizionato *conditional; conditioned*

aria condizionata *air-conditioning*

condominio *condominium*

conoscere *to know, to be acquainted with*

consigliare *to advise, to suggest*

Le consiglio questa medicina. *I suggest this medicine.*

consumare *to consume, to use*

Questa macchina consuma molta benzina? *Does this car use a lot of gas?*

contante *(m.) cash*

Ecco a Lei trecento dollari in contanti. *Here's three hundred dollars in cash.*

contento *happy, glad*

conto *bill, account*

conto sociale *joint account*

conto corrente *checking account*

aprire un conto *to open an account*

Mi prepari il conto? *Can you prepare my bill?*

Il conto, per favore. *The bill, please.*

contorno *side dish*

contorno di verdura *side dish of vegetables*

contratto *contract*

contravvenzione *(f.) infraction; fine, ticket*

pagare una contravvezione *to pay a fine*

contributo *contribution*

contro *against*

pomata contro le scottature *sunburn lotion*

controfirma *countersignature*

controllare *to check, to control*

Controlli i freni, per favore. *Please check the brakes.*

coperto *(n.) cover charge*

coperto *(adj.) covered*

corrente *(n. f.) current, trend*

corrente *(adj.) current*

conto corrente *checking account*

corretto *correct*

caffè corretto *laced coffee*

corridoio *aisle*

corriere *(m.) courier*

corto *short*

capelli corti *short hair*

cosa *(n.) thing*

cosa *(int. pron.) What?*

Cosa fai questo weekend? *What are you doing this weekend? (familiar)*

Cosa vuole? *What do you want? (polite)*

Cosa hai detto? *What did you say? (familiar)*

così *so, thus*

così così *so so*

È proprio così! *That's the way it is!*

costruire *to build*

cotto *cooked*

Voglio la bistecca ben cotta. *I want my steak well done.*

cravatta *tie*

credere *to believe*

credito *credit*

crimine *(m.) crime*

crisi *(f.) crisis*

La donna ha avuto una crisi. *The woman had a crisis.*

crociera *cruise*

fare una crociera *to go on a cruise*

cronaca *commentary, news, column*

cronaca mondana *gossip column*

cronaca nera *crime news*

cuccetta *couchette*

cucchiaio *spoon*

cucina *kitchen*

cugino/a *cousin*

cultura *culture*

cura *cure*

seguire una cura dimagrante *to be on a diet*

custodito *guarded*

parcheggio custodito *guarded parking lot*

D

da *from, since, at, to, by*

Da quanto tempo è in Italia? *How long have you been in Italy?*

Vado dal dottore. *I'm going to the doctor.*

Da dove vieni? *Where are you coming from?*

camera da letto *bedroom*

dado *cube, dice*

dado di manzo *beef bouillon*

dado di pollo *chicken bouillon*

danno *damage*

assicurazione contro i danni *collision damage waiver*

dare *to give*

dare un film *to show a movie*

dare una festa *to have a party*

dare in affitto *to let, to rent*

dare indicazioni *to give directions*

Dammi una mano! *Give me a hand!*

La camera dà sulla strada. *The room overlooks the street.*

data *date*

davanti *in front of, before*

Il museo è davanti alla chiesa. *The museum is in front of the church.*

davvero *really, indeed, truly*

Davvero? *Really?*

debito *debt*

decidere *to decide*

denaro *money*

denaro liquido *cash*

dentifricio *toothpaste*

denuncia *denunciation*
  fare denuncia *to file a complaint*
denunciare *to denounce; to declare*
depositare *to deposit*
derubare *to rob*
  Mi hanno derubato. *I have been robbed.*
desiderare *to want, to desire*
  Desidera? *What would you like?*
  Desidera ordinare adesso? *Would you like to order now?*
  Desidero una camera per una notte. *I would like a room for one night.*
destinatario *addressee, recipient*
destinazione *(f.) destination*
destra *right*
  girare a destra *to turn right*
  sulla destra *on the right*
detersivo *detergent*
di *of*
  Di dov'è Lei? *Where are you from? (polite)*
  Di che colore? *What color?*
diabete *(m.) diabetes*
  Ho il diabete. *I have diabetes.*
dicembre *(m.) December*
dietro *behind, after*
  Non troppo corti di dietro. *Not too short in the back.*
digestivo *digestive*
dilettante *(m./f.) amateur*
dimagrante *slimming*
  seguire una cura dimagrante *to follow a diet*
dipingere *to paint*
dire *to say*
  Cosa ha detto? *What did you say? (polite)*
  Mi dica? *May I help you?*
diretto *(n.) fast train*
direttore *(m.) manager, editor*
  direttore d'orchestra *conductor*
direttrice *(f.) manager, editor*
direzione *(f.) direction*
dirigenziale *managerial*
  lavorare nel settore dirigenziale *to work in the managerial sector*
disco *record*
discoteca *discotheque*
disegnare *to draw, to design*
disinfettante *(m.) disinfectant*
disoccupato *unemployed*
  essere disoccupato *to be unemployed*
dispiacere *to dislike*
  Mi dispiace. *I'm sorry.*
distante *distant*
  È distante un chilometro. *It's a kilometer away.*
distare *to be distant*
  Quanto dista da qui il museo? *How far is the museum?*
dito *finger*
  Mi sono rotto un dito. *I broke my finger.*
ditta *company*
  lavorare in una ditta privata *to work for a private company*
divano *sofa*
diverso *different, several*
divertirsi *to enjoy oneself*

doccia *shower*
  camera con doccia *room with a shower*
documentario *documentary*
documentazione *(f.) documentation, file*
documento *document*
dogana *customs*
dolce *(m.) dessert, cake*
dolce *(adj.) sweet*
dollaro *dollar*
  A quanto è il dollaro oggi? *What is the exchange rate for the dollar today?*
domanda *question*
  fare domanda per un lavoro *to apply for a job*
domani *tomorrow*
  A domani. *See you tomorrow.*
  Domani è il due luglio. *Tomorrow is July second.*
domenica *Sunday*
donna *woman*
  scarpe da donna *women's shoes*
dopobarba *(m.) aftershave lotion*
doppio *double*
  camera doppia *double room*
dormire *to sleep*
  pillole per dormire *sleeping pills*
dose *(f.) dose, ration*
dottore *(m.) doctor*
  andare dal dottore *to go to the doctor*
dove *where*
  Dove sei stato? *Where were you?*
  Dov'è l'ospedale? *Where is the hospital?*
dozzina *dozen*
  una dozzina di uova *a dozen eggs*
dramma *(m.) drama; dramatic literature; theater*
dritto *straight*
dritto *straight*
  Vada sempre dritto. *Go straight ahead.*
dubbio *doubt*
  senza dubbio *without any doubt*
dubitare *to doubt*
duomo *cathedral*

E

e *and*
eccezionale *exceptional*
ecco *here is/are; there is/are*
  Ecco a Lei. *Here you are.*
  Ecco fatto! *All done!*
economico *economic*
  annunci economici *classified ads*
  avviso economico *newspaper ad*
ed *and*
edicola *newsstand*
editoriale *editorial*
elenco *list*
  elenco telefonico *telephone book*
ente *(m.) being; corporation*
  Ente Provinciale per il Turismo *Provincial Tourist Office*
equo *equitable, fair, just*
  equo canone *controlled rent*
esagerare *to exaggerate*
esame *(m.) examination; survey*
escursione *(f.) excursion*

397

esperienza *experience*
  avere esperienza *to have experience*
espressione *(f.) expression*
espresso *(adj.) express*
  lettera espresso *express letter*
  treno espresso *express train*
essere *to be*
  essere gentile *to be kind*
  essere disoccupato *to be unemployed*
  essere assunto *to be hired*
  essere licenziato *to be fired*
  essere in ritardo *to be late*
  essere in orario *to be on time*
  essere sicuro *to be sure*
  essere certo *to be certain*
  essere di servizio *to be on duty*
  essere in ufficio *to be in the office*
  essere stressato *to be under stress*
  essere occupato *to be busy*
  essere contento *to be happy*
estate *(f.) summer*
estero *foreign country*
  francobollo per l'estero *stamp for a foreign country*
  valuta estera *foreign currency*
età *age, period*
evidenziatore *(m.) highlighter*

F

fabbrica *factory*
  lavorare in fabbrica *to work in a factory*
facchino *porter*
fagiolini *(m., pl.) string beans*
fame *(f.) hunger*
  avere fame *to be hungry*
famiglia *family*
famoso *famous*
fan *(m./f.) fan*
  essere un/una fan di *to be a fan of*
fantastico *fantastic*
fare *to do, to make*
  Che tempo fa? *What's the weather like?*
  Fa freddo. *It's cold.*
  Fa caldo. *It's hot.*
  fare carriera *to have a successful career*
  fare una telefonata *to make a telephone call*
  fare colazione *to have breakfast*
  fare il bagno *to go swimming, to take a bath*
  fare un giro *to take a tour*
  fare una passeggiata *to go for a walk*
  fare la spesa *to go grocery shopping*
  fare una fotocopia *to make a photocopy*
  fare una raccomandata *to send a registered letter*
  fare un telegramma *to send a telegram*
  fare benzina *to get gas*
  fare delle compre *to go shopping*
  farsi lo sciampo *to shampoo*
  farsi la barba *to shave*
  Dovremmo farcela. *We should manage.*
  Faccia il pieno, per favore. *Fill it up, please.*
  Ecco fatto. *All done!*
  Non fa niente. *It doesn't matter.*

Non fa male allo stomaco. *It doesn't upset your stomach.*
Potrebbe farmi la permanente? *Could you give me a perm?*
Mi fanno male le orecchie. *My ears hurt.*
farmacia *pharmacy*
  farmacia di turno *pharmacy on duty*
farmacista *(m./f.) pharmacist*
favoloso *fabulous*
  passare delle vacanze favolose *to spend a fabulous vacation*
favore *(m.) favor*
  per favore *please*
favorire *to favor*
fax *fax*
  mandare un fax *to send a fax*
fazzoletto *handkerchief*
  fazzolettino di carta *tissue*
febbraio *February*
febbre *(f.) fever*
  avere la febbre *to have a fever*
ferie *(f., pl.) vacation*
fermare *to stop*
fermata *stop*
  A che fermata devo scendere? *At which stop do I have to get off?*
fermo *firm, still*
  Sta' fermo! *Stay still!*
  fermo posta *poste restante*
ferro *iron, steel*
  pesce ai ferri *grilled fish*
  bistecca ai ferri *grilled steak*
ferrovia *railroad*
  Ferrovie dello Stato *state-owned railroad system*
festa *party, feast, festival*
  dare una festa *to have a party*
festeggiare *to celebrate*
festival *festival*
  festival delle canzone *song festival*
fiammifero *match*
  fiammiferi svedesi *safety matches*
fidanzato/a *fiancé/e*
fiducia *trust, confidence*
  Noi abbiamo fiducia in te. *We trust you.*
figlio *son*
fila *line*
  aspettare in fila *to wait in line*
film *(m.) film*
  dare un film *to show a movie*
filtro *filter*
  Può cambiare il filtro? *Can you change the filter?*
finalmente *finally*
finanziare *to finance*
finanziario *financial*
  rubrica finanziaria *business page*
finestra *window*
finire (isc) *to finish*
fino a *until, as far as*
  fino a Roma *as far as Rome*
  fino a domani *until tomorrow*
fiorino *florin*
firma *signature*
fissare *to fix; to reserve*
  fissare un appuntamento *to make an appointment*

fisso *permanent, fixed*
  stipendio fisso *steady income*
  prezzi fissi *fixed prices*
fondare *to found*
forbici *(f., pl.) scissors*
forchetta *fork*
formaggio *cheese*
fotocopia *photocopy*
  fare una fotocopia *to make a photocopy*
fotocopiare *to photocopy*
fotocopiatrice *(f.) photocopy machine*
fragola *strawberry*
francese *French*
franco *franc*
francobollo *stamp*
  francobollo per l'estero *stamp for a foreign
    country*
fratello *brother*
freccia *arrow; signal*
  La freccia non funziona. *The signal doesn't work.*
freddo *cold*
  Fa freddo. *It's cold.*
  Ho freddo. *I'm cold.*
frenare *to put on the brakes*
freno *brake*
  Controlli i freni, per favore. *Check the brakes,
    please.*
frequentare *to attend*
fresco *fresh*
  frutta fresca *fresh fruit*
  Fa fresco. *It's cool out.*
fretta *haste, hurry; speed*
  avere fretta *to be in a hurry*
frigorifero *refrigerator*
fritto *fried*
  pesce fritto *fried fish*
  patate fritte *French fries*
frizione *(f.) friction; clutch (auto); conflict*
frutta *fruit*
  frutta fresca *fresh fruit*
  succo di frutta *fruit juice*
fruttivendolo *fruit seller*
fumare *to smoke*
  Vietato fumare. *No smoking.*
fumatore *smoker*
  zona fumatori *smoking area*
fumo *smoke*
funzionare *to operate, to function; to act*
  La freccia non funziona. *The signal doesn't work.*
furto *theft*
  assicurazione per il furto *antitheft insurance*
  essere vittima di un furto *to be a victim of a
    robbery*

G

garage *garage*
garza *gauze*
  Ha della garza? *Do you have any gauze?*
gelateria *cafe, ice-cream parlor*
gelato *ice cream*
  gelato al cioccolato *chocolate ice cream*
  gelato alla vaniglia *vanilla ice cream*

genero *son-in-law*
generoso *generous*
genitori *(m., pl.) parents*
gennaio *January*
gentile *gentle*
  essere gentile *to be kind*
gentilmente *politely*
geografico *geographical*
  Ha una carta geografica dell'Italia? *Do you have a
    map of Italy?*
gettone *(m.) telephone token*
giacca *jacket*
giallo *yellow*
  pagine gialle *yellow pages*
giapponese *Japanese*
giardino *garden*
giocare *to play*
giocatore *(m.) player*
giocattolo *toy*
giornalaio *newspaper vendor*
giornale *(m.) newspaper*
  comprare il giornale *to buy the newspaper*
  leggere il giornale *to read the newspaper*
  Cosa dice il giornale? *What does it say in the
    newspaper?*
giornalista *(m./f.) journalist*
giornata *day*
  È una bella giornata. *It's a beautiful day.*
  È una brutta giornata. *It's a miserable day.*
giorno *day*
  Buon giorno. *Good morning.*
  i giorni della settimana *the days of the week*
  Che giorno è oggi? *What day is today?*
  Che bel giorno! *What a beautiful day!*
  tre volte al giorno *three times a day*
giovedì *(m.) Thursday*
girare *to turn*
  girare a destra *to turn right*
  girare a sinistra *to turn left*
  girare la città *to tour the city*
giro *tour; spin*
  giro organizzato *organized tour*
  fare il giro del mondo *to travel around the
    world*
  fare un giro *to take a tour*
giù *down, below*
giudice *(m.) judge*
giugno *June*
goccia *drop*
gola *throat*
  avere mal di gola *to have a sore throat*
gomma *gum; rubber; tire; eraser*
  Mi può riparare la gomma? *Can you fix my
    tire?*
  Ho le gomme a terra. *My tires are low.*
gonna *skirt*
governativo *governmental*
  tassa governativa *government tax*
graffetta *paper clip*
grammo *gram*
  Mi dia cento grammi di formaggio. *I would like a
    hundred grams of cheese.*
grande *big, large, great*
  grande magazzino *department store*

grazie *thank you*
　Mille grazie. *Thanks a million.*
　Molte grazie. *Thanks a lot.*
gruppo *group; musical group*
guanto *glove*
guardare *to look, to watch*
　guardare la televisione *to watch television*
　guardare la partita *to watch the game*
guardia *guard*
　guardia comunale *municipal (traffic) policeman*
guida *guide*
　La guida è molto preparata. *The guide is well
　　prepared.*
　Ha una guida turistica? *Do you have a guidebook?*
guidare *to drive*
　Non guidare velocemente! *Don't drive fast!*

H

hit *(m.) hit, record*
　hit parade *top ten*
　l'ultimo hit *the latest hit*
hotel *(m.) hotel*
　hotel di prima categoria *first-class hotel*
　hotel a tre stelle *three-star hotel*

I

igienico *hygienic*
　carta igienica *toilet paper*
illimitato *unlimited*
　chilometraggio illimitato *unlimited mileage*
imbarco *embarkation*
　carta d'imbarco *boarding pass*
immenso *immense*
immobili *(m., pl.) premises, real estate*
　agenzia immobiliare *real estate agency*
impeccabile *impeccable*
in *in, into*
　in più *more, extra*
　andare in Francia *to go to France*
　andare in città *to go to town*
　tradurre in inglese *to translate into
　　English*
　in campagna *in the country*
　in montagna *in the mountains*
　in casa *at home*
incidere *to cut, to engrave, to record*
　incidere un disco *to cut a record*
incluso *included*
　L'assicurazione è inclusa nel prezzo? *Is the
　　insurance included in the price?*
　I pasti sono inclusi? *Are meals included?*
incontrare *to meet*
　Ci siamo incontrati a Roma. *We met each other in
　　Rome.*
incontro *encounter; game, match*
　incontro di calcio *soccer game*
indicazione *(f.) indication, instruction*
　indicazioni per l'uso *usage instructions*
indietro *back*
　ritornare indietro *to go back*

indirizzo *address*
　Qual è il Suo indirizzo? *What's your address?*
infatti *in fact*
informazione *(f.) information*
　Mi serve un'informazione. *I need some
　　information.*
　Mi potrebbe dare alcune informazioni? *Could you
　　give me some information?*
　ufficio informazioni *information office*
inglese *English*
ingranare *to engage, to go into gear*
　La terza non ingrana. *The car will not go into
　　third gear.*
ingresso *entrance, foyer*
iniezione *(f.) injection*
iniziare *to start*
　A che ora inizia lo spettacolo? *At what time does
　　the show start?*
inquilino *tenant*
insalata *salad*
insegnare *to teach*
　insegnare l'italiano *to teach Italian*
intelligente *intelligent*
interessante *interesting*
interessarsi *to be interested*
　interessarsi di pittura *to be interested in painting*
interesse *(m.) interest*
　Il tasso di interesse è al dieci per cento. *The
　　interest rate is ten percent.*
internazionale *international*
　patente internazionale *International Driving
　　Permit*
interno *(n. m.) interior; apartment number*
interno *(adj.) internal; resident*
interurbana *long-distance call*
intervista *interview*
inventare *to invent*
inverno *winter*
irritazione *(f.) irritation*
　irritazione della pelle *skin rash*
ispezione *(f.) inspection, supervision*
italiano *Italian*
itinerario *itinerary*

L

là *there*
lacca *hair spray*
laccio *lace, string*
　lacci per le scarpe *shoe laces*
ladro *thief*
lamentarsi *to complain*
largo *large, big*
latte *(m.) milk*
lattuga *lettuce*
laurearsi *to graduate*
　laurearsi in commercio *to get a degree in business*
lavare *to wash*
lavarsi *to wash oneself*
lavorare *to work*
　lavorare in proprio *to have one's own business*
　lavorare in fabbrica *to work in a factory*

lavorare in un ufficio *to work in an office*
lavorare nel settore dirigenziale *to work in the managerial sector*
lavorare nel settore privato *to work in the private sector*
lavorativo *working*
orario lavorativo regolare *regular working hours*
lavoro *work*
andare al lavoro *to go to work*
fare domanda per un lavoro *to apply for a job*
cercare lavoro *to look for a job*
colloquio di lavoro *job interview*
leggere *to read*
leggere il giornale *to read the newspaper*
leggero *light*
musica leggera *pop music*
lesso *boiled*
pesce lesso *boiled fish*
lettera *letter*
carta da lettere *stationery*
lettera espresso *express letter*
spedire una lettera *to mail a letter*
imbucare una lettera *to mail a letter*
affrancare una lettera *to put a stamp on a letter*
letteratura *literature*
letto *bed*
camera da letto *bedroom*
vagone letto *sleeping car*
lì *there*
libero *free*
È libero questo posto? *Is this seat free?*
La linea è libera. *The telephone line is free.*
libretto *book*
libretto degli assegni *checkbook*
libretto di risparmi *savings account*
licenziare *to fire*
essere licenziato *to be fired*
lieto *glad, pleased*
Molto lieto. *Very pleased to meet you.*
limonata *lemonade*
limone *(m.) lemon*
linea *line*
La linea è occupata. *The line is busy.*
La linea è libera. *The line is free.*
liquido *liquid*
denaro liquido *cash*
lira *lira*
liscio *smooth; simple*
capelli lisci *straight hair*
lista *list*
lista della spesa *shopping list*
listino *list; timetable; price list*
listino dei cambi *exchange list*
locale *(n. m.) place, house; headquarters*
locale *(adj.) local*
treno locale *local train*
lontano *far*
Abito lontano da qui. *I live far from here.*
È lontano. *It's far.*
luce *(f.) light*
accendere la luce *to turn on the light*
spegnere la luce *to put out the light*
lucidare *to polish, to clean*
lucidare le scarpe *to clean one's shoes*

lucido *(n.) polish*
lucido per scarpe *shoe polish*
lucido *(adj.) bright, shining*
luglio *July*
luna *moon*
luna di miele *honeymoon*
lunedì *(m.) Monday*
lungo *long*
capelli lunghi *to have long hair*

M

ma *but*
macchiato *stained*
caffè macchiato *coffee with a dash of milk*
macchina *car, automobile; machine*
aggiustare la macchina *to fix the car*
noleggiare una macchina *to rent a car*
macchina con le marce *standard car*
Metti in moto la macchina. *Start the car.*
macchina da scrivere *typewriter*
battere a macchina *to type*
madre *(f.) mother*
magazzino *warehouse, store*
grande magazzino *department store*
maggio *May*
maglione *(m.) pullover, sweater*
mai *never*
malato *sick*
male *(n.) evil; harm; ache*
mal di testa *headache*
mal di stomaco *stomachache*
mal di pancia *stomachache*
Ho mal di schiena. *I have a pain in the back.*
male *(adv.) badly, poorly*
Non c'è male. *Not too bad.*
mamma *mommy*
manageriale *managerial*
capacità manageriali *managerial ability*
mancia *tip*
mandare *to send*
mandare un fax *to send a fax*
mangianastro *cassette player*
mangiare *to eat*
manicure *a manicure*
manifestazione *(f.) manifestation, exhibition*
mano *(f.) hand*
Dammi una mano! *Give me a hand!*
stretta di mano *handshake*
chiedere la mano di *to ask in marriage*
battere le mani *to clap*
manzo *beef*
dado di manzo *beef boullion cube*
marca *stamp*
marca da bollo *tax stamps*
marcia *gear*
macchina con le marce *standard-transmission car*
marco *mark*
mare *(m.) sea*
andare al mare *to go to the shore*
marito *husband*
marmellata *jam*
marrone *brown*

martedì *(m.) Tuesday*
marzo *March*
matita *pencil*
matrimoniale *matrimonial*
  camera matrimoniale *double room*
mattina *morning*
  di mattina *in the morning*
meccanico *mechanic*
medicina *medicine*
  prescrivere una medicina *to prescribe a*
    medication
  prendere una medicina *to take a medication*
medico *(n.) doctor*
  Chiamate un medico. *Call a doctor.*
medico *(adj.) medical*
  assicurazione medica *medical insurance*
meglio *better*
  Sto meglio. *I feel better.*
  È meglio. *It's better.*
mela *apple*
melanzana *eggplant*
melone *(m.) melon*
meno *less*
menù *(m.) menu*
mercato *market*
  andare al mercato *to go to the market*
  a buon mercato *at a cheap price*
mercoledì *(m.) Wednesday*
meridionale *southern*
  Italia meridionale *Southern Italy*
mese *(m.) month*
  L'affitto è tre milioni di lire al mese. *The rent is*
    three million lire a month.
messa *mass*
  andare a messa *to go to mass*
messaggio *message*
  messaggio del telegramma *telegram message*
messicano *Mexican*
messinscena *staging*
metà *half, middle*
  pagare metà prezzo *to pay half price*
metro *meter*
  È a cento metri. *It's one hundred meters from*
    here. ·
metropolitana *subway*
  prendere la metropolitana *to take the subway*
mettere *to put; to wear*
  Metti in moto la macchina. *Start the car.*
  Metti la prima. *Put it in first gear.*
  Metti sul/al canale 5. *Put it on channel five.*
mettersi *to put on (clothing)*
  Mettiti il vestito. *Put on your suit (dress).*
  mettersi le scarpe *to put on one's shoes*
miele *(m.) honey*
  luna di miele *honeymoon*
milione *(m.) million*
minerale *(adj.) mineral*
  acqua minerale *mineral water*
minerva *match*
  scatola di minerva *a box of matches*
minuto *(n.) minute*
  È a pochi minuti dal centro. *It's a few minutes*
    from downtown.
minuto *(adj.) minute; petty*

misurare *to measure*
  misurare la pressione *to take someone's blood*
    pressure
mittente *(m./f.) sender*
mobili *(m., pl.) furniture*
modulo *form*
  modùlo per cambiale *promissory note*
  Deve compilare alcuni moduli. *You have to fill in*
    some forms.
moglie *(f.) wife*
molto *a lot of, many, very*
  Molto lieto. *Very pleased to meet you.*
  Sto molto bene. *I am very well.*
  Molte grazie. *Many thanks.*
momento *moment*
  Un momento, per piacere. *One moment, please.*
mondano *worldly*
  cronaca mondana *gossip column*
mondo *world*
  fare il giro del mondo *to travel around the world*
moneta *coin, money*
morire *to die*
mostra *display, show*
moto *motion*
  Metti in moto la macchina. *Start the car.*
moto *(f.) motorcycle*
motore *(m.) motor, engine*
  Il motore scalda. *The engine is overheating.*
multa *fine, penalty, ticket*
murale *(adj.) mural, wall*
  pittura murale *mural painting*
muro *wall*
  armadio a muro *closet*
museo *museum*
musica *music*
  ascoltare un po' di musica *to listen to some music*
  musica di *music by*
  musica classica *classical music*
  musica leggera *pop music*
  musica rock *rock music*
musicale *musical*
  strumento musicale *musical instrument*
musicista *(m./f.) musician*

N

nascere *to be born*
nazionalità *nationality*
né *nor*
  non . . . né . . . né *neither . . . nor*
neanche *not even*
necessario *necessary*
  è necessario *it is necessary*
negozio *store, shop*
  andare al negozio *to go to the store*
  negozio di abbigliamento *clothing store*
  negozio di scarpe *shoe store*
nero *black*
  cronaca nera *crime news*
nervoso *nervous*
nessuno *no one, nobody*
nevicare *to snow*
  Nevica. *It's snowing.*

niente *nothing*
Niente vino, per favore. *No wine, please.*
nipote *(m./f.) grandson, granddaughter, nephew,
niece*
no *no*
noleggiare *to rent*
noleggiare una macchina *to rent a car*
noleggio *rental*
Quanto è il noleggio per una settimana? *How
much is the rental for a week?*
non *not*
Non ho più fame. *I'm not hungry anymore.*
Non sono affatto stanco. *I'm not tired at all.*
Non sono mai andata lì. *I never went there.*
Non vede nessuno. *He doesn't see anyone.*
Non abbiamo ancora mangiato. *We haven't eaten
yet.*
nonna *grandmother*
nonno *grandfather*
normale *normal*
benzina normale *regular gas*
notizia *news; notice; report*
notte *(f.) night*
Buona notte. *Good night.*
di notte *at night*
Desidero una camera per una notte. *I would like
a room for one night.*
novembre *(m.) November*
nulla *nothing*
numero *number*
Che numero porta? *What size do you wear?*
Ho sbagliato numero. *I dialed the wrong
number.*
nuora *daughter-in-law*
nuoto *swimming*
nuovo *new*

O

occasione *(f.) occasion*
Ho avuto l'occasione di andare in Italia. *I had the
opportunity to go to Italy.*
occorrere *to be necessary; to happen, to occur*
Occorre la ricetta? *Do I need a prescription?*
occupato *busy, occupied*
La linea è occupata. *The line is busy.*
Sono molto occupato. *I'm very busy.*
È occupato questo posto? *Is this seat taken?*
offrire *to offer*
oggi *today*
Che giorno è oggi? *What day is today?*
Oggi è lunedì. *Today is Monday.*
Oggi è il primo luglio. *Today is the first of July.*
ogni *every*
olio *oil*
controllare l'olio *to check the oil*
cambiare l'olio *to change the oil*
pittura ad olio *oil painting*
olio da tavola *salad oil*
ondulato *wavy*
capelli ondulati *wavy hair*
onomastico *name day*
Buon onomastico! *Happy Name Day!*

opera *work; opera*
andare all'opera *to go to the opera*
opere di Boccaccio *Boccaccio's works*
mettersi all'opera *to set to work*
operatore *(m.) operator*
operatore turistico *tour operator*
oppure *or*
ora *hour, time*
Che ora è?/Che ore sono? *What time is it?*
A che ora arriva il treno? *At what time does the
train arrive?*
A che ora parte il treno? *At what time does the
train leave?*
orario *(n.) timetable*
in orario *punctual, on time*
orario d'ufficio *office hours*
orario *(adj.) hourly, per hour*
ordinare *to order*
orecchio *ear*
organizzato *organized*
giro organizzato *organized tour*
orientarsi *to find one's bearings*
Non mi posso orientare. *I can't find my way
around.*
oroscopo *horoscope*
ospedale *(m.) hospital*
ottenere *to obtain*
ottenere una promozione *to get promoted*
ottimista *(m./f.) optimist*
ottobre *(m.) October*

P

pacchetto *pack, package*
pacchetto di agevolazione turistica *Incentive
Tourist Package*
pacchetto di sigarette *pack of cigarettes*
pacco *parcel*
assicurare un pacco *to insure a parcel*
spedire un pacco *to send a parcel*
padre *(m.) father*
paga *pay*
pagamento *payment*
pagamento anticipato *payment in advance*
pagare *to pay*
pagare metà prezzo *to pay half price*
pagare la bolletta del telefono *to pay the telephone
bill*
pagina *page*
pagine gialle *yellow pages*
pagina sportiva *sports page*
paio *pair*
un paio di scarpe *a pair of shoes*
palazzina *a small apartment building*
palazzo *palace, an apartment building*
palcoscenico *stage*
pallacanestro *basketball*
pancia *stomach*
mal di pancia *stomachache*
pane *bread*
pane tostato *toast*
panino *sandwich*
pantaloni *(m./pl.) pants*

pantofola *slipper*
papà *(m.) daddy*
parabrezza *windshield*
parcheggio *parking*
  parcheggio custodito *guarded parking*
parente *(m./f.) relative*
parlare *to speak*
  parlare l'italiano *to speak Italian*
  Pronto! Chi parla? *Hello! Who is speaking?*
  parlare al telefono *to speak on the phone*
parola *word*
  parole di *lyrics by*
parrucchiere *(m.) hairdresser*
parte *(f.) part*
  fare la parte di *to play the part of*
partenza *departure*
partire *to leave, to depart*
  A che ora parte il treno per Roma? *At what time does the train for Rome leave?*
partita *game*
  guardare la partita *to watch the game*
  partita di calcio *soccer game*
passaggio *passage, ride*
  Può darmi un passaggio? *Can you give me a ride?*
passaporto *passport*
passare *to pass, to spend*
  passare delle vacanze favolose *to spend a fabulous vacation*
  Come passi il weekend? *How will you spend your weekend?*
passeggero *passenger*
passeggiata *walk*
  fare una passeggiata *to go for a walk*
passo *step*
  È a due passi. *It's very close.*
pasta *pastry, pasta*
pasticca *lozenge, pastille, pill*
  pasticca per la tosse *cough drop*
pasticceria *pastry shop, café*
pasto *meal*
  dopo i pasti *after meals*
  I pasti sono inclusi? *Are meals included?*
patata *potato*
  patate fritte *french fries*
patente *(f.) license, certificate, patent*
  patente internazionale *International Driver's License*
paura *fear*
  avere paura di *to be afraid of*
pazienza *patience*
  Abbi pazienza. *Be patient.*
pelle *(f.) skin*
  irritazione della pelle *skin rash*
pendolare *(m.) swinging; commuting*
  fare il pendolare *to commute*
penicillina *penicillin*
pennarello *marker*
pensare *to think*
  Ci penso io. *I'll take care of it.*
pensione *(f.) pension, allowance; boarding-house*
  riscuotere la pensione *to cash the pension check*

pepe *(m.) pepper*
per *for*
  per favore *please*
  per piacere *please*
  per via aerea *by air mail*
pera *pear*
perdere *to lose*
  perdere il treno *to miss the train*
periferia *suburbs*
  È in periferia. *It's in the suburbs.*
periodo *time period*
permanente *(f.) permanent wave (hair)*
  Potrebbe farmi la permanente? *Could you give me a perm?*
persona *person*
personaggio *personage; character (in a play)*
pesante *heavy*
  Mi sento le braccia pesanti. *My arms feel heavy.*
pesca *peach*
pesce *(m.) fish*
  pesce ai ferri *grilled fish*
  pesce lesso *boiled fish*
  pesce fritto *fried fish*
peseta *peseta*
peso *peso*
pessimista *(m./f.) pessimist*
pettinarsi *to comb one's hair*
pettine *(m.) comb*
piacere *(m.) pleasure*
  Piacere. *Pleased to meet you.*
  Per piacere. *Please.*
pianista *(m./f.) pianist*
piano *(n.) floor, story*
piano *(adv.) softly, slowly*
pianta *plant; map*
  Ha una pianta della città? *Do you have a map of the city?*
piatto *dish*
piazza *square, plaza*
piccolo *small*
piede *(m.) foot*
  andare a piedi *to go on foot*
  Mi sono rotto un piede. *I broke my foot.*
piega *pleat, fold*
  farsi la messa in piega *to have one's hair set*
pieno *full*
  Faccia il pieno. *Fill it up.*
pillola *pill*
  pillole per dormire *sleeping pills*
pinacoteca *art gallery*
piombo *lead*
  benzina senza piombo *unleaded gas*
piovere *to rain*
  Piove. *It's raining.*
pipa *pipe*
piscina *swimming pool*
pisello *pea*
pittore *(m.) painter*
pittura *painting*
  pittura murale *mural painting*
più *more*
  Deve pagare mille lire di più. *You have to pay 1,000 more lire.*
  A più tardi. *See you later.*

pizzetta *small pizza*
poco *a few, a bit, little*
  È a pochi minuti da qui. *It's a few minutes from here.*
poco *little*
  un po' di tutto *a bit of everything*
poi *then, later*
polizia *police*
  polizia stradale *traffic police*
  stazione della polizia *police station*
poliziotto *policeman*
pollo *chicken*
  dado di pollo *chicken bouillon cube*
pomata *ointment, cream, lotion*
  pomata contro le scottature *suntan lotion*
pomeriggio *afternoon*
  di pomeriggio *in the afternoon*
pomodoro *tomato*
portabagagli *(m.) trunk, luggage rack*
portafoglio *wallet*
portare *to bring*
  portare i capelli corti *to have short hair*
  portare i capelli lunghi *to have long hair*
  Che taglia porta? *What size do you wear?*
  Portatemi al Pronto Soccorso. *Bring me to the emergency room.*
portiere *(m.) doorman; goalkeeper*
portinaio *concierge, doorman*
posa *exposure*
  rullino da 24 pose *24-exposure film*
possibile *possible*
  è possibile *it's possible*
possibilità *opportunity, possibility*
posta *post office*
  andare alla posta *to go to the post office*
  fermo posta *poste restante*
postale *postal*
  codice postale *postal code*
  ufficio postale *post office*
postino *mailman*
posto *seat; position; place*
  avere un bel posto *to have a good position (job)*
  È occupato questo posto? *Is this seat taken?*
pranzo *dinner*
  sala da pranzo *dining room*
pratica *practice; habit; documents*
preferibilmente *preferably*
preferire *to prefer*
preferito *favorite*
prefisso *area code*
prego *please; you're welcome*
prelevare *to withdraw*
prendere *to take*
  prendere una medicina *to take medication*
  prendere la metropolitana *to take the subway*
  prendere il tram *to take the streetcar*
  prendere l'autobus *(m.) to take the bus*
  Andiamo a prendere un caffè? *Shall we go for a coffee?*
prenotare *to book*
  prenotare una camera *to reserve a room*
prenotazione *(f.) reservation*
  fare la prenotazione *to make a reservation*
  Ho la prenotazione. *I have a reservation.*

preparare *to prepare*
prescrivere *to prescribe*
  prescrivere una medicina *to prescribe a medication*
presentare *to introduce, to present*
  Ti presento Carla. *Let me introduce you to Carla.*
  Presenti questa ricevuta. *Present this receipt.*
presentatore *(m.) host*
presentazione *(f.) presentation, introduction*
pressione *pressure*
  misurare la pressione del sangue *to take one's blood pressure*
  La pressione è bassa. *Your blood pressure is low.*
prestito *loan*
presto *early*
  A presto. *See you soon.*
pretura *magistrate's court*
previsto *scheduled; foreseen*
prezzo *price*
  Abbiamo prezzi da sogno. *We have fabulous prices.*
  pagare metà prezzo *to pay half price*
prima *before*
  prima dei pasti *before meals*
primavera *spring*
primo *first*
  Metti la prima. *Put it in first gear.*
  prima classe *first class*
  prima colazione *breakfast*
  prima categoria *first class*
privato *private*
  lavorare in una ditta privata *to work in the private sector*
probabile *probable*
  è probabile *it's probable*
prodotto *product*
professionista *(m./f.) professional*
profumo *perfume*
progetto *project, plan*
programma *(m.) program*
  programma speciale *special program*
promemoria *(m.) memorandum*
promozione *(f.) promotion*
  ottenere una promozione *to get promoted*
pronto *ready*
  Pronto! Chi parla? *Hello! Who is speaking?*
proprio *(n.) one's own*
proprio *(adj.) individual; original; exact; neat*
  il proprio figlio *one's own son*
proprio *(adv.) just; really*
  È proprio così! *That's the way it is!*
  È proprio suo. *It's really his.*
prosciutto *prosciutto (cured ham)*
proseguire *to continue*
prossimo *next*
  la prossima volta *next time*
  la settimana prossima *next week*
protagonista *(m./f.) protagonist*
provare *to try*
  Provi questa camicetta. *Try on this blouse.*
prugna *plum*
prurito *itchiness*
pubblicità *commercial, publicity*
pubblico *(n.) public, audience*

pubblico *(adj.) public*
    agente di pubblica sicurezza *policeman*
    telefono pubblico *public phone*
pugilato *boxing*
pulire *to clean*
pulmino *a mini van*
puntata *episode; bet*
puntina *thumbtack*
punto *stitch; period; point*
    Arrivo alle tre in punto. *I arrive at three o'clock*
      sharp.
puntura *injection*

Q

qua *here*
quadro *painting*
qualche *some*
qualcosa *something*
    Qualcosa da bere? *Something to drink?*
    Ha qualcosa di meno caro? *Do you have something*
      less expensive?
    Mi dia qualcosa per la tosse. *Please, give me*
      something for the cough.
    Posso farLe vedere qualcos'altro? *May I show*
      you something else?
qualcuno *someone*
quale *which*
    Quale vuoi? *Which one do you want?*
    Qual'è? *Which one is it?*
quando *when*
    Quando arriva il treno? *When is the train*
      arriving?
quanto *how much, how many*
    Quant'è? *How much is it?*
    Quant'è l'affitto? *How much is the rent?*
    Quanti anni hai/ha? *How old are you?*
      (f., pl.)
    Quanti ne abbiamo oggi? *What's the date today?*
    Da quanto tempo è in Italia? *How long have you*
      been in Italy?
    Quanto costa? *How much does it cost?*
    Quanto costa al chilo? *How much is it a kilo?*
    Quanto è il cambio oggi? *What is the exchange*
      rate today?
quartiere *(m.) neighborhood*
quello *that*
    quello che *what (that which)*
questo *this*
questore *chief of police*
questura *police station*
    andare in questura *to go to the police station*
qui *here*
quotazione *(f.) quotation (of prices)*
quotidiano *(n.) daily newspaper*
quotidiano *(adj.) daily*

R

raccomandata *registered letter*
    fare una raccomandata *to send a registered*
      letter

radio *(f.) radio*
    accendere la radio *to turn on the radio*
    ascoltare la radio *to listen to the radio*
    Cosa c'è alla radio? *What's on the radio?*
    spegnere la radio *to turn off the radio*
    stazione radio *radio station*
radiografia *X ray*
ragazzo *boy*
rapido *(n.) express train*
rapido *(adj.) rapid, quick, swift*
rappresentante *(m./f.) representative*
rasoio *razor*
realizzazione *(f.) accomplishment, creation*
recentemente *recently*
recitare *to recite, to perform*
regalo *gift*
    articoli da regalo *gift items*
regione *(f.) region*
regista *(m./f.) director (cinema)*
registrare *to record*
registratore *(m.) tape recorder*
regolare *regular*
regolarmente *regularly*
reporter *(m./f.) reporter*
residenza *residence*
    Lei ha la residenza in Italia? *Do you have your*
      residence in Italy?
restare *to stay*
    restare a casa *to stay home*
    Resti in linea. *Stay on the line.*
rete *(f.) net, network; goal (soccer)*
    rete portabagagli *luggage rack*
riccio *curly*
    capelli ricci *curly hair*
ricco *rich*
ricetta *prescription, recipe*
    Ci vuole la ricetta? *Is a prescription*
      necessary?
ricevere *to receive*
    ricevere una telefonata *to receive a telephone call*
ricevuta *receipt*
    Presenti questa ricevuta. *Present this receipt.*
richiamare *to call back, to call again*
ricordare *to remember*
ridotto *reduced*
    tariffa ridotta *reduced fare*
riempire *to fill out (forms)*
rifiorire *flourish*
riga *line, stripe; hair part*
rimanere *to stay, to remain*
    rimanere a casa *to stay home*
Rinascimento *Renaissance*
riparare *to repair*
    Mi può riparare la gomma? *Can you repair my*
      tire?
ripostiglio *store-room; closet*
riscuotere *to collect, to cash*
    riscuotere la pensione *to cash the pension*
      check
    riscuotere un assegno *to cash a check*
risparmio *savings*
    libretto di risparmi *savings account*
rispondere *to answer*
    rispondere al telefono *to answer the phone*

ristorante *(m.) restaurant*
andare al ristorante *to go to a restaurant*
vagone ristorante *dining car*
ristretto *restricted, reduced*
caffè ristretto *extra strong coffee*
ritardo *delay, lateness*
essere in ritardo *to be late*
ritornare *to return, to go back*
ritornare indietro *to go back the way you came*
ritorno *return*
biglietto di andata e ritorno *round-trip ticket*
riunione *(f.) reunion, meeting*
sala delle riunioni *meeting room*
rivedere *to see again*
Sono contento di rivederti. *I'm happy to see you again.*
rivista *magazine*
rock *rock and roll*
ballare il rock *to dance to rock and roll*
musica rock *rock music*
rompere *to break*
Mi sono rotto un braccio. *I broke my arm.*
rosa *rose, pink*
rossetto *lipstick*
rosso *red*
rubare *to steal*
Mi hanno rubato il portafoglio! *They stole my wallet!*
rubrica *column, section, page*
rubrica teatrale *theater section*
rubrica finanziaria *business page*
rubrica sportiva *sports page*
rullino *film*
rullino a colori *color film*
rullino da 24 pose *24-exposure film*
russo *Russian*

S

sabato *Saturday*
sala *room*
sala da pranzo *dining room*
sala d'aspetto *waiting room*
sala delle riunioni *meeting room*
salame *(m.) salami*
sale *(m.) salt*
salone *(m.) hall, salon*
salotto *living room*
salutare *to greet*
salutarsi *to greet each other*
saluto *greeting*
sandalo *sandal*
sangue *(m.) blood*
analisi del sangue *blood test*
bistecca al sangue *steak cooked rare*
sapere *to know, to know how*
sapone *(m.) soap*
sapone per la barba *shaving cream*
sbagliare *to make a mistake*
Scusi, ho sbagliato numero. *I'm sorry, I dialed the wrong number.*
scaldare *to warm up*
Il motore scalda. *The engine is overheating.*

scarpa *shoe*
scarpe da tennis *tennis shoes*
scarpe di camoscio *suede shoes*
scarpe da donna *women's shoes*
scarpe da uomo *men's shoes*
allacciarsi le scarpe *to tie one's shoes*
lucidare le scarpe *to clean one's shoes*
negozio di scarpe *shoe store*
spazzola per scarpe *shoe brush*
togliersi le scarpe *to take off one's shoes*
mettersi le scarpe *to put on one's shoes*
scarpone *(m.) boot*
scarponi da sci *ski boots*
scatola *box*
scatola di cerini *box of wax matches*
scatola di minerva *a box of matches*
carne in scatola *canned meat*
scendere *to get down, to get off*
A che fermata devo scendere? *At which stop do I have to get off?*
schiena *back*
Ho mal di schiena. *I have a pain in the back.*
sci *(m.) skiing*
scarponi da sci *ski boots*
sciampo *shampoo*
farsi lo sciampo *to shampoo one's hair*
scippatore *(m.) bag snatcher*
scippo *bag snatching*
sciroppo *syrup*
sciroppo per la tosse *cough syrup*
scolpire *to sculpt*
scompartimento *compartment*
scorso *past, last*
l'anno scorso *last year*
la settimana scorsa *last week*
scrittore *(m.) writer*
scrivania *desk*
scrivere *to write*
macchina da scrivere *typewriter*
scultore *(m.) sculptor*
scultura *sculpture*
scusare *to excuse*
Scusa. *Excuse me.*
Scusi, ho sbagliato numero. *I'm sorry, I dialed the wrong number.*
seccante *annoying*
Sei seccante! *You're a pain!*
sedano *celery*
sedativo *sedative*
sedere *to sit*
sedersi *to sit down*
segretaria *secretary*
segreteria *secretary's office*
la segreteria telefonica *answering machine*
seguire *to oversee, to follow*
seguire una cura dimagrante *to follow a diet*
sempre *always*
Vada sempre dritto. *Go straight ahead.*
senape *(f.) mustard*
sensibilità *sensibility, sensitivity*
sentire *to hear*
sentirsi *to feel*

senza *without*
  senz'altro *certainly*
  senza dubbio *without any doubt*
sera *evening*
  Buona sera. *Good evening.*
  di sera *in the evening*
servire *to serve; to be necessary; to need*
  Che cosa ci serve? *What do we need?*
  Mi serve dello sciroppo per la tosse. *I need some cough syrup.*
servizio *report*
  servizio di attualità *news report*
  servizio speciale *special report, feature*
  stazione di servizio *gas station*
  essere di servizio *to be on duty*
  Il servizio è compreso? *Is the service charge included?*
sete *(f.) thirst*
  avere sete *to be thirsty*
settembre *(m.) September*
settimana *week*
  i giorni della settimana *the days of the week*
  la settimana prossima *next week*
settimanale *(m.) weekly newspaper*
settore *(m.) sector*
  lavorare nel settore dirigenziale *to work in the managerial sector*
sfogliare *to skim through*
  sfogliare il giornale *to skim through the newspaper*
sfortunatamente *unfortunately*
sì *yes*
sicurezza *security*
  agente di pubblica sicurezza *policeman*
  cassetta di sicurezza *safety deposit box*
  cintura di sicurezza *seat belt*
sicuro *sure*
  essere sicuro *to be sure*
sigaretta *cigarette*
  sigarette con filtro *filtered cigarettes*
  sigarette senza filtro *nonfiltered cigarettes*
  una stecca di sigarette *a carton of cigarettes*
  un pacchetto di sigarette *a pack of cigarettes*
simpatico *nice*
singola *single*
  camera singola *single room*
sinistra *left*
  girare a sinistra *to turn left*
  a sinistra *to the left*
  sulla sinistra *on the left*
sipario *curtain*
siringa *syringe*
smalto *enamel*
  smalto per le unghie *nail polish*
soccorso *help*
  Portatemi al Pronto Soccorso. *Bring me to the emergency room.*
sociale *social*
  conto sociale *joint account*
soggiorno *stay, sojourn*
  Azienda Autonoma Soggiorno *City Tourist Board*
  soggiorno *living room*
sogno *dream*
  Abbiamo prezzi da sogno. *We have fabulous prices.*

soldi *(m., pl.) money*
  soldi in contanti *cash money*
soletta *insole*
solo *only*
soltanto *only*
sopra *on, on top, above*
sorella *sister*
spaghetti *(m., pl.) spaghetti*
  spaghetti al sugo *spaghetti with sauce*
spagnolo *Spanish*
spazzola *brush*
  spazzola per scarpe *shoe brush*
speciale *special*
  servizio speciale *special report, feature*
  programma speciale *special program*
spedire *to mail, to send*
  spedire una lettera *to mail a letter*
  spedire un pacco *to send a parcel*
spegnere *to turn off, to blow out*
  spegnere la televisione *to turn off the television*
  Spenga il motore. *Turn off the engine.*
sperare *to hope*
spesa *shopping*
  fare la spesa *to go grocery shopping*
spettacolo *show*
  assistere ad uno spettacolo *to attend a show*
  spettacolo di varietà *variety show*
  A che ora inizia lo spettacolo? *At what time does the show start?*
  A che ora termina lo spettacolo? *At what time does the show end?*
spiaggia *beach*
  andare alla spiaggia *to go to the beach*
spiccioli *(m. pl.) small change*
spillatrice *(f.) stapler*
spinaci *(m., pl.) spinach*
spirito *spirit; intellect; alcohol*
sport *(m.) sport*
sportello *door, window*
  sportello della macchina *car door*
  sportello dei cambi *exchange window*
  Si accomodi allo sportello numero cinque. *Please go to window number five.*
sportivo *sporting*
  pagina sportiva *sports page*
spremuta *squeeze*
  spremuta d'arancia *freshly squeezed orange juice*
spuntatina *trim*
spuntino *snack*
squadra *team*
stagione *(f.) season*
stanco *tired*
stanza *room*
stare *to stay*
  Come stai? *How are you?*
  Sto bene. *I'm fine.*
  Sta' attento! *Be careful!*
  Sto per uscire. *I'm about to go out.*
  Stiamo mangiando. *We're eating.*
  Sta' fermo! *Stay still!*
stasera *tonight*
stazione *(f.) station*
  stazione radio *radio station*
  stazione televisiva *TV station*

stazione di servizio *gas station*
stazione ferroviaria *railroad station*
stazione della polizia *police station*
stecca *stick*
stecca di sigarette *carton of cigarettes*
stella *star*
albergo a tre stelle *three-star hotel*
sterlina *pound, sterling*
stipendio *salary, wage*
stivaletto *ankle boot*
stivale *(m.) boot*
stomaco *stomach*
bruciore allo stomaco *heartburn*
mal di stomaco *stomachache*
Fa male allo stomaco. *It upsets the stomach.*
stradale *of the road*
Ha una carta stradale? *Do you have a road map?*
straniero *foreigner*
stressato *stressed*
essere stressato *to be under stress*
stretto *strict, tight*
La camicia è un po' stretta. *The shirt is a bit tight.*
La camicia mi sta stretta. *The shirt is too tight.*
studiare *to study*
studiare l'italiano *to study Italian*
stupendo *stupendous*
su *up, above, on*
sulla destra *on the right*
sulla sinistra *on the left*
successo *success*
succo *juice*
succo di frutta *fruit juice*
sud *south*
suggerire *to suggest*
Le suggerirei questa tintura. *I would suggest this color.*
suocero *father-in-law*
suonare *to play (an instrument)*
suonare la chitarra *to play the guitar*
suonare il violino *to play the violin*
super *super*
supposta *suppository*
surgelato *frozen*
svedese *Swedish*
fiammiferi svedesi *safety matches*
svegliarsi *to wake up*

T

tabaccheria *tobacco shop*
tabacco *tobacco*
tacco *heel*
tacco alto *high heel*
tacco basso *low heel*
tacco a spillo *stiletto heel*
taglia *size*
Che taglia porta? *What size do you wear?*
tagliacarte *(m.) letter opener*
tagliando *coupon*
tagliare *to cut*
tagliarsi i capelli *to get a haircut*
tagliarsi i capelli a zero *to get a crewcut*
taglierina *paper cutter*

taglio *cut, length; style*
biglietti di grosso taglio *big bills*
biglietti di piccolo taglio *small bills*
tanto *so much, so many, so*
Tanti auguri! *Best wishes!*
Tante grazie. *Many thanks.*
tardi *late*
A più tardi. *See you later.*
tariffa *fare*
tariffa ridotta *reduced fare*
tassa *tax*
tassa governativa *government tax*
tasso *rate*
tasso del cambio *exchange rate*
Il tasso di interesse è al dieci per cento. *The interest rate is ten percent.*
tavolo *table*
tè *(m.) tea*
teatrale *theatrical*
rubrica teatrale *theater section*
teatro *theater*
andare a teatro *to go to the theater*
tecnica *technique*
tedesco *German*
telecomando *remote control*
telefonare *to telephone*
telefonata *phone call*
fare una telefonata *to make a telephone call*
ricevere una telefonata *to receive a telephone call*
fare una telefonata "erre" *to call collect*
telefonico *telephonic*
carta telefonica *telephone card*
cabina telefonica *telephone booth*
elenco telefonico *telephone book*
segreteria telefonica *answering machine*
telefono *telephone*
rispondere al telefono *to answer the telephone*
telefono pubblico *public phone*
bolletta del telefono *telephone bill*
telegiornale *(m.) television news*
telegramma *(m.) telegram*
fare un telegramma *to make a telegram*
messaggio del telegramma *telegram message*
telenovela *soap opera*
teleromanzo *soap opera*
televisione *(f.) television*
guardare la televisione *to watch television*
accendere la televisione *to turn on the television*
spegnere la televisione *to turn off the television*
Cosa c'è alla televisione? *What's on television?*
televisivo *of television*
stazione televisiva *TV station*
televisore *(m.) television set*
tempo *time; weather*
Che tempo fa? *What's the weather like?*
Fa bel tempo. *The weather's nice.*
Non ho neanche il tempo di mangiare. *I don't even have the time to eat.*
Da quanto tempo è in Italia? *How long have you been in Italy?*
tenere *to hold, to keep, to have*
Tenga pure. *Keep the change.*
tennis *(m.) tennis*
scarpe da tennis *tennis shoes*

tenore *(m.) tenor*
terminare *to finish*
termometro *thermometer*
terra *earth, land*
   Ho le gomme a terra. *My tires are low.*
terza *third*
   terza pagina *cultural page*
testa *head*
   mal di testa *headache*
   Mi gira la testa. *My head is spinning.*
testata *headline*
testo *text*
   elaboratore *(m.)* di testi *word processor*
timbro *postmark*
tingere *to dye, to tint*
   tingersi le unghie *to paint one's nails*
   tingersi i capelli biondi *to dye one's hair blond*
tintura *color, shade, dye*
tipico *typical*
tipo *type*
   Che tipo di musica preferisce? *What kind of music do you like?*
tirare *to pull*
   Tira vento. *It's windy.*
titolo *title*
togliere *to take away, to remove*
   togliersi le scarpe *to take off one's shoes*
tonico *tonic*
   acqua tonica *tonic water*
tonno *tuna*
torta *cake*
tosse *(f.) cough*
   pasticca per la tosse *cough drop*
   sciroppo per la tosse *cough syrup*
totale *total*
tovagliolo *napkin*
tragedia *tragedy*
tram *(m.) streetcar*
   prendere il tram *to take the streetcar*
trama *plot*
trasmissione *(f.) transmission, broadcast*
   trasmissione in diretta *live broadcast*
treno *train*
   treno rapido *express train*
   treno locale *local train*
   treno espresso *express train*
   treno diretto *through train*
   viaggiare in treno *to travel by train*
   perdere il treno *to miss the train*
   prendere il treno *to take the train*
   A che ora arriva il treno? *At what time does the train arrive?*
   A che ora parte il treno? *At what time does the train leave?*
   Su quale binario arriva il treno? *On which track is the train arriving?*
tribunale *(m.) tribunal, court*
troppo *too much, too many, too*
   È troppo caro. *It's too expensive.*
trovare *to find*
   Dove posso trovare . . . ? *Where can I find . . . ?*
   trovare lavoro *to find a job*
trucco *makeup*
turista *(m./f.) tourist*

turistico *tourist*
   carta carburante turistica *highway toll card*
   classe turistica *economy class*
   guida turistica *guidebook*
   operatore turistico *tour operator*
   ufficio informazioni turistiche *tourist information office*
tutto *all*
   Tutto qui? *Is that all?*

U

ufficio *office*
   ufficio informazioni *information office*
   essere in ufficio *to be in the office*
   lavorare in un ufficio *to work in an office*
   ufficio postale *post office*
ultimo *last*
   Un'ultima cosa. *One last thing.*
unghia *nail*
   smalto per le unghie *nail polish*
università *university*
uomo *man*
   scarpe da uomo *men's shoes*
uovo *(m.) egg*
   una dozzina di uova *(f., pl.) a dozen eggs*
urbano *urban*
   vigile urbano *municipal policeman*
urina *urine*
   analisi dell'urina *urine analysis*
usato *used*
uscire *to go out*
uscita *exit, gate*
uso *use, usage*
   indicazioni per l'uso *usage instructions*
utilitaria *compact car*
uva *grape*

V

vacanza *vacation, holiday*
   andare in vacanza *to go on vacation*
   passare delle vacanze favolose *to spend a fabulous vacation*
vaglia *money order*
   fare un vaglia *to draft a money order*
vagone *(m.) railroad car*
   vagone ristorante *dining car*
   vagone letto *sleeping car*
valigia *suitcase*
valuta *currency*
   valuta estera *foreign currency*
vaniglia *vanilla*
   gelato alla vaniglia *vanilla ice cream*
varietà *variety*
   spettacolo di varietà *variety show*
vecchio *old*
vedersi *to see oneself/each other*
velocemente *fast*
venerdì *(m.) Friday*
venire *to come*
   Di dove vieni? *Where do you come from?*

ventisette *twenty-seven*
  il ventisette *payday for state employees (the 27th)*
verde *green*
  benzina verde *unleaded gas*
verdura *vegetables*
vero *true*
  essere vero *to be true*
vestire *to dress*
vestirsi *to get dressed*
vestito *suit, dress*
via *street*
viaggiare *to travel*
  viaggiare in treno *to travel by train*
viaggio *trip, voyage, journey*
  Buon viaggio! *Have a nice trip!*
  fare un viaggio *to take a trip*
  agenzia di viaggi *travel agency*
  agente *(m./f.)* di viaggi *travel agent*
  viaggio d'affari *business trip*
vicino *near, next to, close by*
  Abito vicino al centro. *I live close to downtown.*
  È vicino. *It's close by.*
  vicino di casa *neighbor*
video *video*
videoregistratore *(m.) VCR*
vigile *(m.) traffic policeman*
  vigile urbano *municipal (traffic) policeman*
villa *villa, single family house*
vincere *to win*
vino *wine*
viola *purple*
violento *violent*
violino *violin*
  suonare il violino *to play the violin*
visitare *to visit*
  visitare una città *to visit a city*
  visitare un paese *to visit a country*
vitamina *vitamin*
vittima *victim*
  essere vittima di un furto *to be a victim of a robbery*

vivace *lively*
  essere vivace *to be lively*
vocabolario *vocabulary*
volere *to want*
  Ti voglio bene. *I love you.*
  Ci vuole la ricetta? *Is a prescription necessary?*
  Cosa vuoi? *What do you want?*
volo *flight*
  assistente *(m./f.)* di volo *flight attendant*
volta *time*
  la prossima volta *next time*
  tre volte al giorno *three times a day*
volume *volume*
  abbassare il volume *to lower the volume*

W

week-end *(m.) weekend*
  Cosa fai questo week-end? *What are you doing this weekend?*
  Come passi il week-end? *How will you spend your weekend?*

Y

yen *yen*

Z

zia *aunt*
zio *uncle*
zoccolo *clog*
zona *area, zone*
  zona fumatori *smoking area*
  zona non fumatori *nonsmoking area*
zucchero *sugar*
zucchini *(m., pl.) zucchini*

ENGLISH–ITALIAN

A

a *un, una, uno, un'*
ability *abilità, capacità*
  to look for someone with managerial abilities *cercare qualcuno con capacità manageriali*
above *sopra*
accelerate (to) *accelerare*
acceptance *accettazione (f.)*
accomplishment *realizzazione*
account *conto*
  joint account *conto sociale*
  checking account *conto corrente*
  savings account *libretto di risparmi*
  to open an account *aprire un conto*
ache *dolore (m.), male (m.)*

  stomachache *mal di stomaco, mal di pancia*
  headache *mal di testa*
  backache *mal di schiena*
active *attivo*
actor *attore (m.)*
actress *attrice (f.)*
ad *pubblicità*
  classified ads *annunci economici (m., pl.)*
  newspaper ad *avviso economico*
address *indirizzo*
  What's your address? *Qual' è il Suo indirizzo?*
addressee *destinatario*
advanced *avanzato, anticipato*
  advanced payment *pagamento anticipato*
afraid *spaventato, impaurito*
  to be afraid *avere paura*

411

after *dopo*
 after meals *dopo i pasti*
afternoon *pomeriggio*
 in the afternoon *nel pomeriggio*
aftershave *dopobarba (m.)*
against *contro*
age *età*
agency *agenzia*
 travel agency *agenzia di viaggio*
 real estate agency *agenzia immobiliare*
agent *agente (m./f.)*
 travel agent *agente di viaggio*
 real estate agent *agente immobiliare*
air *aria*
 air conditioning *aria condizionata*
airline *compagnia aerea*
airplane *aereo*
airport *aeroporto*
aisle *corridoio*
album *album*
alcohol *alcool*
 rubbing alcohol *spirito*
all *tutto*
 not at all *non . . . affatto*
 I'm not tired at all. *Non sono affatto stanco.*
 Is that all? *Tutto qui?*
 All done! *Ecco fatto!*
allergic *allergico*
also *anche*
always *sempre*
amateur *dilettante (m./f.)*
ambulance *ambulanza*
 I need an ambulance. *Ho bisogno di un'ambulanza.*
American *americano*
analysis *analisi*
anatomy *anatomia*
and *e, ed*
announcement *annuncio*
answer (to) *rispondere*
 to answer the phone *rispondere al telefono*
anymore *non . . . più*
 I'm not hungry anymore. *Non ho più fame.*
apartment *appartamento*
 furnished apartment *appartamento ammobiliato*
 to rent an apartment *affittare un appartamento*
 to look for an apartment for rent *cercare un appartamento in affitto*
 a small apartment building *palazzina*
aperitif *aperitivo*
appetite *appetito*
applaud (to) *applaudire*
apple *mela*
apply *fare domanda*
 to apply for a job *fare domanda per un lavoro*
appointment *appuntamento*
 to make an appointment *fissare un appuntamento*
approximately *circa*
 It's approximately a kilometer away. *È distante circa un chilometro.*
April *aprile*
architect *architetto*
architecture *architettura*

area *area, zona*
 smoking area *zona fumatori*
 nonsmoking area *zona non fumatori*
arm *braccio*
 My arms feel heavy. *Mi sento le braccia pesanti.*
arrival *arrivo*
arrive (to) *arrivare*
 At what time does the train arrive? *A che ora arriva il treno?*
art *arte (f.)*
 Fine Arts *Belle Arti*
 art gallery *pinacoteca*
article *articolo*
 articles of clothing *articoli di abbigliamento*
artist *artista*
artistic *artistico*
ask (to) *chiedere*
 to ask for an encore *chiedere il bis*
 to ask for directions *chiedere indicazioni*
aspirin *aspirina*
assistant *assistente (m./f.)*
at *a, da*
 at a cheap price *a buon mercato*
 at the supermarket *al supermercato*
 at the outdoor market *al mercato*
 at the real estate agency *all'agenzia immobiliare*
 at the police station *alla questura*
 at the train station *alla stazione ferroviaria*
 at the currency exchange office *all'ufficio di cambio*
 at the mechanic *dal meccanico*
 at the doctor's *dal dottore*
attend (to) *frequentare, assistere (a)*
 to attend a show *assistere ad uno spettacolo*
audience *pubblico*
August *agosto*
automatic *automatico*
 automatic transmission *cambio automatico*
autonomous *autonomo*
 Autonomous City Tourist Board *Azienda Autonoma Soggiorno*
away *lontano*
 It's a kilometer away. *È distante un chilometro.*
 Go away. *Va' via.*

B

back *(n.) schiena*
 I have back pain. *Ho mal di schiena.*
back *(adv.) indietro*
 to go back the way you came *ritornare indietro*
bad *male*
 Not too bad. *Non c'è male.*
bag *borsa, busta*
 bag snatching *scippo*
 bag snatcher *scippatore*
ballerina *ballerina*
ballet *balletto*
banana *banana*
bandage *cerotto*
bank *banca*

bank note *banconota*
bar *bar*
barber *barbiere (m.)*
bartender *barista (m./f.)*
basketball *pallacanestro*
bath *bagno*
   to take a bath *fare (farsi) il bagno*
bathroom *bagno*
   room with a bathroom *camera con bagno*
   room without a bathroom *camera senza bagno*
   to go to the bathroom *andare al bagno*
be (to) *essere*
   to be kind *essere gentile*
   to be unemployed *essere disoccupato*
   to be hired *essere assunto*
   to be fired *essere licenziato*
   to be late *essere in ritardo*
   to be on time *essere in orario*
   to be sure *essere sicuro*
   to be certain *essere certo*
   to be active *essere vivace*
   to be in the office *essere in ufficio*
   to be under stress *essere stressato*
   to be busy *essere occupato*
   to be happy *essere contento*
   It's hot. *Fa caldo.*
   It's cold. *Fa freddo.*
   to be . . . years old *avere . . . anni*
   to be thirsty *avere sete*
   to be patient *avere pazienza*
   to be afraid *avere paura*
   to be in a hurry *avere fretta*
   to be hungry *avere fame*
   to be hot/warm *avere caldo*
   How are you? *Come stai?*
   I'm fine. *Sto bene.*
   Be careful. *Sta' attento!*
   I'm about to go out. *Sto per uscire.*
beach *spiaggia*
   to go to the beach *andare alla spiaggia, andare al mare*
beans *fagioli*
   string beans *fagiolini*
beard *barba*
beautiful *bello*
   It's a beautiful day. *È una bella giornata.*
bed *letto*
   bedroom *camera da letto*
beef *manzo*
   beef bouillon cube *dado di manzo*
beer *birra*
before *prima, prima di*
   before meals *prima dei pasti*
behind *dietro*
believe (to) *credere*
belt *cintura*
   seat belt *cintura di sicurezza*
beside *accanto a*
   The museum is beside the art gallery. *Il museo è accanto alla pinacoteca.*
   Sit down beside me. *Siediti accanto a me.*
better *meglio*
   I feel better. *Sto meglio.*
   It's better. *È meglio.*

big *grande*
bill *conto, biglietto*
   big bills *biglietti di grosso taglio*
   small bills *biglietti di piccolo taglio*
   Can you prepare my bill? *Mi prepari il conto.*
   The bill, please. *Il conto, per favore.*
   to pay the telephone bill *pagare la bolletta del telefono*
birthday *compleanno*
   Happy Birthday! *Buon compleanno!*
bit (a) *poco, po'*
   a bit of bread *un po' di pane*
   a bit of everything *un po' di tutto*
black *nero*
blond *biondo*
   blond hair *capelli biondi*
   to dye one's hair blond *tingersi i capelli biondi*
blood *sangue (m.)*
   blood test *analisi del sangue*
blouse *camicetta*
blue *blu*
boarding *imbarco*
   boarding pass *carta d'imbarco*
boiled *lesso*
   boiled fish *pesce lesso*
book *libro*
   checkbook *libretto degli assegni*
   telephone book *elenco telefonico*
   guidebook *guida turistica*
boot *stivale (m.), scarpone (m.)*
   ski boots *scarponi da sci*
   ankle boot *stivaletto*
booth *cabina*
   telephone booth *cabina telefonica*
boring *noioso*
born (to be) *nascere (pp. nato)*
   I was born in Rome. *Sono nato/a a Roma.*
box *scatola, cassetta*
   box of wax matches *scatola di cerini*
   a box of (book) matches *scatola di minerva*
   safety deposit box *cassetta di sicurezza*
   post office box *casetta postale*
   mailbox *cassetta postale*
boxing *pugilato*
boy *ragazzo*
brake *freno*
   Can you check the brakes, please? *Controlli i freni, per favore.*
bread *pane (m.)*
break (to) *rompere*
   I broke my arm. *Mi sono rotto un braccio.*
breakdown *collasso, esaurimento*
   The woman had a nervous breakdown. *La donna ha avuto un esaurimento nervoso.*
breakfast *colazione (f.)*
   to have breakfast *fare colazione*
bright *lucido*
bring (to) *portare*
   Bring me to emergency. *Portatemi al Pronto Soccorso.*
broadcast *trasmissione (f.)*
   live broadcast *trasmissione in diretta*
brother *fratello*
   brother-in-law *cognato*

413

brown *bruno, marrone, castano*
  brown hair *capelli castani*
brush *spazzola*
  shoe brush *spazzola per scarpe*
build (to) *costruire*
burn (to) *bruciare*
bus *autobus*
  bus ticket *biglietto per l'autobus*
  to take the bus *prendere l'autobus*
business *affare (m.)*
  to own a business *lavorare in proprio*
  business trip *viaggio d'affari*
busy *occupato*
  The telephone line is busy. *La linea è occupata.*
but *ma*
butter *burro*
buy (to) *comprare*
  to buy the newspaper *comprare il giornale*
by *da, per*
  by air mail *per via aerea*
bye *arrivederci, arrivederLa, ciao*

C

cabinet *armadio*
  filing cabinet *casellario*
café *caffè (m.), bar (m.)*
cake *torta*
call (to) *chiamare*
  to be called *chiamarsi*
  Call a doctor, please. *Chiami un medico per favore.*
  Call the operator. *Chiami il centralino.*
  to call collect *fare una telefonata "erre"*
  to call back *richiamare*
call *chiamata*
  phone call *telefonata*
  to make a telephone call *fare una telefonata*
  to receive a telephone call *ricevere una telefonata*
Canadian *canadese*
cancellation *cancellazione (f.)*
capacity *capacità, abilità*
  to look for someone with managerial capacity *cercare qualcuno con capacità manageriali*
car *macchina, automobile (f.), vagone (m., on trains)*
  car racing *automobilismo*
  car rental *autonoleggio*
  standard car *macchina con le marce*
  Start the car. *Metti in moto la macchina.*
  compact car *utilitaria*
  sleeping car *vagone letto*
  dining car *vagone ristorante*
card *carta*
  telephone card *carta telefonica*
  highway toll card *carta carburante turistica*
care *cura*
  I'll take care of it. *Ci penso io.*
career *carriera*
  to have a successful career *fare carriera*
careful *attento*
  Be careful! *Sta' attento!*

carrot *carota*
carton *stecca*
  carton of cigarettes *stecca di sigarette*
cartoons *cartoni animati*
cash *contante (m.)*
  cash money *soldi in contanti*
  Here's three hundred dollars in cash. *Ecco a Lei trecento dollari in contanti.*
cash (to) *riscuotere*
  to cash a traveler's check *cambiare un traveler's check*
  to cash the pension check *riscuotere la pensione*
  to cash a check *riscuotere un assegno*
cashier *cassiere (m.)*
  Please go to the cashier's window. *Si accomodi alla cassa.*
cassette *cassetta*
  cassette player *mangianastri*
cathedral *duomo, cattedrale (m.)*
CD (compact disc) *CD*
  the latest CD *l'ultimo CD*
celery *sedano*
center *centro*
  commercial center *centro commerciale*
certain *certo*
  It's certain. *È certo.*
certainly *certamente*
championship *campionato*
chance *possibilità*
  chance for a successful career *possibilità di fare carriera*
change (to) *cambiare*
  to change channels *cambiare canale*
  to change dollars into lire *cambiare dollari in lire*
  to change the oil *cambiare l'olio*
change *spiccioli (m., pl.)*
channel *canale (m.)*
  to change channels *cambiare canale*
charcoal *carbone (m.)*
charge *prezzo*
  cover charge *coperto*
cheap *economico*
  at a cheap price *a buon mercato*
check *assegno*
  checkbook *libretto degli assegni*
  to cash a check *riscuotere un assegno*
check (to) *controllare*
  Please check the brakes. *Controlli i freni, per favore.*
cheese *formaggio*
cherry *ciliegia*
chicken *pollo*
  chicken bouillon cube *dado di pollo*
chief *capo*
  chief of police *questore (m.)*
child *bambino*
Chinese *cinese*
chocolate *cioccolato*
  chocolate ice cream *gelato al cioccolato*
church *chiesa*
cigarette *sigaretta*
  filtered cigarettes *sigarette con filtro*
  nonfiltered cigarettes *sigarette senza filtro*

a carton of cigarettes *una stecca di sigarette*
a pack of cigarettes *un pacchetto di sigarette*
city *città*
to tour the city *girare la città*
map of the city *pianta della città*
class *classe (f.), categoria*
first-class hotel *albergo di prima categoria*
I always travel in first class. *Viaggio sempre in prima classe.*
economy class *classe turistica*
I'm going to class. *Vado a lezione.*
classical *classico*
classical music *musica classica*
clean (to) *pulire, lucidare*
to clean one's shoes *lucidare le scarpe*
clog *zoccolo*
close *vicino*
It's very close. *È a due passi.*
It's close by. *È vicino.*
closed *chiuso*
closet *armadio a muro, ripostiglio*
clothes *abiti (m., pl.), vestiti (m., pl.)*
clothing *abbigliamento*
articles of clothing *articoli di abbigliamento*
clothing store *negozio di abbigliamento*
clutch *frizione (f.)*
coach *allenatore (m.)*
coat *cappotto*
code *codice (m.)*
postal code *codice postale*
area code *prefisso*
coffee *caffè (m.)*
espresso coffee *espresso*
laced coffee *caffè corretto*
coffee with a dash of milk *caffè macchiato*
weak coffee *caffè lungo*
extra strong coffee *caffè ristretto*
coffee with milk *caffellatte (m.)*
Shall we go for coffee? *Andiamo a prendere un caffè?*
cold *freddo*
It's cold. *Fa freddo.*
color *colore (m.)*
What color? *Di che colore?*
color film *rullino a colori*
column *colonna, rubrica*
gossip column *cronaca mondana*
comb *pettine (m.)*
comb (to) *pettinare*
to comb one's hair *pettinarsi*
come (to) *venire*
Where are you coming from? *Da dove vieni?*
comedy *commedia*
comfort *comodità*
comfortable *comodo*
comfortably *comodamente*
commercial *pubblicità*
commission *commissione (f.)*
commodity *comodità*
commute (to) *fare il pendolare*
company *compagnia, ditta, azienda*
compartment *scompartimento*
complain (to) *lamentarsi*

complaint *protesta, lamentela, denuncia*
to file a complaint *fare denuncia*
computer *computer*
concert *concerto*
open-air concert *concerto all'aperto*
to go to a concert *andare a un concerto*
conditioner *condizionatore (m.)*
hair conditioner *balsamo per i capelli*
conditioned *condizionato*
air-conditioning *aria condizionata*
condominium *condominio*
conductor *conduttore (m.)*
orchestra conductor *direttore d'orchestra*
continue (to) *continuare, proseguire*
contract *contratto*
contribution *contributo*
control *controllo*
remote control *telecomando*
corporation *ente (f.), corporazione (f.)*
correct *corretto*
couchette *cuccetta*
cough *tosse (f.)*
cough drop *pasticca per la tosse*
cough syrup *sciroppo per la tosse*
counter *banco*
check-in counter *banco d'accettazione*
countersignature *controfirma*
country *nazione (f.), paese (m.)*
foreign country *estero*
stamp for a foreign country *francobollo per l'estero*
coupon *buono*
gas coupon *buono benzina*
courier *corriere (m.)*
court *tribunale (m.), corte (f.)*
magistrate's court *pretura*
cousin *cugino/a*
craftsmanship *artigianato*
credit *credito*
crime *crimine*
crime news *cronaca nera*
cruise *crociera*
to go on a cruise *fare una crociera*
cube *cubo; dado*
beef bouillon cube *dado di manzo*
chicken bouillon cube *dado di pollo*
cucumber *cetriolo*
culture *cultura*
curly *riccio*
curly hair *capelli ricci*
currency *valuta*
foreign currency *valuta estera*
curtain *sipario*
customs *dogana*
cut *taglio*
cold cuts *affettati (m.,pl.)*
cycling *ciclismo*
cylinder *cilindro*
How many cylinders does the car have? *A quanti cilindri è la macchina?*

D

daddy *papà*

damage *danno*
    collision damage waiver *assicurazione contro i danni*

dance (to) *ballare*
    to dance to a slow song *ballare il liscio*
    to dance to rock and roll *ballare il rock*

date *data*

daughter *figlia*
    daughter-in-law *nuora*

day *giorno, giornata*
    the days of the week *i giorni della settimana*
    What day is today? *Che giorno è oggi?*
    What a beautiful day! *Che bel giorno!*
    three times a day *tre volte al giorno*
    It's a beautiful day. *È una bella giornata.*
    It's a miserable day. *È una brutta giornata.*

dear *caro*

debt *debito*

December *dicembre (m.)*

decide (to) *decidere (pp. deciso)*

delay *ritardo*

department *dipartimento*
    department store *grande magazzino*

deposit (to) *depositare*

desk *scrivania*

dessert *dolce (m.)*

destination *destinazione (f.)*

detergent *detersivo*

diabetes *diabete (m.)*

die (to) *morire (pp. morto)*

diet *dieta, cura dimagrante*
    to follow a diet *seguire una cura dimagrante*

different *diverso, differente*

digestive *digestivo*

dinner *pranzo*

direction *direzione (f.)*
    to ask for/to give directions *chiedere/dare indicazioni (f., pl.)*

director *regista (m./f.), direttore (m.)*

discotheque *discoteca*

dish *piatto*

disinfectant *disinfettante (m.)*

display *mostra*

doctor *dottore (m.), dottoressa (f.), medico*
    to go to the doctor *andare dal dottore*
    Call a doctor, please. *Chiami un medico, per favore.*

document *documento*

documentary *documentario*

dollar *dollaro*
    What is the exchange rate for the dollar? *A quanto è il dollaro?*

door *porta*
    car door *sportello della macchina*

doorkeeper *portinaio, portiere (m.)*

dosage *dose (f.)*

dossier *pratica*

double *doppio, duplice*
    double room *camera doppia/matrimoniale*

doubt *(n.) dubbio*
    without any doubt *senza dubbio*

doubt (to) *dubitare*

down *giù*

downtown *centro*
    downtown (city center) *in centro*
    to go downtown *andare in centro*

dozen *dozzina*

draw (to) *disegnare*

dress *(n.) veste (f.), abito*

dress (to) *vestire*
    to get dressed *vestirsi*

drink (to) *bere*

drive (to) *guidare*
    Don't drive fast! *Non guidare velocemente!*

drop *goccia, pasticca*
    cough drop *pasticca per la tosse*

dry (to) *asciugare*
    to dry one's hair *asciugarsi i capelli*

duty *dovere (m.)*
    to be on duty *essere di servizio*

dye *tintura*

dye (to) *tingere*
    to dye one's hair blond *tingersi i capelli biondi*

E

ear *orecchio*

early *presto*

eat (to) *mangiare*

economic *economico*

editor *direttore (m.)*

editorial *editoriale (m.)*

egg *uovo (m.)*
    a dozen eggs *una dozzina di uova (f., pl.)*

eggplant *melanzana*

elevator *ascensore (m.)*

embassy *ambasciata*

emergency *emergenza*
    Emergency Room *Pronto Soccorso*

encore *bis (m.)*
    to give an encore *concedere il bis*
    to ask for an encore *chiedere il bis*

engine *motore (m.)*
    The engine is overheating. *Il motore scalda.*

English *inglese*

enjoy (to) *piacere*
    to enjoy oneself *divertirsi*

enough *abbastanza*

envelop *busta*

episode *puntata*

eraser *gomma*

estate *proprietà*
    real estate agency *agenzia immobiliare*

evening *sera*
    Good evening. *Buona sera.*
    in the evening *di sera*

every *ogni*

exaggerate (to) *esagerare*

exceptional *eccezionale*

exchange *cambio*
What is the exchange rate today? *Quanto è il cambio oggi?*
The exchange rate is high. *Il cambio è alto.*
exchange rate *tasso del cambio*
excursion *escursione (f.)*
excuse (to) *scusare*
Excuse me. *Scusa./Scusi.; Permesso.*
expensive *caro, costoso*
Do you have something less expensive? *Ha qualcosa di meno caro?*
experience *esperienza*
to have experience *avere esperienza*
exposure *posa*
24-exposure film *rullino da 24 pose*
express *espresso*
express letter *lettera espresso*
express train *treno espresso*
express train *rapido*
expression *espressione (f.)*

F

fabulous *favoloso*
to spend a fabulous vacation *passare una vacanza favolosa*
factory *fabbrica*
to work in a factory *lavorare in fabbrica*
fall *autunno*
fall (to) *cadere*
to fall asleep *addormentarsi*
family *famiglia*
famous *famoso*
fan *fan*
to be a fan of . . . *essere un/una fan di . . .*
fantastic *fantastico*
far *lontano, distante*
I live far from here. *Abito lontano da qui.*
It's far. *È lontano.*
fare *tariffa*
reduced fare *tariffa ridotta*
fast *velocemente*
father *padre (m.)*
father-in-law *suocero*
favor *favore (m.)*
favor (to) *favorire*
favorite *preferito*
fax *fax (m.)*
to send a fax *mandare un fax*
to receive a fax *ricevere un fax*
fear *paura*
February *febbraio*
feel (to) *sentirsi*
fever *febbre (f.)*
to have a fever *avere la febbre*
few *pochi/e*
fiancé *fidanzato*
fiancée *fidanzata*
file *documentazione (f.), cartella*
fill (to) *riempire, compilare*
You have to fill out some forms. *Deve compilare alcuni moduli.*

Fill it up, please. *Faccia il pieno, per favore.*
film *film, rullino*
color film *rullino a colori*
24-exposure film *rullino da 24 pose*
filter *filtro*
Can you change the filter? *Può cambiare il filtro?*
finally *finalmente*
finance (to) *finanziare*
financial *finanziario*
find (to) *trovare*
to find a job *trovare lavoro*
I can't find my way around. *Non mi posso orientare.*
fine *multa, contravvenzione*
finger *dito*
I broke my finger. *Mi sono rotto un dito.*
finish (to) *finire (isc)*
fire (to) *licenziare*
to be fired *essere licenziato*
firm *fermo*
first *primo*
Put it in first gear. *Metti la prima.*
first class *prima classe, prima categoria*
fish *pesce (m.)*
grilled fish *pesce ai ferri*
boiled fish *pesce lesso*
fried fish *pesce fritto*
fix (to) *aggiustare*
flight *volo*
flight attendant *assistente (m./f.) di volo*
floor *piano*
What floor is it on? *A che piano è?*
florin *fiorino*
flourish (to) *rifiorire*
folder *cartella*
follow (to) *seguire*
food *cibo*
frozen food *surgelati (m., pl.)*
foot *piede (m.)*
to go on foot *andare a piedi*
I broke my foot. *Mi sono rotto un piede.*
for *per*
foreign *estero, straniero*
foreign currency *valuta estera*
foreign country *estero*
stamp for a foreign country *francobollo per l'estero*
foreigner *straniero*
fork *forchetta*
form *modulo*
You have to fill out some forms. *Deve compilare alcuni moduli.*
found (to) *fondare*
foyer *ingresso*
franc (money) *franco*
free *libero*
The telephone line is free. *La linea è libera.*
French *francese*
french fries *patate fritte*
fresco *affresco*
fresh *fresco*
fresh fruit *frutta fresca*
Friday *venerdì (m.)*

417

fried *fritto*
  fried fish *pesce fritto*
friend *amico*
from *da, di*
  Where do you come from? *Di dove vieni?*
front *fronte (f.)*
  in front of *di fronte, davanti (a)*
  The museum is in front of the church. *Il museo è davanti alla chiesa.*
fruit *frutta*
  fresh fruit *frutta fresca*
  fruit juice *succo di frutta*
fruit seller *fruttivendolo*
fuel *gas, carburante (m.)*
full *pieno*
furnish (to) *arredare*
  The room is furnished. *La stanza è arredata.*
furnished *ammobiliato*
  furnished apartment *appartamento ammobiliato*
furniture *mobili (m., pl.)*

G

gallery *galleria*
  art gallery *pinacoteca*
game *partita*
  to watch the game *guardare la partita*
  soccer game *partita di calcio*
garage *garage (m.)*
garden *giardino*
garlic *aglio*
gasoline (gas) *benzina*
  gas station attendant *benzinaio*
  gas station *stazione di servizio*
gasoline *benzina*
  super (gas) *benzina super*
  regular gas *benzina normale*
  unleaded gas *benzina senza piombo, benzina verde*
  gas coupon *buono benzina*
gate *uscita*
gauze *garza*
gear *marcia, cambio*
  to change gears *cambiare marcia*
  The car won't go into third gear. *La terza non ingrana.*
generous *generoso*
gentle *gentile*
German *tedesco*
get up (to) *alzarsi*
get off (to) *scendere*
  At which stop do I have to get off? *A che fermata devo scendere?*
get (to) *ottenere, ricevere*
  to get a haircut *tagliarsi i capelli*
gift *regalo*
  gift items *articoli da regalo*
give (to) *dare*
  to give directions *dare indicazioni*
  Give me a hand! *Dammi una mano!*
  Could you give me some information? *Mi potrebbe dare alcune informazioni?*
  to give an encore *concedere il bis*
glad *contento, lieto*

glass *bicchiere (m.)*
  glass of mineral water *bicchiere d'acqua minerale*
gloves *guanti (m., pl.)*
go out (to) *uscire*
go (to) *andare*
  to go to work *andare al lavoro*
  to go to the doctor *andare dal dottore*
  to go downtown *andare in centro*
  to go to a restaurant *andare al ristorante (m.)*
  to go to the shore *andare al mare*
  to go to the store *andare al negozio*
  to go to a concert *andare al concerto*
  to go on vacation *andare in vacanza*
  to go to the post office *andare alla posta*
  to go to the movies *andare al cinema*
  to go to church *andare in chiesa*
  to go to Rome *andare a Roma*
  to go to Italy *andare in Italia*
  to go on foot *andare a piedi*
  Shall we go for coffee? *Andiamo a prendere un caffè?*
  Let's go for a ride. *Andiamo a fare un giro.*
  Go slow. *Vu' piano.*
  Go straight. *Vada sempre dritto.*
good *buono*
  Have a good trip! *Buon viaggio!*
  Good morning. *Buon giorno.*
  Good night. *Buona notte.*
  Good evening. *Buona sera.*
good-bye *(familiar) arrivederci*
good-bye *(polite) arrivederLa*
governmental *governativo*
  government tax *tassa governativa*
graduate (to) *laurearsi*
  to graduate with a degree in Economics and Business *laurearsi in economia e commercio*
gram *grammo*
  I would like a hundred grams of cheese. *Mi dia cento grammi di formaggio.*
granddaughter *nipote (f.)*
grandfather *nonno*
grandson *nipote (m.)*
grape *uva*
green *verde*
greet (to) *salutare*
  to greet each other *salutarsi*
greeting *saluto*
grilled *ai ferri*
  grilled fish *pesce ai ferri*
  grilled steak *bistecca ai ferri*
guard *guardia*
guarded *custodito*
guide *guida*
guitar *chitarra*
  to play the guitar *suonare la chitarra*

H

hair *capelli (m.,pl.)*
  hair conditioner *balsamo per i capelli*
  short/long hair *capelli corti/lunghi*
  curly/straight hair *capelli ricci/lisci*
  blond/brown hair *capelli biondi/castani*

hair spray *lacca*
to dry one's hair *asciugarsi i capelli*
to dye one's hair blond *tingersi i capelli biondi*
How would you like your hair? *Come vuole i capelli?*
hairdresser *parrucchiere/a*
half *metà*
to pay half price *pagare metà prezzo*
hand *mano (f.)*
Give me a hand! *Dammi una mano!*
handkerchief *fazzoletto*
happy *felice, contento*
I'm happy to see you. *Sono contento di rivederti.*
hardly *appena*
hat *cappello*
have (to) *avere*
to have breakfast *fare colazione*
to have the opportunity to . . . *avere occasione di . . .*
to have a good position *avere un bel posto*
to have a fever *avere la febbre*
to have a sore throat *avere mal di gola*
to have a stomachache *avere mal di stomaco*
to have heartburn *avere bruciore allo stomaco*
to have a mustache *avere i baffi*
to have a party *dare una festa*
head *testa*
My head is spinning. *Mi gira la testa.*
headache *mal di testa*
headline *testata*
heavy *pesante*
My arms feel heavy. *Mi sento le braccia pesanti.*
heel *tacco*
high heel *tacco alto*
low heel *tacco basso*
hello *ciao, pronto (phone)*
help *aiuto*
help (to) *aiutare*
May I help you? *Mi dica? Desidera?*
here *qui, qua*
Here it is. *Ecco.*
Here you are. *Ecco a Lei.*
hi *ciao*
highlighter *evidenziatore (m.)*
hire (to) *assumere*
to be hired *essere assunto*
hit *hit (m.)*
the latest hit *l'ultimo hit*
holiday *vacanza*
home *casa*
at home *a casa*
to stay home *restare a casa*
honey *miele (m.)*
honeymoon *luna di miele*
hope (to) *sperare*
horoscope *oroscopo*
hospital *ospedale (m.)*
host *presentatore (m.), ospite (m.)*
hot *caldo*
It's hot. *Fa caldo.*
to be hot *avere caldo*
hotel *albergo, hotel (m.)*
three-star hotel *albergo a tre stelle*
first-class hotel *albergo di prima categoria*

hour *ora*
regular working hours *orario lavorativo regolare*
house *casa*
how *come*
How are you going to spend your weekend? *Come passi il weekend?*
How long have you been in Italy? *Da quanto tempo è in Italia?*
How are you? *Come stai?*
How much is it? *Quant'è?*
How much does it cost? *Quanto costa?*
How much is it a kilo? *Quanto costa al chilo?*
hundred *cento*
hungry *affamato*
to be hungry *avere fame*
hurry *fretta*
to be in a hurry *avere fretta*
hurt (to) *fare male*
My ears hurt. *Mi fanno male le orecchie.*
husband *marito*

I

ice cream *gelato*
chocolate ice cream *gelato al cioccolato*
vanilla ice cream *gelato alla vaniglia*
ice-cream parlor *gelateria*
immense *immenso*
impeccable *impeccabile*
in *in, a*
in fact *infatti*
included *incluso, compreso*
Is the insurance included? *L'assicurazione è inclusa?*
Are meals included? *I pasti sono inclusi?*
Is the service charge included? *Il servizio è compreso?*
income *reddito*
steady income *reddito fisso*
information *informazione (f.)*
I need some information. *Mi serve un'informazione.*
information office *ufficio informazioni*
injection *puntura, iniezione (f.)*
insole *soletta*
inspection *ispezione (f.)*
instruction *istruzione (f.), indicazione (f.)*
usage instructions *indicazioni per l'uso*
insurance *assicurazione (f.)*
theft insurance *assicurazione per il furto*
medical insurance *assicurazione medica*
insure (to) *assicurare*
to insure a parcel *assicurare un pacco*
intelligent *intelligente*
interest *interesse (m.)*
The interest rate is ten percent. *Il tasso di interesse è al dieci per cento.*
interested *interessato*
to be interested in literature *interessarsi di letteratura*
interesting *interessante*

international *internazionale*
   International Driver's License *patente*
   internazionale
interview *intervista, colloquio*
   job interview *colloquio di lavoro*
introduce (to) *presentare*
   Let me introduce you to Carla. *Ti presento*
   Carla.
introduction *introduzione (f.), presentazione (f.)*
invent (to) *inventare*
itchiness *prurito*
item *articolo*
   gift items *articoli da regalo*
itinerary *itinerario*
Italian *italiano*

J

jacket *giacca*
jam *marmellata*
January *gennaio (m.)*
Japanese *giapponese*
job *lavoro*
   job interview *colloquio di lavoro*
journalist *giornalista (m./f.)*
judge *giudice (m.)*
juice *succo*
   fruit juice *succo di frutta*
jukebox *juke-box*
July *luglio*
June *giugno*
just *appena*

K

keep (to) *tenere*
   Keep the change. *Tenga pure.*
ketchup *ketchup (m.)*
key *chiave (f.)*
   room keys *chiavi della camera*
kilogram *chilo*
   Five thousand lire a kilo. *Cinquemila lire al*
   chilo.
kilometer *chilometro*
kind *gentile*
   to be kind *essere gentile*
kitchen *cucina*
knife *coltello*
know (to) *conoscere, sapere*

L

lace *laccio*
   shoe laces *lacci per le scarpe*
landlord *proprietario (m./f.)*
large *grande*
last *scorso, ultimo*
   last year *l'anno scorso*
   last week *la settimana scorsa*
   December is the last month of the
     year. *Dicembre è l'ultimo mese dell'anno.*

late *tardi*
   to be late *essere in ritardo*
later *più tardi*
   sooner or later *prima o poi*
   See you later. *A più tardi.*
lead (to) *dirigere, guidare*
least *il meno*
   not in the least *niente affatto*
   at least *almeno*
leave (to) *partire*
   At what time does the train for Rome leave? *A*
   che ora parte il treno per Roma?
left *sinistra*
   on the left *a sinistra*
   to turn left *girare a sinistra*
lemon *limone (m.)*
lemonade *limonata*
less *meno*
   Beer is less expensive than wine. *La birra è*
   meno cara del vino.
letter *lettera*
   express letter *lettera espresso*
   to mail a letter *spedire/imbucare una lettera*
   to put a stamp on a letter *affrancare una lettera*
   letter opener *tagliacarte (m.)*
lettuce *lattuga*
license *patente (f.)*
light *(n.) luce (f.)*
light *(adj.) leggero*
lighter *accendisigari, accendino*
like *come*
   What's the weather like? *Che tempo fa?*
like (to) *piacere*
   I like the theater. *Mi piace il teatro.*
   What would you like? *Desidera?*
   I would like a room for the night. *Desidero una*
   camera per una notte.
line *linea; fila, coda*
   The telephone line is busy. *La linea è occupata.*
   The telephone line is free. *La linea è libera.*
   to wait in line *aspettare in fila, fare la coda*
lipstick *rossetto*
liquid *liquido*
lira *lira*
list *lista, listino*
   exchange list *listino dei cambi*
   shopping list *lista della spesa*
listen (to) *ascoltare*
   to listen to the radio *ascoltare la radio*
literature *letteratura*
little *piccolo*
little (a) *poco*
live (to) *abitare*
   to live on the second floor *abitare al primo piano*
   to live in Italy *abitare in Italia*
   to live in Rome *abitare a Roma*
loan *prestito*
local *locale*
   local train *treno locale*
long *lungo*
   to have long hair *capelli lunghi*
   long-distance call *interurbana*
look (to) *guardare*
   to look for *cercare*

to look for a job *cercare lavoro*
to look for an apartment for rent *cercare un appartamento in affitto*
lot (a) *molto*
a lot of money *molto denaro*
lotion *lozione (f.), pomata*
suntan lotion *pomata contro le scottature*
love *(n.) amore (m.)*
love (to) *amare, volere bene*
I love you. *Ti amo. Ti voglio bene.*
low *basso*
luggage *bagaglio, valigie (f., pl.)*
luggage rack *portabagagli*
hand luggage *borsa a mano*

M

machine *macchina*
answering machine *la segreteria telefonica*
magazine *rivista*
mail (to) *spedire, imbucare*
to mail a letter *spedire/imbucare una lettera*
to send a parcel *spedire un pacco*
mailbox *buca delle lettere, cassetta postale*
mailman *postino*
make (to) *fare*
to make a telephone call *fare una telefonata*
to make a photocopy *fare una fotocopia*
to make an appointment *fissare un appuntamento*
makeup *trucco*
man *uomo*
men's shoes *scarpe da uomo*
manage (to) *farcela*
We should manage. *Dovremmo farcela.*
manager *manager, direttore (m.)*
managerial *manageriale*
to look for someone with managerial ability *cercare qualcuno con capacità manageriali*
to work in the managerial sector *lavorare nel settore dirigenziale*
manicure *manicure (f.)*
manifestation *manifestazione (f.)*
many *molto, tanto*
Many happy returns! *Tanti auguri!*
Many thanks. *Tante grazie.*
map *carta, mappa, pianta*
Do you have a map of Italy? *Ha una carta geografica dell'Italia?*
Do you have a road map of the region? *Ha una carta stradale della regione?*
Do you have a map of the city? *Ha una pianta della città?*
March *marzo*
mark (currency) *marco*
marker *marcatore (m.)*
marker *pennarello*
market *mercato*
to go to the market *andare al mercato*
stock market *borsa*
mass *messa*
to go to mass *andare a messa*
masterpiece *capolavoro*

match *partita, incontro*
boxing match *incontro di pugilato*
match *fiammifero, cerino*
box of matches *scatola di cerini*
safety matches *fiammiferi svedesi*
matter (to) *importare*
It doesn't matter. *Non importa./Non fa niente.*
May *maggio*
meal *pasto*
after meals *dopo i pasti*
Are meals included? *I pasti sono inclusi?*
meat *carne*
mechanic *meccanico*
at the mechanic *dal meccanico*
medical *medico*
medical insurance *assicurazione medica*
medication *medicina*
to prescribe a medication *prescrivere una medicina*
to take medication *prendere una medicina*
medicine *medicina*
meet (to) *incontrare, conoscere*
We met each other in Rome. *Ci siamo incontrati a Roma.*
I met two American girls. *Ho conosciuto due ragazze americane.*
meeting *riunione (f.)*
meeting room *sala delle riunioni*
melon *melone (m.)*
memo *promemoria (m.)*
menu *menù (m.)*
message *messaggio*
telegram message *messaggio del telegramma*
meter *metro*
It's two hundred meters from here. *È a duecento metri.*
Mexican *messicano*
mileage *chilometraggio*
unlimited mileage *chilometraggio illimitato*
milk *latte (m.)*
coffee with milk *caffellatte (m.)*
million *milione (m.)*
mineral *minerale*
mineral water *acqua minerale*
minute *minuto*
It's a few minutes away from downtown. *È a pochi minuti dal centro.*
miss (to) *perdere*
to miss the train *perdere il treno*
mistake *errore (m.), sbaglio*
to make a mistake *sbagliare*
moment *momento, attimo*
One moment, please. *Un attimo, per favore.*
mommy *mamma*
Monday *lunedì (m.)*
money *denaro*
money order *vaglia (m.)*
to draft a money order *fare un vaglia*
month *mese (m.)*
The rent is three million lire a month. *L'affitto è tre milioni di lire al mese.*
moon *luna*
honeymoon *luna di miele*

more *più*
> more, extra *di più*
> You have to pay a hundred dollars more. *Deve pagare cento dollari in più.*

morning *mattina*
> in the morning *di mattina*
> Good morning. *Buon giorno.*

mortadella *mortadella*

mother *madre (f.)*

motor *motore (m.)*

motorcycle *moto (f.)*

mustache *baffi (m., pl.)*
> to have a mustache *avere i baffi*

move (to) *muovere, trasportare*
> to move (one's home) *cambiare casa*

movie *film (m.)*
> to show a movie *dare un film*
> to go to the movies *andare al cinema*
> movie theater *cinema (m.)*

much *molto*
> How much is it? *Quant'è?*
> How much is the rent? *Quant'è l'affitto?*
> How much does it cost? *Quanto costa?*
> How much is it a kilo? *Quanto costa al chilo?*

museum *museo*

music *musica*
> music by . . . *musica di . . .*
> classical music *musica classica*
> pop music *musica leggera*
> rock music *musica rock*

musical *(n.) operetta*

musical *(adj.) musicale*
> musical group *complesso*
> musical instrument *strumento musicale*

musician *musicista (m./f.)*

mustard *senape (m.)*

N

nail (human) *unghia*
> nail polish *smalto per unghie*

name *nome (m.)*
> What's your name? *Come ti chiami?*
> Name Day *onomastico*
> My name is Anthony. *Mi chiamo Antonio.*

napkin *tovagliolo*

nation *nazione (f.)*

nationality *nazionalità*

near *vicino, vicino a*
> I live near downtown. *Abito vicino al centro.*

necessary *necessario*
> Is a prescription necessary? *Ci vuole la ricetta?*

need (to) *servire, avere bisogno (di)*
> What do we need? *Che cosa ci serve?*
> I need some cough syrup. *Mi serve dello sciroppo per la tosse.*
> I need a pen. *Ho bisogno di una penna.*

neighbor *vicino di casa*

neighborhood *quartiere (m.)*

neither *né*
> neither . . . nor *non . . . né . . . né*

nephew *nipote (m.)*

nervous *nervoso*
> nervous breakdown *esaurimento nervoso*

net *rete (f.)*

never *mai*

new *nuovo*

news *telegiornale (m.), notizia*
> crime news *cronaca nera*

newspaper *giornale (m.)*
> What's in the newspaper? *Cosa c'è sul giornale?*
> What does the newspaper say? *Cosa dice il giornale?*
> daily newspaper *quotidiano*
> weekly newspaper *settimanale (m.)*
> newspaper vendor *giornalaio*

newsstand *edicola*

next *prossimo*
> next time *la prossima volta*
> next week *la settimana prossima*

next (to) *vicino, accanto*

nice *gentile, simpatico, carino*

niece *nipote (f.)*

night *notte (f.)*
> Good night. *Buona notte.*
> at night *di notte*
> I would like a room for one night. *Desidero una camera per una notte.*

no *no*
> no longer *non . . . più*
> No wine, please. *Niente vino, per favore.*

nobody *nessuno*

no one *nessuno*

not *non*
> I'm not American. *Non sono americano(a).*
> not at all *non . . . affatto*
> I'm not tired at all. *Non sono affatto stanco.*
> not even *neanche*

nothing *niente, nulla*

notice *annuncio, avviso*
> newspaper ad *avviso economico*

November *novembre (m.)*

now *adesso*

number *numero*
> I'm sorry, I dialed the wrong number. *Scusi, ho sbagliato numero.*

O

occasion *occasione (f.)*
> I had the opportunity to go to Italy. *Ho avuto l'occasione di andare in Italia.*

occur (to) *succedere*

October *ottobre (m.)*

of *di*

offer (to) *offrire*

office *ufficio*
> information office *ufficio informazioni*
> to work in an office *lavorare in un ufficio*
> post office *ufficio postale*
> tourist information office *ufficio informazioni turistiche*

oil *olio*
to check the oil *controllare l'olio*
to change the oil *cambiare l'olio*
The car is leaking oil. *La macchina perde olio.*
okay *va bene, okay*
old *vecchio*
on *su, sopra*
on the right/left *sulla destra/sinistra*
on the table *sulla tavola*
onion *cipolla*
only *solo, soltanto*
open *aperto*
open-air concert *concerto all'aperto*
open (to) *aprire*
to open an account *aprire un conto*
opera *opera*
to go to the opera *andare all'opera*
operator *operatore (m.); centralino, centralinista (m./f.)*
tour operator *operatore turistico*
optimist *ottimista*
or *o, oppure*
orange *arancia* (fruit); *arancione* (color)
freshly squeezed orange juice *spremuta d'arancia*
orange drink *aranciata*
order (to) *ordinare*
organized *organizzato*
organized tour *giro organizzato*
other *altro*
outfit *abito, vestito*
overheat (to) *scaldare*
The engine is overheating. *Il motore scalda.*

P

pack *pacchetto*
a pack of cigarettes *pacchetto di sigarette*
package *pacco*
page *pagina*
business page *rubrica finanziaria*
sports page *rubrica sportiva*
yellow pages *pagine gialle*
cultural page *terza pagina*
pain *dolore (m.)*
You're a pain! *Sei seccante!*
pain killer *antidolorifico*
paint (to) *dipingere*
to paint one's nails *tingersi le unghie*
painter *pittore (m.)*
painting *quadro, pittura*
mural painting *pittura murale*
pair *paio*
a pair of shoes *un paio di scarpe*
palace *palazzo*
pants *pantaloni (m., pl.)*
paper *carta*
paper clip *graffetta*
paper pad *blocchetto*
writing paper *carta da lettere*
government-stamped paper *carta da bollo*
toilet paper *carta igienica*

paper cutter *taglierina*
carbon paper *carta carbone*
parcel *pacco*
to insure a parcel *assicurare un pacco*
to send a parcel *spedire un pacco*
parents *genitori (m., pl.)*
parking *parcheggio*
supervised parking lot *parcheggio custodito*
part *parte (f.)*
to play the part of *fare la parte di*
party *festa*
to have a party *dare una festa*
passenger *passeggero*
passport *passaporto*
pasta *pasta*
pastry *pasta*
pastry shop *pasticceria*
patience *pazienza*
patient *paziente*
Be patient. *Abbi pazienza.*
pay (to) *pagare*
to pay half price *pagare metà prezzo*
to pay the telephone bill *pagare la bolletta del telefono*
pay *paga*
payment *pagamento*
advance payment *pagamento anticipato*
peach *pesca*
pear *pera*
peas *piselli (m., pl.)*
pencil *matita*
penicillin *penicillina*
pension *pensione (f.)*
pepper *peperone (m.); pepe (m.)*
perform (to) *recitare*
perfume *profumo*
period *periodo*
perm *permanente (f.)*
Could you give me a perm? *Potrebbe farmi la permanente?*
person *persona, personaggio*
pessimist *pessimista (m./f.)*
pharmacist *farmacista (m./f.)*
pharmacy *farmacia*
photocopier *fotocopiatrice (f.)*
The photocopier doesn't work. *La fotocopiatrice non funziona.*
photocopy (to) *fotocopiare*
photocopy *fotocopia*
to make a photocopy *fare una fotocopia*
pianist *pianista (m./f.)*
pill *pillola*
sleeping pills *pillole per dormire*
pin *spillo*
stiletto heel *tacco a spillo*
pink *rosa*
pipe *pipa*
plate *piatto*
play *gioco; dramma (m.)*
in play *per scherzo*
play (to) *giocare, suonare*
to play the guitar *suonare la chitarra*
to play tennis *giocare a tennis*

player *giocatore (m.)*
please *per favore, per piacere, per cortesia*
pleased *contento*
   Very pleased to meet you. *Molto lieto.*
   Pleased to meet you. *Piacere.*
plot *trama, intrigo*
plum *prugna*
police *polizia*
   police station *commissariato, questura*
   to go to the police station *andare al*
     commissariato/in questura
   traffic police *polizia stradale*
policeman *poliziotto, agente di pubblica sicurezza*
   traffic policeman *vigile (m.)*
polish *lucido*
   shoe polish *lucido per scarpe*
politely *gentilmente*
porter *facchino*
position *posizione (f.); posto*
   to have a good position *avere un bel posto*
possible *possibile*
   It is possible. *È possibile.*
post *posta*
   post office *posta, ufficio postale*
   to go to the post office *andare alla posta*
   post office box *casella postale*
postal *postale*
   postal code *codice (m.) postale*
postcard *cartolina*
postmark *timbro*
potato *patata*
   french fried potatoes *patate fritte*
prefer (to) *preferire (isc)*
preferably *preferibilmente*
prepare (to) *preparare*
prescribe (to) *prescrivere*
   to prescribe a medication *prescrivere una*
     medicina
prescription *ricetta*
   Is a prescription necessary? *Ci vuole la ricetta?*
present (to) *presentare*
   Present this receipt. *Presenti questa ricevuta.*
pressure *pressione (f.)*
   to take one's blood pressure *misurare la*
     pressione del sangue
   Your blood pressure is low. *La pressione è bassa.*
price *prezzo*
   to pay half price *pagare metà prezzo*
   We have fabulous prices. *Abbiamo prezzi da*
     sogno.
private *privato*
   to work in the private sector *lavorare in una ditta*
     privata
probable *probabile*
   It is probable. *È probabile.*
product *prodotto*
professional *professionista (m.)*
program *programma (m.)*
   special program *programma speciale*
project *progetto*
promote (to) *promuovere*
   to get promoted *ottenere una promozione*
promotion *promozione (f.)*

prosciutto *prosciutto*
protagonist *protagonista (m./f.)*
public *pubblico*
   public phone *telefono pubblico*
purple *viola*
put (to) *mettere*
   to put a stamp on a letter *affrancare una lettera*
   to put on the brakes *frenare*
   to put in first gear *mettere la prima*
   Put it on channel five. *Metti al canale 5.*
   to put on (clothing) *mettersi*
   Put on your suit. *Mettiti il vestito.*
   to put on one's shoes *mettersi le scarpe*

Q

quarter *quarta; quarto* (fraction)
question *domanda*
quotation *quotazione (f.)*

R

radio *radio (f.)*
   to turn on the radio *accendere la radio*
   to listen to the radio *ascoltare la radio*
   What's on radio? *Cosa c'è alla radio.*
   to turn off the radio *spegnere la radio*
   radio station *stazione radio*
railroad *ferrovia*
   railroad car *vagone (m.)*
rain (to) *piovere*
   It's raining. *Piove.*
rash *irritazione (f.)*
   skin rash *irritazione della pelle*
rate *tasso*
   exchange rate *tasso del cambio*
   What is the exchange rate today? *Quant'è il*
     cambio oggi?
razor *rasoio*
read (to) *leggere*
   to read the newspaper *leggere il giornale*
ready *pronto*
really *veramente*
   Really? *Davvero?*
reason *ragione (f.), motivo*
receipt *ricevuta*
   Present this receipt. *Presenti questa ricevuta.*
receive (to) *ricevere*
   to receive a telephone call *ricevere una telefonata*
   to receive a fax *ricevere un fax*
receiver *destinatario*
recently *recentemente*
record (to) *registrare*
record *disco*
   to cut a record *incidere un disco*
red *rosso*
reduced *ridotto*
   reduced fare *tariffa ridotta*
referee *arbitro*
refrigerator *frigorifero*

register *registro, registratore (m.)*
  cash register *cassa*
registered *registrato*
  to send a registered letter *fare una raccomandata*
regular *regolare, normale*
  regular gas *benzina normale*
relative *parente (m./f.)*
remember (to) *ricordare, ricordarsi*
remote *remoto*
  remote control *telecomando*
Renaissance *Rinascimento*
rent (to) *affittare*
  for rent *affittasi*
  Do you have rooms for rent? *Ha camere da affittare?*
  to look for an apartment to rent *cercare un appartamento in affitto*
  to rent out *dare in affitto*
  to rent a car *noleggiare una macchina*
rent *(n.) affitto*
  controlled rent *equo canone*
rental *affitto, noleggio*
  How much is the rental for a week? *Quant'è il noleggio per una settimana?*
repair (to) *riparare*
  Can you repair my tire? *Mi può riparare la gomma?*
report *servizio*
  news report *servizio di attualità*
  special report *servizio speciale*
reporter *reporter*
representative *rappresentante*
reservation *prenotazione (f.)*
  to make a reservation *fare la prenotazione*
reserve (to) *prenotare*
  to reserve a room *prenotare una camera*
residence *residenza*
  Do you have your residence in Italy? *Lei ha la residenza in Italia?*
restaurant *ristorante (m.)*
  to go to a restaurant *andare al ristorante*
return *ritorno*
rich *ricco*
ride *passaggio*
  Can you give me a ride? *Può darmi un passaggio?*
right *destra*
  on the right *a destra*
  to turn right *girare a destra*
rob (to) *derubare*
  I have been robbed. *Mi hanno derubato.*
rock *roccia*
  rock and roll *rock*
  to dance to rock and roll *ballare il rock*
  rock music *musica rock*
room *stanza, camera*
  living room *salotto*
  dining room *sala da pranzo*
  waiting room *sala d'aspetto*
  bedroom *camera da letto*
  I would like a room with bathroom. *Vorrei una camera con bagno.*
  room without bathroom *camera senza bagno*

room with shower *camera con doccia*
single room *camera singola*
double room *camera doppia, camera matrimoniale*
Do you have rooms for rent? *Ha camere da affittare?*
to reserve a room *prenotare una camera*
meeting room *sala delle riunioni*
ruler *riga*
Russian *russo*

S

safe *cassaforte (f.)*
safety *sicurezza*
  safety deposit box *cassetta di sicurezza*
salad *insalata*
salami *salame (m.)*
salesman *commesso*
salon *salone (m.)*
salt *sale (m.)*
sandals *sandali (m., pl.)*
sandwich *panino*
Saturday *sabato*
save (to) *salvare; risparmiare (money)*
saving *risparmio, economia*
  savings account *libretto di risparmi*
say (to) *dire*
  What did you say? *Cosa hai detto?*
scheduled *previsto*
scissors *forbici (f., pl.)*
sculptor *scultore (m.)*
sculpt (to) *scolpire*
sculpture *scultura*
sea *mare (m.)*
season *stagione (f.)*
seat *posto*
  Is this seat vacant/taken? *È libero/occupato questo posto?*
secretary *segretaria*
  secretary's office *segreteria*
section *sezione (f.)*
  theater section *rubrica teatrale*
sector *settore (m.)*
  to work in the managerial sector *lavorare nel settore dirigenziale*
sedative *calmante (m.), sedativo*
see (to) *vedere*
  to see oneself/each other *vedersi*
  See you later. *A più tardi.*
  See you soon. *A presto.*
  See you tomorrow. *A domani.*
  See you! *Ci vediamo!*
send (to) *mandare*
  to send a fax *mandare un fax*
  to send a registered letter *fare una raccomandata*
sender *mittente (m./f.)*
sensitivity *sensibilità*
September *settembre (m.)*
set (to) *mettere*
  to set in place *mettere a posto*

several *parecchi; diversi*
shampoo *sciampo*
  to shampoo *farsi lo sciampo*
sharp *acuto*
  I will arrive at three o'clock sharp. *Arrivo alle tre in punto.*
shave (to) *farsi la barba*
  shaving cream *sapone (m.) per la barba*
shirt *camicia*
shoe *scarpa*
  tennis shoes *scarpe da tennis*
  suede shoes *scarpe di camoscio*
  women's shoes *scarpe da donna*
  men's shoes *scarpe da uomo*
  to tie one's shoes *allacciarsi le scarpe*
  a pair of shoes *un paio di scarpe*
  to clean one's shoes *lucidare le scarpe*
  shoe brush *spazzola per scarpe*
  to take off one's shoes *togliersi le scarpe*
  to put on one's shoes *mettersi le scarpe*
  shoe store *calzoleria, negozio di scarpe*
  shoehorn *calzascarpe (m.)*
shoemaker *calzolaio*
shop (to) *fare delle spese*
shopping *spesa*
  to go shopping *fare la spesa*
short *corto*
  short hair *capelli corti*
show *spettacolo*
  to attend a show *assistere ad uno spettacolo*
  variety show *spettacolo di varietà*
  At what time does the show end? *A che ora termina lo spettacolo?*
  to show a movie *dare un film*
shower *doccia*
  room with shower *camera con doccia*
sick *malato*
sideburns *basette (f., pl.)*
side dish *contorno*
  side dish of vegetables *contorno di verdura*
signal *segnale (m.), freccia*
  The signal doesn't work. *La freccia non funziona.*
signature *firma*
since *da*
sing (to) *cantare*
singer *cantante (m./f.)*
single *singola*
  single room *camera singola*
sister *sorella*
  sister-in-law *cognata*
sit (to) *sedere*
  to sit down *sedersi*
  Please sit down. *Si accomodi.*
size *numero, taglia*
  What size do you wear? *Che numero/taglia porta?*
ski *sci (m.)*
  ski boots *scarponi (m., pl.) da sci*
skim (to) *sfogliare*
  to skim through the newspaper *sfogliare il giornale*
skin *pelle (f.)*
  skin rash *irritazione della pelle*

skirt *gonna*
sleep (to) *dormire*
  sleeping pills *pillole per dormire*
  sleeping car *vagone (m.) letto*
  to be sleepy *avere sonno*
slipper *pantofola*
small *piccolo*
smoke (to) *fumare*
  nonsmoking area *zona non fumatori*
  smoking area *zona fumatori*
smoke *fumo*
snack *spuntino, merenda*
snow (to) *nevicare*
  It's snowing. *Nevica.*
so *così*
  so so *così così*
  so much *tanto*
  so many *tanti/e*
soap *sapone (m.)*
  soap opera *teleromanzo, telenovela*
soccer *calcio*
  soccer game *partita di calcio*
sofa *divano*
some *alcuni/e, qualche*
  I have some questions. *Ho alcune domande./Ho qualche domanda.*
someone *qualcuno*
something *qualcosa*
  Something to drink/eat? *Qualcosa da bere/ mangiare?*
  Do you have something less expensive? *Ha qualcosa di meno caro?*
  Please, give me something for my cough. *Mi dia qualcosa per la tosse.*
  May I show you something else? *Posso farLe vedere qualcos'altro.*
son *figlio*
  son-in-law *genero*
song *canzone (f.)*
  to listen to a song *ascoltare una canzone*
  song festival *festival della canzone*
  singer-songwriter *cantautore*
soon *presto*
  See you soon. *A presto.*
sorry *spiacente*
south *sud (m.)*
southern *meridionale*
  Southern Italy *Italia meridionale*
spaghetti *spaghetti (m., pl.)*
  spaghetti al dente *spaghetti al dente*
  spaghetti with sauce *spaghetti al sugo*
Spanish *spagnolo*
speak (to) *parlare*
  to speak Italian *parlare (l') italiano*
  Hello! Who is speaking? *Pronto! Chi parla?*
  to speak on the phone *parlare al telefono*
special *speciale*
  special report *servizio speciale*
  special program *programma speciale*
spend (to) *passare*
  to spend a fabulous vacation *passare una vacanza favolosa*
  How are you going to spend your weekend? *Come passi il weekend?*

spinach *spinaci (m., pl.)*
spoon *cucchiaio*
sport *sport (m.)*
  sports page *pagina sportiva*
spray *lacca*
  hair spray *lacca per capelli*
spring *primavera*
square *piazza* (place); *quadrato* (geom.)
squeeze (to) *spremere*
  freshly squeezed orange juice *spremuta
    d'arancia*
stage *palcoscenico*
staging *messinscena*
stamp *francobollo, marca*
  tax stamp *marca da bollo*
  stamp for a foreign country *francobollo per
    l'estero*
  government-stamped paper *carta da bollo*
stand *bancarella*
stapler *spillatrice (f.)*
star *stella*
  three-star hotel *albergo a tre stelle*
start (to) *cominciare, iniziare*
  At what time does the show start? *A che ora
    inizia lo spettacolo?*
  The car won't start. *La macchina non si mette in
    moto.*
station *stazione (f.)*
  radio station *stazione radio*
  TV station *stazione televisiva*
  gas station *stazione di servizio*
  gas station attendant *benzinaio*
  police station *questura*
stay (to) *stare, restare, rimanere*
  to stay at home *rimanere a casa*
  Stay still. *Sta' fermo.*
  Stay on the line. *Resti in linea.*
steady *fisso*
  steady income *reddito fisso*
steak *bistecca*
  I want my steak well done. *Voglio la mia bistecca
    ben cotta.*
  I would like my steak rare. *Desidero la mia
    bistecca al sangue.*
steal (to) *rubare*
  They stole my wallet. *Mi hanno rubato il
    portafoglio.*
sterling *sterlina*
still *ancora, sempre; fermo*
  I'm still hungry. *Ho ancora fame.*
  Stay still! *Sta' fermo!*
stomach *stomaco, pancia*
  stomachache *mal di stomaco/pancia*
  It upsets your stomach. *Fa male allo
    stomaco.*
stop (to) *fermare*
stop *fermata*
  At which stop do I have to get off? *A che fermata
    devo scendere?*
store *negozio*
  department store *grande magazzino*
  clothing store *negozio di abbigliamento*
  shoe store *negozio di scarpe, calzoleria*
stove *cucina*

straight *dritto*
  Go straight ahead. *Vada sempre dritto.*
strawberry *fragola*
street *via, strada*
streetcar *tram*
  to take the streetcar *prendere il tram*
stress *tensione (f.)*
  to be under stress *essere stressato*
study (to) *studiare*
  to study Italian *studiare l'italiano*
stupendous *stupendo*
suburbs *periferia*
  It's in the suburbs. *È in periferia.*
subway *metropolitana*
  to take the subway *prendere la metropolitana*
success *successo*
suede *camoscio*
  suede shoes *scarpe di camoscio*
sugar *zucchero*
suggest (to) *suggerire*
suit *abito, vestito*
suitcase *valigia*
summer *estate (f.)*
sunburn *scottatura*
Sunday *domenica*
super *super*
  super (gas) *benzina super*
suppository *supposta*
sure *sicuro*
  to be sure *essere sicuro*
sweater *maglione (m.)*
sweet *dolce*
swim (to) *nuotare*
  to go swimming *fare il bagno*
swimming *nuoto*
  swimming pool *piscina*
syringe *siringa*
syrup *sciroppo*
  cough syrup *sciroppo per la tosse*

T

table *tavolo*
take (to) *prendere*
  to take a medication *prendere una medicina*
  to take the subway *prendere la metropolitana*
  to take the streetcar *prendere il tram*
  to take the bus *prendere l'autobus (m.)*
  Is this seat taken? *È occupato questo posto?*
  to take off *togliere*
  to take off one's shoes *togliersi le scarpe*
  to take one's blood pressure *misurare la
    pressione*
  to take a tour *fare un giro*
tall *alto*
tape recorder *registratore (m.)*
tax *tassa*
  tax stamps *marca da bollo*
  government tax *tassa governativa*
tea *tè (m.)*
teach (to) *insegnare*
  to teach Italian *insegnare l'italiano*
team *squadra*

technique *tecnica*
telegram *telegramma (m.)*
  to send a telegram *fare un telegramma*
  telegram message *messaggio del telegramma*
telephone (to) *telefonare*
telephone *telefono*
  public phone *telefono pubblico*
  telephone bill *bolletta del telefono*
  to answer the phone *rispondere al telefono*
  telephone token *gettone (m.)*
  telephone card *carta telefonica*
  telephone booth *cabina telefonica*
  telephone book *elenco telefonico*
  telephone call *telefonata*
  to make a telephone call *fare una telefonata*
  to receive a telephone call *ricevere una telefonata*
television *televisione (f.)*
  to watch television *guardare la televisione*
  to turn on the television *accendere la televisione*
  to turn off the television *spegnere la televisione*
  What's on television? *Cosa c'è alla televisione?*
  television set *televisore (m.)*
teller *cassiere (m.)*
  instant teller *bancomat*
ten *dieci*
  top ten *hit parade*
tenant *inquilino*
tennis *tennis (m.)*
  tennis shoes *scarpe (f.) da tennis*
tenor *tenore (m.)*
test *test (m.); analisi (f.); prova*
  to have some tests done *fare degli accertamenti*
  blood test *analisi del sangue*
  urine test *analisi dell'urina*
thank (to) *ringraziare*
  Thank you. *Grazie.*
  Thanks a lot. *Mille grazie./Molte grazie.*
that *che, quello*
  that which *quello che*
theater *teatro*
  to go to the theater *andare a teatro*
  theater section *rubrica teatrale*
theft *furto*
  to be a victim of a theft *essere vittima di un furto*
then *allora, poi*
there *lì, là; ci*
  They're over there. *Sono là.*
  I'm going there tomorrow. *Ci vado domani.*
  Are there any shows? *Ci sono delle mostre?*
  Are there any special events? *Ci sono delle manifestazioni?*
thermometer *termometro*
thief *ladro*
thing *cosa*
thirsty *assetato*
  to be thirsty *avere sete*
this *questo*
throat *gola*
  to have a sore throat *avere mal di gola*
thumb *pollice (m.)*
  thumb tack *puntina*
Thursday *giovedì (m.)*
ticket *biglietto*

ticket collector *bigliettaio*
ticket booth *biglietteria*
one-way ticket *biglietto di andata*
round-trip ticket *biglietto di andata e ritorno*
first/second-class ticket *biglietto di prima/seconda classe*
bus ticket *biglietto per l'autobus*
tie *cravatta*
tie (to) *allacciare*
  to tie one's shoes *allacciarsi le scarpe*
tight *stretto*
  The shirt is a bit tight. *La camicia è un po' stretta.*
time *tempo, ora, volta*
  What time is it? *Che ora è?/Che ore sono?*
  At what time does the train arrive? *A che ora arriva il treno?*
  At what time does the train leave? *A che ora parte il treno?*
  to be on time *essere in orario*
  I don't even have the time to eat. *Non ho neanche il tempo di mangiare.*
  the first time I saw it . . . *la prima volta che l'ho visto . . .*
  Once upon a time . . . *C'era una volta . . .*
tip *mancia*
tire *gomma*
  My tires are low. *Ho le gomme a terra.*
tired *stanco*
tissue *fazzolettino di carta*
title *titolo*
to *a, da, in*
toast *pane tostato*
tobacco *tabacco*
tobacconist *tabaccaio*
today *oggi*
  What day is today? *Che giorno è oggi?*
  Today is Monday. *Oggi è lunedì.*
  Today is the first of July. *Oggi è il primo luglio.*
toilet *bagno*
  toilet paper *carta igienica*
tomato *pomodoro*
tomorrow *domani*
  See you tomorrow. *A domani.*
  Tomorrow is July second. *Domani è il due luglio.*
tonic *tonico*
  tonic water *acqua tonica*
tonight *stasera*
  See you tonight! *Ci vediamo stasera!*
too *troppo; anche*
  It's too expensive. *È troppo caro.*
  She is going, too. *Anche lei va.*
toothpaste *dentifricio*
total *totale*
tour (to) *girare*
  to tour the city *girare la città*
tour (n.) *giro*
  organized tour *giro organizzato*
  to take a tour *fare un giro*
  to go on tour (art) *fare una tournée*
  tour operator *operatore turistico*
tourist *turista (m./f.)*
  tourist information office *ufficio informazioni turistiche*

toy *giocattolo*
track *binario*
   Which track is the train arriving on? *Su quale binario arriva il treno?*
traffic *traffico*
   traffic policeman *vigile (m.), vigile urbano*
tragedy *tragedia*
train *treno*
   express train *rapido, espresso*
   local train *locale*
   through train *diretto*
   to travel by train *viaggiare in treno*
   to miss the train *perdere il treno*
   to take the train *prendere il treno*
   At what time does the train arrive? *A che ora arriva il treno?*
   At what time does the train leave? *A che ora parte il treno?*
training *allenamento*
transmission *trasmissione (f.), cambio*
   automatic transmission *cambio automatico*
travel (to) *viaggiare*
   to travel by train *viaggiare in treno*
   to travel around the world *fare il giro del mondo*
   travel agency *agenzia di viaggi*
   travel agent *agente (m./f.) di viaggi*
tribunal *tribunale (m.)*
trim *spuntatina*
trip *viaggio*
   Have a nice trip! *Buon viaggio!*
   to take a trip *fare un viaggio*
   business trip *viaggio d'affari*
   round-trip ticket *biglietto di andata e ritorno*
true *vero*
trunk (of a car) *portabagagli (m.)*
trust *fiducia*
   We trust you. *Noi abbiamo fiducia in te.*
try (to) *provare*
   to try on *provarsi*
   Try on this blouse. *Provi questa camicetta.*
Tuesday *martedì (m.)*
tuna *tonno*
turn off (to) *spegnere*
   to turn off the television *spegnere la televisione*
   Turn off the engine. *Spenga il motore.*
turn (to) *girare*
   to turn right *girare a destra*
   to turn left *girare a sinistra*
turn on (to) *accendere*
   to turn on the television *accendere la televisione*
   to turn on the radio *accendere la radio*
type *tipo*
   What kind of music do you like? *Che tipo di musica preferisce?*
type (to) *battere a macchina*
typewriter *macchina da scrivere*
typical *tipico*

U

understand (to) *capire (isc)*
unemployed *disoccupato*
   to be unemployed *essere disoccupato*

unfortunately *sfortunatamente*
university *università*
unleaded *senza piombo*
   unleaded gas *benzina senza piombo/verde*
unlimited *illimitato*
   unlimited mileage *chilometraggio illimitato*
up *su*
urine *urina*
   urine test *analisi dell'urina*
us *ci*
   to us *ci*
usage *uso*
   usage instructions *indicazioni per l'uso*
use (to) *usare, consumare*
   This car uses a lot of gas? *Questa macchina consuma molta benzina?*
used *usato*

V

vacant *vacante, libero*
   Is this seat vacant? *È libero questo posto?*
vacation *vacanza, ferie (f., pl.)*
   to go on vacation *andare in vacanza*
   to spend a fabulous vacation *passare una vacanza favolosa*
van *furgone (m.)*
   mini van *pulmino*
vanilla *vaniglia*
   vanilla ice cream *gelato alla vaniglia*
variety *varietà*
   variety show *spettacolo di varietà*
VCR *videoregistratore (m.)*
vegetables *verdura*
very *molto*
   Very pleased to meet you. *Molto lieto.*
   I am very well. *Sto molto bene.*
victim *vittima*
   to be a victim of a robbery *essere vittima di un furto*
video *video*
villa *villa*
vinegar *aceto*
violent *violento*
violin *violino*
   to play the violin *suonare il violino*
visit (to) *visitare*
   to visit a city *visitare una città*
vitamin *vitamina*
vocabulary *vocabolario*
volume *volume*
   to lower the volume *abbassare il volume*

W

wait (to) *aspettare*
   to wait in line *aspettare in fila, fare la coda*
   to wait for the bus *aspettare l'autobus*
waiter *cameriere (m.)*
wake up (to) *svegliarsi*
walk *passeggiata*
   to go for a walk *fare una passeggiata*

walk (to) *camminare, andare a piedi*
wall *muro*
  (wall) closet *armadio a muro*
wallet *portafoglio*
want (to) *volere*
  What do you want? *Cosa vuoi?*
wardrobe *armadio*
warehouse *magazzino*
wash (to) *lavare*
  to wash oneself *lavarsi*
watch (to) *guardare*
  to watch television *guardare la televisione*
  to watch the game *guardare la partita*
water *acqua*
  mineral water *acqua minerale*
  tonic water *acqua tonica*
watermelon *anguria*
wavy *ondulato*
  wavy hair *capelli ondulati*
way *modo*
  That's the way it is! *È proprio così!*
wear (to) *portare*
  What size do you wear? *Che taglia/numero porta?*
weather *tempo*
  What's the weather like? *Che tempo fa?*
Wednesday *mercoledì (m.)*
week *settimana*
  next week *la settimana prossima*
weekend *weekend*
  What are you doing this weekend? *Cosa fai questo weekend?*
welcome *benvenuto*
welcome (to) *dare il benvenuto*
  You're welcome! *Prego!*
well *bene*
what *che, cosa, che cosa*
  What a beautiful day! *Che bel giorno!*
  What day is today? *Che giorno è oggi?*
  What's the weather like? *Che tempo fa?*
  What time is it? *Che ora è?*
  What size do you wear? *Che taglia/numero porta?*
  What are you doing this weekend? *Cosa fai questo weekend?*
  What do you want? *(Che) cosa vuoi?*
  What did you say? *Cosa hai detto?*
when *quando*
  When are you arriving? *Quando arrivi?*
where *dove*
  Where were you? *Dove sei stato?*
  Where is the hospital? *Dov'è l'ospedale?*
which *che*
  The show (which) I saw was good. *Lo spettacolo che ho visto era buono.*
which *quale*
  Which one do you want? *Quale vuoi?*
  Which one is it? *Qual'è?*
white *bianco*
who *che, chi*
  Hello! Who is speaking? *Pronto! Chi parla?*
wife *moglie (f.)*

win (to) *vincere*
window *finestra; sportello*
  car window *finestrino*
  Please go to the cashier's window. *Si accomodi alla cassa.*
  exchange window *sportello dei cambi*
  Please go to window number five. *Si accomodi allo sportello numero cinque.*
windshield *parabrezza (m.)*
windy *ventoso*
  It's windy! *Tira vento!*
wine *vino*
  wine cellar *cantina*
winter *inverno*
withdraw (to) *prelevare*
without *senza*
  without any doubt *senza dubbio*
word *parola*
word processor *elaboratore (m.) di testi*
work (to) *lavorare, funzionare*
  The turn signal doesn't work. *La freccia non funziona.*
  The photocopy machine doesn't work. *La fotocopiatrice non funziona.*
  to work in a factory *lavorare in fabbrica*
  to work in an office *lavorare in ufficio*
  to work in the managerial sector *lavorare nel settore dirigenziale*
  to work in the private sector *lavorare nel settore privato*
  to go to work *andare al lavoro*
  to look for work *cercare lavoro*
working *lavorativo*
  regular working hours *orario lavorativo regolare*
world *mondo*
  to travel around the world *fare il giro del mondo*
write (to) *scrivere*
writer *scrittore (m.), scrittrice (f.)*

X

X ray *radiografia*

Y

year *anno*
  last year *l'anno scorso*
  I am 20 years old. *Ho vent'anni.*
yellow *giallo*
  yellow pages *pagine gialle*
yen *yen*
yes *sì*

Z

zone *zona, area*
zucchini *zucchini (m., pl.)*

ACKNOWLEDGMENTS

Thanks to Crown Publishers' Living Language™ staff: Kathryn Mintz, Jacqueline Natter, Helga Schier, Victoria Su, Ana Suffredini, Evelyn Ch'ien, Peter Davis, Jennifer Harper, Patricia Slezak, and Kim Hertlein. Special thanks to Clifford Browder, Graziana Lazzarino, Marcel Danesi, and Raffaella Maiguashca.

431

INDEX